AF600272

Tao Yuanming & Manuscript Culture

TAO YUANMING & MANUSCRIPT CULTURE:

The Record of A Dusty Table

XIAOFEI TIAN

A China Program Book

UNIVERSITY OF WASHINGTON

SEATTLE & LONDON

This publication was supported in part by the China Studies Program, a division of the Henry M. Jackson School of International Studies at the University of Washington.

Printed in the United States of America
17 16 15 14 13 12 11 5 4 3 2
Designed by Ashley Saleeba

University of Washington Press
P.O. Box 50096, Seattle, WA 98145, U.S.A.
www.washington.edu/uwpress

Library of Congress Cataloging-in-Publication Data
Tian, Xiaofei.
Tao Yuanming and manuscript culture : the record of a dusty table / Xiaofei Tian.
p. cm.
Includes bibliographical references and index.
ISBN 978-0-295-98553-4 (hardback : alk. paper)
1. Tao, Qian, 372?–427—Criticism and interpretation. 2. Transmission of texts. I. Title.
PL2665.T3Z8985 2005
895.1′124—dc22 2005014428

The paper used in this publication is acid-free and 90 percent recycled from at least 50 percent post-consumer waste. It meets the minimum requirements of American National Standard for Information Sciences—Permanence of Paper for Printed Library Materials, ANSI Z39.48-1984.♾♻

Cover illustration: Traditionally attributed to Yan Liben. *Northern Qi Scholars Collating Classic Texts,* Northern Song dynasty, eleventh century. Handscroll, ink and color on silk, 10 7/8 × 44 7/8 in. Museum of Fine Arts, Boston: Denman Waldo Ross Collection 31.123

For my parents

Contents

ACKNOWLEDGMENTS ix

INTRODUCTION 3

1 POSSESSION & LOSS 23

2 "WHO THE MASTER IS, NO ONE KNOWS" 56

3 LOST HOMESTEADS: RETURNING TO TAO 95

4 FOOD, DEATH, & NARRATION 132

5 BECOMING A VESSEL 174

6 HARD EVIDENCE: READING A STONE 196

CONCLUSION 220

NOTES 226

CHINESE GLOSSARY 275

EDITIONS OF TAO YUANMING'S COLLECTION 289

SELECTED BIBLIOGRAPHY 299

INDEX 309

Acknowledgments

In writing this book I am indebted to many people for their inspiration and support. I would particularly like to thank Alan Berkowitz, Kang-i Sun Chang, Wilt Idema, and David Knechtges, who read through the entire manuscript and gave detailed, thoughtful comments, and whose warm friendship brings much joy to my work in this field.

The book has been enriched by the questions and feedback from the audiences before whom I presented parts of the manuscript: the conference on the Six Dynasties organized by Jack Chen and held at Harvard University in May 2000, the China Humanities Seminar at Harvard Fairbank Center chaired by Michael Puett in October 2002, the hermeneutics conference organized by Kang-i Sun Chang and held at Yale University in May 2003, and a panel on Tao Yuanming organized by Wendy Swartz for the Association of Asian Studies Annual Meeting in March 2004. I have also benefited from my exchanges with Professor Yuan Xingpei of Beijing University over the years, whose fine work on Tao Yuanming remains a source of inspiration; from my conversations with Sarah Allen and Christopher Nugent, who both did extensive and outstanding research on textual transmission in the Tang literature in their

Ph.D. dissertations (Harvard University, 2004). I am thankful to my editors at University of Washington Press, Lorri Hagman, for her enthusiasm and encouragement when this book was still an unpolished manuscript, and Kerrie Maynes, for her careful copyediting; and to production manager John Stevenson, for patiently answering all my questions about the jacket illustration.

But above all I wish to thank my parents and brother, whose faith in me and whose loving support are the foundation of everything important in my life. My greatest debt is to my beloved husband, Stephen Owen, for having made me fall in love with classical Chinese poetry all over again, for reading every chapter of this book in its every stage and offering stimulating criticism, and for understanding his wife's long hours of intense work and cheerfully taking over many a domestic chore. I am eternally grateful for our finding each other—two people who share the same birthday, and who share the same passion for work, life, and poetry.

Tao Yuanming & Manuscript Culture

Introduction

Thou didst convert my loving dream
To loathing, and to hate extreme;
So copyists have oft times slipped
And quite transformed a manuscript.

In the early eleventh century in Moorish Spain, an aristocratic Arab scholar, Ibn Hazm (994–1069), wrote a book entitled *The Ring of the Dove.* In this book, Ibn Hazm explored various aspects of love: its origin, signs, and the misfortunes suffered by people in love. The lines above are quoted from a section of the book in which Ibn Hazm maintains that a person may fall in love through merely hearing the description of the other party, without ever setting eyes on him or her. However, if the person someday actually sees the object of his speculative passion, "either his love is confirmed, or it is wholly nullified." Ibn Hazm then relates a personal story in which love turned to hate when the two parties met each other in real life, and cites his own verse quoted above.[1]

What is of interest here is Ibn Hazm's reference to the transformation of a manuscript in the hands of copyists and the ambiguity of his simile. If we make the common assumption that a copy is "inferior" to the original, we may then regard a scribe's copy as the reality in which the two parties meet: it falls so much short of the original manuscript (that is, the description of the beloved) that the reader's (lover's) ardor is turned into disgust. However, we might just as well understand the scribe's copy as being the extravagant description of the beloved, who would be, in this case, compared to the original. But if this is so, then the scribe's copy cannot be said to have "corrupted" the master copy: it must have improved the original version so much as to cause someone to fall in love—with an illusion. In the second reading of the verse, Ibn Hazm would be suggesting that the scribe, through "slipping," has in fact enhanced the quality of the original manuscript.

Hand copying a book may be a practice quite alien to us now, but it was the single most important means of transmission of knowledge and information in the age of manuscript culture. Unlike a printed book, which is always absolutely identical to its fellow copies of the same print run, each hand-copied manuscript is a unique entity. In John Dagenais' words, it "takes on features of orality" in the sense that a handwritten manuscript resembles an oral performance in its occasional and singular nature.[2] Oral poetry is often anonymous: we do not know its exact time and place of origin or its author; a hand-copied text may have an author, but we often no longer have the master copy written out by the author himself or herself. This is particularly true in Chinese manuscript culture, in which the medium of transmission was easily destructible paper, and not, for instance, the more durable parchment or vellum employed in medieval Europe. In such cases, when we do not possess an original master copy made "authoritative" by the author's own hand, we are left only with multiple copies of an illusory source text. The beloved is absent: all we have are descriptions of the beloved, which unfortunately can never convey to us the full picture.

Such a way of thinking about manuscript culture fits a Christian religious model only too well: what we see in this fallen world are no more than imperfect manifestations of the divine. Even in China, where the religious model is missing, the passion for the one and only "origin" prompts scholars to a ceaseless quest. The truth, however, is that any quest for the "original" and hence the "authentic" is rendered essentially meaningless by the unrecoverable absence of a master copy; only such a master copy would give us grounds to decide that one version is superior and another inferior. Ultimately one discovers that the beloved is merely an imagined being who exists in the descriptions only.

Ibn Hazm was an older contemporary of Su Shi (1037–1101), an eminent Chinese literary figure, who lived during the Northern Song dynasty (960–1126). During this period, printing was becoming widespread and replacing manuscript copying as the dominant mode of transmission of knowledge and information—although, as we shall see, it never completely eclipsed manuscript culture. We may be quite certain that the two men, Ibn Hazm and Su Shi, had never even heard of each other, and yet Su Shi undertook that very task of looking in manuscripts for his beloved: an earlier poet whose works had come down to him in dozens of handwritten copies, each different from the others. He berated the copyists for their careless mistakes, which, in his opinion, had defiled the image of the beloved for more than five hundred years until he, Su Shi, recovered its original brilliance. He thought he had discovered the beloved—the true one—and was elated by his discovery.

Su Shi not only believed that he alone knew what kind of person his beloved poet "really" was, he also felt that this knowledge gave him a particular authority in interpreting the poet's works and identifying "errors" made by mindless copyists. There is, as we can easily see, one problem with Su Shi's project: his very understanding of what kind of person the earlier poet was could have come only from those imperfect manuscript copies of his works, passed on to Su Shi by many generations of scribes, editors, and compilers. In order to arrive at the true, uncorrupted image of the beloved earlier poet, Su Shi would have to make corrections to those "bad" manuscript copies. If, by this point, the reader detects a certain irony in Su Shi's passionate undertaking, he or she is not too far from the truth.

The current book focuses on the poetry of Su Shi's beloved poet and a cultural icon, Tao Yuanming (also known as Tao Qian, 365?–427), one of the greatest, perhaps also one of the most misunderstood, classical Chinese poets. If he is misunderstood, it is because he has been made into an eternal presence, rather than surviving as an image in texts that were shaped by the force of manuscript culture and subsequent editors.

Tao Yuanming lived towards the end of the Eastern Jin dynasty (317–420), when northern China was under non-Chinese rule. The last years of the fourth century were marked by constant uprisings against the declining Jin royal house, until finally Liu Yu (r. 420–422), a powerful general who had earlier helped suppress a major rebellion, replaced the Jin with his own regime, the Song dynasty, usually referred to as the Liu Song to differentiate it from the later dynasty under the same name. Tao Yuanming was born to a once-illustrious family; his great-grandfather was Tao Kan (259–334), a native of the south and one of the most influential political and military figures in early Eastern Jin. By the time Tao Yuanming was born, the Tao family had already lost most of its influence, though it still maintained some contacts in the court and was obviously considered a prominent southern noble family. Tao Yuanming served in several official posts during his lifetime, but never rose to any high position. His last appointment was that of a county magistrate at Pengze, a place not far from his native town Xunyang (in present-day Jiangxi Province). He was not happy in his post, and in 405, upon the death of his sister, he resigned and went home. He spent the rest of his life at his home estate in quiet reclusion, although he apparently kept up his friendships with local and court officials, drinking and exchanging poetry with them. These friends included the contemporary literary celebrity Yan Yanzhi (384–456), who wrote an elegy for Tao after his death in 427.

Tao Yuanming's poetry and prose were known to his contemporaries, and after his death his works continued to circulate. The first well-known editor of Tao Yuanming's works was Xiao Tong (501–531), the Crown Prince of Resplendent Brilliance (Zhaoming Taizi) of the Liang, and the compiler of the most influential pre-Tang literary anthology. Xiao Tong deeply admired Tao Yuanming's writings. During the Tang (618–907), Tao Yuanming was appreciated largely as a drinker and as a recluse who held fast to his principles. Although a small number of well-known Tang poets were obviously influenced by him, including Wang Ji (590?–644), Wang Wei (701–761), and Wei Yingwu (ca. 733–793), he remained only one of many famous pre-Tang poets—until he was singled out as *the* pre-Tang poet by Su Shi and his coterie about five hundred years after his death.

This book originated from a simple observation. A few years ago, in the course of preparing for a graduate seminar, I reread Tao Yuanming's poetry. The modern critical edition I was using, compiled by the great Shandong scholar Lu Qinli (1910–1973), contains a number of textual variants. These textual variants have not usually been taken very seriously by Chinese commentators and scholars of past and present—the only exception to the rule being a variant in one of Tao Yuanming's poems on drinking, which was made famous by none other than Su Shi himself as an example of how copyists could "transform a manuscript" in an unforgivable way. Many modern editions choose to exclude textual variants, no doubt considering them superfluous and irrelevant, or they include only a small number of them. In Lu Qinli's edition, however, the variants conveniently appear in a smaller font under the poetic lines, which are printed vertically, starting from right to left, in keeping with the traditional Chinese book format. As I was reading along, I noticed that if I inserted one of those variants in smaller fonts into the poem proper, I would have a completely different poetic line—sometimes exactly opposite to the meaning of the commonly accepted version. In more than one case, the choice of a different textual variant altered not just the line but also changed the whole poem.

From my "discovery," many questions naturally follow: since an "authoritative" or "definitive" edition stamped with the author's approval is nowhere to be found, what makes an editor of Tao Yuanming's works decide to choose one variant over another? Certainly we can exclude "later" variants; but our repertoire of variants comes largely from the Northern Song, which produced the editions on which modern editions are based. How many variants have been lost in the course of well more than a thousand years as a result of copyists' and editors' dismissal and exclusion? And what does it mean to ask such questions? One thing, however, remains certain: just underneath the smooth, fixed surface of a modern printed edition is a chaotic and unstable world. This is the world of manuscript culture, a few of whose traces remain in these variants.

As mentioned previously, because of the fragility of their medium, early manuscripts produced in China have largely disappeared. The famous manuscripts of the Tang and the Five Dynasties (907–960) from the Dunhuang grottos of northwestern China, protected by the dry weather of the desert and by their geographical isolation, are a rare case of survival. From some of the writings of the same period, however, we may still catch a glimpse of the fascinating process of a manuscript's metamorphosis, and recognize the essential fluid nature of manuscript culture. I will give two examples, one being the author himself changing the text after he discovered, to his indignation, that his poetry had been altered beyond his own recognition; the other being a woman "fixing" the text she was given to copy. The first example is the account given to us by the late-Tang monk Guanxiu (late ninth–early tenth century) in his preface to a series of twenty-four quatrains "On Dwelling in the Mountains" (Shanju shi):

> I wrote a set of twenty-four quatrains, "On Dwelling in the Mountains," during my stay at Zhongling in the fourth and fifth year of the Xiantong reign [860–873]. As soon as I put down my brush, someone took away the draft. Afterwards, some of the poems were written on the walls; some passed from mouth to mouth, and I occasionally heard one or two chanted by people. They were all full of errors. Since the *xinchou* year of the Qianfu reign [881], I have been hiding in the mountain monastery

> from the bandits.[3] I happened to get hold of a complete copy; the style was uncultivated and vulgar, the tone base and low. How could I bear letting gentlemen of refined taste hear them like this? So one day I took out my brush and revised them: some I kept, some I deleted, some I corrected, and some I added to. Then again I completed twenty-four of them, and they shine with elegance.[4]

Guanxiu's preface shows us that the poems were literally like the poet's progeny, taken away from him when first born and then growing up into something he could no longer recognize. The poet seems to have completely lost control of his products; only by sheer chance did he "get hold of a complete copy."

The next example provides us with the missing link by allowing us to see exactly *how* a text undergoes transformation when it is out of the hands of the author. We have a story told by Gao Yanxiu, a writer living in the ninth century. The story says that there was a young man surnamed Wei who had acquired a sixteen-year-old courtesan as his concubine. He was infatuated with her, not only because she was beautiful and had talent in music but also because she was very literary. "He asked her to transcribe the poetry of Du Fu [712–770], but the copy they acquired was full of errors and lacunae. As she was copying, she made corrections along the way, and the writings became clear and comprehensible. Because of this Wei was quite taken with her."[5]

The second example shows us just how differently, how vigorously, and indeed how aggressively, a medieval Chinese reader related to literary works. Such a realization might be baffling and troublesome for a modern reader, who is used to the stability and fixity of printed books, definitive editions, copyright laws, and the notion of intellectual property. In modern times, we can still be changed by our reading, but we usually do not change our reading materials. In the age of manuscript culture, however, a scribe—a particular sort of reader—could participate actively, confidently, in the reproduction of the works of Du Fu, one of the greatest classical Chinese poets, and the scribe might have been just about any literate person—a professional copyist, an illustrious member of the literati, a nobleman, a literate but hardly learned commoner, or a talented courtesan. He or she could have worked for pay, for love of poetry, or for love of a person. To the degree that they were engaged in the production of manuscript copies by copying, editing, altering, and revising, we are no longer talking about the readers' reception of a stable text, but about the readers' dynamic participation in the very process of creating a text that is essentially protean. In such a paradigm, the author is still important, but the author no longer occupies the stable central position as an all-powerful and controlling presence in relation to his or her work.

In an article entitled "Book Culture and Textual Transmission in Sung China," Susan Cherniack discusses textual volatility in the Song in relation to the rise of printing. She argues that errors in printed texts affected a much larger readership because each manuscript was unique and so "the impact of errors occurring in any single manuscript was limited to a comparatively small circle of readers."[6] This is certainly true, but printed copies also "contain" or limit the number of variants produced every time a new copy is made, while every handwritten copy is liable to produce new variants, sometimes copy errors and sometimes deliberate alterations, and so increase the total number of variants.

From the anecdote about Wei's concubine, we also learn that textual variants do not come only from copyists' careless mistakes; they are also a consequence of self-conscious editing: filling in lacunae and correcting what are regarded as errors. To a large measure, this was what the Northern Song editors were doing when preparing a printed edition. Faced with not just one handwritten copy of a poet's collection but sometimes many copies, they had to choose "the right reading" from a variety of variants; in some cases, they were faced with the discrepancy between words transmitted on paper and those in stele inscriptions. Ouyang Xiu's (1007–1072) collated edition of the Tang writer Han Yu (768–824) was universally acclaimed as a "fine edition" (*shanben*), but when he later compared it with the stele inscriptions of Han Yu's prose, to his dismay he discovered "many errors," and "from now on I know it is very common for texts to lose their genuineness during the long course of their transmission."[7]

Northern Song scholars, critics, and commentators inherited the scattered and messy remains of Tang manuscript culture; and, perhaps in part because of the increasingly prominent role of printing, for the first time in history disagreements among handwritten manuscript copies were noticed with passionate concern. This may be a good example of how material culture and technology can change people's perception of the world. Ye Mengde's (1077–1148) *Remarks Recorded While Avoiding the Heat* (Bishu luhua) tells the story of a fanatic lover of Du Fu, who would pester his colleagues by constantly talking about Du Fu's poetry. Sometimes, in the heat of an argument, he would ask one of the clerks to go and fetch his copy of Du Fu's poems; if the clerk brought him a copied version (*luben*), he would look at the clerk angrily and yell at him, "Why didn't you get the genuine copy (*zhenben*) in my collection?"[8] We do not quite know what a *zhenben* was as opposed to a *luben*—was it an original handwritten copy from the Tang as opposed to what had been copied out by the man himself?—but the point of the anecdote is the intense awareness of the "genuineness" (implying "the original") of an edition, a concern that one rarely finds in the Tang. Collation, ever an important activity, took on a particularly poignant urgency in the Northern Song. In extreme cases, finely collated editions even affected the real estate business: Zhu Bian (?–1144) writes in *Old Stories Heard at Quwei* (Quwei jiuwen) that the books in Song Minqiu's (1019–1079) family book collection had all been collated three or five times and were therefore considered "fine editions" (*shanben*). Song Minqiu lived in Chunming Ward (Chunming Fang), and those elite literati members who loved reading would often choose to live in the same neighborhood to be able to borrow books from him. As a result, houses in Chunming Ward became twice as expensive as those in other areas.[9]

We know that Tao Yuanming's poetry was already disseminated during his lifetime, at least among his friends. In his preface to the series of poems "On Drinking" (Yinjiu), he recounts how he "asked my old friend [or friends] to copy the poems out, so as to provide some diversion." By the beginning of the Northern Song, there existed a large number of manuscript copies of Tao Yuanming's writings. According to a colophon written to Tao Yuanming's collection by Song Xiang (996–1066),

> Nowadays there are a number of private and official editions [of Tao Yuanming's works], all different from what is documented in the two historical records [i.e., *The Sui History* and *The Old Tang History*].[10] The one divided into eight *juan* [originally a scroll, later a unit of division for a Chinese book] was edited by the Crown Prince Zhaoming of Liang. The preface, Tao Yuanming's biography, and his elegy are collected into one *juan* and put at the very beginning, followed by the collection proper, but the table of contents has been lost. The one divided into ten *juan* was edited by Vice Director Yang[11]. . . . Over the years I have acquired only a paltry number of copies, which comes to no more than several dozens, and I never knew which version was the right one.[12]

Another Northern Song scholar, Cai Qi (or Cai Juhou, ca. 1109), gives us to understand that "there are so many editions of Tao Yuanming's poetry these days that collators encounter endless variants. Sometimes for one character there are dozens of variants, which cannot possibly be all listed."[13]

To know "which version was the right one" plagued Northern Song literary scholars, and they spent much time and effort sorting out this bewildering manuscript legacy. Liu Kai (947–1000), an aggressive editor, tampered with more than five thousand and seven hundred characters when he was collating the Tang writer Han Yu's collection.[14] Tao Yuanming's writings, like the rest of pre-Song literary output, have come down to us through the mediation of the Song literary values, and to understand this editorial practice is of vital importance to our approach to Tao Yuanming's poetry, whose deceptive simplicity is partially the doing of the Northern Song editors.

To a modern scholar, this editorial practice may often seem alarmingly arbitrary. Su Shi once cited a line by Du Fu, in which a character, *mo* 沒, "to disappear," was reportedly changed by Song Minqiu into *bo* 波, "the waves," so that "The white gull disappears into the boundless waters" became something like "The white gull [flies] over the boundless waves," as Song Minqiu believed that gulls did not know how to "disappear into the waters."[15] The anonymous collection of anecdotes *Pure Chat at Daoshan* (Daoshan qinghua, ca. early twelfth century) reports the following story:

> Du Fu's poem "Sleeping over at Longmen" [Su Longmen] has a line, "Constellations' woof presses close against the Heaven's towers" [Tian que xiang wei bi 天闕象緯逼]. Wang Anshi [1021–1086] changed the second character *que* 闕 to *yue* 閱. Huang Tingjian [1045–1105] strongly endorsed the change in public. Liu Gongfu [Liu Bin, 1022–1088], upon hearing of this, said, "You've got to be afraid of that guy!"[16]

Wang Anshi's confident editorial approach also caught the attention of Cai Qi:

> Du Fu's collection circulating nowadays was collated by Imperial Academician Wang Yuanshu [the courtesy name of Wang Zhu, 997–1057]. Whenever he saw a variant, he would preserve it in a note and did not want to do away with it. By the time Wang Jinggong [the honorary title of Wang Anshi] edited *The Anthology of A Hundred Masters*, he would ponder the question and then choose his preferred version to make a definitive edition. For example, the line "The master is more talented

> than Qu and Song" has an editorial note [by Wang Zhu] saying, "Or as 'Sometimes the master talks about Qu and Song.'" Wang Anshi then replaced the character in the text proper with the variant. . . . Such examples are so numerous that they cannot be listed one by one. The appropriateness of his choices is obvious.[17]

Cai Qi also notes that Wang Anshi sometimes simply changed what he thought was unreasonable in the text to something that he believed would make the most sense.

What "aggressive" editors such as Liu Kai, Song Minqiu, and Wang Anshi did to the manuscripts is little different from what Wei's concubine had done; and exactly how they decided which variant to choose or what alternative character to "fill in" is an intriguing question. As we can see from Wang Anshi's editorial principles, the usual tactic seems to choose what "makes the most sense" in the context. Such a preference for the "easier reading," of course, is a highly problematic criterion in textual scholarship: "sense" is historically contingent, and what makes sense to contemporary readers may easily lose its transparency in a later age. This, as I will try to show in later chapters, is in fact what happens regarding the choice of textual variants in Tao Yuanming's poetry: the word that makes the most obvious sense often prevails over the word that does not fit into the context in any self-evident way—and yet the rejected, "more difficult" reading may be explained by allusions and references probably quite familiar to Tao Yuanming's contemporaries. Literature is not a transcendental, self-contained entity immune to the interaction of a field of historical, social, and cultural forces; but for premodern Chinese readers, faith in direct communication with an ancient author often eclipsed the sense of temporal distance between them—to the degree that the ancient author became an eternally present figure, impervious to change and unbound by the mores of his or her times.

This is particularly true in the case of Tao Yuanming, who is considered the archetypal recluse, and who, in the modern age, has been treated as a poet who represents something "quintessentially Chinese." In other words, Tao Yuanming is not only taken out of his historical circumstances, but is also restricted to a rather fixed image. Although scholars and critics have tried to complicate such an image by pointing out Tao Yuanming's discontent and struggle with his decision to give up public service for a reclusive life, the basic aspects of Tao Yuanming as a man and a poet have been set in place: a lofty-minded recluse, intensely loyal to the declining and later overthrown Jin dynasty; a spontaneous, willful, unconventional person who is often portrayed as drinking excessively, both in his own works and in visual arts of the later period (mostly post-Tang); a poet who chooses to pursue self-fulfillment through a set of private values rather than through public life, who finds contentment and pleasure in retirement and leisure, who defies material hardship for the sake of adhering to his personal principles, and who writes natural, unaffected, and simple poetry of nature in celebration of such a lifestyle. The perception of Tao Yuanming as an intense Jin loyalist, although with a long history, was particularly endorsed by Southern Song neo-Confucians, who must have discovered a special pathos in Tao Yuanming's loyalty, in that it could be easily related to their own times. The fall of the Northern Song into the hands of the "barbarian" rulers was only too similar to the end of the Western Jin (265–317), and the constantly threatened security of the Southern Song reminded them of the situation of Tao Yuanming's own dynasty, the Eastern Jin. Although there is in fact nothing in Tao Yuanming's own poetry and prose that suggests such loyalist sentiment, it has not only become one of the hallmarks of Tao Yuanming's personality since the Song but also a guiding principle in the interpretation of his writings, sometimes leading to extremely tenuous and distorted explications, as in the famous case of his most obscure poem, "An Account of Ale" (Shu jiu). In the modern age, the issue of loyalty in Tao Yuanming studies does not provoke the same kind of passionate interest as it did in imperial China, but other aspects of the traditional image of Tao Yuanming still prevail, and sometimes take on a no less poignant urgency, for, in the nation-building project of the twentieth century, elements of Tao Yuanming's works—such as the harmony between man and nature believed to be exemplified in his poetry about farming—have for many people come to define the essence of "Chinese art" and "Chinese culture." The argument that Tao Yuanming's poetry is "not really unadorned and plain," that he was able to endure inner conflicts and doubts about his life decisions, and that he suffered from anger and anguish at the usurpers and rebels of his age, only serves to confirm the established image of Tao Yuanming and his works.

We cannot know which variant is "right," but we can see to some degree the historical motivation for choosing one variant over another and the version of Tao Yuanming that has been suppressed by such choices. These commonplace opinions about Tao Yuanming and the desire for the stability of his image have had a profound impact on the choice of textual variants in Tao

Yuanming's works. Which character may be kept in the text proper and which must be removed to a note (typically beginning with *yi zuo* 一作, "also as X," and, if there are more variants for the same character, *you zuo* 又作, "or as Y") becomes an editorial decision invested with ideological significance. The most famous example is the controversy over *jian* 見 (to see) and *wang* 望 (to gaze at) initiated by Su Shi; we will discuss this controversy at some length in the first chapter. Elsewhere in the Tao Yuanming collection, however, we see many more cases in which a textual variant makes a great difference in understanding a poem. In the aggregate such cases alter the entire landscape of Tao Yuanming's poetry and prompt us to reconsider many things about the poet: he may turn out, as this book shall endeavor to show, both much more embedded in the literary and philosophical interests of his age and much more innovative, playful, quirky, and wistful than his accepted image. In counterpoint to the earnestness celebrated by generations of scholars and critics, we may in fact find in Tao Yuanming's poetry a strong sense of irony about the world and about himself, a more perverse turn of mind, and great discomfort and anxiety about the dark forces of nature—despite the pious repetition about how the poet yearns for the liberating power of nature and feels at home in his "gardens and fields."

In a study of various editions of Tao Yuanming's collection, contemporary scholar Yuan Xingpei points out that the number of variants recorded in various printed editions of Tao Yuanming's works from the Southern Song to early Yuan seem to have decreased: the edition dating roughly from after 1124 (the Jigu ge edition), for example, has over seven hundred and forty places where the editor notes variants (in a corpus of one hundred and twenty-seven poems and various prose pieces—by no means a large body of work); these include both single characters and phrases or even whole lines, not to mention those cases in which one character has two or three variants (so that the total number of textual variants in this edition could well exceed a thousand). An edition with a colophon dated 1140 only has somewhat over two hundred textual notes, and the extent of its recorded variants does not go beyond the Jigu ge edition; Tang Han's edition (ca. mid-thirteenth century) has about a hundred and forty-three notes for textual variants;[18] and finally, the later Li Gonghuan edition has no more than six.[19] We should be aware that what we have now are no more than a fraction of the Song and Yuan printed editions no longer extant; and yet, if we only look at these editions and these figures, there seems to be a steady pattern of reducing and limiting the number of variants, a process that parallels the increasing stabilization of the image of Tao Yuanming.

Yuan Xingpei discusses three kinds of textual variants which could affect the meaning of a line: those that have to do with "rhetorical merit," those that contain correct or incorrect information, and those that concern the chronology of Tao Yuanming's life.[20] Of the three categories, the last could become a point of controversy among the numerous scholars devoted to compiling Tao Yuanming's chronology, determining the year of his birth, and dating Tao Yuanming's writings; but such variants are not of central concern to the current book, nor do they affect our reading of Tao Yuanming's works in any significant way. In the second category, we find that variants appear due to the discovery of "error" in Tao Yuanming's quotations from ancient sources. That is, if an editor or scribe noticed that the poet "made a mistake" in citation, he would correct the mistake and delegate, if he were so disposed, the "erroneous" text to a footnote. This is regarded as "improving" a manuscript, and we may be reasonably sure that the editor or scribe may not have deemed it necessary to record every such emendation. Such an "error," however, might simply have come from a manuscript copy of the source different from what we have now, available in Tao Yuanming's age, but no longer extant. It is, of course, also possible that Tao Yuanming made a mistake.

The first category of textual variants discussed by Yuan Xingpei is of particular interest and importance to us here, and yet it seems that finer differentiation is called for than simply describing such variants in terms of "rhetorical merit" (*xiuci*). There are editorial choices based on relatively straightforward aesthetic grounds: in the line cited by Yuan Xingpei as an example, "Days and months toss a person away and leave him behind," "to toss" (*zhi* 擲), which is generally favored by editors and appears in all standard editions in the text proper, has a textual variant, "to sweep off" (*sao* 掃). There are, however, also textual variants that embody fierce ideological differences beneath a thin veil of aesthetic concerns: *jian* and *wang*, for instance, can hardly be said to merely imply a preference for superior artistry. While *jian*, "to see," is considered more spontaneous, more accidental, and so more natural, *wang*, "to gaze at," is seen as entailing too much effort. Since Tao Yuanming is regarded as *the* genuine person who always acts according to the dictates of his nature, only *jian* could represent the "genuine" Tao Yuanming.

This word play on "genuine" took on particular significance in late imperial China, when discovering the true Tao Yuanming and acquiring a rare early printed edition of Tao Yuanming's collection were passions so closely intertwined that they became hardly separable. This coincided with the popularization of printing (especially the explosive growth of publishing during the second half of the sixteenth century), the booming book market, the obsession with private book collecting, and a rise in the value of Song and Yuan editions. There were over two hundred famous book collectors in the Ming and more than five hundred in the Qing, their total number far exceeding any previous period in Chinese history.[21] For such collectors, Song books were the most prized—for being the earliest printed editions (and so best representing the "original" texts), for their legendary printing quality and elegant script styles, and for their scarcity. From the book collectors' ecstatic celebration of the appearance, the smell, and the "feel" of a rare Song edition, one is tempted to conclude that texts were in fact treasured less for their content than for their materiality: an old book is definitely not just for reading; it is also to be cherished as a beautiful, costly, much-desired object. There are numerous stories about how book dealers produced fake Song editions to make a profit,[22] as well as stories of how book collectors used every means—from economic reward, political pressure, sexual attraction, to outright hoodwinking and cheating—to acquire a coveted rare book. As we shall see, Song and Yuan editions of Tao Yuanming's collection, particularly one supposedly written out by Su Shi (or more likely in the calligraphic style of Su Shi), became just such objects of desire, much sought after and fought over.

Many of the Ming and Qing book collectors were also scholars, collators, and bibliographers. There was a correlation between the high commercial value put on the increasingly rare early editions and the intense preoccupation with recovering the "true essence" of ancient authors. It was during the Qing that study of editions (*banben xue*) and textual studies (*jiaokan xue*) became independent and reflective branches of scholarship.[23] Huang Pilie (1763–1825), one of the greatest book collectors and bibliographers of the Qing, is a representative figure. Living during the peaceful reigns of the Qianlong and Jiaqing emperors, he was very much part of the so-called Qian-Jia school (*Qian Jia xuepai*), which focused its attention on philology and bibliography, on collation and annotation of the classics, and on textual studies in general. True to the spirit of the Qian-Jia school, Huang Pilie believed in "seeking the ancient" and "seeking the genuine," the two goals often seen as being one. He once wrote, "Each and every single thing written by an ancient author has his soul and spirit in it. It is where his thread of life was attached, which is why it could live so long. However, as time passes by, it may become hidden, and to shine forth again it must depend on posterity's collecting what has been scattered and consulting the old records. This is why it is so important for us to seek out the ancient."[24] In terms of his concrete collecting and collating activities, seeking the ancient and the genuine meant that the earlier printed editions (which should be understood as Song editions) or earlier handwritten manuscript copies were invariably considered better than the later ones, for they could, in Huang Pilie's opinion, best reflect the "original" form of a classic and bring out the spirit of an ancient author. The one good thing about Huang Pilie's devout reverence for early editions is that he was extremely cautious in his collation, always recording every textual variant he encountered; but the negative aspect is also obvious: the refusal to realize the intrinsically unstable nature of texts in manuscript culture reinforces the illusion that despite great problems in textual transmission, we can still perfectly recover antiquity. It must be added here that the fluidity of manuscript culture did not stop in the Northern Song with the spread of printing. For one thing, people continued to copy books on a large scale throughout imperial China: Chen Xianxing points out that of the fifty-six thousand, seven hundred and eighty-seven titles recorded in *A Catalogue of Fine Editions of Chinese Classics* (Zhongguo shanben guji shumu), more than half are handwritten manuscripts.[25] For another thing, in Chinese woodblock printing, even a printed edition requires copying a manuscript—this is how printing blocks are prepared.[26] And yet, the particular nature of manuscript culture and the various issues it raises have yet to be recognized by Chinese scholars today. Although books on print culture sometimes include a section or two on manuscripts, it is often no more than a perfunctory mention, and the focus largely remains on the "correct," the "original," the "authentic."

As said before, the quest for the genuine (*zhen*) acquires a special resonance in reading Tao Yuanming. Textual variants are rejected or criticized because they do not represent the "genuine" Tao Yuanming and so they cannot be "genuine"—they are either careless errors or changes made by "shallow" or "vulgar" people who have failed to understand Tao Yuanming's intention—then the purged and purified text is used as an evidence of Tao Yuanming's "genuineness," which implies both the authenticity of the "original" Tao Yuanming and the spontaneity and total lack of self-consciousness that is seen as the quintessential characteristic of Tao Yuanming's personality. The desire for textual stability blends in perfectly with the ideological desire for the poet as a more or less one-dimensional monument, the foundation on which the stable text is based. Tao Yuanming and his poetry are woven into a grand cultural myth which figures prominently in the construction of a modern national culture.[27] In such a myth, the man and his work represent something "born of nature" and miraculously retaining its "natural" state, an artlessness held as the highest literary and moral ideal. Tao Yuanming is regarded as an inherent constituent of the "Chinese national character," and for this reason, his person and his poetry have to be perfectly consistent (because we get to know the person mainly through his poetry). He is not even allowed any self-consciousness in writing about himself, for in many people's eyes self-consciousness compromises a person's earnestness and even amounts to being a "fake." This lack of self-consciousness does not mean lack of self-doubt, which Tao Yuanming is permitted to have in abundance (because it only highlights his nobility in his final decision to follow the dictates of his heart); it means that he did not think of himself as a "poet"—he was just "living" and then happened to write some poetry, which fortuitously happened to have been very well preserved; he was also totally unaware of how he looked in the eyes of the world because he did not care for it. In all these portrayals Tao Yuanming somehow emerges as extremely simple and transparent (just like his poetry), a monolithic figure untouched by the institutions and mores of his age. Any challenge to such an image of Tao Yuanming—any suggestion that Tao Yuanming was actually a sophisticated poet—is resisted with a vehemence rarely seen in discussions of any other premodern Chinese poet, not even Du Fu, commonly acknowledged as perhaps the greatest.[28]

Instead of showing how readers received Tao Yuanming's works, this book will demonstrate how they actually participated in a most active manner in producing Tao Yuanming, and will outline the trajectory along which Tao Yuanming was constructed in manuscript culture and afterward. There is a significant difference between studying readers' reception of a poet's works and studying the impact of manuscript culture on a poet's works; while the former presumes textual stability and the authoritative control of an author, the latter seeks to expose any such comfortable conventional notion of text and authorship as an illusion. Readers do not simply interpret a work differently over time, but shape the very text to their interpretation. This book also intends to bring Tao Yuanming back into the historical, social, cultural, and literary contexts in which he was deeply embedded. Only when we see to what a great extent he was one with his age can we better appreciate his departures from tradition. Rather than seeking to subvert the established assumptions about Tao Yuanming, I hope to add new dimensions to them, so that one may finally come to recognize the protean world of manuscript culture, and discover not just one "Work" by the essentialized Tao Yuanming, but multiple texts continuously produced long after the author's physical demise. The following chapters will strive to show that the "genuine" Tao Yuanming is no more than one version of realization of the image of Tao among many, a product of ideological and social assumptions that prove too partial, too historically unspecific, to be effective.

Chapter one revolves around the concept of acquisition in reading Tao Yuanming's poetry: how a desire to acquire the true meaning of the master leads to actively controlling the texts of his poems—by choosing the "right" variants—and how such a desire is intricately bound up with the intellectual and cultural issues of the Northern Song. In late imperial China, acquiring the essence of the poet became physically embodied in the possession of a Song printed edition of his works: such a printed edition was a thing of great cultural and commercial value. Chapter two discusses "who Tao Yuanming really is" by comparing and contrasting his four biographies, which are often used as an independent "historical context" to interpret Tao Yuanming's works and edit them. Scholars and commentators either try to reconcile any discrepancy between the biographies and Tao Yuanming's writings, or, if there is anything that contradicts the conventional view of the poet, they choose to ignore it. In this chapter, I will show how the construction of Tao Yuanming in the biographies is, in fact, based on Tao Yuanming's own projection of his image in his poetry and prose, guided by the Six Dynasties discourse of reclusion, and influenced by different ideological inclinations.

Tao Yuanming is regarded as the fountainhead of a kind of poetry called "farmstead poetry" (*tianyuan shi*), whose main theme is a reclusive life (as opposed to active service in the government) lived out in "the fields and gardens"—a pastoral setting. Much ink has been spilled on Tao Yuanming's basic contentment with his farming life and his whole-hearted enjoyment of nature. Chapter three will take up some of his best-known farming poems, and, by considering those textual variants that are usually left in notes, reveal a Tao Yuanming who perhaps had a much more troubled relationship with nature than is usually thought, and a Tao Yuanming who is quite self-conscious about "being a farmer"—and yet can only be a spectator standing outside the farming community, reflecting on his own alienation and "difference/strangeness" (*yi* 異).

Perhaps because Tao Yuanming's poetry is characterized as essentially artless and plain, and because his poems have been reduced to rather transparent readings by ideological editorial practice, much critical energy in modern Tao Yuanming studies has been directed to discussions about whether Tao Yuanming is primarily Confucian or Daoist or both, and whether one can discern a hint of Buddhism in his writings as well. These philosophical inclinations are often seen as exerting a combined influence on the poet. Sometimes he is identified more exclusively with one philosophical orientation than with another, and great ideological weight is often invested in the differentiation. The unfortunate consequence is that the "poetry" in Tao Yuanming's poetry is ignored; we may tend to forget that Tao Yuanming is, first of all, a poet, and a great one. Poetry may certainly contain philosophical points, but good poetry is always more than its philosophical points, and it is this "surplus" that makes it poetry in the first place. Unlike philosophical treatises, poetry is less systematic and more occasional, emerging from those fleeting moments whose historical circumstances frequently elude us. Despite passionate efforts by later scholars and critics to reconstruct a poet's life year by year or even day by day, so that those moments from which a poem is born may be recovered, we know that any such reconstruction will always remain imperfect. We have only the poems themselves to work with; these may echo the intellectual issues of an age, but such issues are fused into something which cannot be pinned down to a consistent, well-organized system of thought. Chapters four and five will treat some of Tao Yuanming's central concerns as concretely realized in the poetic images and motifs of his poetry. These chapters will attempt to delineate Tao Yuanming's complicated relationship with his contemporary world by demonstrating how his favorite subjects grow out of conventional literary themes and are closely intertwined with concurrent cultural practices, yet manage to emerge in unique and unusual ways.

Finally, chapter six takes us away from Tao Yuanming's poetry to a rock found in Tao Yuanming's home region, "The Drunken Stone," on which it is said the poet left behind bodily traces. Going through strange mutations and mutilations, generating numerous, often conflicting, accounts, inscribed over and over again, the material embodiment of Tao Yuanming in a stone provides us with a good allegory of how the poet becomes petrified in a hard surface and yet how even then he manages to elude us, through textual fluctuation, corruption, and permutations.

In her engaging book *Unediting the Renaissance*, which offers refreshing insights into the "vast array of possibilities" denied to us by modern standard editions, Leah S. Marcus eloquently argues for the particular relevance textual instability and materiality have for contemporary students and scholars:

> As both computer technology and poststructuralist theory have made inroads into the field of literary studies, most of us have come to think of texts as more malleable, less fixed, than we did before. If texts are generated by computer, the idea of the "original" loses much of its charisma: how can we reliably differentiate "originals" from copies? Printing out our own computer-generated work, we have ourselves become printers and designers on a small scale, and may therefore take more interest in past modes of book production and the ways in which format can influence interpretation. The "new philology" investigates textual instability at a grassroots, material level.[29]

On this level, literary writings should no longer be considered as existing "in the mind or intent of the author," rising above the material form of manuscripts and printed books which are "'simply objects of utility,' 'vessels' for conveyance of their contents."[30] Indeed, each manuscript and printed edition is a unique historical performance by copyists, editors, commentators, woodblock cutters, and book collectors who one after another leave their traces on it and therefore change it.

We are living in a transition period much like the one experienced by the editors and scholars of the Northern Song, who felt anxiety and discomfort about the rise of printing; people no longer related to reading as they had when the main method of transmitting knowledge was to copy everything. Although the Internet culture in which the younger generation feels right at home is rather immaterial, it curiously resembles manuscript culture in its multiplicity, its very lack of center, certainty, and authority. Having grown up with the printed book myself, I realize that this could be very unsettling, but it could also be liberating. It is, as a matter of fact, an allegory of the human condition.

Song Shou (991–1041), the father of Song Minqiu (who did not believe in gulls merging with waves), was an avid book collector as well as a collator. He once said that collating manuscripts was like sweeping dust: as soon as one brushed it off, it began to gather again.[31] The dusty table is therefore a perfect metaphor not only for collating and editing but also for an excursion into the messy world of manuscript culture. Tao Yuanming would certainly understand, as he knew better than anyone else about the chaos of nature, which is constantly threatening the fragile human order imposed on it.

1 Possession & Loss

Someone came at midnight and carried the mountain away.

—Huang Tingjian

This chapter is about the ways in which a person may relate to a mountain: catching sight of it, looking at it with longing, desiring it, acquiring it by obtaining its "spirit" through painting or writing, buying it, or stealing it. Our question of mountains intersects with issues of acquisition (*de* 得)—of mountains large and miniature, of states of mind, and even of truth. Let me begin with a poem, arguably the most famous one written by Tao Yuanming. Cited in *An Anthology of Literature* (Wen xuan) compiled by Xiao Tong and the early Tang encyclopedia *Classified Extracts from Literature* (Yiwen leiju; comp. 624) as an "unclassified poem" (Za shi), it is now generally known as the fifth in a series of twenty poems entitled "On Drinking" (Yinjiu):

結廬在人境	*I built my cottage in the human world,*
而無車馬喧	*yet there is no noise of horse and carriage.*
問君何能爾	*How then did you manage to achieve this?*
心遠地自偏	*When the heart is far away, the locale naturally becomes remote.*

采菊東籬下	*Picking chrysanthemum flowers by the eastern hedge,*
悠然望南山	*I gaze at South Mountain in the distance.*
山氣日夕佳	*The mountain air is lovely at dusk,*
飛鳥相與還	*and birds fly back with one another.*
此還有真意	*In this return there is a fundamental truth,*
欲辯已忘言	*I am going to explain it, but already forgot the words.*[1]

The noise of horse and carriage is not that of common traffic: it refers to the coming and going of aristocrats and officials. In the opening poem of the "On Reading *The Classic of Mountains and Seas*" (Du Shanhai jing) series, the poet graciously suggests that his friends have been kept from visiting him because he lives in such an out-of-the-way narrow lane. But in this poem, he simply says: "When the heart is far away, the locale naturally becomes remote." This is pure Zhuangzi (late fourth century B.C.E.): it does not matter whether the location is distant from the "human realm" or not; it is all about one's state of mind, one's perspective.

Then, as he is picking chrysanthemum flowers, the poet raises his eyes to South Mountain in the distance. Later readers not only regard this as Tao Yuanming's hallmark image but also consider the flowers blooming in the chilly season as a natural symbol of the poet's ability to preserve moral integrity in adverse circumstances. What we often forget is that it is primarily because of Tao Yuanming that the chrysanthemum flowers acquire such significance. As we will often see in the course of this study, the later associations that grew up in the tradition of reading Tao Yuanming return in the guise of a dehistoricized context for reading Tao Yuanming; such resonant meaning invested in the chrysanthemums derived largely from this well-known line. In Tao Yuanming's own age, the most immediate connotation of chrysanthemums, as Wang Yao (1914–1989) correctly points out, would have been as a means of obtaining longevity.[2] The third and fourth couplets skillfully weave together the images of permanence and immensity with that of delicateness and evanescence: while the mountain is massive and majestic, the flowers and birds, in the descending darkness, seem small, frail, and transient.[3]

The last couplet echoes Zhuangzi:

> The fish trap exists because of the fish; once you've gotten the fish, you can forget the trap. The rabbit snare exists because of the rabbit; once

you've gotten the rabbit, you can forget the snare. Words exist because of the meaning; once you've gotten the meaning, you can forget the words. Where can I find a man who has forgotten the words so I can have a word with him?[4]

The allusion to the *Zhuangzi* passage in the last couplet implies that the poet can now afford to discard words only because he has acquired the essential message, the fundamental truth (*deyi wangyan*). Certainly the irony does not escape us, that the poet has to use words (*yan*) to tell us this. But what kind of "fundamental truth" the poet has "acquired" (*de*) remains a mystery. He withholds it from us just as he refers to his acquisition only indirectly, by way of a Zhuangzi allusion.

But we do know one thing: Zhuangzi desires more than just truth; once he has found the truth, he longs for someone who "has forgotten the words." The loneliness of the philosopher is implied in this self-contradictory yearning, and the loneliness of the poet is implied in his becoming the very person who "has forgotten the words" but has also lost the philosopher:

少時壯且厲	*When I was young, I was stalwart and passionate;*
撫劍獨行游	*grasping my sword, I went on a journey all alone.*
誰言行游近	*Who says that the journey was a short one?*
張掖至幽州	*I had gone as far as Zhangye and Youzhou.*[5]
飢食首陽薇	*When hungry, I ate the bracken of Shouyang;*
渴飲易水流	*when thirsty, I drank from the Yi River.*[6]
不見相知人	*Instead of seeing anyone who understood me,*
惟見古時邱	*I only saw ancient grave mounds.*
路邊兩高墳	*Two high graves by the roadside—*
伯牙與莊周	*the tombs of Boya and Zhuang Zhou.*
此士難再得	*Gentlemen like those are hard to acquire again,*
吾行欲何求	*so what am I seeking on my journey!*[7]

In this poem, Tao Yuanming relates that he had, when he was a young man, gone on a trip seeking someone who could understand him. Boya is the famous zither player who, after his friend Zhong Ziqi died, broke his zither and vowed never to play again, for nobody would ever be like Zhong Ziqi in "knowing the tune" (*zhiyin*). At first glance, Boya and Zhuangzi (referred to as Zhuang

Zhou) seem to be an odd pair, but they were matched before in *Huainanzi* and *The Garden of Tales* (Shuo yuan), two Western Han works produced from the second to first century B.C.E.: "After Zhong Ziqi died, Boya broke the strings and smashed the zither, for nobody else in the world would truly appreciate his music; Huishi died and Zhuangzi stopped discoursing, for nobody else in the world was worth talking to."[8] In Tao Yuanming's poem, not only was the poet unable to find anyone who understood him, but even those ancients who had lamented over the loss of their own understanding friends (*zhiyin*) were long dead. In the last couplet Tao Yuanming explicitly uses the word *de*, to "get" or "acquire," even though he uses it in a negative sense: it is difficult to acquire people such as Boya and Zhuang Zhou again.

Although the word *de* emerges in the South Mountain poem only by implication, it is a central concept that wraps up and helps make sense of the whole poem. To understand this concept properly, we must realize that the *Zhuangzi* passage cited above and echoed in the South Mountain poem was such that Tang Yongtong (1893–1964), one of the best modern scholars on Wei-Jin "arcane learning" (*xuanxue*), suggested that the relationship between *yan* (words or language) and *yi* (intent or concept) provides the basic premise upon which Wei-Jin metaphysical discourse rests.[9] It would be impossible to go into detail here about *yan* and *yi*, but a brief description might be helpful. A section called "Clarification of the Image" (Ming xiang) from Wang Bi's (226–249) exegesis of *The Classic of Changes* (Yi jing) is generally considered the fountainhead of *yan/yi* discourse:

> Language is what clarifies the image, and once one acquires the image, one can forget about language; the image is what preserves the concept, and once one acquires the concept, one can forget about the image. . . . Therefore, those who preserve language are not those who acquire the image; those who preserve the image are not those who acquire the concept.[10]

Wang Bi believes that "nothing can equal Image in giving the fullness of concept; nothing can equal language in giving the fullness of Image."[11] This is the point at which he sets himself in opposition to the alternative proposition in another *Zhuangzi* passage that language is no more than the dregs of the ancients.[12] Still, for Wang Bi, both language and image are reduced to a medium, as is the fish-trap. Wang Bi's theoretical position had an immense impact on the development of the Wei-Jin "arcane learning."

What concerns us here, however, is not getting rid of language (*wangyan*), but the acquirement of the concept (*deyi*), or more precisely, the central importance of *de*. *De* is a fine verb of "acquisition" because it can be applied to a variety of things, from land to a concept to a poetic couplet. It refers to the establishment of ownership. The fifth-century work *A New Account of Tales of the World* (Shishuo xinyu) records an anecdote about the Eastern Jin minister Chi Chao's (336–377) generous funding of recluses, which sounds very much like a "Reclusion Fellowship Program":

> Every time Chi Chao heard of someone who was going to become a high-minded recluse, he would provide a million cash to fund his reclusion as well as build a residence for him. He had a house constructed for Dai Kui [?–396] in the Shan mountains, which was well-built and quite elegant. When Dai first went there, he felt he was in an official's mansion. Chi also prepared a million cash for Fu Yue [fl. fourth century], but Fu's reclusion did not come to fruition, so Chi Chao eventually did not give him the money.[13]

Reclusion, being cultural capital itself, also requires a certain amount of more ordinary capital to begin. It comes at a price and usually occurs at a special locale. The same section of *Tales of the World* on reclusion relates the story of Kang Sengyuan (fl. ca. 300–350), a monk of non-Chinese origin, who went to Yuzhang (in modern-day Jiangxi Province) around 340. There he built a lovely residence for himself miles away from the city: "It was right beside the mountain ranges, surrounded by a long river; fragrant trees were ranged in the court, and a clear stream gushed under the walls of his hall." There he devoted himself to studying Buddhist sutras and meditating. The whole court paid him frequent visits, observing him while he was practicing his breathing techniques. "Moreover, as he was very happy with his life and had a way to be self-content, his reputation was on the rise. Finally, unable to endure it any more, he gave up his reclusion."[14] Presumably, it was the court officials' visits and observation that the monk found unbearable.

The description of Kang Sengyuan's residence seems rather lavish in the usually succinct narrative, and it is only in such an environment that Kang Sengyuan is said to have been "self-content," literally, "acquiring himself" (*zide*). The fact that reclusion is closely associated with a well-defined physical space is shown in another *Tales of the World* anecdote. In this anecdote, it is not enough to just live beside the mountain; the recluse feels compelled to possess the mountain in a more tangible way:

> The monk Zhi Daolin [314–366] through a friend asked to purchase Ang Hill from Master Fashen [286–374]. Master Fashen said, "I have never heard that Chaofu and Xu You purchased mountains for reclusion."[15]

Chaofu (Nest-Dweller) and Xu You are two famous recluses from antiquity.[16] According to a fourth-century work, *Biographies of Lofty and Reclusive Monks* (Gaoyi shamen zhuan), Zhi Daolin was much embarrassed by Fashen's taunting remark, although he still settled down at Ang Hill in his later years.[17]

It is against such a background that we should read Tao Yuanming's South Mountain poem. His claim that he built his cottage right in the middle of the human world can be seen as a gesture directed against the common practice of his contemporaries who required the acquisition of more remote and potentially more expensive settings for their spiritual development. Tao Yuanming's own uncle, Tao Dan (ca. fourth century), was one of those recluses who not only built a cottage on the mountain, but also responded to the summons of the prefect by escaping to another mountain and never coming back.[18] Unlike Kang Sengyuan, Tao Yuanming's avoidance of the importunate visits of admiring court nobility is a clear sign of his success in "concealing [*yin*] himself." His successful concealment, Tao Yuanming tells us, has been achieved by the aloofness of his heart, not by physical isolation. A "great recluse" (*dayin*) can hide himself in the most noisy public places, such as the court or the market, while only "lesser recluses" (*xiaoyin*) need to stay on mountains and in caves.[19]

Tao Yuanming is, in fact, careful to maintain a distance from the mountain, a conventional site of reclusion. The hedge fences off the human world, but it also separates him from the mountain he gazes at. Yet in spirit he very much identifies himself with the birds flying back to South Mountain. In the seventh of the "Unclassified Poems," a poem reflecting on old age and mortality, he compares life to traveling and says, "On and on—where am I supposed to go? / There is my old home on South Mountain." Commentators generally take "my old home" as referring to the Tao family cemetery ground. In a way, South Mountain is home to the birds as well as to the poet himself. Tao Yuanming did finally attain the mountain, but only by keeping his distance and looking at it.

By maintaining a contemplative distance, Tao Yuanming's poem anticipates the famous "Preface to a Painted Landscape" (Hua shanshui xu) by his contemporary, Zong Bing (375–443), the Buddhist painter-recluse. In the preface Zong Bing relates how, unable to climb mountains in his old age, he chooses to represent them with brush and paper so as to experience the landscape through paintings:

> I am attached to Mount Lu and Mount Heng, and miss roaming the hills of Jing and Wu: [they make me] forget that old age is approaching. I am ashamed that I cannot perfect my body with the breathing technique, nor am I able to catch up with those who visited Stone Gate.[20] Therefore, I have drawn images and arranged colors, constructing these cloudy peaks. Those things whose principles had been lost beyond middle antiquity may be sought out by concepts a thousand years later; those things whose meaning transcends language and image may be obtained by the mind within books and scrolls. How even more true of those things one experiences in person and sees with one's own eyes, whose forms one delineates with forms, and whose colors are imitated with colors?[21]

Zong Bing argues for the truthfulness of representation because, he says, if one can grasp the principle of something from a thousand years ago by reading books, then how much more so for paintings which, after all, describe form for form and color for color? Through an exertion of imagination one can comprehend, by means of language and images, what is beyond language and images. This possibility clearly grows out of the metaphysical discourse on the relationship between words (*yan*), image (*xiang*), and concept (*yi*). Zong Bing's application of such a discourse to the theory of painting is typical of the aesthetic discourse of his time, when great emphasis was put on the transmission of "spirit" (*chuan shen*) through the depiction of form.[22]

Zong Bing goes on to describe how one may acquire a mountain by way of grasping its spirit in a painting:

> With the greatness of Kunlun Mountain and the smallness of the eyes, if one looks at it closely within inches, then one cannot see its shape; but if one keeps a distance of many miles, then the mountain can be encompassed by the inch-small pupils. This is because the further away one is from the mountain, the smaller the mountain appears. Now if one

> spreads silk to reflect it from afar, then the form of Langfeng Peak [the highest peak of Mount Kunlun] may be encompassed within square inches. A vertical stroke of three inches is as good as the height of thousands of feet; a horizontal stretch of ink may represent the distance of hundreds of miles. Therefore those who look at a painting only worry about its likeness, but do not think that its diminutive size hurts its verisimilitude; this is only natural. In this way, the lofty grace of Mount Song and Mount Hua as well as the numinous spirit of dark valleys can all be acquired in one drawing.

Unlike South Mountain, the legendary Langfeng Peak is where immortals are said to dwell, yet even such a remote location is made easily accessible by a painting. For Zong Bing, there is no need to buy a mountain: the painting is the perfect means of acquiring its numinous spirit and lofty elegance. The representation is so satisfying that it may perfectly replace the real experience:

> Response by the eye leads to understanding by the mind: for a painter who takes this as a principle and achieves similitude with skill, the eyes that look upon his paintings will also respond and the heart of the viewer will understand the same thing. Responding and understanding then move the spirit; the spirit soars and the truth is obtained. So even if one emptily seeks for the truth under secluded cliffs, what more could be added?

Gazing at the landscape leads to the acquisition of its "truth" or its "spirit." With craftsmanship, then, a painter can transmit the truth or the spirit of the landscape to the viewer. Zong Bing does not speculate on whether the painted landscape may reflect the spirit of the painter: he is solely concerned with the capacity of the painting to perfectly represent a landscape and transmit the truth—a cosmic principle—already inherent in the landscape.

Zong Bing doubtlessly believes that "language may give the fullness of the concept" (*yan jin yi*): "Besides, the spirit is limitless; it resides in forms and moves all species. As the truth enters reflections and traces, if one can indeed depict them skillfully, then one can indeed give the fullness of the truth." Then he gives a description of his reflection on the painted image: "Thereupon I live in leisure and regulate my breath, hold my wine cup and stroke my zither; as I open the painting scrolls and face them in solitude and quiet, I reach the four ends of the earth while sitting here." Here we seem to catch a glimpse of our poet Tao Yuanming, who manages to acquire the "truth" of the mountain scene by simply looking.

For Song literati seven centuries later, however, fascinated with acquisition of works of art as well as objects of nature, to acquire a mountain is no longer such a simple matter. It was in the hands of such Northern Song literati that Tao Yuanming was transformed from one of many Six Dynasties poets to the greatest Six Dynasties poet, and then into a cultural icon. Perhaps not accidentally, his transformation was in part centered around this South Mountain poem, or, more specifically, a textual variant—one of the many—in this poem. What is at stake is eventually not only the acquisition of the mountain but also the way in which the poet acquires (*de*) the mountain.

Seeing & Gazing

The contested textual variant in this poem appears in the third position of the sixth line: the verb *wang* (to gaze at) is also read *jian* (to see). Cai Qi cites it as a primary example of the serious problem posed to editors and collators by "bad" manuscript copies: "The poet's relaxation, detachment and complacency is expressed as such that he seems to have gone beyond the bounds of the universe. The vulgar editions usually have *wang* instead of *jian*. If so, then the line would be spoiled." Such bad choices, Cai Qi alerts us, "simply destroy the fine tone of the entire poem."[23]

Cai Qi's opinion originates from the great literary master of the age, Su Shi, who argues passionately for the reading *jian*:

> Because of picking the chrysanthemum flowers, he happened to *see* the mountain, and what he saw corresponded perfectly to his state of mind. This line is most marvelous. In recent years all the vulgar editions have "*gazing* at South Mountain," which takes away the life of the whole poem. The intention of the ancients was deep and subtle, but vulgar people carelessly alter the text as they wish. This is most abominable.[24]

Thus, for Su Shi, the act of seeing implies a casual effortlessness, the gift of acquiring something without looking for it; but "gazing" would indicate a longing on the poet's part, too ardent, too eager, for the Northern Song master's taste.

Elsewhere Su Shi again uses this couplet as an example to express his annoyance with what he considers thoughtless tampering with the ancient texts. He says, "In recent years, people carelessly altered texts according to their own whims. Vulgar and shallow people usually share the same likes and dislikes, so many chime in agreement. The ancient texts are thereupon getting more and more incorrect and corrupted each day, which is deeply abhorrent."[25] In fact, Northern Song poets often suffered from changes, "corrections," and imperfect transmission in general, even in their own times, and Su Shi himself figures in the Song collections of "random jottings" (*biji*) as someone whose texts frequently escaped authorial control. This may partially account for his anger at the "vulgar and shallow people" altering texts "according to their own whims."[26]

Su Shi may well have been scornful of how "vulgar and shallow" people tend to agree with each other, suggesting both a normative reading and a consensus; but the irony is that his opinion about the advantage of *jian* over *wang* has since become so widely accepted that later commentators often feel embarrassed by the very existence of *wang*.[27] That *jian* is superior to *wang* and therefore must have been the correct or original version is constantly echoed in "remarks on poetry" (*shihua*), promoted mostly by Su Shi's followers or admirers.

In the account of Peng Cheng (fl. ca. 1105), a supporter of Su Shi and a close friend of Su Shi's protégé Huang Tingjian, Su Shi's position regarding the variant is attributed to Huang Tingjian: "Luzhi [Huang Tingjian's courtesy name] once said, 'People of vulgar taste changed [*jian*] into *wang*. If one character is different, the mood and manner of the ancient poet are lost to us. Scholars must keep this in mind.'"[28] The monk Hui Hong (1071–1128?) also records the quotation as Huang Tingjian's in his *Night Chat of the Cold Studio* (Lengzhai yehua).[29]

The retelling of the same story in the prolific "remarks on poetry" of the Song formed a formidable cultural force, effectively perpetuating the assumption about who or what Tao Yuanming was. Even Shen Gua (ca. 1031–1095), who did not necessarily endorse Su Shi's political views, supported the reading of *jian* over *wang*. He says in *Continuation of the Notes of Dream Creek* (Mengxi xubitan), composed between 1088 and 1095:

> Tao Yuanming's couplet from the "Unclassified Poems"—"Picking chrysanthemum flowers by the eastern hedge, / I catch sight of South Mountain in the distance"—was changed into "I gaze at South Mountain in the distance" when *Wen xuan* was collated in the past. This alteration

seems inappropriate. If it were "I gaze at South Mountain," then the meaning of this line would not fit the context, and the poem would not have been a fine piece.[30]

When Shen Gua uses the term "change into," he seems to suggest that there had been a "correct" text of *Wen xuan* which had *jian*, "to see," but that the correct text had been erroneously altered to *wang*, "to gaze at." And yet, neither the earliest extant copy of *Wen xuan* surviving from the Tang nor *Classified Extracts from Literature*, the encyclopedia compiled in 624, has *jian*; they both have *wang* instead. It is not entirely impossible that Su Shi himself invented the variant *jian*, just as many people were wont to do, or misremembered having seen it in some version of the text.[31] Ye Mengde once borrowed a copy of Tao Yuanming's collection from Zhao Delin (the courtesy name of Zhao Lingzhi, 1061–1134), which turned out to have been read by Su Shi: "from time to time I see words changed [by him]."[32] Did Su Shi change these words according to some other edition available to him, or did he simply change them "according to [his] own whims"? It is an interesting practice to make changes—no doubt considered "corrections"—on someone else's book, or perhaps Su Shi had passed on his own book to Zhao Delin, who was a very good friend.

The significance of *jian* lies in the fact that it is an ideological choice. Of all the early comments on *jian* and *wang*, the elucidation of Chao Buzhi (1053–1110), one of Su Shi's most faithful followers, is particularly important. In a colophon written to Tao Yuanming's poetry in 1104, Chao Buzhi gives a further exposition of Su Shi's view:

> In poetry, one can tell fine craftsmanship from clumsiness from one word. For instance, "His body light: a single bird in passage"—or "His body light: a single bird sinks." From "in passage" [*guo*] to "sink" [*xia*] and "goes swiftly" [*ji*] and "descend" [*luo*]—each is different and yet each is not nearly as fine as the original. It is easy to tell [which word is superior or inferior] simply by comparison. Just as what Luzhi [Huang Tingjian] said, it is like comparing jade-like stone with real jade. This, however, is still no more than the kind of comparison one can make between craft and clumsiness, finesse and crudity: the poet's thought and feelings are not immediately clear. I remember when I was at Guangling, Dongpo [Su Shi] said to me, "Tao Yuanming's

heart was not set on poetry; his poems were written to lodge his heart. 'Picking chrysanthemum flowers by the eastern hedge, / I gaze at South Mountain in the distance'—picking chrysanthemum flowers and gazing at the mountains at the same time would have left no room for further thought, which is not the original intention of Yuanming. If the couplet goes 'Picking chrysanthemum flowers by the eastern hedge, / I catch sight of South Mountain in the distance,' then it shows that the poet was just picking chrysanthemum flowers and did not mean to look at the mountains; only accidentally did he raise his head and see them, and thereupon in a detached manner he forgot about his feelings, his mood one of relaxation, and his mind remote." Something like this cannot be sought in the finesse or crudity of words: comparing the difference between *wang* and *jian* to that between stone and jade would be misleading. Written by Chao Buzhi on the last day of the tenth month in the third year of the Chongning reign.[33]

The variants for the Du Fu line "His body light: a single bird in passage" are from an anecdote in Ouyang Xiu's *Liuyi's Remarks on Poetry* (Liuyi shihua). Ouyang Xiu relates how Secretary Chen Congyi once acquired an old copy of Du Fu's poetry "which was full of errors and lacunae." One character, *guo*, was missing from the line in question, and his friends tried to fill in the empty space, giving in turn *ji* (fast), *xia* (sink), and *luo* (descend). But "no one could get it just right. Later Chen got hold of a good edition, and found that the line was, in fact, 'His body light: a single bird in passage.' Chen accepted his defeat with a sigh: as he saw it, even though it was a question of only one word, neither he nor any of his friends could equal Du Fu's choice."[34]

Chao Buzhi makes a fine distinction between the variants for the Du Fu line and those for the Tao Yuanming line. In the former case, he argues, it is a mere matter of "craftsmanship or clumsiness," and everyone can immediately see which word is the best; but in the latter case, it would be difficult to tell which version is better, because what is at stake here is much more than poetic language—it is the poet's intention, attitude, state of mind, his "thought and feelings." Here we see no mention of the issue of manuscript copies or printed editions, and the discussion even transcends aesthetic concerns: it is an elucidation of the superiority of *jian* over *wang* from a purely ideological perspective, based on the person one believes Tao Yuanming to have been. Suddenly the difference between *jian* and *wang* takes on a significance that goes far beyond admiration for ancient masters, anxiety about textual corruption, or even a desire to "find the perfect word" for the missing space. We are dealing with a poet whose heart is believed to be "not set on poetry" (*yi bu zai shi*): if a poet manages to transcend poetry, he does so not by his poetry, but by a particular state of mind. In other words, he prevails by an idealized personality created from scratch by the Song literati members led by Su Shi.

Chao Buzhi's observation recalls Chen Shidao (1053–1101), another illustrious figure of the Su Shi group. In *Houshan's Remarks on Poetry* (Houshan shihua), Chen Shidao tells the students of poetry: "Yuanming did not compose poetry—he was merely writing out the wonders in his heart. Even if one learns from Du Fu and fails, one can still manage to be adroit; but if one is without the talent of a Han Yu or the wonders of a Tao Yuanming and yet tries to learn from their poetry, one would only end up like Letian [Bai Juyi, 772–846]."[35] The distinction between "talent" and "wonders" is again a significant way of differentiation: the former refers to a poet's literary and intellectual capacity; the latter is directed toward the poet as a person.

From this period on, the view that Tao Yuanming's poetry was "nature" or "naturalness" itself became dominant. Huang Tingjian comments: "Xie Kangle [Xie Lingyun, 385–433] and Yu Yicheng [Yu Xin, 513–581] worked at their poetry without sparing any effort, and yet they fall far short of Tao Yuanming, the magistrate of Pengze. Why is this? It is because the two of them cared about the criticism and praise of vulgar people regarding their poetic craftsmanship or lack of poetic skill, while Yuanming simply lodged his heart in his poetry."[36] In a colophon to the poetry of someone named Yike, Huang Tingjian says in similar terms,

> When we come to Yuanming, his poetry is the so-called "just right without having to be cut to a straight line." Even so, those who are skilled at axes often suspect its clumsiness; those who are confined by rulers and measurements complain about its lack of restraint. . . . Yuanming's clumsiness and lack of restraint—how can one talk about these to someone who does not understand![37]

Yang Shi (1053–1135) claims, "The reason why Tao Yuanming's poetry cannot be matched is because his blandness, profundity, and purity are all spontaneous and natural. If one tries hard to emulate it, then one realizes that Yuanming's poetic style cannot be achieved by effort."[38] Huang Che (fl. ca. 1124–1141) in his *Remarks on Poetry at Gong Creek* (Gongxi shihua) seems to have combined the above statements into the following: "The reason why Yuanming cannot be matched is because he had no interest in [poetic] criticism and fame, craftsmanship and clumsiness."[39] The world of Tao Yuanming is thus characterized by an ostensible lack of self-consciousness, represented by *jian*, "to see," not by seeking and desiring, which is represented by *wang*, "to gaze." The mountain must be acquired in a seemingly casual way, as a matter of accident, not sought after earnestly, or desired too passionately.

During the transition period between the Northern Song and Southern Song, one can see how people still sought more tangible evidence to support Su Shi's claim about *jian* being superior to *wang*. Wu Zeng (fl. ca. 1050) says in his *Casual Records from Nenggai Studio* (Nenggaizhai manlu):

> Dongpo believed that ignorant people mistook *jian* as *wang* in the Tao Yuanming couplet "Picking chrysanthemum flowers by the eastern hedge, / I catch sight of South Mountain in the distance," and that the difference between the two characters is like that between jade-like stone and real jade. When I, however, see Letian's poem in imitation of Tao Yuanming, in which a couplet reads, "From time to time I would pour myself a cup of wine, / sitting and gazing at the south-eastern mountains," I realize that the erroneous vulgar version has been there for a long time. Only two lines in Wei Suzhou's [Wei Yingwu] "In Reply to Magistrate Pei Shui of Chang'an"—"I pick chrysanthemum flowers when the dews are still wet / Raising my head and seeing the autumn hills"—have truly acquired the essence of Yuanming's poem, and I thereupon know Dongpo's theory is credible.[40]

It is fascinating to observe the fluidity of the property rights of an idea among the members of a loosely defined literary group, as Huang Tingjian's metaphor of stone and jade, rejected by Chao Buzhi as not discerning enough, is assigned to Su Shi here. But more interesting is Wu Zeng's effort to justify Su Shi's "theory." The Bai Juyi couplet is cited from the ninth of his "Sixteen Poems in Imitation of Tao Qian's Style" (Xiao Tao Qian ti shi shiliu shou; written in 813).[41] If Bai Juyi had indeed written those lines with this particular

Tao Yuanming couplet in mind, then his copy of Tao Yuanming's poetry not only had *wang* for *jian* but most probably had *shishi wang nanshan* 時時望南山 ("from time to time I gaze at South Mountain"), a variant version that, judged from the silence of the commentators, is beyond being dignified with a dismissal.

The Wei Yingwu quotation is, however, more problematic, for the original does not bear a title in which Wei Yingwu claims to be imitating the Tao Yuanming style, as he usually did.[42] It has eighteen lines altogether, and, apart from the two lines cited by Wu Zeng, does not evoke Tao Yuanming in any way. It is a polite poem thanking Magistrate Pei for taking time from his busy official duties to visit a recluse like the poet himself. The two couplets from which Wu Zeng culls out the lines are: "Facing the stream and turning melancholy, / I pick chrysanthemum flowers when the dews are still wet. / Raising my head and seeing the autumn hills, / I feel as though myriad things had been left behind me."

Another Southern Song literary figure, Ge Lifang (?–1164), criticizes Wei for not being able to measure up to Tao Yuanming: "Because Yingwu felt melancholy, he went to pick chrysanthemum flowers; because he saw the autumn hills, he felt he could leave behind myriad things: what he acquired is very different from what Tao had acquired."[43] Once again we see the verb "acquire," and in Ge Lifang's opinion, Wei Yingwu obviously fails to acquire the "fundamental truth" inherent in the mountain scene.

For the Tang poet Wei Yingwu, however, *jian* and *wang* might not have been so profoundly different after all. Another of Wei Yingwu's poems, "Gazing South at the Autumn Scenery in an Idle Courtyard Together with Director Han" (Tong Han langzhong xianting nanwang qiujing), is much closer to Tao Yuanming's South Mountain poem both in spirit and in phrasing. In this poem about the "acquisition" of the mountain scene, "seeing" and "gazing" occur side by side:

朝下抱餘素	*Retiring from the court, I harbor ample plainness;*
地高心本閒	*the place is high, but the heart is always detached.*
如何趨府客	*Why does the person who rushes to the call of service,*
罷秩見秋山	*upon quitting his job, see the autumn hills?*
疏樹共寒意	*Sparse trees share the feeling of cold;*
遊禽同暮還	*roaming birds return home with the dusk.*

因君悟清景	*Because of you, I understand the clear scene;*
西望一開顏	*gazing west, we both break into a smile.*[44]

Carrying off the Mountain

Let me, for the time being, move to another mountain, albeit a miniature one. In 1094, Su Shi saw an unusual rock with nine little peaks belonging to Li Zhengchen of Hukou. He was going to purchase it with a hundred pieces of gold, but before he had time to do it, he was banished to the far south. He wrote a poem to commemorate this experience and named the rock Nine Glories Mountain in a Jug (Huzhong Jiuhua).[45] Eight years later, in 1101, Su Shi was pardoned and summoned back from his exile. Returning to Hukou, he discovered to his disappointment that the rock had been acquired by someone else for eighty thousand cash. He wrote another poem, matching rhymes with his previous piece, to console himself. In this poem, he compared himself to Tao Yuanming, who had come home from official service.[46] But we know that unlike Su Shi, Tao Yuanming returned because he had given up his official post; besides, if Tao Yuanming may write in his literary exposition "Return" (Guiqulai ci) that "the pines and chrysanthemums still remain" upon his homecoming, then Su Shi could only lament that what he left behind—a miniature mountain—had been irrevocably lost.

In a colophon to Li Zhengchen's poem, Chao Buzhi fills us in on the rock's whereabouts:

> The family of Li Zhengchen of Hukou has been collecting strange-looking stones for generations. There are several hundred rocks in his collection. He once had a rock, about five feet tall, with a remarkable shape. When Master Dongpo was banished to Huizhou, he passed by Li Zhengchen's home and named the rock Nine Glories in A Jug, as it has nine peaks. In the ninth month of the second year of the Yuanfu reign [1099], I was banished to Shangrao, and I moored my boat by the temple of Bell Mountain. The monk told me how marvelous the rock was, but Zhengchen did not show up, and I did not have time to visit him. In the seventh month of the third year of the Yuanfu reign [1100], I was pardoned by the emperor and went back north. The first thing I asked the monks of the temple was the whereabouts of the rock, and I learned that it had already been taken away by Guo Xiangzheng of Dangtu for

the price of eighty thousand cash several months ago. And yet Master Dongpo will certainly pass though this place again, and in the collection of Mr. Li there are still many extraordinary and strange-looking rocks. Once the Master writes about them, they would all become more valuable than the Nine Glories.[47]

Chao Buzhi firmly believes that the words of the Master will add value to the rocks in Li Zhengchen's collection if only he cares to write about them, or, more literally, "give them a name." The things of nature, however extraordinary in themselves, lack a name, an identity, and a voice, and they must wait for the recognition of a man—a masterful poet—to become distinguished, just as the poetry of Tao Yuanming must also await the recognition and valuation of the Master to become invaluable. For Chao Buzhi, value also means commodity value: a price in monetary terms. Both Su Shi and Chao Buzhi took care to record the exact cost—anticipated or actual—of the miniature mountain. The last sentence of the colophon, "they would all become more valuable than the Nine Glories," is literally "they would all become more weighty than the Nine Glories." The double entendre of "the Nine Glories"—both the rock with nine little peaks admired by Su Shi and the real Nine Glories Mountain—can hardly escape any reader. The word *zhong,* "weighty," "important," could also mean "costly," as in *guizhong,* a literary and commercial value that perfectly corresponds, in Chao Buzhi's mind, to the grand status of the Master. There is, however, one thing that Chao Buzhi, the faithful disciple, fails to realize: once a rock acquires a name from the Master, it starts to take on an identity, an individuality, and just like the beloved, it becomes unique and so irreplaceable. Su Shi did return to Hukou, just as Chao Buzhi had predicted, less than a year after Chao Buzhi wrote the colophon; but the Master did not name any other rock in Li Zhengchen's collection, but merely wrote with fond recollection about the one rock he had desired and lost.

Ronald Egan states that one of Su Shi's most recurrent themes is "that of non-attachment, that is, not allowing oneself to become attached to things or possessive of them."[48] The obsession with non-attachment, however, always bespeaks a passion for the alternative, and Su Shi indeed deeply cared about acquirement and possession (*de*). There is a poem in his collection with the long, self-explanatory title "The Mate Pool Rock in My Collection Is a Rare Treasure. Wang Jinqing Asks to Borrow It with a Little Poem, and I Know He Intends to Snatch It from Me. I Do Not Dare Not to Lend It to Him, but I Precede the Rock with This Poem."[49] In the poem, he beseeches Wang Jinqing to return the rock to him as soon as possible. The irony is, of course, that this same Wang Jinqing was the very person for whose Hall of Precious Artworks (Baohui Tang) Su Shi wrote an account about fifteen years before in 1077. In that account, Su Shi advised Wang to enjoy the artworks without holding onto them, and that he should not care when such things are taken by someone else.[50]

It is only through knowing Su Shi and his passionate attachment to things that we can understand his admiration of Tao Yuanming, a poet who could look at a mountain without longing for it in the way Su Shi himself longed for a rock, a miniature mountain. Unlike Su Shi, Tao Yuanming did not have to buy the mountain to acquire it. The nature of the acquisition nonetheless remains the same; it is just that Tao Yuanming did it with such apparent ease that Su Shi became fascinated with his gesture. Yet this "apparent ease" is partially Su Shi's creation: his insistence on *jian* (to see) as opposed to *wang* (to gaze at), spontaneous versus deliberate, set the tone for understanding Tao Yuanming in future ages. Su Shi seems to have projected onto the Eastern Jin poet the concerns of his own age as well as his own ideal cultural image.

This would have been merely another case of "reader's reception" had it not involved the choice of a textual variant. To interpret Tao Yuanming is one thing, but to shape the interpretation of Tao Yuanming by actively controlling the texts of his poems is another thing altogether. The image of Tao Yuanming that guided premodern and modern editors' choices of textual variants was, however, no more than a creation, first of the biography writers, and then, more significantly, of the Northern Song literati led by Su Shi. The image acquired its urgency in relation to Northern Song intellectual issues and their own anxieties about acquisition. We are left with a vicious circle here: the supposed character of the historical person determines the choice of the variant, and then the chosen variant is used to support the image of the person. Generation after generation of Tao Yuanming readers have been trapped in such a circle, and few have been able to break free.

In grasping and publicizing the significance of the profound distinction between the variants "seeing" and "gazing," a distinction missed by the "vulgar" crowd, Su Shi proclaims himself to be the person who truly "got" the "fundamental truth" (*zhenyi*) of the former master; after Tao Yuanming, Su Shi is the one to acquire (*de*) South Mountain once again.

Let us turn to another poem by Tao Yuanming. Again this is a poem about possession and loss, and its power is again centered around one textual variant in which is hidden a stolen mountain. The poem is entitled "In the Third Month of the Year of *Yisi*, I Passed through the Qian Creek on a Mission to the Capital When I Was Aide to the General of Jianwei" (Yisi sui sanyue wei Jianwei canjun shi du jing Qianxi):[51]

我不踐斯境	*Since I last set foot on this land,*
歲月好已積	*many months and years have stored up.*
晨夕看山川	*From morning to dusk, I look at the hills and rivers,*
事事悉如昔	*everything happens just like before:*
微雨洗高林	*a light rain cleanses the tall grove;*
清飆矯雲翮	*a fresh wind lifts the wings of cloud.*
眷彼品物存	*I am attached to the myriad things that remain,*
義風 [在義] 都未隔	*never separated from the righteous wind.*[52]
伊余何為者	*And I—what am I doing here?*
勉勵從茲役	*—strive to carry out this service.*
一形似有制	*This solitary form may seem curbed,*
素襟不可易	*but the heart of old is not to be altered.*
園田日夢想	*I dream of gardens and fields every day,*
安得久離析	*how can I be kept away from them for long?*
終懷在歸 [壑] 舟	*In the end I think of* the returning boat / the boat in the ravine;
諒哉負[宜] 霜柏	*steadfast is the cypress* bearing / appropriate for *frost.*[53]

On the surface level, the poem voices a desire to withdraw from public service; but if we look more closely, we see a much more intense preoccupation with what is lost and what may be preserved. Hills and rivers, wind and rain, always remain the same despite the fall of dynasties, wars, chaos—birds too, the short-lived creatures that become immortalized by being reduced to the metonymic "wings of cloud" (*yunhe*) and so retain their faceless, eternal anonymity. A light rain washes the trees clean; then a fresh breeze, which presumably dries the wings of the birds, lifts them up into the clouds. Everything is related to everything else in nature. The phrase *dou wei ge* (not at all separated) stands out in the eighth line, as the poet implicitly sets up a contrast between the harmony of nature and the complications of the human world, in which all kinds of separations exist, such as his own absence from this land, or his severance from home. Revisiting the familiar landscape, the poet nonetheless experiences a new severance, which makes him intensely aware of his dissonant intrusion into a harmonious scene:

> And I—what am I doing here?
> —strive to carry out this service.

Despite his attachment to the things he sees, the poet feels oddly out of place; he is merely a passerby. The solitude of *yixing* (lit., "one form") is clearly set off by the pairing of things in nature—rain and forest, wind and birds. This form is, furthermore, "curbed" by external factors. He is, however, not without consolation: "the heart of old," he says, "is not to be altered." This unalterable ideal is the counterpart of what is permanent in nature, something that proves constant in contrast with the volatile political world and the fragile physical body.

Then, in the final couplet, we find an intriguing variant:

> In the end I think of *the returning boat,*
> steadfast is the cypress bearing frost.

Or alternatively,

> In the end I think of *the boat in the ravine,*
> steadfast is the cypress bearing frost.

The allusion in the last line is doubtlessly to Confucius's famous remark: "It is only when the cold season is here that we know the pines and cypresses are the last to wither."[54] It would be a symbol of the "heart of old" that is not to be altered by circumstances. The first reading, with "the returning boat" instead of "the boat in the ravine," is quite transparent—the poet is probably traveling on water, and so the image of "the returning boat" is most appropriate to indicate his decision to withdraw from public service and go home. In fact, *guizhou* ("the returning boat") is the reading most premodern and modern editors choose to follow.[55] Unfortunately, it makes the poem a much less interesting one.

But if we opt for *hezhou*, "boat in the ravine," then Tao Yuanming's contemporaries would almost certainly not have missed the allusion to a *Zhuangzi* passage:

> You hide a boat in the ravine and a mountain in the swamp, and tell yourself that they will be safe.[56] But in the middle of the night a man of strength shoulders them and carries them off, and in your ignorance you have no idea what happened. It is proper to hide small things in big ones, and yet they get away from you. Now if you were to hide the world in the world, then nothing would get away, and this would be the ultimate reality of permanent things. It is an accident that you have taken on human form, and yet you are delighted. The human form has ten thousand changes that never come to an end—how could one's delights be counted! Therefore, the sage wanders in the realm where things cannot get away from him and all remain.[57]

In this beautiful passage, Zhuangzi discusses the mutability of human life, declaring that one can only find permanence in being resigned to the endless transformations of things. The man of strength (*youlizhe*) who can steal the boat in the ravine and even the mountain in the marsh is a powerful image of the process of transformation. In the context of Tao Yuanming's poem, this image brings the whole poem together in an illuminating way. Months and years accumulate, but the myriad things "remain" (*cun*) in their transformations, which is the same verb used in *Zhuangzi*. The eternal renewal of nature is contrasted with the irrevocable decay of "the human form"—this solitary body (*yi xing*), called into laborious public service. Traveling perhaps in a boat, the poet recalls the image of the boat in the ravine, carried off by a mysterious man of strength in the darkness of the night. The realization that he must make haste to fulfill his cherished desire before his boat is taken to a dark mooring place prompts him to write the last line of the poem, which is the poet's reconfirmation of his decision to return home: life is short, and his only way to contest the whirlwind forces of change is to choose the kind of life he truly loves. The tension between constancy and change is thus sustained until the very end.

In the fifth of his "Unclassified Poems," Tao Yuanming uses the image of the boat in the ravine to describe the rapid course of human life—his life:

壑舟無須臾	*The boat in the ravine hardly stays a moment;*
引我不得住	*it carries me on, giving me no rest.*

前途當幾許　*How much longer is the voyage ahead?*
未知止泊處　*I do not yet know where we will moor.*

The thief carrying away the boat hidden in the ravine is clearly a figure of mutability. But in Tao Yuanming's poem on passing through Qian Creek, this figure of change has itself been tampered with by change, in the form of a textual variant.

The boat thief also carries off something of much larger dimensions: a mountain hidden in a marsh. When Su Shi came back from his exile and discovered he had lost the Nine Glories Mountain in a Jug (the unusual rock with nine peaks), he lamented his loss with a poem. Soon afterwards, he passed away. Then, a year later, his friend Huang Tingjian responded to Su Shi's poem, matching its rhymes.[58] The poem opens with the poignant line: "Someone came at midnight and carried the mountain away." For Huang Tingjian, the loss is double: the loss of the rock to another buyer, and the loss of Su Shi himself. Both are mountains, carried off by an audacious midnight thief.[59]

Possession & Loss

Quite apart from its many hidden and explicit associations with Tao Yuanming, the story revolving around the miniature mountain in a jug may be taken as a fitting metaphor of what happens to Tao Yuanming's poetry. Just as the rock is transformed into a miniature mountain of immortality and becomes both "weighty" and costly upon Su Shi's recognition, Tao Yuanming's poetry acquired unprecedented value ever since the appraisal of Su Shi and his followers such as Huang Tingjian and Chao Buzhi; and, just as with the rock, the value of Tao Yuanming's poetry became both aesthetic and commercialized.

Su Shi himself often talked about writing out Tao Yuanming's poems and prose by hand.[60] An accomplished calligrapher, Su Shi's handwritings were sought out and cherished by many collectors, both his contemporaries and posterity. It is no wonder therefore that of all the Song printed editions of Tao Yuanming's collection, there was one edition that attracted the particular attention of connoisseurs—this was handwritten in beautiful large characters in the calligraphic style of Su Shi himself. Since it has a colophon dated the tenth year of the Shaoxing reign (1140), it is often dubbed as the Shaoxing edition; sometimes it is also called the "printed edition in Su Shi's handwriting" (*Su xie keben* or *Su Shi edition,* hereafter referred to as the Su Shi edition).

It is suspected to have been a reprint of an edition collated and printed by Wang Houzhi (Zhongliang) in the fourth year of the Xuanhe reign (1122). Hu Zi (1108?–1168?) mentions such an edition in his *Collected Comments of the Fisherman Recluse of Tiao Creek, Second Series* (Tiaoxi yuyin conghua houji, preface dated 1167): "I have in my private possession the collection of Master Jingjie's works. It was printed by Wang Zhongliang when he was magistrate at Xinyang in the *renyin* year of the Xuanhe reign [1122]. The characters are large and so particularly easy on my old eyes. The calligraphic style is in imitation of that of Dongpo: it is wonderfully done and very lovely."[61]

It seems to me that a printed edition of Su Shi's handwritten copy of Tao Yuanming's entire collection is no more than a myth, as nowhere in Su Shi's writings did he mention the existence of such an edition. Regarding the so-called Su Shi edition or Shaoxing edition, Liu Shengmu (1878–1959) has made a convincing argument:

> The ten chapters of the collection of Tao Yuanming written in the calligraphic style of Su Shi is commonly regarded as a hand-copy of Su Shi. In fact it was done only in Su Shi's style but not by Su Shi himself. According to the colophon dated the eleventh month of the tenth year of the Shaoxing reign: "I recently acquired the Master's collection, which has been collated by many worthies. Thereupon I carve it on woodblocks, so that it may be immortalized," and so forth. It does not make clear who wrote the colophon, but looking at the calligraphic style, we can ascertain that the colophon and the whole collection were written out by the same hand, and it is quite doubtless that the colophon was written by the person who had the collection carved.[62]

At least for Mao Yi (1640–1713), the claim of Su Shi's handwritten copy of Tao Yuanming's collection was a real one—and one fraught with the pain of family history. His colophon spells out another story of renewed appraisals, recognition, loss, and desire to possess.

> My late father once told me: "Your maternal grandfather had a Northern Song edition of Tao Yuanming's collection, which was handwritten by Su Wenzhong [Su Shi's posthumous title] and then carved onto woodblocks. It was obtained by someone with power in our hometown, and eventually was destroyed in a fire. Wenzhong admired Master Tao

to such an extent that he not only matched the rhymes of all his poems, but also copied out his entire collection by hand to be printed. How devoted he was! A precious edition such as this is like the pearl of Marquis Sui and the jade of Bian He: it is really very rare to obtain one." I remember these words and do not dare to forget them.[63]

Mao Yi's father was Mao Jin (1599–1659), one of the most famous late Ming book collectors and publishers, who built the private library Jigu ge. A Southern Song edition that used to belong to Jigu ge and so is dubbed the "Jigu ge edition" is currently still in the Chinese National Library. It contains a large number of textual variants and is supposedly the same edition that was sold by Mao Yi in his later years to Pan Lei (1646–1708). But Mao Yi is talking about a different edition of Tao Yuanming here, the one his mother's family had lost to "someone with power" (*youlizhe*), the very phrase used in *Zhuangzi* to refer to the one who carries away the hidden boat in the ravine. The *youlizhe* seems to take Tao Yuanming editions as well as mountains and boats.

Although Mao Yi did not mention this "someone" by name, any contemporary reader or anyone familiar with the historical context would immediately know that it was probably none other than the late Ming poet, writer, scholar, and the controversial minister serving two dynasties, Qian Qianyi (1582–1664), who, like Mao Jin and Mao Yi, was from Changshu of Jiangsu. Qian Qianyi in fact wrote a colophon in the summer of 1643 to an edition referred to as "The Collected Works of Tao Yuanming Copied by Dongpo," in which he praised the edition extravagantly:

> The calligraphy is bold and elegant, and looks extremely similar to the tomb inscription of Sima Guang [1019–1086; written by Su Shi]. There is no doubt that it was by the hand of Dongpo. The woodblock carving is exquisite. Between the lines one senses an aura of nobility and dignity that come with age. Indeed this is a treasure rare to find in this world.[64]

We do not know if this is the edition that Mao Yi claims had been snatched away from his family collection, but it seems likely. In 1643, Qian Qianyi built the Tower of Crimson Cloud (Jiangyun Lou) to house his recently acquired concubine and the famed former courtesan Liu Shi (1618–1664) as well as many rare editions. Both Liu Shi and the rare Song editions are, of course, *youwu*—"the most lovely creatures"—and Qian Qianyi's eight poems written upon the completion of the tower adequately describe his pleasure in both: "Together we rise and retire in this tower of a hundred feet, playing with both zither and books on the third-tier terrace."[65] But the name Qian Qianyi chose for his tower—Crimson Cloud—could not have been more unfortunate: the crimson color of something as transient and changeable as wisps of cloud seems to have foretold the great fire of 1649, which burned down the tower and destroyed many of the rare books in Qian Qianyi's possession.

Mao Yi's colophon does not end here. In the subsequent account, he relates a story of taking revenge in a family feud as well as playing the chivalrous role of Lin Xiangru (third century B.C.E.), the resourceful Zhao minister who successfully recovered the priceless jade of Bian He (seventh century B.C.E.) from the greedy King of Qin:

> One day I met Qian Zunwang [1629–1701], who showed me this edition. I opened and examined it closely: it was written in the style of Su Dongpo, but after the colophon of Si Yue there is a colophon dated the tenth year of the Shaoxing reign by an anonymous person, so it cannot be a Northern Song edition. But the calligraphic style is distinctly that of Su Shi, and I know it must have been a reprint of the original Su Shi edition. At first, Gu Mei [fl. 1653] [Yiren] of Taicang put this edition up for sale, and he showed it to Zunwang. Zunwang said, "This is only a Yuan edition and not worth much." Yiren asked, "How do you know this?" Zunwang answered, "It says, 'The Song edition has such and such variant characters.' So it has to be a Yuan edition." Yiren had nothing to say upon hearing this, and so he sold the edition to Zunwang at a discount price. When I heard of this, I smiled and said, "The so-called Song edition refers to the edition of Prime Minister Song Xiang [not to the Song Dynasty]. If Zunwang did not know this and told Yiren those words, it was unwise of him; if he did know this and still told Yiren those words, it was dishonest of him. But I have long received instructions from my deceased father and so I know it is a good edition." Yiren heard this and so he redeemed the edition with the original price, and subsequently named his studio Tao Lu [Tao Cottage]. He also asked some contemporary celebrity figure to write an account in commemoration of this event.

Qian Zunwang is Qian Zeng, a grand-nephew of Qian Qianyi and an avid book collector himself.[66] We do not know if he was being dishonest when he misinformed Gu Mei of the date of the edition, for it was much more common to regard the phrase "Song edition" (Song ben) as referring to a Song Dynasty edition than to the "Song Xiang edition" (Song Xiang ben). The fact that Qian Zeng allowed Gu Mei to redeem the edition for the original price (which was a cheaper price than the cost of a Song edition) seems to indicate that he was not aware that he had in his possession a Song edition after all. By helping Gu Mei repossess the Song edition he lost in ignorance, Mao Yi in a way "got back" at the Qian family, and he did not specify who the "contemporary celebrity figure" was; it was none other than Qian Qianyi.

Mao Yi acquired more than just a sense of satisfaction from the incident:

> I said to Yiren, "If not for my words, then your bright pearl would have been thrown away to a dark place for a long time, and how could you have obtained your so-called Tao Cottage? Now how about lending your edition to me to make a copy of it?" My teacher Master Qian Meixian is a great calligrapher, and so I asked him to copy out the edition by hand. He completed the task in a year. The brushwork and ink shine forth from the paper, clearly in the style of the original. Those who obtain my edition later must not take it lightly.
>
> My maternal grandfather's first name was Zhan and his courtesy name was Dexin. He called himself Yue'an. He was the grandson of Yan the Duke Wenjing [Yan Na, a Ming minister; 1511–1584] and the fourth son of Palace Secretary Master Dongting. In the last quarter of the fourth month of the year of *shenxu* [1694], Mao Yi, the descendent of Jigu, wrote the above.

To return to his maternal grandfather at the end of the colophon is a clear indication that Mao Yi intends it to be read as a narrative about settling scores: the anonymous "someone with power" (*youlizhe*) who snatched away his maternal grandfather's precious Northern Song edition is now completely eclipsed by the detailed account of his grandfather's name, courtesy name, style name, as well as his illustrious lineage; and Mao Yi, the descendant of the wronged ancestor, claims a victory by helping Gu Mei repossess his rare book as well as by making a copy of it for himself. And we must note that it is not just to reproduce the words of the original: it is to duplicate the original as closely as possible in terms of calligraphic style. Mao Yi's father Mao Jin was the person who began the practice of hiring good calligraphers to copy those

Song editions he could not acquire on paper of the best quality. The product was dubbed "facsimile of the Song [edition]" (*ying Song chao*). The price for copying a book was sometimes even higher than the buying price.[67]

The story told in Mao Yi's colophon is an intricate one about possession, exchange, and value. Like the rare book itself, information and knowledge also acquire a price in the economic system of exchange, as the correct identification of a rare Song edition earns Mao Yi the right to make a personal copy of the rare edition. It is not just any copy, but a copy done with care and craftsmanship, a work of art in itself. This is why Mao Yi takes the trouble to let us know exactly how much time Qian Meixian had spent copying the entire book, as the time and labor spent on it only served to increase the value of this copy of a copy.

In the end, however, this is a story about power: power exerted and flaunted in vain, power contested in the site of a rare book—an edition of the collection of someone who is supposed to be the least interested in power. The "someone with power" who carried away the rare book like a hidden boat in the ravine lost the book to the fearful force of nature, and his descendent lost another rare book through ignorance and bad luck, while the descendent of the deprived Yan Zhan got back what had been taken away from the family—both in the form of a handwritten copy and in the form of a colophon written to publicize the balancing of accounts in a quiet family feud.[68]

No less than a painting, a garden, or a precious piece of bronze or jade work from antiquity, a rare book was a much desired commodity in late imperial China, as well as a site of displaying and contesting power—economic, political, and cultural. A Southern Song edition of Tao Yuanming's poetry (with his literary exposition "Return" appended at the end) annotated by Tang Han (1202–1272) is the subject of another story of possession and loss. Gu Zixiu's 1787 colophon details how his friend Zhou Chun (1729–1815) obtained this precious edition. In the year of *xinchou* (1781), Bao Tingbo (Yiwen; 1728–1814) and Wu Qian (Kuili; 1733–1813) visited Zhou Chun; that night, they mentioned a collection of Tao Yuanming's poetry with a preface by Tang Han, of whose identity they knew nothing. Zhou Chun slapped the table and cried out: "That's a wonderful book!" He started telling them who Tang Han was, and Bao Tingbo, realizing he had just missed a rare edition, "looked devastated, as if he had lost something." When Zhou Chun asked him if he had the book with him, Bao Tingbo answered that he had given it to Zhang Yanchang (Qitang; 1738–1814) of Haiyan. On the fifth day of the fifth month, Zhou Chun borrowed the book from Zhang, and what happened next, euphemistically described by Gu Zixiu as Zhang's pressing for a return of the book and then Zhou's compromise in offering an exchange, is obviously an audacious case of deprivation: "At first, Zhou offered Zhang calligraphy pieces, paintings, bronzes, porcelains, as well as the Duan ink stones, but Zhang refused them all." Finally, Zhou got away with a grand old ink stick, which weighed about one catty and was worth a certain amount in white gold. The whole negotiation process took about two years, and was settled in 1783: "This book then became the possession of Master Zhou, and it was so difficult to obtain it!"[69]

Then, in 1786, Bao Tingbo finally got hold of a copy of the edition. Zhang Yanchang urged Wu Qian—a book collector himself and famous for his Baijing Lou—to carve the book on a set of woodblocks and reprint it.[70] Then Gu Zixiu praised Zhou Chun, without whose exquisite recognition and evaluation, he argued, the book would not have been able to come into circulation. He also referred to Bao, Zhang, and Wu as "enthusiastic people" or "connoisseurs" (*haoshizhe*) "rare to find among the crowd." The rarity of the people who sponsored the printing of the edition in certain ways complemented the rare book.

Zhou Chun, according to his own account, was "overwhelmed with joy" when he "acquired this book from a friend." He repaired the worn places of the book himself and then had someone rebind it. Somewhat troubling, however, is that he wrote the account three days after the summer solstice of 1781, when the book was still supposed to be borrowed property. It is amusing to note that on the back of this page with Zhou Chun's account, which obviously had been inserted at the very beginning of the book (before Tang Han's original preface) during the rebinding, there is an elegant seal inscription: "I regard myself as a person of the age before the Fuxi emperor" ("Zi wei shi Xi huang shang ren"). This is a phrase taken from Tao Yuanming's "Letter to My Sons: Yan and the Others" (Yu zi Yan deng shu). In the letter Tao Yuanming tells of lying under the northern window (the coolest spot in the house) in the fifth and sixth months, and when a breeze comes, he thinks of himself as a person of the age before the Fuxi emperor.[71] The fifth and sixth months were exactly the season in which Zhou Chun wrote his happy account of "acquiring the book," and his joy indeed seems to have spilled out into the seal inscription.

Zhou Chun also named his studio Li Tao Zhai. *Li* (rites) refers to the Song edition of a book on rites he owned, but it may be also taken as a verb, in which sense the studio's name means "Treating Tao Respectfully with Proper Rites." We may remember that Gu Mei, after he repossessed his lost Song edition, named his studio Tao Lu (Tao Cottage), as well as asking a literary celebrity to write a record of it—this is an interesting way of flaunting one's possession indeed, by naming the studio after the author of a rare book. Yet the ostensible display of possession by naming the studio after the book was coupled with a tantalizing gesture of reclusion and exclusion: it is said that for the rest of his life Zhou Chun never showed the book to anyone, and told people that after his death he was going to have it buried with him. Zhou Chun was perhaps quite aware that by allowing access to his rare book he risked being deprived of it by "someone with power" (*youlizhe*), just as Qian Zeng's showing his edition to Mao Yi led to his loss of the book. Zhou Chun's refusal to show the book, however, served only to arouse a stronger desire. Huang Pilie, the book collector and bibliographer who called himself the Master of Being Servile to the Song [Editions] (Ning Song Zhuren), confessed in his colophon eventually added to this Southern Song book, "I heard all about it from the Wuxing book dealers and had been thinking of the book for a long time."

The year was 1808, the season between summer and autumn. "A rumor saying that bookseller so and so had gotten hold of this book and was going to put it up for sale in the Wu region created a big splash." Huang waited and waited, but never heard anything else. Then he got a letter from a friend saying that he had offered forty taels of silver for the book, but unfortunately did not win the bid; the book had been carried away by a family of Xiashi. By this time, Huang had given up all hope of obtaining the book.

Then, in the summer of 1809, an opportunity presented itself to Huang Pilie in the form of Wu Xiu (Zixiu, 1764–1827), a connoisseur of paintings, calligraphy, bronzes, and stones. He had borrowed the book from the family of Xiashi, and showed it to Huang Pilie during his visit. Huang learned that it was possible to "talk business with" the Xiashi family. Wu Xiu's role in the whole transaction was a little ambiguous: did he also covet the book, but could not offer a better price than Huang? Or was he a mere medium in the business transaction? It is not immediately clear from Huang's narrative. One clear thing is that "the negotiation took a long time," and the final price was fixed at a hundred taels of silver—more than twice as much as Huang's friend had offered before. The cost was, however, only partially paid in the form of silver; the rest was fulfilled by "literati's objects"—perhaps ink stones, brush holders, or first-class ink sticks.

Huang Pilie wrote the colophon on the mid-autumn day of 1809. Above the neatly written colophon, in the empty margin of the page, he had scribbled out an additional note in smaller characters and with a more casual hand, saying that

Zhou Chun, upon selling his Song book on rites, had changed his studio name from Li Tao Zhai to Bao Tao Zhai (Studio of Treasuring Tao); then, after he sold the Tao collection, he again changed his studio name to Meng Tao Zhai (Studio of Dreaming of Tao). As for Huang himself, since this is the second Song edition of Tao Yuanming's collection in his possession, he named his studio Tao Tao Shi (Chamber of the Double Taos). The phrase *taotao* also describes pleasure and enjoyment, as in *qile taotao* (something like "giddy with joy").

The "Tao" embedded in these various studio names does not represent so much Tao Yuanming the poet or his poetry as an edition of his collection. The identification of Tao Yuanming with a Song edition makes it possible to literally obtain and own him in the physical form of a book. Tao Yuanming's poetry is quite beside the point here; rather, it is an obsession with things of value that prevails. A rare book is, to be sure, a rather peculiar thing of value; the passion for books carries with it the cachet of a particular social class. Looking at the many seals stamped on the Tang Han edition (more than forty, as it has changed hands many times, both before and after Huang Pilie), one cannot help noticing the similarity between the book and many mountains in China, which are often inscribed to various degrees, sometimes so heavily that it becomes hard to find an empty spot on an entire cliff. The point in both cases is to leave a mark of oneself on the desired object and so establish an actual or symbolic ownership. Many have commented on "reading a landscape" as if a landscape were a book; but in the case of Tao Yuanming's poetry, the literary works of Tao Yuanming became more and more like the inscribed flat surface of a cliff: a petrified object, appreciated less for its inner content than for its surface. To obtain a rare edition of Tao Yuanming was like obtaining a rock: if one could not acquire the whole mountain, then at least one could seize a part of it in the form of a rock that resembles the mountain. In the same way, one thinks one can possess the elusive poet—the poet whose texts have appeared differently in different manuscript copies, so much so that sometimes one character may have "dozens of variants."

In his letter to his sons, before he tells them about the pleasure of lying in a cool, breezy spot in early summer, Tao Yuanming describes another pleasure:

> I studied zither and books when I was young, and I happened to love leisure and peace. If I opened a scroll and acquired something from it, then I would be so delighted that I forgot to eat.

It is the pleasure of reading, but not just of reading; it is also the pleasure of *youde*—"acquiring something" from the books. Tao Yuanming's remark accords perfectly with what he says of himself in "The Biography of Master Five Willows" (Wuliu xiansheng zhuan): "He likes reading, but does not seek hard to understand; and yet, whenever he comprehends the concept, he becomes so happy that he forgets to eat." In both quotations, we hear the echo of "obtaining the concept and forgetting the words" (*deyi wangyan*).

This lineage of moments across a millennium and a half in the story of Tao Yuanming is, as I hope the reader can see, something of an allegory of the changes in "acquiring" the mountain and the truth. Tao Yuanming "acquired" his mountain by keeping his distance, and there seems a peculiar relation between such distance and the fluid and elusive nature of both the poet and the text of his works in manuscript culture. The more later ages tried to take possession of Tao Yuanming, his truth, and his mountain, the more these became a fixed thing, a commodity that passed from hand to hand and could be snatched away by that dark "someone with power." The poet's text was "fixed," in several senses of the word, and became an antiquarian object, whose meaning was also "fixed" by the antiquarian structure of values that belonged far more to the age of those who "fixed" it than to Tao Yuanming himself. Yet this peculiar object, the Tao Yuanming embodied in his poetry, remained there, gesturing outside the sphere of those who acquired and possessed him.

The Tang monk Jiaoran (720?–796?) once wrote a poem entitled "The Tenth Day of the Ninth Month" (Jiuyue shiri). In the last couplet, he, too, talks about "gazing south":

愛殺柴桑隱	*I am damn fond of the recluse of Chaisang;*
名溪近訟庭	*the famous stream is close to the legal court.*
掃沙開野步	*Sweeping the river bank to open up a wild dock,*
搖舸出閒汀	*I steer a little boat around the lazy sandbar.*
宿簡邀詩伴	*A note from last night to invite poet companions;*
餘花在酒瓶	*in the wine jar there are still remaining flowers.*
悠然南望意	*The intent of gazing south in the distance*
自有峴山情	*naturally contains the feelings for Mount Xian.*[72]

While most people write about the ninth day of the ninth month, Jiaoran chose to write about the "aftermath" of the Double Ninth, when there are only "remaining [chrysanthemum] flowers" in the wine jar. They are the "leftovers" from yesterday: a superfluous abundance that paradoxically indicates a lack, a presence denoting absence and the passage of time.

Chaisang was Tao Yuanming's hometown. In Tao Yuanming's poetry collection, there are three poems addressed to the Magistrate of Chaisang, one to Magistrate Ding, and two to Magistrate Liu. The latter is often identified as Liu Yimin (359?–415), who once served as a magistrate but then withdrew from the office to become a recluse and a devout Buddhist. The last couplet evokes the famous Western Jin minister Yang Hu (221–278), the capable governor of Jingzhou. Yang Hu, when stationed at Xiangyang, often went off to Mount Xian. There he would drink, talk, and recite poetry all day long. Once, in the middle of a party, he sighed with emotion, saying to his attendants,

> As long as the universe has been, so long has this mountain been. Many have been the worthy and great men who, just as you and I now, have climbed here to gaze afar. They have all perished and are heard of no more—this is what gives me sorrow. If after my lifetime I still have any consciousness, then surely my soul will climb to this spot.[73]

After Yang Hu died, the people of Xiangyang erected a stele on the mountain to commemorate the man. Whoever gazed at the stele would always shed tears, and so Yang Hu's appointed successor, Du Yu (222–284), named it the "stele for shedding tears" (*duo lei bei*). Du Yu himself, who "loved to make a posthumous name," made two steles on which he carved his accomplishments; then he sank one into the river beneath Mount Wan and set the other atop Mount Xian, saying, "How do we know that in the future the river will not turn into a hill and the hill into a valley?"[74]

We do not know where Jiaoran wrote this poem and what mountain he was gazing at in the south. One thing is clear: in Jiaoran's poem, Mount Xian is no longer the site from which one gazes afar, but becomes the object of a gaze—even if it is just in the mind's eye. In many ways, Jiaoran's poem is reminiscent of Tao Yuanming (and we may speculate that the version of Tao Yuanming's South Mountain poem seen by Jiaoran must have had *wang* instead of *jian*): the closeness of the stream to the legal court clearly echoes the sentiment that when the heart is far away, the locale naturally becomes remote. We also see all the familiar motifs: the chrysanthemum flowers, the wine, and the southward gaze into the distance. Mount Xian, massive and heavy, is placed side by side with those "remaining flowers in the wine jar," and serves as both a sign of permanence and a reminder of human fragility. It is vain, after all, to pick chrysanthemum flowers on the Double Ninth, a festival associated with longevity and durability which itself has turned into yesterday.

From Yang Hu and Tao Yuanming to Jiaoran, several hundred years had passed, but the desire for permanence remained the same, even though everything else in the "human realm" proved more transient. Jiaoran, who claimed to be the tenth generation descendent of Xie Lingyun, Tao Yuanming's contemporary poet who often obtained "metaphysical truth" in the landscape, described his own attainment not so much in terms of *de* but in terms of *you*—"'having' rather than specifically owning."[75] In fact, it is *zi you*, an unforced, unstrained "having," untainted by the kind of anxiety about possession and loss shown by the later-born. And rather than obtaining the mountain itself, Jiaoran claims that his gaze "naturally contains" feelings for Mount Xian, the yearning for an immortal name that moved Yang Hu to sighs and Du Yu to carving the steles. This is a different way of possessing the mountain, even though the nature of appropriation is unchanged.

2 "Who the Master Is, No One Knows"

Language is the body's pattern [wen].
When the body is going to hide,
what need does one have for wen?
[Speaking up] would be to seek to be known.

—*Zuo zhuan*, Duke Xi 24

There has been much debate and speculation about the detailed chronology of Tao Yuanming's life. The biographies of Tao Yuanming preserved in various historical sources do not contribute much toward a clarification of the poet's dates; instead, the biographies and the way in which scholars have dealt with the biographies present some interesting and interrelated issues regarding the reconfiguration of the poet's image, the construction of history, and the problems of manuscript culture. Although the main body of the various biographies remains basically the same, there are a number of additions and deletions in the details, which, taken together, present us with subtly different pictures of the poet, as well as disclosing the different dispositions of the biographers themselves. All of the biographies, moreover, have incorporated Tao Yuanming's writings, varying from one to four pieces, which present us with many significant textual variants. Scholars, however, tend to look to modern editions of Tao Yuanming's work, which either eliminate the variants or keep them while ignoring their implications. This leads to many new problems, such as the questionable claim that there are discrepancies between Tao Yuanming's writings and his biographies, which will be taken up later in this chapter.

Unlike his great-grandfather Tao Kan, Tao Yuanming never served in a prominent official post, nor was he one of the most notable members (or even the only recluse) of the Tao clan.[1] It seems reasonable to assume that, apart from the poet's communications with his more distinguished contemporaries and their subsequent (written or oral) accounts of him, which found their way into various historical writings forming the sources of the earliest extant official biography of Tao Yuanming, the other likely source for biographical information about the poet would be his own writings, which were already circulating during Tao Yuanming's lifetime. A. R. Davis once commented,

> For the family and appointment details some kind of official source may be presumed, but for the character anecdotes it seems to me probable that T'ao's own writings were in most cases the prime source. Before they were gathered into the histories, they had acquired a greater or less degree of exaggeration and had been sometimes set for the sake of verisimilitude in particular but doubtful contexts. If this view is correct, to use the anecdotal material of the biographies to provide a context for particular poems of T'ao is clearly a risky proceeding.[2]

This is an insightful observation that may be taken further in new directions. Looking closely, we notice that even a large part of "the family and appointment details" could be easily assembled from Tao Yuanming's poetry and prose. For instance, almost all of the official posts served by Tao Yuanming and mentioned in his biographies, except for the initial appointment of Libationer of Jiangzhou prefecture, appeared, in one place or another, in his writings. The poem discussed in the previous section, "In the Third Month of the Year of *Yisi* [405], I Passed through the Qian Creek on a Mission to the Capital When I Was Aide to the General of Jianwei," furnishes a good example. There is another poem with a similarly explicit narrative title (though not explicit enough to satisfy the curiosity of many a Tao'ologist): "Upon Passing through Qu'e When Beginning My Service as Aide to the General of Zhenjun" (Shi zuo Zhenjun canjun jing Qu'e). The preface to the well-known literary exposition "Return" relates the complete story of the poet's short service as the magistrate of Pengze County. In the poem "Charge to My Son" (Ming zi), Tao Yuanming sketches his family genealogy, indicating in no ambiguous terms that Tao Kan, the Duke of Changsha, was his ancestor, and that both his grandfather and father had held office. We will examine in what way the "anecdotal material of the biographies" accords with Tao Yuanming's writings by and by; for the moment, it suffices to suggest that in the sense that Tao Yuanming's works provided his biographers with both background information and testimony of what they knew, the phrase "poetry as autobiography" is rendered literal.[3]

Canonical statements of Chinese literary theory always point to the paramount importance of knowing "who an author is." Ever since Mencius (fourth century B.C.E.) first phrased it in those terms, "to know what kind of person the author was and to consider the age in which he lived" (*zhi ren lun shi*) has held sway over Chinese literary critics even to the present.[4] This exegetical imperative develops from the canonical proposition that poetry is "that to which what is intently on the mind goes,"[5] and therefore a function of the poet's unique personality, identity, thoughts, and feelings. Such a poetics, however, gave rise to a series of problems. The insistence on a perfect correspondence between "what is intently on the mind" and what comes out in language is the source of an enduring anxiety about the "truthfulness" or "genuineness" (*zhen*) of one's words and the transparency of one's intentions. Mencius, for instance, warns against being deceived by elusive words that seek to escape and hide.[6] Confucius mistrusts "crafty words" (*qiaoyan*) and emphasizes the potential discrepancy between one's words and one's action: "I used to listen to what a person said and believed that was what he did; now I listen to what a person says but observe what he does."[7]

A critical theory that claims to be based on the knowledge of what kind of person the author is requires, first of all, a context in which we can make sense of the text. In the case of Tao Yuanming, we face an apparently irresolvable difficulty: if the poet's biographies are to a large extent constructed on the basis of his own writings, then the attempt to seek a context for Tao Yuanming's poetry and prose outside his poetry and prose is doomed to a vicious circle. Indeed, all the biographies we have of Tao Yuanming begin with Tao Yuanming's own pseudo-autobiographical account, the famous "Biography of Master Five Willows." After quoting the short piece in its entirety, the biographers unanimously conclude in these very same words, "His contemporaries considered it a factual record [of himself]."

Already in this statement do we see the tendency to use a person's writings to understand and define the person, and the boundary between reality and literary configuration becomes blurred. While the biographers employ the poet's writings to construct the life of the man, readers begin to use the poet's writings to support the claims made by his biographies and hence prove the poet's "transparency" or "genuineness" (regarded not so much as the opposite of hypocrisy but as the equivalent of an utter lack of self-consciousness). As contemporary scholar Wang Guoying points out, "Ever since the Song Dynasty, whenever people were writing a chronological account of Tao Yuanming's life and works or any critical biography, or even when they were just analyzing or annotating Tao Yuanming's poetry and prose, they would almost always rely on these biographies as supportive evidence of a viewpoint or an argument."[8] Expounding Tao Yuanming's poems with bits and pieces from the biographies, critics and scholars began putting together a composite portrait of the poet. When we look at this portrait, it is almost impossible to tell Tao Yuanming's own writings and his "life stories" apart.

Finally, when editors and annotators encountered the problems with textual variants that inevitably arose in a manuscript culture, it became common practice to use a shared image of Tao Yuanming as a standard to decide which word would be the best choice and which word must have been "an inferior substitute filled in by a shallow person"—a common phrase used by an annotator to refer to a variant he does not like. This is exactly what happened in the case of "gazing" and "seeing" discussed in the previous chapter. A full circle is thus completed: we see that the poet's biographies are based on his writings; then his writings are edited and altered on the basis of the poet's image as presented in his biographies; eventually, this relatively fixed version of the poet's writings is used to substantiate the poet's image.

The field of classical Chinese literary studies in China is characterized by a passionate desire to know. The desire is not necessarily utilitarian, for to know precisely who the Jianwei General was does not contribute a better understanding or appreciation of the poem in any obvious way, and yet it has sent many a scholar to painstaking research and generated a great deal of discussion and speculation. This desire to know represents a particular form of acquiring a sense of belonging and retains its central importance in a poetics built on and around social relations.

Yet in his fictive autobiography Tao Yuanming declares that the identity of Master Five Willows is unknown: "Who the Master is, no one knows; nor is his name identified. Since there are five willows beside his residence, he is called Master Five Willows."[9] This opening statement, troping on the famous poet Ruan Ji's (210–263) "Biography of Master Great Man" (Daren xiansheng zhuan),[10] uncannily foretells Tao Yuanming's own fate in Chinese literary history. Hardly had half a century passed before his very name had already become a point of doubt. Shen Yue, Tao Yuanming's first biographer, states at the opening of Tao Yuanming's biography, "Tao Qian's courtesy name was Yuanming; some say his name was Yuanming and his courtesy name Yuanliang." In another fifty years the second biographer, Xiao Tong, reversed the order of Shen Yue's statement, so that in his version Qian is the courtesy name and Yuanming the name. *The Jin History* (Jin shu) and *The Histories of the Southern Dynasties* (Nan shi) both come up with more ingenious combinations, though the essential ingredients are kept.[11] The ambiguity shrouding the name of Tao Yuanming finally led to the theory that after the Eastern Jin fell Tao Yuanming changed his name as an expression of his loyalist sentiments,[12] a hypothesis which, however clever, was much more consonant with the thirteenth-century context of the Southern Song than with the Southern Dynasties, when loyalism was not yet as serious an issue. During the Southern Dynasties, it was in fact extremely common for a person to serve more than one dynasty, sometimes even up to three.

Because of the multiple meanings of the phrase *hexu* 何許 in classical Chinese, the first sentence of the "Biography of Master Five Willows" could also be understood as "where the Master came from / what age he lived in, no one knows." Even though *hexu* is generally understood as "whence" in the context of the biography, a play with words would not be entirely improper when dealing with Tao Yuanming, a supreme manipulator of words.

Before we undertake a close comparison of the different versions of Tao Yuanming's biography as a "recluse" (*yinshi* 隱士) in dynastic histories, perhaps we should look at how the poet constructs his own image in his "autobiography," and set up some of the contemporary issues around Tao Yuanming as a "recluse."

What Is at Stake in Naming: Constructing Master Five Willows & the "Terms" of Reclusion in the Six Dynasties

Any reconstruction of Tao Yuanming must begin with his own construction of Master Five Willows:

> Who the Master is, no one knows; nor is his name identified. Since there are five willows beside his residence, he is called Master Five Willows. He is a quiet man of few words, admiring neither glory nor gain. He

likes reading, but does not seek hard to understand; and yet, whenever he comprehends the concept, he becomes so happy that he forgets to eat.[13] By nature he loves wine, which he cannot often obtain due to his poverty. Relatives and old friends know this and sometimes invite him to a drinking party. He arrives and finishes what is in his cup right away, always expecting to get drunk. As soon as he is drunk, he withdraws, never begrudging either leaving or staying. His house is bare, the roof and walls hardly providing a shelter against wind or sun; his hemp clothes are plain and shabby; his food basket and gourd ladle frequently go empty; he is at peace. Often he composes literary works to entertain himself, revealing his aims quite well. Forgetting about gain and loss, he lives out his life like this.

Appraisal: Qianlou's wife once said, "He [Qianlou] was not upset about poverty and low station; nor did he eagerly pursue wealth and honor."[14] Such words might be able to describe what kind of person the Master is. Enjoying wine and writing poetry, he rejoices in his aims. Is he a person of the age of Wuhuai? Or is he a person of the age of Getian?[15]

Apart from a disregard of glory and gain, this is a self-portrait that emphasizes spontaneity (*ziran*): the Master's love of reading is combined with a lack of interest in a zealous quest for knowledge, and this lack of interest in arduous exertion is qualified by a more spontaneous pleasure in "getting" something by accident. Essentially the Master does not "seek" to understand, but waits for understanding to occur more "naturally." The spirit of spontaneity is further illustrated in the act of coming to a party and finishing his wine right away and then withdrawing as soon as he gets drunk, a description that implies this is a person who cares more for the wine than for social formalities.

Another emphasis in this short piece is on spiritual happiness. After listing a series of life's necessities, which for Master Five Willows are clearly in short supply—"His house is bare, the roof and walls hardly providing a shelter against wind or sun; his hemp clothes are plain and shabby; his food basket and gourd ladle frequently go empty"—the author concludes with a terse statement: "he is at peace." Such a state of mind is not a result of abundant material possessions but is closely associated with reading and writing: when he "gets" something in the books, "he becomes so happy that he forgets to eat"; he "composes literary works to entertain himself"; and, finally, "Enjoying wine and writing poetry, he rejoices in his aims." The echo of *The Analects* is unmistakable, in particular the two passages concerning Confucius's favorite disciple Yan Hui: "The Master said, 'How worthy was Hui! With one basket of food and one ladle of water in a shabby lane, others could hardly bear the sorrows brought by such hardship, but Hui never lost his joy. How worthy was Hui!'" and "The Master said, 'One could say that Hui had come very close to it [the Way]. He often suffered from emptiness [e.g., poverty].'"[16]

This is not a person, however, who is blissfully oblivious of social formalities and the necessities of life (or the lack of them). He is aware of the kind intentions of his relatives and friends who invite him, a person too poor to buy wine himself, and he is aware of all the things he claims he does not care about or has forgotten—it does not matter whether it is merely one meal or some larger "gain and loss." The modern scholar Qian Zhongshu (1910–1998) once pointed out that the key word of this piece is *bu* (not), the term of negation.[17] What Qian did not point out is that each negation paradoxically contains (and so reminds the reader of) what it negates. This becomes ironic only through reading the piece as autobiography—that is, considering the narrator and Master Five Willows as one and the same person.

Finally, we must call the reader's attention to this statement: "Often he composes literary works to entertain himself, revealing his aims quite well." The word "aims" (*zhi* 志) is a loaded word in the Chinese cultural tradition, carrying with it both political and literary implications. The basic meaning of the word, however, is "what is intently on the mind." The problem here is the apparent conflict between the stated objective of his writings, which is to amuse himself, and the nature of the writings, which reveal (*shi*) his aims. If one's purported reader is oneself (writing for one's own amusement), then to whom does he have to demonstrate what is on his mind?

Here it becomes necessary for us to examine how the terms of reclusion have been constructed during the Six Dynasties, and how these contemporary issues around "reclusion" may help us understand Tao Yuanming in a larger, historical context.

Shen Yue (441–513) is the first to have written Tao Yuanming's biography, which is included in "Biographies of Recluses" in *The Song History* (Song shu). His foreword is a reflective elucidation on the paradox of *yin* (to go in hiding and become a recluse) and *xian* (to show oneself and become known). Shen Yue distinguishes between the reclusion of "the worthy man" (*xian ren*) and that of the recluse (*yin zhe*). We might particularly note his attention to the word *ji*, "trace," which was an important concept in Lao-Zhuang thought:[18]

> The meaning of *yin* is that the traces are not overtly manifested and that one's way cannot be known. When no sage emerges for a thousand years of silence, then great worthies keep themselves hidden and lower themselves to the level of the common folks. But they do so merely to preserve their lives and keep out of harm's way, so they do not necessarily have to reside in caves or dwell under cliffs. They are a repository of experiences and, grasping the principles of success and failure, are close to sagehood, but no one in the age descries them and nothing in this world detects them. For someone like this, how can he wash his ears at the Ying River and, by doing so, explicitly reveal his aims of rising above the crowd?
>
> To flee and shun the world—this is the doing of a worthy man. Wherever one goes, one is always within the world, and yet there are reasons to evade the world. Hence we know that the basic principle is to veil one's way, but not to hide one's body. "Nest-Dweller" is the very name by which the [nameless] person is designated; and the designation "Furry Elder" has come into being because there are overt traces that can be transmitted.[19] This is the kind of reclusion practiced by the old man who hefted baskets,[20] but not the reclusion of the worthy man: the difference is that the deep significance of the reclusion of the worthy man lies in hiding himself, while in the reclusion of the old man who hefted baskets, the matter is confined to going against the world.
>
> When we discuss the traces these two kinds of recluses leave, we find that they differ; when we examine their motivations, so too there is a distinction: when one hides oneself in accordance with the times, there is nothing we can know him by; but treating a guest with a chicken and millet meal, the old man who hefted baskets was demonstrating his virtue of rising above the world. When the times are closed off and one practices reclusion, the traces of his being a recluse are unseen; but when one practices reclusion to go against the world, he does so in order to be considered a recluse. One who conceals his physical presence, I shall

call a "recluse" [*yin zhe*]; one who conceals his Way, I shall call him a "worthy man" [*xian ren*].[21]

Shen Yue, a man who served three dynasties and enjoyed an illustrious official career, could hardly hide his distaste for those self-righteous recluses who he felt had sought to be known as recluses. For him a "known recluse" was an oxymoron. He also took the opportunity to express contempt for a work entitled *Biographies of Genuine Recluses* (Zhen yin zhuan) by Yuan Shu (408–453), which had supposedly recorded all nameless recluses from antiquity down to the present times (only one fragment of which is still extant). For Shen Yue, leaving behind no personal name (*ming*) was not sufficient to prove the genuineness of a recluse. Though not a personal name, is not "Nest-Dweller" an appellation (*hao*)? An appellation comes into being because the person left observable traces, *ji*. Shen Yue's argument may be squarely set within the then immensely influential discourse of Daoist philosopher Laozi on the paradoxical relationship between the Way (the Dao) and "name": the Way is unnamable and cannot be reduced to names or concepts, and yet Laozi has no other way of conveying or expounding the Way except by making use of names and concepts. Hence the statement: "I do not know Its name; I grant It the designation of 'Dao' and force on It the name of 'Great.'"[22] In the same way, if Shen Yue had strictly applied his standard, he would have had no "Biographies of Recluses" in *The Song History*, for the only recluses for whom he begrudgingly granted respect seem to have been those who had left no traces at all, and hence were completely unknown and unknowable.

If "well-known recluses" had always been suspicious in the eyes of the cynical or shrewd, then during Tao Yuanming's times, as Berkowitz states, "the phenomenon of disengagement as a marketable pose, adapted and adopted by attention-seeking profiteers or insincere freeloaders, became a recurrent topic of discussion."[23] The word "marketable" is aptly used, for reclusion could turn out to be not just an expedient way of inviting public fame and official appointment, but also the means of procuring material gains.[24] The ancient antithesis between *lu* (official salary) and *geng* (plowing in the fields) could hardly be sustained in this new context. Shen Yue had good reasons to be skeptical, and this may be why the chroniclers of reclusion in the Six Dynasties often took special care to note how a recluse would reject material help from state officials and sometimes even from the emperor himself. But the question about how to distinguish the "genuine recluses" from the rest remains.

Earlier in the fifth century, Fan Ye's (398–445) foreword to "Biographies of Disengaged People" (Yimin zhuan) in *Hou Han shu*, the first extant dynastic history that carves out a niche for recluses, articulates the anxiety by trying to delineate a clearly defined space for *yimin*—literally, "people who have broken loose": "Although there is something stubborn and self-righteous about them [the recluses] that bears similarity to those who put their names up for sale, they nevertheless cast off their burdens like cicadas, escape from the madding crowd, and go off beyond the boundaries of the world; and that certainly makes them different from those who decorate themselves with cleverness and craftiness in order to pursue superficial gain."[25]

Although Fan Ye's *Yimin zhuan* "was not the first such section included in historical compilations of particular dynasties" or "the first compilation of biographical accounts devoted to practitioners of reclusion,"[26] setting up a category of "disengaged people" in the dynastic history instead of simply writing an independent *Biographies of High-minded Gentlemen* as the third-century writers Xi Kang (223–262) or Huangfu Mi (215–282) had done is nonetheless significant: it may be regarded as an attempt to situate the recluses in a larger historical context, and to rein in the "people who have broken loose" by categorizing them as such and granting them a fixed place. Categorizing, cataloguing, and classifying are the means of identifying species and hence knowing them, which in turn leads to power and control. As in natural history, classifying a group of people, a species, requires a means to distinguish its members from others. As Michel Foucault says, "Identity and what marks it are defined by the differences that remain. An animal or a plant is not what is indicated—or betrayed—by the stigma that is to be found imprinted upon it; it is what the others are not; it exists in itself only in so far as it is bounded by what is distinguishable from it."[27] So is a recluse. If a recluse is a person who has "broken loose," he is now effectively recaptured in Fan Ye's dynastic history, which contains many new categories that previous dynastic histories did not have. The recluse is an identifiable species that must be carefully set apart from those who "put their names up for sale" (despite the overlapping qualities of self-righteousness and stubbornness) and from those who blatantly pursue worldly gain. Fan Ye's inclusion of the *yimin* (disengaged people) category in the writing of dynastic history arose from a larger need to establish and delineate the meaning of the recluse, to distinguish a genuine recluse from a false one.

In terms of Lao-Zhuang thought, which held a particularly powerful sway in the Six Dynasties, naming is equal to distinguishing and vice versa; in naming or distinguishing, one risks destroying the unnamable, indistinguishable Way. In fact, naming/distinguishing is the beginning of destruction, as in the *Zhuangzi* story in which the allegorical Hundun (Undifferentiated), who has no eyes, ears, nose, or mouth, is killed when he is endowed with these organs of perception.[28] To leave traces (*ji*), to do deeds or say things that become known to the world, leads to being "named," being distinguished from others, even if the person in question remains anonymous. In the cases of "Nest-Dweller" and "Furry Elder," both are not personal names but simply *hao*, nicknames or appellations by which people refer to them: "'Nest-Dweller' is the name by which the [nameless] person is designated; and the designation of 'Furry Elder' has come into being because there are overt traces that can be transmitted." Shen Yue sees this as essentially in conflict with *yin*, "to go into hiding and practice reclusion," and his articulation of anxiety about the oxymoron of "a known recluse" is very much a translation of the Lao-Zhuang discourse on the inherently paradoxical nature of the Way, which is unnamable and yet must be named.

A person who goes into hiding and practices perfect reclusion should then by definition not reveal or demonstrate himself in any way. But with all the "attention-seeking profiteers or insincere freeloaders" floating around, how could a serious, genuine recluse distinguish himself from the rest and therefore keep the name of recluse untarnished? If the very practice of reclusion itself cannot remain hidden from the world and has to become a visible trace, then one way of avoiding the bad name of a "bogus recluse" is to reconcile one's intentions or inner motivations (*xin*) with the outer manifestations (*ji*); in other words, as in the teachings of Confucius, there should be perfect accord between the inner and the outer, the substance (*shi*) and the name (*ming*).

As far as we know, Tao Yuanming is the earliest Chinese poet who weighs, discusses at length, explains, and often plainly seeks to justify his resolve to withdraw from office and become a recluse. He makes a very specific point of revealing his aims or demonstrating his intentions by means of literary writings. Master Five Willows has no name, but he does have an appellation. The five willow trees mark his house and mark the man who dwells in the house; however, he is designated Master Five Willows not because of the trees but because he has left visible traces. In other words, it is not that the man is known because of the trees but rather the trees become known because of the man. Considering his quiet, unassuming nature, his lack of interest in glory and gain, his non-attachment to people as manifested in the statement that "As soon as he is drunk, he withdraws, never begrudging either leaving or staying," the only "traces" left by Master Five Willows seem to be his writings, with which he amuses himself and in which he manifests his aims.

But the biography of Master Five Willows was written by someone who, unlike Shen Yue or Fan Ye, was himself a recluse; according to Shen Yue, this fictional biography was intended as a self-portrayal, and its authenticity was acknowledged by his contemporaries. Such an evaluation means that the autobiographical account was already circulating during the poet's lifetime and among people who knew, or knew about, him. This account would then be viewed as the visible trace left by its recluse-author, Tao Yuanming. Announcing anonymity from the outset, the biography nevertheless gave Tao Yuanming a name that was immortalized in Chinese culture. Opening the nationally standard textbook of Chinese intended for sixth graders (last edited in 2001), on the third page of the illustrations at the beginning of the book we see a colored painting done in the traditional Chinese ink and brush style—a portrait of none other than Tao Yuanming entitled "Master Five Willows."

Reconstructing Master Five Willows: The Biographies

If, in Chinese historiography, history is often considered to be a mirror that is used to reflect on the present, then this mirror can also function as a looking glass that catches the reflection of the person who holds it. When writing a biography, what is at stake in the deliberate selection and arrangement of the materials at the historian's disposal? In the case of Tao Yuanming's biographies, we may never be able to answer this question; the wanton destructiveness of history has taken from us the majority of the source materials once available to Southern Dynasties and Tang historians. However, the existence of the four biographies written within two centuries of Tao Yuanming's death grants us an opportunity to make a close comparison of the variations in a group of texts that show clear traces of mutual consultation and possibly share certain sources.

Of the four formal biographies of Tao Yuanming, the earliest appears in *The Song History*, compiled about sixty years after Tao Yuanming's death. Then there is the one written by an admirer of Tao Yuanming's literary writings, Xiao Tong. Xiao Tong appended this biography to a collection of Tao Yuanming's works he had edited, presumably in the 520s. This edition has been lost, but the biography has been preserved in several Song printed editions of Tao Yuanming's collection. The third biography is included in *The Jin History*, the official history of Jin collectively completed in 648 under the auspices of Li Shimin (598–649), Emperor Taizong of Tang (r. 626–649). The fourth is contained in Tang historian Li Yanshou's (618–676) *The Histories of the Southern Dynasties. The Histories of the Southern Dynasties* was a private undertaking, started by Li Yanshou's father, Li Dashi (570–628), and finished by the son, who presented it to the throne in 659.

According to Li Yanshou's account in *Histories of the Northern Dynasties* (Bei shi), this was a project that took him more than a decade to accomplish, and his participation in the official compilation of *The Jin History* as well as *The Sui History* enabled him to gain access to a wealth of historical materials and documents that contributed a great deal to his compilation of *The Histories of the Southern and Northern Dynasties.*[29] Despite the earlier completion of *The Jin History*, it is quite impossible to determine whether the actual composition of the *Jin History* version of the Tao Yuanming biography precedes the *Histories of the Southern Dynasties* version or vice versa; we can only be reasonably certain that Li Yanshou was fully aware of the *Jin History* version of the Tao Yuanming biography, and therefore any divergence of the *Histories of the Southern Dynasties* version from the *Jin History* version would have been a self-conscious departure.

Below is a comparison of the four versions of Tao Yuanming's biography.[30] We have the *Song History* version, the Xiao Tong version, the *Jin History* version, and the *Histories of the Southern Dynasties* version.[31]

> SONG HISTORY: Tao Qian's courtesy name was Yuanming; some say his name was Yuanming and his courtesy name Yuanliang. He was a native of Chaisang of Xunyang. His great-grandfather was Tao Kan, the Jin Commander. From his youth Tao Qian had had lofty inclinations. He once wrote "The Biography of Master Five Willows" as a self-portrayal. . . . This is the way he described himself, and his contemporaries considered it a factual record.

> XIAO TONG: Tao Yuanming's courtesy name was Yuanliang; some say his name was Qian and his courtesy name Yuanming. He was a native of Chaisang of Xunyang; his great-grandfather was Tao Kan, the Jin Commander.
>
> From his youth Tao Qian had had lofty inclinations. He was learned

and good at literary compositions. An extraordinary person rising above the crowd, he followed his natural impulses and was content with his choices. He once wrote "The Biography of Master Five Willows" as a self-portrayal. . . . and his contemporaries considered it a factual record.

JIN HISTORY: Tao Qian's courtesy name was Yuanliang. He was the great-grandson of Tao Kan, the Jin Commander. His grandfather Tao Mao was magistrate of Wuchang. From his youth Tao Qian had cherished lofty feelings. He was learned and good at literary compositions. An extraordinary, unrestrained person, he followed his natural impulses and was content with his choices. He was highly regarded by his townsmen. He once wrote "The Biography of Master Five Willows" as a self-portrayal. . . . He described himself in this way, and his contemporaries considered it a factual record.

HISTORIES OF THE SOUTHERN DYNASTIES: Tao Qian's courtesy name was Yuanming; some say his name was Shenming and his courtesy name Yuanliang. A native of Chaisang of Xunyang, he was the great-grandson of Tao Kan, the Jin Commander. From his youth Tao Qian had had lofty inclinations. By his residence were five willow trees, so he wrote "The Biography of Master Five Willows". . . . He described himself in this way, as he intended it to be a self-portrayal. His contemporaries considered it a factual record.

All versions set the tone with Tao Yuanming's self-portrayal in "The Biography of Master Five Willows," even though the "encomium" or "appraisal" in Tao Yuanming's piece is not found in any of them, as if the historian or the biographer wished to retain the right to write the concluding and conclusive remarks on the subject's life. The *Histories of the Southern Dynasties* version is slightly different from the others in that it takes a line from the fictional autobiography and integrates it into the biographical text: the five willow trees, the reason for the appellation of Master Five Willows, were turned into the occasion on which Tao Yuanming composed the piece. Such a move provides us with a good example of how Tao Yuanming's own writings may have been put to use by his biographers.

There are also some other interesting divergences. Xiao Tong made a few additions to the *Song History* version, which proved to be central to the image-building of Tao Yuanming: the first was an emphasis on Tao Yuanming's learning; the second, on his literary skills; and the third, on his intrinsic qualities. The portrayal of Tao Yuanming as *ren zhen* ("following his natural impulses") is an apt summary of the image of Tao Yuanming presented as Master Five Willows; such a portrayal is also what Tao Yuanming celebrated in his poetry, most notably in "Drinking Alone during Incessant Rain" (Lianyu duyin), which shall be discussed in detail in chapter four.

The *Jin History* version follows Xiao Tong's version closely, but adds one sentence after the appraisal of Tao Yuanming's personality: "He was highly regarded by his townsmen." Granted this is a minor addition, it nonetheless foreshadows a general tendency in the *Jin History* version to portray Tao Yuanming as more affable and cautious in his dealings with the world.

Tao Yuanming's great-grandfather, Tao Kan, did not come from an illustrious family. He was probably not even a Han Chinese,[32] as Wen Qiao (288–329) once referred to him contemptuously as a "Xi dog" (*Xi gou*, Xi being the name for a southern non-Han people).[33] The historian's concluding observation in Tao Kan's *Jin History* biography states that "Shixing [Tao Kan's courtesy name] did not come from an aristocratic clan, and his customs differed from those of the Han Chinese," which is a clearer indication of Tao Kan's family and ethnic background.[34] The *Jin History* biography claims that Tao Kan's mother (surnamed Zhan) was a concubine. If it were true, then Tao Kan's social status would have been further compromised. Li Xiang's (1859–1931) commentary on *Shishuo xinyu* opposes this claim because he believes that the verb used for marrying Zhan in the *Jin History* biography, *pin,* was for taking a wife, not for taking a concubine.[35] Li Xiang's assumption, however, has no basis: *pin* was used in either case in the Southern Dynasties period.[36] According to Yan Zhitui's (ca. 529–591) *Yanshi jiaxun*, one of the differences between the south and north was that unlike in the north, people in the south did not look down upon children born of concubines.[37] *Yanshi jiaxun*, however, was composed three hundred years after Tao Kan's time; besides, the Eastern Jin elite was mostly composed of the northern émigrés.

Although Tao Kan's father had served in a military post in the Kingdom of Wu, when Tao Kan grew up his family was not wealthy. His mother reputedly had to sell her hair to provide for one of her son's visitors.[38] This act was paid off handsomely, when the visitor, touched by Tao Kan's hospitality, recommended him to the magistrate of Lujiang, who appointed Tao Kan to be an inspector. Tao Kan gradually rose in position by his administrative ability, his military talent, and his persistence. Because of his pivotal role in suppressing the rebellion of Su Jun in 328, Tao Kan was elevated to the rank of Duke of Changsha and Minister of Defense.

According to his *Jin History* biography, Tao Kan had a pragmatic and austere personality; he did not like the prevalent "arcane discourse" (*xuan yan*) or "pure talk" (*qing tan*) and he detested displays of unrestrained behavior such as an ostentatiously unkempt personal appearance. While the people of the Eastern Jin generally regarded these as marks of aristocratic breeding and cultivation, Tao Kan denounced them as mere superficial decoration and not befitting the teachings of former kings. He was frugal in the use of both material resources and time. He advocated the importance of farming. He hated idleness; in his own spare time he would carry a hundred bricks out of his house in the morning and then carry them back into the house at night. When he was asked why he did so, he answered that he did not want to become lax and lazy. He imposed a strict limit on his drinking; sometimes he reached that limit long before the end of the banquet, but he would never exceed it. In many ways, Tao Kan represented the very opposite of the values upheld by the Eastern Jin aristocracy. He rose to power through sheer ability and will, and the aristocrats—including members of the most well-known noble clans, such as the Wangs and Xies—had to pay him grudging respect. Nevertheless, there was a rumor that Tao Kan had harbored ambitions not appropriate for a minister, and was only stopped by a sense of insecurity and peril. Although he started his official career by the sale of his mother's hair, when he reached old age, he "had dozens of concubines and more than a thousand servants; his hoard of treasures and valuables exceeded the imperial storage." The historian's judgment of Tao Kan at the end of his biography shows a mixture of praise and criticism of Tao Kan's character.[39]

In several of his poems, Tao Yuanming refers to his family line with pride,[40] even though Tao Yuanming's account of his love of drinking, his idleness, and his poverty seems to have been antithetical to the values of his illustrious great-grandfather.[41] Tao Yuanming's great-grandfather would never have approved of Master Five Willows, but Master Five Willows was only a self-image, and Tao Yuanming had inherited many concerns from his paternal ancestor, as we shall see in subsequent chapters.

> SONG HISTORY: As his parent was old and his family poor, he began his official career as the Libationer of the [Jiangzhou] prefecture.[42] But

he could not bear the bureaucratic work, and resigned from office not long after. When the Prefecture asked him to be Recorder, he did not accept. Supporting his family by plowing in the fields, he became frail and sickly.

XIAO TONG: As his parent was old and his family poor, he began his official career as the Libationer of the [Jiangzhou] prefecture. But he could not bear the bureaucratic work, and resigned from office not long after. When the Prefecture asked him to be Recorder, he did not accept. Supporting his family by plowing in the fields, he became frail and sickly.

JIN HISTORY: As his parent was old and his family poor, he began his official career as the Libationer of the [Jiangzhou] prefecture. But he could not bear the bureaucratic work, and resigned from office not long after. When the Prefecture asked him to be Recorder, he did not accept. Supporting his family by plowing in the fields, he became frail and sickly.

HISTORIES OF THE SOUTHERN DYNASTIES: As his parent was old and his family poor, he began his official career as the Libationer of the [Jiangzhou] prefecture. But he could not bear the bureaucratic work, and resigned from office not long after. When the Prefecture asked him to be Recorder, he did not accept. Supporting his family by plowing in the fields, he became frail and sickly.

Regardless of whether it was one parent or both parents that the biographers referred to in the first line of this section, providing for one's aging parents had been a conventional pretext for starting a public career.[43] In the preface to his famous literary exposition "Return," Tao Yuanming's opening statement is that poverty was the main reason why he had sought an official post. He also mentioned that his house was full of children to be fed, and that farming was not enough to provide for the little ones.[44] *Gonggeng* (plowing in person) is likewise an ambiguous phrase: we cannot determine how much farm labor Tao Yuanming personally engaged in, but it would be preposterous to assume that Tao Yuanming worked in the fields as much as a real peasant.

It is important to understand that these phrases, including the term *leiji*, "frail and sickly," are part of the discourse of the recluse and were used time and again in official biographies, personal records, letters, and so forth.[45]

> XIAO TONG: Tan Daoji, the governor of Jiangzhou prefecture, paid him a visit, and found him lying wasted and hungry for days. Daoji said to him, "The way a worthy man deals with the world is to retire when the Way falls into decay, but to come forward when the Way reigns. Now that you live in such an enlightened age, why do you abuse yourself like this?" Tao answered: "How do I dare expect to be considered a worthy man? My aspirations do not reach that far." Daoji presented him with grain and meat, but he dismissed the gifts.

> HISTORIES OF THE SOUTHERN DYNASTIES: Tan Daoji, the governor of Jiangzhou prefecture, paid him a visit, and found him lying wasted and hungry for days. Daoji said to him, "The way a worthy man deals with the world is to retire when the Way falls into decay, but to come forward when the Way reigns. Now that you live in such an enlightened age, why do you abuse yourself like this?" Tao answered, "How do I dare expect to be considered a worthy man? My aspirations do not reach that far." Daoji presented him with grain and meat, but he dismissed the gifts.

What is interesting here is the addition of the Tan Daoji (?–436) anecdote in Xiao Tong's version, later adopted in *The Histories of the Southern Dynasties*; since it appears right after the description of Tao Yuanming's hard work in the fields and his consequent illness, the reader is easily lured into thinking that he is reading a linear narrative. But Tan Daoji did not become the governor of Jiangzhou until 426, one year before Tao Yuanming's death.[46] The lateness of this event in Tao Yuanming's life, provided it did happen, makes its early appearance in Xiao Tong's version chronologically confusing. Xiao Tong persistently attempts to create the impression of temporal linearity by using time words such as "later," "by the end of the year," "before this," and "at the time," and yet, as many have observed, the chronology in his version is a mess.

This anecdote is important in that it not only portrays Tao Yuanming as uncompromising despite adverse circumstances but also gives Tao Yuanming an opportunity to defend himself against one of the most common objections a recluse had to face: namely, that a worthy man only hides himself in troubled times, so why should he do so in an enlightened age? Tao Yuanming's answer makes clear that his aspirations do not reach as far as the "worthy man"—a polite way of saying that his aspirations are of a different order altogether. A recluse (*yin shi*) is literally "a gentleman who hides"; ironically enough, he has to constantly speak out to reveal his intentions.

Although the *Song History* and *Jin History* versions do not include this self-explanatory anecdote, the *Song History* biography quotes more from Tao Yuanming's own writings than any other version and so adequately represents Tao Yuanming's self-representation, and the *Jin History* biography provides us with an episode unique to itself, in which Tao Yuanming explains himself at length to some unknown "person" or "people" (in Chinese simply given as *ren*).

> SONG HISTORY: He also became Aide to the Zhenjun General and then to the Jianwei General. Once he told his relatives and friends, "I would like to support my 'three-path' life with some zither and song. How about that?"[47] When the authorities heard of it, he was made magistrate of Pengze County.

> XIAO TONG: Later, he became Aide to the Zhenjun General and then to the Jianwei General. Once he told his relatives and friends, "I would like to support my 'three-path' life with some zither and song. How about that?" When the authorities heard of it, he was made magistrate of Pengze County.

> JIN HISTORY: He also became Aide to the Zhenjun General and then to the Jianwei General. Once he told his relatives and friends, "I would like to support my 'three-path' life with some zither and song. How about that?" When the authorities heard of it, he was made magistrate of Pengze County.

> HISTORIES OF THE SOUTHERN DYNASTIES: He also became Aide to the Zhenjun General and then to the Jianwei General. Once he told his relatives and friends, "I would like to support my 'three-path' life with some zither and song. How about that?" When the authorities heard of it, he was made magistrate of Pengze County.

Contemporary scholars generally agree that Tao Yuanming became Aide to the Zhenjun General in 404 and then Aide to the Jianwei General in 405.[48] According to Tao Yuanming's preface to "Return," he was appointed the magistrate of Pengze in the eighth month of the same year (405) and resigned from his post in the eleventh month after a little more than eighty days in office. "The authorities," mentioned in the preface to "Return," were none other than his uncle.[49] Again, to use poverty, support of a large family, accumulation of retirement funds, and love of wine or of the local landscape as a pretext for requesting to serve was a common ruse.[50]

> Xiao Tong: He did not take his family with him, but he sent a servant to his sons, along with a letter saying, "It is hard for you to provide for your daily needs all by yourselves, so I am sending you this servant to help you out with your daily chores of gathering firewood and drawing water. He, too, is a son of his parents; you should treat him well."

> Histories of the Southern Dynasties: He did not take his family with him, but he sent a servant to his sons, along with a letter saying, "It is hard for you to provide for your daily needs all by yourselves, so I am sending you this servant to help you out with your daily chores of gathering firewood and drawing water. He, too, is a son of his parents; you should treat him well."

Again, this is an addition in Xiao Tong's version later adopted in *The Histories of the Southern Dynasties.* We do not know the source of this anecdote. In Tao Yuanming's letter to his five sons, he says, "I regret that you are all still young, and that our family is poor and has no servant. How can you be exempt from the daily chores of collecting firewood and drawing water? I think of this often and do not know what to say."[51] This is kept in his *Song History* biography, but Xiao Tong removed it. Xiao Tong's anecdote does accord with the statement in "Return," supposedly written by Tao Yuanming right after he resigned his post at Pengze, that "the servant boy cheerily welcomes me, and my little son waits at the door."

For the above quotation from Tao Yuanming's letter to his five sons, a noticeable variant occurs in the later printed editions of Tao Yuanming's collected works. They generally read, "You are all very young, and our family is poor, so you are always burdened with the daily chores of gathering firewood and drawing water. When can you ever be exempt from this?" *Wu yi* (having no servant) becomes *mei yi* (are always burdened with). Not only has the word class of *yi* changed from noun (servant) to verb ("work hard on" or "be burdened with the work of"), but the meaning of the word and the punctuation are also different. This convenient variant ingeniously solves the problem of whether the Tao household had a servant or not, and there needs to be no conflict between Tao Yuanming's personal letters and his biography authored by Xiao Tong. Incidentally, Xiao Tong's version is the one that has been most frequently included in Tao Yuanming's collected works.

> SONG HISTORY: He demanded to have glutinous rice planted in all the public fields. His wife and children earnestly begged him to plant some non-glutinous rice, so he had two *qing* and fifty *mu* planted with glutinous rice and fifty *mu* with non-glutinous rice.
>
> An inspector was sent down to the county by the commandery, and Tao Yuanming's subordinates told him that he should tie his girdle and call on the inspector. Tao Qian gave a sigh, "I cannot bow before a country bumpkin for the sake of five pecks of rice." On that same day he untied his seal ribbon and left the post. Later he composed "Return". . . . Toward the end of the Yixi period [405–418], he was called to the post of assistant archivist; he did not accept.

> XIAO TONG: He demanded to have glutinous rice planted in all the public fields, saying, "I would be satisfied if I could always get drunk with ale." His wife and children earnestly begged him to plant some non-glutinous rice, so he had two *qing* and fifty *mu* planted with glutinous rice and fifty *mu* with non-glutinous rice.
>
> At the end of the year, an inspector was sent down to the county by the commandery, and Tao Yuanming's subordinates told him that he should tie his girdle and call on the inspector. Tao Qian gave a sigh, "How can I bow before a country bumpkin for the sake of five pecks of rice!" On that same day he untied his seal ribbon and left the post. Later he composed "Return." He was called to the post of archivist; he did not accept.

> JIN HISTORY: He demanded to have glutinous rice planted in all the public fields, saying, "I would be satisfied if I could always get drunk

with ale." His wife and children earnestly begged him to plant some non-glutinous rice, so he had one *qing* and fifty *mu* planted with glutinous rice and fifty *mu* with non-glutinous rice.

He had always been proud and would not curry favor with his superiors. An inspector was sent down to the county by the commandery, and Tao Yuanming's subordinates told him that he should tie his girdle and call on the inspector. Tao Qian gave a sigh, "I cannot bow for the sake of five pecks of rice and subserviently serve a country bumpkin." In the second year of the Yixi reign [406], he untied his seal and left the county. He composed "Return". . . . Soon after, he was called to the post of archivist; he did not accept.

HISTORIES OF THE SOUTHERN DYNASTIES: He demanded to have glutinous rice planted in all the public fields. His wife and children earnestly begged him to plant some non-glutinous rice, so he had two *qing* and fifty *mu* planted with glutinous rice and fifty *mu* with non-glutinous rice.

An inspector was sent down to the county by the commandery, and Tao Yuanming's subordinates told him that he should tie his girdle and call on the inspector. Tao Qian gave a sigh, "I cannot bend and bow before a country bumpkin for the sake of five pecks of rice." On that same day he untied his seal-ribbon and left the post. Later he composed "Return" to express his feelings. . . . Toward the end of the Yixi period [405–418], he was called to the post of assistant archivist; he did not accept.

This is the most famous part of Tao Yuanming's life story—so much so that it largely eclipses the other anecdotes and becomes Tao Yuanming's hallmark—and yet this is the least credible part in the biographical account. A. R. Davis says,

> The poet's own statement in the preface to "Return Home!" ("the harvest [or 'the glutinous rice'] of the public fields would be sufficient for making wine") was clearly responsible for the appearance of this anecdote, as Xiao Tong's small insertion underlines. . . . This story is certainly a clumsy invention, if one takes into account the poet's own statement that he was at Pengze only from the eighth to the eleventh month (September to December) 405, i.e. not the rice-planting season.[52]

The invention may be clumsy, but it is a generic one: we notice the remarkable similarity between Tao Yuanming's statement, the glutinous rice story, and several anecdotes recorded in *Shishuo xinyu*. Ruan Ji, for instance, had supposedly asked to become a commandant of infantry because several hundred jugs of wine were stored in the commissary. Kong Qun (ca. mid-fourth century) once wrote to his relatives and old friends, "From this year's harvest I received seven hundred jars of glutinous rice—not quite enough for fermentation."[53]

But it is also possible that Tao Yuanming's preface to "Return" had been changed to fit the anecdote in his biographies. Zeng Ji's (twelfth–thirteenth century) 1192 edition records a variant reading for the statement in his preface. Instead of "the harvest of the public fields would be sufficient for making wine" (*zuyi wei jiu*), we have "the harvest of the public fields *would be more than sufficient as nourishment*" (*guozu weirun;* my italics). Ma Yongqing (*jinshi* degree, 1109), in his *Lanzhenzi* (completed after 1136), claims the same variant reading as seen in "an old copy" of Tao Yuanming's collection.[54] Ma Yongqing also points out that Tao Yuanming's term at Pengze was not rice-planting season, and yet he places too much trust in the textual stability of Tao Yuanming's preface to "Return" by saying that if one encounters any inconsistency between the preface and Tao Yuanming's biographies, one should look to the preface for truth. In fact, even of the preface we have two versions. The one appearing in Xiao Tong's *Wen xuan* is considerably shorter than the one in later printed editions of Tao Yuanming's collection, and the shorter version contains none of the detailed biographical information given in the longer version, such as his uncle's intervention, his sister's death, the season, or the duration of his service at Pengze, including the statement cited above. It simply says, "My family was poor, and yet I was apprehensive of serving far away from home. Pengze County is only a hundred *li* away, so I asked for the office there. Not many days passed before I felt a longing for returning home. I gave up my office and left of my own accord. Events have made it possible for me to follow my heart's desire, and I have entitled my piece 'Return.'"[55] While the longer version of the preface may have appeared in one or more of the early manuscript copies, its credibility is nonetheless in question.

In the longer version of the preface, Tao Yuanming states that the immediate reason for his resignation was his sister's death; there is not a word about the inspector's visit. In the *Jin History* version, the date given for his resignation (the second year of the Yixi reign) does not fit Tao Yuanming's self-account either (the eleventh month of the first year of the Yixi reign). Davis speculates that *The Song History* and *The Jin History* included the text of "Return" but omitted the preface "presumably because the compilers were conscious that there was some contradiction."[56]

Hong Mai (1123–1202) chose a different reading of the conflict between the biographies and Tao Yuanming's own version of the event: "I suspect that Tao Yuanming's claim about 'discipline and restraint' and 'going against myself' must have had a reason, and he did not want to express it explicitly. We may see this from the content of his 'Return,' which only speaks about the joy of returning home but does not mention Wuchang [where his sister died] at all."[57]

Hong Mai's interpretation embodies an important cultural change in early modern China: if earlier readers were not troubled by inconsistencies in a text, by Hong Mai's time the impulse was to provide a rational explanation for everything. No discrepancy, oddity, or accident was allowed to stand without a justification; in some cases, even if the problem was insoluble, there would at least be a show of attempting to solve it. In such a context, a textual variant or even the text itself is seen as a "person who broke loose" (*yimin,* the term Fan Ye had used to classify recluses in his dynastic history), and must be captured and contained in an all-inclusive historical system.

It is ironic to recall that Tao Kan, Tao Yuanming's great-grandfather, had initially served as an inspector, and at the beginning of his official career had been referred to as a "low-born person" (*xiaoren*).[58] The process of social ascent culminates in the great-grandson, who is now too proud to bow to an inspector he calls a "country bumpkin" ("rustic low-born person").

> JIN HISTORY: Although he gave up paying visits to the officials of the prefecture or commandery, when his fellow countryman Zhang Ye and his friends Yang Songling, Chong Zun, and others invited him to a drink or to go to some drinking party with them, he would go cheerfully even if he did not know the host. When he was drunk, he would leave. He would never call on anyone, and the only places he visited were his farms or Mount Lu. Wang Hong, who became the governor of Jiangzhou during the Yuanxi period [419–420], had great respect for Tao Qian, and paid a visit to Tao in person. Tao Qian claimed to be ill and refused to see him. Later he told his friends, "By nature I am not inti-

mate with the world, and because of my illness I live a reclusive life. I am not doing this for some pure ideal or a desire for reputation, so how do I dare consider Mr. Wang's visit as adding to my personal glory! To mistake an unworthy person as worthy—this is what Liu Gonggan thought would have brought blame on a gentleman; it is not a small offence."[59]

Zhang Ye, Yang Songling, and Chong (presumably a corrupted character for Pang) Zun, because of their surnames, have all been identified with the people who appear in the titles of Tao Yuanming's poems "At the End of the Year, Answering a Poem by Attendant Zhang" (Suimu he Zhang changshi),[60] "To Chief of Staff Yang" (Zeng Yang zhangshi),[61] and the two poems both entitled "In Reply to Aide Pang" (Da Pang canjun), as well as "Resentful Poem in the Chu Mode, to Registrar Pang and Secretary Deng" (Yuan shi Chu diao shi Pang zhubu Deng zhizhong). There is no evidence to either support or refute these identifications. A person named Pang Tongzhi appears in the *Song History* version (see below), and has been identified with Pang (Chong) Zun in the above *Jin History* section and hence with Aide Pang. Again, this is a hypothesis based on nothing but a common surname.

That Tao Yuanming would cheerfully go to a drinking party even if he did not know the host and then retire as soon as he got drunk is certainly an elaboration of the statement in "Biography of Master Five Willows." But it is also a conventional characteristic of an "unrestrained" gentleman in the Jin. Looking at *Shishuo xinyu*, we see that many famous drinkers behaved in the same way. Liu Chang (ca. mid-third century) is described as undiscriminating about his drinking company, and the Ruans outdid him by having a happy drinking party with pigs.[62] Withdrawing upon satisfying one's desire, without further lingering, demonstrated spontaneity and simplicity. Liu Yimin, Tao Yuanming's contemporary, is said to have come to the boat of a traveling official and asked to borrow his utensils to cook some fresh fish; upon hearing this was the well-known recluse Liu Yimin, the official became excited and tried to talk to him longer, but Liu Yimin had no intention of staying, and left as soon as he finished his fish fillets. The official followed him to his house, and Liu Yimin did treat him to some bad wine, which the official had to drink down on account of his great respect for the host. During their drinking, Liu Yimin rose and started to leave again, saying that he was in the middle of cutting the reeds (for making mats) and should not be away from it for too long.[63] Two anecdotes about Luo You (ca. mid-fourth century) in the same section say similar things about Luo

You's instant withdrawal upon satisfying his appetite. In one case he even said, "Now I have eaten my fill; there is no need to stay on any more."[64]

The anecdote concerning Wang Hong merits a few words. Wang Hong (379–432) was a member of the illustrious Wang clan, the great-grandson of Prime Minister Wang Dao (276–339), the central figure in the naissance of the Eastern Jin. Wang Hong himself played a conspicuous role in both Liu Yu's founding of the Liu Song and Liu Yilong's (Emperor Wen of Song, r. 424–454) rise to the throne. He was appointed governor of Jiangzhou in 418 and remained in the post until 425.[65]

Wang Hong's political and cultural significance, as indicated by his high position as well as his noble family line, is a necessary piece of information for us to appreciate Tao Yuanming's refusal to receive him. Yet the additional anecdote contained in the *Jin History* version, which consists of Tao Yuanming's explanation of why he claims illness to avoid Wang Hong, again betrays an anxiety on the historian's part about revealing a recluse's motivation and inner world, for fear that he may be misinterpreted. Tao Yuanming emphasizes that he lives a reclusive life not because of any "pure ideal" or "desire for reputation," but because of his delicate health, and that he does not want to be mistaken for a "worthy man." This coincides with the anecdote in Xiao Tong's version, in which Tao Yuanming answers Tan Daoji that his aspirations do not reach those of a worthy man. Yet the *Jin History* story lacks the defiant flavor of the Xiao Tong version: Tao Yuanming's words are not uttered as a direct retort to someone's question but as a self-initiated explanation of his motives to some unidentified audience. It shows the man as cautious and self-conscious in his dealings with the world—anything but "following his natural impulses." Understandably, this is the later readers' least favorite of all the Tao Yuanming stories, despite the fact that it has a good chance of being true; no other version of Tao Yuanming's biography has included it.

> SONG HISTORY: Wang Hong, the governor of Jiangzhou, wished to make his acquaintance, but did not succeed in securing a visit from Tao. Tao Qian once went to Mount Lu, and Wang Hong asked Tao Yuanming's old friend Pang Tongzhi to prepare a drinking party and wait for him halfway at Lili. Having some sort of foot disease, Tao came in a sedan-chair carried by a retainer and his two sons, and shared drinks with Pang quite cheerfully. After a while Wang Hong arrived, and yet Tao was not offended.

Xiao Tong: Wang Hong, the governor of Jiangzhou, wished to make his acquaintance, but did not succeed in securing a visit from Tao. Tao Qian once went to Mount Lu, and Wang Hong asked Tao Yuanming's old friend Pang Tongzhi to prepare a drinking party and wait for him halfway at Lili. Having some sort of foot disease, Tao came in a sedan-chair carried by a retainer and his two sons, and shared drinks with Pang quite cheerfully. After a while Wang Hong arrived, and yet Tao was not offended.

Jin History: Wang Hong wished to make his acquaintance, but did not succeed in securing a visit from Tao. Once Tao was going to Mount Lu, and Wang, who had someone constantly watching over him, learned of Tao Yuanming's trip, and so he sent Tao Yuanming's old friends such as Pang Tongzhi to wait for Tao halfway with wine. Seeing there was wine, Tao Qian sat down to drink in a roadside pavilion, and became so merry that he forgot to leave. Then Wang Hong turned up, and they had a happy banquet all day.

Histories of the Southern Dynasties: Wang Hong, the governor of Jiangzhou, wished to make his acquaintance, but did not succeed in securing a visit from Tao. Tao Qian once went to Mount Lu, and Wang Hong asked Tao Yuanming's old friend Pang Tongzhi to prepare a drinking party and wait for him halfway at Lili. Having some sort of foot disease, Tao came in a sedan-chair carried by a retainer and his two sons, and shared drinks with Pang quite cheerfully. After a while Wang Hong arrived, and yet Tao was not offended.

Wang Hong's initial failure to secure a visit from Tao Yuanming contrasts with the final meeting that occurs "naturally" through Wang Hong's crafty arrangement. When the encounter occurs "naturally," then Tao Yuanming is shown to go with the flow. The noticeable thing in this section is Lili, or Chestnut Village, which appears in all but the *Jin History* version; clearly located somewhere in between Tao Yuanming's residence and Mount Lu, it was later transformed into Tao Yuanming's home village.[66]

Jin History: Tao Qian had no shoes, and Wang Hong wanted his attendants to provide shoes for him. When the attendants asked for

> measurements, Tao Qian stretched his feet out right in the midst of company and had them take the measurements. Wang Hong then invited Tao to go back to the prefecture, and inquired how he had traveled. He replied, "I have some foot problem, so I always ride in a sedan chair, which is good enough for me to get back in." So he had one retainer and his two sons carry him to the prefecture; he was totally comfortable with it, and one did not feel that he envied an elegant carriage in the least. From then on, if Wang Hong wanted to see him, he would always seek him out among the woods and valleys; and he would from time to time supply Tao with wine and food if he ran short.
>
> His relatives and friends sometimes took wine and food to Tao Qian, which he never rejected. Every time he was drunk, he would be left in a genial mood. He never cared about his livelihood, but turned everything over to his sons and servants. He never made a public show of emotions, be it anger or happiness. He just drank whenever he had wine; and even when he did not have wine, he would not stop chanting [poetry]. He once said that when, in some leisurely summer month, as he lay down under the north window, a light breeze came upon him, he would then think of himself as a person of the age before the Fuxi emperor.

These sections appear only in the *Jin History* version. The shoe story is to highlight Tao Yuanming's easygoing and casual nature, and has an earlier source in Tan Daoluan's (ca. early fifth century) *A Sequel to the Chronicles of Jin* (Xu Jin yangqiu).[67] The *Jin History* version makes much of the bamboo sedan chair in which Tao Yuanming was carried around, so as to emphasize his complete sense of ease in the face of all the pomp and circumstance of a grandee.

Tao Yuanming's cheerful acceptance of Wang Hong's gifts of ale and food forms a contrast with his proud dismissal of Tan Daoji's offerings in the Xiao Tong version (later adopted in *The Histories of the Southern Dynasties*). Tao Yuanming's image as an uncompromising recluse is considerably softened in the *Jin History* version by the absence of the Tan Daoji incident and the addition of his associations with Wang Hong. The identities of the two officials may also provide a clue to the portrayals of Tao Yuanming's different reception of them: Tan Daoji was a general, a military figure, from a humble background, while Wang Hong was an aristocrat from the highly esteemed Wang clan. The difference between the two people may be illuminated by an anecdote that involves Tao Yuanming's own family member, Tao Fan (fl. ca. 376), Tao Kan's son. Wang Huzhi (d. ca. 364), a member of the Wang clan living in reclusion, was offered a boatload of rice by Tao Fan, who was serving as the magistrate in the area. Wang declined and said, "If Wang Xiuling [Wang Huzhi's courtesy name] were hungry, he would of course ask for food from Xie Renzu [Xie Shang's courtesy name, 308–357]. He has no need of Tao Hunu's [Tao Fan's baby name] rice."[68] Instead of classifying this anecdote under "Contempt and Insults" (*Jian ao*), *Shishuo xinyu* categorizes it under "The Square and Proper" (*Fang zheng*), which shows the author's approving attitude toward Wang's bluntness. The key to understanding this anecdote as well as the *Shishuo xinyu* author's standard of classification is to realize that Xie Shang was a member of the illustrious Xie clan, while Tao Fan, though the son of Tao Kan and a well-known official himself, was nevertheless looked down upon as a military man from a family background much inferior to that of the Wangs and Xies. Similarly, it would be deemed more "appropriate" for Tao Yuanming to accept financial assistance from Wang Hong than from Tan Daoji.

The last part is apparently transformed from "Biography of Master Five Willows" and Tao Yuanming's letter to his sons:

> Song History: Before this, Yan Yanzhi was Personnel Secretary to Liu Liu, General of the Rear Army. When he was in Xunyang, he became good friends with Tao Qian. Later he was appointed magistrate of Shi'an commandery. On his way to Shi'an he stopped by Xunyang and visited Tao every day. Every time they gathered together, they drank until they were both drunk. Before he went away, Yan left Tao twenty thousand cash. Tao turned all of the money over to the tavern and then went there to get wine bit by bit.
>
> Once, on the ninth day of the ninth month, Tao ran out of wine. He sat among the chrysanthemum flowers by his house for a long time. Then it happened that Wang Hong sent him some wine. Tao drank until he was drunk; only then did he go back into the house.

> Xiao Tong: Before this, Yan Yanzhi was Personnel Secretary to Liu Liu, General of the Rear Army. When he was in Xunyang, he became good friends with Tao Qian. Later he was appointed magistrate of

Shi'an commandery. On his way to Shi'an he stopped by Xunyang and visited Tao every day. Every time they gathered together, they drank until they were both drunk. Wang Hong tried to invite Yan Yanzhi, but to no avail. Before he went away, Yan left Tao twenty thousand cash. Tao turned all of the money over to the tavern and then went there to get wine bit by bit.

Once, on the ninth day of the ninth month, Tao sat among the chrysanthemum flowers by his house for a long time, blossoms filling his hands. Then it happened that Wang Hong sent him some wine. Tao drank until he was drunk; only then did he go back into the house.

HISTORIES OF THE SOUTHERN DYNASTIES: Before this, Yan Yanzhi was Personnel Secretary to Liu Liu, General of the Rear Army. When he was in Xunyang, he became good friends with Tao Qian. Later he was appointed magistrate of Shi'an commandery. On his way to Shi'an he stopped by Xunyang and visited Tao every day. Every time they gathered together, they drank until they were both drunk. Wang Hong tried to invite Yan Yanzhi, but to no avail. Before he went away, Yan left Tao twenty thousand cash. Tao turned all of the money over to the tavern and then went there to get wine bit by bit.

Once, on the ninth day of the ninth month, Tao ran out of wine, and he sat among the chrysanthemum flowers by his house for a long time. Then it happened that Wang Hong sent him some wine. Tao drank until he was drunk; only then did he go back into the house.

Liu Liu (?–416) was appointed the governor of Jiangzhou before Wang Hong, from the year 415 to 416. Yan Yanzhi, one of the two best-known literary figures of the early fifth century (the other being Xie Lingyun), had started his official career serving under Liu Liu. Yan Yanzhi became the magistrate of Shi'an in 422.[69] After Tao Yuanming died, Yan Yanzhi wrote an elegy—the first extant piece of writing about Tao Yuanming by someone other than Tao Yuanming himself.[70]

The *Jin History* biography noticeably does not contain these passages. While the three versions are practically identical at this point, Xiao Tong's version makes one interesting addition adopted in *The Histories of the Southern Dynasties*: "Wang Hong tried to invite Yan Yanzhi, but to no avail." Xiao Tong's version seems to have established a gradually ascending social hierarchy among the three well-known people Tao Yuanming associated with—Tan Daoji, Wang Hong, and Yan Yanzhi—determined not so much by actual political power as by cultural power. Xiao Tong, the Crown Prince of the Liang, lived in the first half of the sixth century. As was typical of the period, even though the great aristocratic families of the Eastern Jin still retained a kind of aura, in terms of social, political, and cultural prestige, they were slowly giving way to those who climbed the social ladder on the basis of merit—especially people who excelled in literature. Xiao Tong's account, however, again goes directly against the *Jin History* portrayal of Tao Yuanming as an extremely agreeable fellow.

Sitting among chrysanthemum flowers, with or without ale, on the Double Ninth Festival—apart from the Pengze story, this is another well-known image of Tao Yuanming. As Wang Guoying points out, it seems to have been inspired by Tao Yuanming's preface to a poem entitled "Living at Leisure on the Ninth Day" (Jiuri xianju), which states, "Autumn chrysanthemum blossoms fill the garden, and yet there is no way to hold a cup of wine."[71]

> SONG HISTORY: Tao did not understand music, but he kept a plain zither with no strings. When he became tipsy, he would stroke the zither to express his feelings.
>
> XIAO TONG: Tao did not understand music, but he kept a plain zither with no strings. When he became tipsy, he would stroke the zither to express his feelings.
>
> JIN HISTORY: Tao did not understand music, but he kept a plain zither with no strings or harmonic nodes. Whenever there was a drinking party, he would stroke the zither, saying, "As long as one knows the appeal of the zither, what is the need for the sound of strings?"
>
> HISTORIES OF THE SOUTHERN DYNASTIES: Tao did not understand music, but he kept a plain zither. When he became tipsy, he would stroke the zither to express his feelings.

Again, this anecdote is seen as conflicting with Tao Yuanming's own writings, in which he often mentions the pleasures of "zither and books"—unless, of course, by "playing zither" he invariably means "stroking the zither with no strings," or, as Davis suggests, "zither and books" is "a phrase which is part of the terminology of withdrawal . . . so that it may be unnecessary to understand the references to 'zither' literally."[72]

It is interesting to observe that there is a relevant variant in Tao Yuanming's letter to his sons. Both the *Song History* and *Histories of the Southern Dynasties* versions of the letter contain this line: "I have loved books since youth" (*Shao lai hao shu* or *Shaonian lai hao shu*). The line remains almost exactly the same in the early Tang encyclopedia *Classified Extracts from Literature* and the early Song encyclopedia *Cefu yuangui* (comp. 1013), neither of which makes any reference to the zither.[73] In the collected works of Tao Yuanming, however, this line reads, "I have loved [or studied] *zither and books* since youth" (*Shao hao qin shu* or *Shao xue qin shu;* my italics). Did the historians notice the discrepancy and change Tao Yuanming's letter so as to preserve the wonderful story? Or did the Northern Song editors emend the text so as to accord with the letter as contained in the historians' records? There is no way for us to determine, due to the extreme textual fluidity in the manuscript culture, but these questions point to interesting possibilities.[74]

Su Shi may have been one of the earliest people to notice the discrepancy:

> In the old days it was said that Yuanming did not understand music. . . . This is nonsense. Yuanming himself had said "I sing to the seven strings," so how could he not understand music? It must have been that his zither had strings but the strings were worn and slackened, and he did not bother to replace them, so he simply stroked the zither to express his intentions. Only by interpreting it this way can we acquire the truth of things.[75]

People were reading texts in a different way than ever before in the Song: they were meticulous, they noticed inconsistencies, they tried to find ingenious rational explanations for them, and they believed that there was a "truth" which they must do their utmost to "acquire." The Song desire to "acquire" integrates beautifully with the firm belief in the existence of one single truth, which allows for no accident, fortuity, or irrationality. Such a desire started with the Song and has become an integral part of interpretive assumptions.

> SONG HISTORY: Noble or humble, whoever visited him, he would treat them to a drink if he had it. If he was drunk first, he would tell the guest, "I am drunk and I want to sleep; you may leave now." This is how genuine and frank he was.

The prefect once visited him when the wine was ready. Tao Qian took off his head cloth to strain the wine; after he finished, he put it back on again.

XIAO TONG: Noble or humble, whoever visited him, he would treat them to a drink if he had it. If he was drunk first, he would tell the guest, "I am drunk and I want to sleep; you may leave now." This is how genuine and frank he was.

The prefect once visited him when the wine was ready. Tao Qian took off his head cloth to strain the wine; after he finished, he put it back on again.

HISTORIES OF THE SOUTHERN DYNASTIES: Noble or humble, whoever visited him, he would treat them to a drink if he had it. If he got drunk first, he would tell the guest, "I am drunk and I want to sleep; you may leave now." This is how genuine and frank he was.

The prefect once visited him when the wine was ready. Tao Qian took off his head cloth to strain the wine; after he finished, he put it back on again.

These anecdotes emphasize both Tao Yuanming's characteristic "following his natural impulses" and his love of drinking. The first story seems to be a reversal of his statement in "Biography of Master Five Willows" that as soon as he gets drunk at a friend's or relative's house, he withdraws. The second story may have derived from a couplet in the last of Tao Yuanming's "On Drinking" series: "If I fail to drink to my heart's content, / I would let down the cloth on my head." Without the anecdote, the meaning of these two lines would have been enigmatic.[76]

The *Jin History* version, however, does not contain this portrayal of Tao Yuanming's spontaneous and casual nature.

JIN HISTORY: At the time, Zhou Xuzhi went to Mount Lu and became a disciple to the monk Hui Yuan [334–416]. Liu Yimin of Pengcheng also led a reclusive life at Mount Kuang [another name for Mount Lu]. Yuanming did not respond to the calls of the government. They were referred to as "the three recluses of Xunyang." Later, Governor Tan Shao [366–421] pleaded with Zhou Xuzhi to come forward, who, together with the scholars Zu Qi and Xie Jingyi, gave lectures on Confucian ritual texts in the north of the city. The official quarters they stayed in were close to the stable, so Yuanming showed them a poem, saying, "Master Zhou transmitted the teachings of Confucius, / Zu and Xie follow like echoes. . . . A stable is, alas, no lecture hall, / no matter how diligently you collate the texts."

The first part of the above section in Xiao Tong's version is almost taken verbatim from the biography of Zhou Xuzhi (377–423) in "Biographies of Recluses" in Shen Yue's *Song History*.[77] The second part is virtually a footnote to Tao Yuanming's poem "To be Shown to Secretary Zhou, and Zu and Xie" (Shi Zhou yuan Zu Xie).[78] Tan Shao, the older brother of Tan Daoji, became governor of Jiangzhou in 416 and stayed until Wang Hong replaced him in 418.[79] That Xiao Tong's version alone contains this anecdote seems to suggest Xiao Tong's passion for poetry and his familiarity with Tao Yuanming's works.

SONG HISTORY: Tao Qian held minor offices when he was young and was not rigid about public service. But because his great-grandfather had been a chief minister under the Jin, he felt too ashamed to submit to a later dynasty. Ever since Gaozu's imperial accomplishments became more and more pronounced, he would not serve again. He always dated his literary works; up to the Yixi period [405–418], he would use the reign name to designate dates, but from the Yongchu period [420–422] on, he would only sign the calendar year.

He wrote his sons a letter to express his inclinations as well as to instruct them. . . . He also wrote a poem entitled "Charge to My Son". . . . He died in the fourth year of the Yuanjia reign at the age of sixty-three.

XIAO TONG: Tao Yuanming's wife, neé Zhai, was also able to endure toil and hardship and shared his aims.

Because his great-grandfather had been a chief minister under the Jin, he felt too ashamed to submit to a later dynasty. Ever since Gaozu's imperial accomplishments became more and more pronounced, he would not serve again.

In the fourth year of the Yuanjia reign, the emperor was going to call him to service again, when he died. He was granted this posthumous title: Master Jingjie.

JIN HISTORY: He died during the Yuanjia reign, at the age of sixty-three. The collection of his literary works is still circulating in the world.

HISTORIES OF THE SOUTHERN DYNASTIES: Tao Qian held minor offices when he was young and was not rigid about public service. But because his great-grandfather had been a chief minister under the Jin, he felt too ashamed to submit to a later dynasty. Ever since Emperor Wu of Song's imperial accomplishments became more and more pronounced, he would not serve again. He always dated his literary works; up to the Yixi period [405–418], he would use the reign name to designate dates, but from the Yongchu period [420–422] on, he would only sign the calendar year.

He wrote his sons a letter to express his inclinations as well as to instruct them. . . . He also wrote a poem entitled "Charge to My Son."

In the fourth year of the Yuanjia reign, the emperor was going to call him to service again, when he died. He was granted this posthumous title: Master Jingjie.

His wife, neé Zhai, shared his inclinations and was also able to endure toil and hardship. As they say, the husband ploughed in front and the wife hoed behind; this was how they were.

Shen Yue himself was not a loyalist, having served three dynasties. One possible dimension of Shen Yue's assertion about Tao Yuanming's reason for reclusion has rarely been brought to attention: that Tao Yuanming felt too ashamed to serve a later dynasty was because his ancestor was a high-level minister of Jin. Although Shen Yue was not clear on this point, in the cultural context of the age, his statement could mean that in Shen Yue's eyes, the concept of "aristocratic clan membership" or "family background" (a clumsy translation of *mendi*) played a larger role in Tao Yuanming's decision to withdraw than a sense of loyalty to the Jin Dynasty, as Liu Yu, the founding emperor of Song, came from a humble family of minor gentry.[80]

Yongchu is the reign name of Liu Yu. The avoidance of using the Liu Song reign names to date his writings was taken to indicate the poet's refusal to acknowledge the legitimacy of the Liu Song rule. However, Si Yue, an eleventh-century monk, first raised a question about Shen Yue's statement. In a piece of commentary inserted at the beginning of the third *juan* in a printed edition of Tao Yuanming's collection (with a colophon dated 1066), he argues that of Tao Yuanming's extant poems, there are altogether nine (that is, counting two poems under the same title as one) dated by calendar year. These were composed between the year *gengzi* (400) and the year *bingchen* (416), all under the rule of Emperor An of Jin (r. 397–418). As the Liu Song replaced the Eastern Jin in 420, "how could he have felt ashamed of serving two dynasties and so date his poems with calendar years to mark a difference some twenty years before the change of dynasty?" Si Yue further states, "Moreover, there is no poem in his collection that contains any Jin reign name. I suppose that he incidentally used the calendar year to record one event, and later people simply imitated that practice and ordered his poems this way, which was not Yuanming's original intention."[81]

Scholars' opinions have long been divided on this issue: some agree with Si Yue's judgment, while many others oppose it.[82] Interestingly, neither Xiao Tong nor *The Jin History* followed Shen Yue on this point. While we do not know about the compilers of *The Jin History*, Xiao Tong was a great lover of Tao Yuanming's writings, and since he edited Tao Yuanming's collection, we may assume that he had read through all of Tao Yuanming's works. His silence on Tao Yuanming's dating method is rather significant. The debate culminates in the modern scholar Zhu Ziqing's (1898–1948) suggestion that Shen Yue must have made a careless remark.[83] Zhu Ziqing endorses Wu Renjie (*jinshi* degree, 1244), one of the earliest compilers of Tao Yuanming's chronology, who emphasizes that although Tao Yuanming had used different ways to date a piece of writing before the Jin fell, he never once mentioned any Liu Song reign name.[84] While Wu's statement is true, there is only one piece of Tao Yuanming's writing that carries a Song date ("In Sacrifice for Myself"), and so it is simply impossible to determine on the evidence of Tao Yuanming's transmitted works whether Tao Yuanming deliberately avoided using a Song reign name or not. What is rarely taken into account in this debate is textual fluidity; it was not uncommon to change the title of a poem while copying a manuscript, and it would have been too credulous to hold on to a title or the order of arrangement in a collection from before the age of print culture as fixed throughout centuries.

Shen Yue's terse statement, however, has been used to support the reading of the loyalist sentiments expressed in Tao Yuanming's poetry, and then the loyalist sentiments henceforth discovered in Tao Yuanming's poetry become evidence that supports Shen Yue's statement in the biography. In fact, Tao Yuanming never explicitly voiced any such sentiment in his writings; the many exemplary historical figures praised by Tao Yuanming and taken by later commentators to be subtle allusions to his own loyalism to the fallen Jin, such as the brothers Boyi and Shuqi (eleventh century B.C.E.), who refused to eat the grain of the new dynasty and starved to death, were popular topics of Jin poetry and prose. People frequently look for poetic images in Tao Yuanming's works that allude to the fall of Jin, and sure enough, those who look for something in a text will almost always find it (in later chapters, I will, however, show how misleading some of those attempts are). Bai Juyi's ninth-century reading of Tao Yuanming is very telling. In 816, Bai wrote a poem entitled "Visiting Master Tao Yuanming's Former Residence" (Fang Tao gong jiuzhai). It opens with these lines:

垢塵不污玉	*Dust cannot stain a piece of jade,*
靈鳳不啄羶	*nor will a numinous phoenix peck at foul food.*
嗚呼陶靖節	*Alas, Master Tao of Pure Integrity—*
生彼晉宋間	*he was born at the turn of Jin and Song.*
心實有所守	*In his heart there were principles he indeed abided by,*
口終不能言	*but in the end he was unable to utter a word.*[85]

Tao Yuanming claims he "forgot the words" in the South Mountain poem, but Bai Juyi describes him as "unable" to utter a word. Nevertheless, Bai Juyi apparently "acquires" the truth beyond the silence of the poet and sees the hidden principles by which Tao Yuanming "indeed" abided. The process of transforming Tao Yuanming into a solid, grand, and unchanged mountain to be "intuitively" understood and deciphered had already begun.

Shen Yue's claim that Tao Yuanming was a loyalist to the Jin ruling house became firmly established by the Song, when Tao Yuanming first gained status. Despite Si Yue's argument, most Song literati members held Tao Yuanming up as a loyal Jin subject, and one of their favorite pieces of evidence was this story about dating his writings with calendar years. As Ge Lifang says in *Yunyu yangqiu*, "The world, in discussing Yuanming, differs from the opinion of Si Yue, and agrees that he only used calendar years instead of reign names since the Yongchu period."[86] Once again, myth has proved more powerful than truth.

In summary, in the four biographies we see both overlapping passages and differences. Since Xiao Tong's version is part of a collection of Tao Yuanming's works, he has no need to include Tao Yuanming's writings in the biography—except for "The Biography of Master Five Willows." Xiao Tong shows his familiarity with Tao Yuanming's writings by adding the anecdote about sending home a servant from Pengze (which accords better with Tao Yuanming's "Return" than Shen Yue's biography) or the anecdote about the stable (which becomes a narrative context for Tao Yuanming's poem) and also by characterizing Tao Yuanming as "learned and good at literary compositions" at the beginning (which accentuates Tao Yuanming's literary achievements). The addition of the anecdote of Tan Daoji, on the other hand, highlights Tao Yuanming's insistence on principles in the face of dire poverty. A wonderful final touch is the introduction of Tao Yuanming's wife: is this an implicit refutation of Tao Yuanming's "*Fu* on Stilling the Passions" (Xianqing fu), which Xiao Tong disliked so much because in his eyes it was not consistent with Tao Yuanming's image as a high-minded recluse? It certainly goes against Tao Yuanming's own claim about not having "Lai's wife"—meaning a wife sharing his high-minded aspirations.[87]

In contrast, the Tao Yuanming in the *Jin History* biography is much softened. He is portrayed as very cautious in his dealings with Wang Hong, very agreeable, very carefully casual, unwilling to offend anyone. His love of wine is not so strongly stressed as in the other biographies, mainly because of the prominent absence of the anecdotes about his turning the money over to the tavern, his getting drunk on the Double Ninth, his treating his guests to drinks, and his straining the wine with his turban. One small difference, nonetheless interesting, occurs in the description of Tao Yuanming's stringless zither. While the other three biographies have "When he became tipsy, he would stroke the zither to express his feelings," the *Jin History* version has "Whenever there was a drinking party, he would stroke the zither, saying. . . ." Tao Yuanming's stroking the zither becomes a very public gesture, and, once again, Tao Yuanming is explaining himself to others. Finally, the most conspicuous difference is that the *Jin History* biography removes any mention of Tao Yuanming's refusal to serve the Liu Song.

The *Histories of the Southern Dynasties* biography follows Shen Yue's and Xiao Tong's versions more closely than it does the *Jin History* version. This is certainly an interesting choice for a historian who participated in the compilation of *The Jin History*. The choice might very well have been an ideological one.

All four biographies, however, begin with Tao Yuanming's self-construction. The biographies become intertwined with Tao Yuanming's own words, and later they are used to support the interpretation of Tao Yuanming's own words, and, in some cases, perhaps as a basis to change Tao Yuanming's own words. Many attempts have been made to resolve any tension that might exist between Tao Yuanming's writings and the biographies: some sections considered irreconcilable with the image of Tao Yuanming as a spontaneous person, such as Tao Yuanming's explanation of his refusal to see Wang Hong, are simply left in silence.

3 Lost Homesteads: Returning to Tao

Mencius believed that an ideal reader should, in his reading, seek to understand and befriend ancient authors. When we try to return to Tao Yuanming, we find that the man is shrouded in a haze of generalized anecdotes and the poet is lost in a body of texts filled with indeterminate variants, arbitrary editorial choices, and conflicting ideological claims. The sense of loss, triggered by an awareness of the problems of manuscript culture in our case, is what Tao Yuanming himself once experienced when he gave up his official post and came home—or so he tells us in his famous series of five poems, "Returning to Dwell in Gardens and Fields" (Gui yuan tian ju).

Almost every time he went into public service, Tao Yuanming expressed his yearning for an undisturbed private life; sometimes his official career seemed no more than a necessary pretext for the grand gesture of resigning and going home. In order to return to a place, one first has to leave it. The pleasure in entertaining the idea of withdrawal to private life and declaring one's resolve to resign is nothing more than an aftermath. Yet it is much more important, though often less exhilarating, to face the consequences of such a major decision. What if life at home is, contrary to one's expectation, every bit as frustrating as life in the public world? Or worse—what if the home itself is transient and part of a grand illusion?

Unwelcome Plants

The figure of loss is embedded in the very text of "Returning to Dwell in Gardens and Fields." There is a sixth poem in this series, which may be traced back at least to Su Shi's time, since Su Shi wrote a poem matching rhymes with it, taking it to be by Tao Yuanming. Later, however, it was recognized as an imitation written by Jiang Yan (444–505) that somehow got mixed up in Tao Yuanming's collection. But even if this poem is inauthentic, there does seem to have been another missing sixth poem. Hu Zi recorded the following remarks of Han Ju (courtesy name Zicang, ?–1135) in *Collected Comments of the Fisherman Recluse of Tiao Creek, First Series* (Tiaoxi yuyin conghua qianji, preface dated 1148):

> The last of the six "Gardens and Fields" poems describes a journey, which is unlike the first five poems. Now all the popular/vulgar editions take Jiang Yan's poem beginning with "I plant seedlings in the eastern fields" as the sixth poem; even Dongpo wrote a poem matching its rhymes by mistake. On the other hand, Chen Shugu's (?–1090) edition only has five poems [under this title]. I think neither version is correct. There should be six poems entitled "Unclassified Poems," as in Prime Minister Zhang's edition.[1]

According to Han Ju, by the twelfth century there were at least three versions of Tao Yuanming's series of poems known as "Returning to Dwell in Gardens and Fields"; the "popular editions" had six poems under the current title, the sixth being Jiang Yan's imitation; Chen Shugu's edition (either a printed or a manuscript copy) had only five poems under this title, presumably the same five poems as in all the modern editions; in the third case, we have a series of six poems under a completely different title, "Unclassified Poems" (Za shi), a much looser title that does not necessarily imply any internal "connection" between the poems—moreover, in this series the sixth poem is apparently about a journey, which even more forcefully refutes the current title, "Returning to Dwell in Gardens and Fields," unless, of course, we presume that the poet leaves his "fields and gardens" again at the end of the series. This mysterious sixth poem has never been located, but in the twelve poems under the title "Unclassified Poems" in Tao Yuanming's collection there are three poems describing a journey, and in fact the ninth poem is explicitly about going away for official business and longing to return home. If we recall that even the South Mountain poem, now the fifth of the "On Drinking" series, is invariably cited as an "Unclassified Poem" in such early sources as *An Anthology of Literature* and *Classified Extracts from Literature*, we realize that poem titles, just like the poetic text itself, are in flux and at the mercy of later editorial efforts. Poems, particularly from before the age of print culture, often seem to pick up titles and authors along the way and are made to fall into place where they "belong." In any case, we should keep in mind that our subsequent reading of this series of poems must be put in the context of the textual fluidity of manuscript culture. In other words, we work with what we have, but what we know about "Tao Yuanming" has been very much mediated and compromised by generations of textual adulteration and imperfect transmission.

The first poem in this series portrays Tao Yuanming's initial delight upon first coming home, a delight not yet rendered stale by familiarity and routine. Even in the opening line, we embark on a journey beset with troubling variants that obstruct our progress at almost every step:

少無適俗韻 *In my youth my disposition was ill-suited for the common world;*
性本愛丘山 *by nature I loved hills and mountains.*

Zeng Ji's 1192 edition gives a variant, *yuan* 願 (desire) for *yun* 韻 (disposition), so that the line reads, "In my youth, I had no desire to suit the common world." *Yun*, however, remains the traditional reading, and most modern anthologists choose *yun*, either without explanation or on the ground that *yun* was a common word used in describing a person's character in the Six Dynasties.[2] If we want a better reason for the preference for *yun*, we have to take into consideration the subtle difference in meaning between the two words: *yun*, originally a musical term indicating the harmonious sound of a tune, emphasizes a person's innate quality, while *yuan* ("desire" or "wish") is not inherent in a person as an inborn characteristic, but represents an act of will. A citation from Wang Tanzhi's (330–375) letter to Xie An (320–385) may best illustrate the implications of *yun*: "I suppose a person's form [*ti*] and nature [*yun*] are like the square or round shape of a vessel: just as the square or round shape of one vessel cannot be transferred to another, how can one's form and nature be exchanged with someone else's?"[3] If *yun* is intrinsic and effortless, then *yuan* involves striving and exertion. The point here is not which word is "correct," but which word is favored by commentators and why.

The poet then describes his official career as a mistake, which he now has happily corrected:

誤落塵網中	*I erred and fell into the snares of dust,*
一去三十年	*away from home for thirty years in all.*
羈鳥戀舊林	*The caged bird craves the woods of old,*
池魚思故淵	*a fish in a pond fancies former depths.*
開荒南野/畝際	*Clearing wastelands at the edge of the southern* wilds / acres,
守拙歸園田	*I abide by my clumsiness and return to my gardens and fields.*

To give the source of the then unusual term *chen wang* ("dusty snares" or "dusty net"), Ding Fubao (1874–1952) cites a line from a letter by Dongfang Shuo (154–93 B.C.E.): "One should not be confined by the dusty snares and reins of fame."[4] But the source of this letter is not reliable. On the other hand, Fan Ning (339–401), Tao Yuanming's elder contemporary, used the term in a treatise praising Confucianism and denouncing He Yan (190–249) and Wang Bi, two famous figures advocating the Lao-Zhuang philosophy. In this treatise, a fictional interlocutor claims that He Yan and Wang Bi had "raised high the net that went into decline for a thousand years, and drew down the dusty snares of the Duke of Zhou and Confucius [*luo Zhou Kong zhi chen wang* 落周孔之塵網]."[5] We notice that although *luo* here is used in a very different sense from the *luo* in Tao Yuanming's *luo chen wang* (falling into the snares of dust), the phrasing and the syntax are remarkably similar. Fan Ning bitterly argues against the imaginary interlocutor in his treatise, but the *Jin History* tells us that Fan Ning was in the minority during his age in his upholding of Confucian values: "Ning admired Confucianism and opposed what was popular [i.e., the Lao-Zhuang philosophy]."[6] Zhou Xuzhi, who for his teaching of Confucian texts became the target of Tao Yuanming's satire in "To be Shown to Secretary Zhou, and Zu and Xie," was Fan Ning's student since the age of twelve, and, as Fan Ning's favorite disciple, was dubbed "Yanzi" [Yancius].[7] Since Tao

Yuanming was familiar with Zhou Xuzhi, we have good reason to suspect that he might have had knowledge of Fan Ning's treatise and so was deliberately subverting the phrase *luo chen wang* in his poem; both the Duke of Zhou and the public-minded Confucius represent the world of official service, which Tao Yuanming denounces as the "snares of dust."

The phrase "thirty years" has no textual variant, but it has inspired many emendations and ingenious speculations because of the problems it poses for the passionate chroniclers of Tao Yuanming's life. What concerns us here, however, is the incongruity looming in the next four lines, which introduce an implicit contrast between the conventional metaphor of a confined bird and fish longing for their former freedom and the image of clearing wasteland. On the one hand, nature loathes being fettered and desires to break free; on the other hand, humankind needs to constrain and cultivate. To clear up wasteland is to cut down the space for creatures of wilderness—the home of birds and fish. In the line "Clearing wastelands at the edge of the southern *wilds / acres*," the variant character "acres" (*mu*) turns out to be interesting. To open up some land for farming on the margin of the wilderness is the modest gesture of a man who negotiates with nature and strives to make a living, but in the alternative reading, we see him expanding the farming land he already has, in an attempt to enlarge the territory of civilization.[8]

One word of note here: *kai huang*, "to clear wastelands," is a large and toilsome project. According to Jia Sixie (sixth century), the author of the agricultural work *Essential Techniques for the Peasantry* (Qimin yaoshu), "When clearing wastelands in mountains or marshes for new fields, always cut down the weeds in the seventh month; the weeds should be set on fire once they have dried out. Cultivation should begin only in the spring."[9] When there are larger trees and shrubs, we are told, it may take as long as three years before the land can be used for farming. As Francesca Bray points out, "most reclamation work required heavy initial investment and was beyond the means of all but the rich." She quotes from an eighteenth-century agricultural manual: "'Only households with many workers and much land can afford to open up new land.'"[10]

方宅十餘畝	*My estate spans more than a couple of acres,*
草屋八九間	*my thatched cottage contains a few rooms.*[11]
榆柳蔭後簷	*Elms and willows shade the back eaves;*
桃李羅堂前	*peach and plum spread in front of the hall.*

曖曖遠人村	*The distant community is lost in a haze;*
依依墟里煙	*smoke from the village hearths lingers in the air.*
狗吠深巷中	*A dog barks in the deep lanes;*
雞鳴桑樹顛	*on top of a mulberry tree a rooster crows.*
戶庭無塵雜	*There is no dust or disorder in house or yard;*
虛室有餘閑	*the empty chambers are filled with leisure.*

This poem has long been considered a sketch of the rustic environment to which Tao Yuanming returns. And yet, looking closely, we discover that it is more a portrayal of Tao Yuanming's own home than of the village; there is, as a matter of fact, quite some distance between them. Tao Yuanming's home estate is a space well protected by the shady elms and willows, peach and plum trees. It is set apart from the remote community lost in a haze, and the cooking smoke rising from the villagers' chimneys and hearths both indicates and conceals their presence. There is no clear visual impression of the villagers' life; the noises made by their chickens and dogs are the only sounds that reach the poet.

Many commentators have noticed that the last couplet of the passage is taken almost verbatim from a supposedly Eastern Han ballad "Cockcrow" (Jiming),[12] but a famous passage in *Dao de jing* (or *Tao te ching*), the canonical work attributed to the Daoist philosopher Laozi, may have been the true origin of these lines. Given the familiarity of Tao Yuanming's contemporaries with Lao-Zhuang texts, this passage is more likely to have emerged in the reader's mind. In this passage, Laozi depicts an ideal utopia, where "neighboring states may look at one another, and the sound of dogs and roosters may be overheard, and yet their people grow old and die with no comings and goings between them."[13]

Gazing at the distant village, the poet shows no desire to go beyond the boundary clearly defined by the trees surrounding his house. Enclosed within is a space small enough to be manageable; it is clean and orderly, with no dust, no mess. Lu Ji's (261–303) lines on the hardship of being in official service come to mind: "Luoyang, the capital city, is very windy and dusty, / white clothes are turned black."[14] Characterizing his dealings with the common (*su*) world as being trapped in dusty snares, the poet is glad that his own home is unsoiled. The couplet echoes *Zhuangzi*: "An empty chamber gives birth to brightness" (Xu shi sheng bai), which commentators gloss as a metaphorical way of saying "the heart, when devoid [of desires, concerns, worries], becomes enlightened by the Way."[15] With this the poet brings the poem to the concluding statement:

久在樊籠裏	*For a long time I have been in a cage,*
復得返自然	*now again I return to the natural way of life.*

The image of the caged bird returns briefly only to be negated. The poet claims that he is free now, as he has come back to nature (*ziran*), and once again leads a "natural" life. The nature he comes back to embrace, however—the neat rows of trees lined up in the front and back of his house, the spotless, uncluttered, well-organized interiors—is a highly idealized state of nature, just like the vision of utopia in *Dao de jing*. It can hardly be sustained for long if completely left to itself; it requires vigilant control. It is, to put it simply, a very unnatural nature, a nature that needs constant artificial care, a nature, like a garden, that has been "naturalized" and made accessible to human comfort and affection. The phrase *kai huang*, "clearing up wastelands," already points to the immense human efforts to keep nature in check. The last line, however, has an unfortunate textual variant, which radically changes the ending and complicates the whole poem:

久在樊籠裏	*For a long time I have been in a cage,*
安得返自然	how *can I get to return to the natural way of life?*

This unexpected question completely shatters the calm and complacency built up in the previous lines; we suddenly realize that anxiety and doubt still beset our poet, despite his return to the gardens and fields. He seems to be saying, "For a man who has been kept captive so long in the dusty snares of the common world, how can I ever learn to get used to this new, simple, natural way of life again?"

We decide that this reading cannot make any sense. The poet has already broken free from the former constraints of the world of red dust; he should be at peace now. The ample leisure that, like stored grain, becomes overabundant (*yu*), should help ensure a relaxed state of mind. Every scene—from the enclosed physical space, the trees, the sound of a dog barking and a cock crowing, the distant village, and the cooking smoke rising from hearths, to the neat courtyard and the empty room—is infused with a sense of serenity. Or is it?

Commentators, while sometimes taking time to justify their dismissal of a variant, are almost unanimously silent on this one. "The joy of returning to the fields" is the focal point. We only hear what we want to hear and believe what we want to believe. What Tao Yuanming has really written becomes irrelevant, as long as we are convinced that he has returned to the countryside and all is well. We thereupon regard the variant as a mere error, a "word weed" that must be plucked out and discarded from this neat garden of a poem. What is a "weed" anyway? Nothing but an "unwanted, invasive, unwelcome plant."

Weeds, however, are proliferating. The second poem in the "Return" series opens by reiterating the poet's resolve to keep to his dust-free, solitary purity, which is manifested in the gesture of closing the door against the outside world. The initial delight upon coming home, however, already begins to wane as the poet tries to establish a new, more "natural," way of life:

野外罕人事 *Beyond the wilderness, few human affairs;*
窮巷寡輪鞅 *to the narrow lane rarely come wheels and yokes.*
白日掩荊扉 *In broad daylight I close my wicker door,*
虛室絕塵想 *ceasing dusty thoughts in empty chambers.*

If in the first poem Tao Yuanming declares that dust is absent from his home, here he makes sure to tell us that he has even managed to get rid of all "dusty thoughts" from his mind: the spiritual abode is just as clean as the physical dwelling. The phrase "empty chambers" (*xu shi*), which echoes the first poem and is the term from *Zhuangzi* figuratively used for the mind, has a variant, given in Zeng Ji's 1192 edition: "*Facing the wine* and ceasing dusty thoughts" (*Dui jiu jue chen xiang* 對酒絕塵想). What the "dusty thoughts" are we do not know—does the poet secretly miss the world he has renounced?—but it is certain that they belong to the "dusty snares" from which he has just escaped, the remaining traces of those thirty years of entrapment. The memory of the world he foregoes is so powerful that only by drinking can the man avoid getting mentally involved in it again.[16] But "facing the wine" is not a popular choice with the anthologists, despite Tao Yuanming's famous love of drinking. Wang Shumin explains that "empty chamber" forms a better, more interesting parallel with "broad daylight" (lit., "bright sun" or "bright day"), as he is thinking of the Zhuangzi remark "An empty chamber gives birth to brightness."[17]

"Human affairs" (*renshi*) in the first line are glossed by Chinese commentators as social interactions. This is immediately illustrated by the next line: "to the narrow lane rarely come wheels and yokes." The wheels and yokes are the carriages used by officials. And yet, for the character "few" (*gua*) there is a variant, "to unfasten or undo" (*jie* 解). So, instead of receiving no visits from carriage-riding officials, the poet may be saying that his own carriage has been disassembled and put to disuse. Perhaps he has come home in such a carriage, but it proves too large for the narrow lane, and he has decided not to ride in it anyway, which is tantamount to saying that he gives up visiting a certain class of people. In "Return," he makes a promise: "May my fellowship be severed and my wanderings come to an end" (Qing xi jiao yi jue you).

As we will see, neither undoing the wheels and yokes nor severing fellowship means that he is going to become a misanthropic hermit, but simply that he will not carry on social intercourse with people from the official world. Just as the phrase *renshi* (human affairs) does not encompass the very human worries and concerns in the rural world but instead specifically points to "a political domain quite distinct from this agrarian society,"[18] so we learn that what the poet refers to as "fellowship" does not include his mingling with "non-carriage folks." Indeed, Tao Yuanming's poetry "speaks to and for our flurried world of carriage-riders and poetry readers."[19] And yet, they themselves being part of the complicated world of poetry readers, traditional Chinese commentators love the romanticized image of a simple, outspoken poet who is almost indistinguishable from a (romanticized) farmer.

As the poem goes on, we see that the poet is not completely indifferent to the human world:

時復墟曲中　　*Now and then on the winding village paths,*
披草共來往　　*pushing back grasses, we visit one another.*[20]

For these lines, if we follow the alternative reading, we will have:

時復墟里人　　*Now and then people of the village,*
披衣共來往　　*throwing on their clothes, visit one another.*

In this alternative reading, it is even more difficult to tell whether the poet himself participates in the communion among the villagers, or if he is once again simply observing and listening, as in the first poem. Commentators generally opt for the former interpretation (and they mostly reject the variant) and see the poet as coming out from behind his closed door.

相見無雜言　*When we meet, there is no mixed talk;*
但道桑麻長　*we only discuss how mulberry and hemp grow.*[21]

Mixed talk (*za yan*) recalls the phrase *chen za* in the preceding poem: from the lack of dusty thoughts to the lack of mixed talk, the poet is reaffirming the absence of either dust or mess and the sense of purity. One may mingle with the world, but the poet insists that it is a better world, more neat and tidy, than the political arena. The reverberation of the two words, "dust" (*chen*) and "mess" (*za*), is so exquisite that one cannot but discard the textual variant, "other talk" (*bie yan* 別言).

Even in such a rustic community, however, where everything seems so simple and innocent, a person is not completely free of anxiety—though the anxiety is of a different order from that caused by the dusty snares of the political world. The new anxiety is about the harvest. The idealized rural scene in the first poem has become more real and less romantic.

桑麻日已長　*Mulberry and hemp grow taller every day,*
我土日已廣　*every day my land grows more broad.*
常恐霜霰至　*Yet I always fear that frost and sleet will come,*
零落同草莽　*and there will be withering and falling, as with the weeds.*

When mulberry and hemp grow and the cultivated land becomes larger (the result of "clearing up wastelands"), nature is giving way, and it is the farmer's delight. But as mulberry and hemp grow taller every day, so is a man getting older, and nature is taking revenge in its own way. If mulberry and hemp wither and fall in the frost, there will not be any difference between them and the weeds of the wilderness the poet tries so hard to pluck out: the cherished and unwanted plants will eventually share (*tong*) the same fate. Here the withering and falling are not just of the crops.[22] In the background of the last lines, we hear the anxious cry of Qu Yuan (fourth–third century B.C.E.), the poet of "Encountering Sorrow" (Li sao): "As grass and trees wither and fall, / I fear the aging of the beautiful one."[23] This, however, is not something a simple farmer ordinarily feels concerned about.

There is a variant for "land" (*tu*) in the second line, which is *zhi* 志: "aspiration," "intention," and sometimes "ambition." In this case, the line becomes, "every day my aspiration grows more expansive." The Song critic Cai Qi says that even if one adopts the variant *zhi*, it does not make much difference in meaning.[24] He is wrong. If we choose *zhi*, a loaded term in the Chinese literary and intellectual tradition, then the last two lines are given extra weight: the fear of a life cut short would be directly related to and contrasted with the daily expansion of the poet's aspirations. He would then seem to be saying that as time flies by, he is afraid that he will not be able to accomplish what he aspires to do. The poet is filled with worries that can only be eased with hard work in the fields.

The following is the third poem of the series:

種豆南山下 *I plant beans at the foot of South Mountain,*
草盛豆苗稀 *weeds prosper, the bean sprouts are few.*[25]
晨興理荒穢 *I rise in the morning to tend the weeds;*
帶月荷鋤歸 *I come back in moonlight, hoe over my shoulder.*
道狹草木長 *The path is narrow, weeds and shrubs growing tall,*
夕露霑我衣 *the evening dew soaks my clothes.*
衣霑不足惜 *I do not regret if the clothes are soaked,*
但使願無違 *as long as my wish is not thwarted.*

The threat of wilderness is always present in this series of poems. While mulberry and hemp are growing every day, so are grass and weeds. The paths and ploughed land, signs of human civilization, are both being invaded. The cheerful poet opening up the wastelands in the first poem and the anxious poet concerned about frost in the second is now driven out of his closed door to clear away the weeds from dawn to dusk. The key word in the third poem is again *gui*, "to return"; in this case the poet is returning home after a day's hard work in the fields. The path may be narrow, the dew cold, and the night dark, but the prospect of a home lit up by a hearth fire waiting for him at the end of the journey is very comforting. This comforting vision, however, is shattered in the next poem by a philosophical awakening.

Taking a break from farm work, in the fourth poem the poet goes on a pleasure outing with the youngsters:

久去山澤遊 *Long have I left wandering in hills and marshes,*
浪莽林野娛 *deprived of the pleasures of woods and moors;*[26]

試攜子姪輩	*now taking along my sons and nephews,*
披榛步荒墟	*pushing back the thicket, we walk to a ruined village.*

Once again we see the verb *pi* (push back); in the second poem, the villagers have had to "push back" grass to visit one another. We also see the word *xu* (village); the same word used in the first poem for the distant farming community and in the second poem for the village, but here it has a gloomy prefix, *huang*—"desolate," "deserted," and "overgrown," the very condition the poet tries to eliminate in the first poem as he "clears up wastelands" (*kai huang*).

徘徊丘壟間	*We linger among the grave mounds:*
依依昔人居	*vaguely recognizable are places where people once lived.*
井灶有遺處	*There are remains of wells and hearths,*
桑麻殘朽株	*rotten stumps of mulberries and hemp.*
借問採薪者	*I ask someone gathering firewood,*
此人皆焉如	*"Where did all the people go?"*
薪者向我言	*The wood gatherer says to me,*
死沒無復餘	*"All dead and gone—nothing is left."*
一世異朝市	*In one lifetime court and market change—*
此語真不虛	*these truly are not empty words.*
人生似幻化	*Human life is like a conjured illusion:*
終當歸空無	*in the end, it will return to nothingness.*

We constantly hear the echoes of words and phrases used in the first poem. The hazy quality of the cooking smoke coming from the village hearths, *yiyi*, is now transferred to the hearths falling into ruins. The plants—mulberry and hemp, happily growing under human care in the second poem—turn into rotten stumps. And, of course, there is no more rooster crowing in the treetops. But the saddest thing is that, while traces of wells, hearths, and trees can still be found, those people who once attended to them leave nothing behind (*wu fu yu*). From the first poem in the series to this one, we have witnessed a *huan hua* (a game of illusion conjured up by the poet's word magic). We must read these two poems side by side while keeping in mind what goes in between: the worries, the hopes, the toils, the hard work to keep the boundary between civilization and nature clear and to fend off the invasion of weeds—in a word, the stuff of human life, which is now reduced to ruins and nothingness. In the last line of this poem we once again encounter the word *gui* (to return) at its most poignant. For it is the "grand homecoming" (*da gui*),[27] as indicated by the concluding line of "Return": "I will just ride the transformations and go back to the ultimate end" (Liao cheng hua yi gui jin). Everything will eventually revert to emptiness. That is, everything but the words that tell you such; they "truly are not empty."

Throughout the series Tao Yuanming is deeply concerned with *huang*, a chaotic wilderness that must be brought back to order by human care. But what is the use of clearing up the wastelands and plowing and planting, if everything, including the plowman, is going to end in naught? We cannot find a reply in the poems. And yet, instead of losing himself in despair and anguish, the poet decides to make the best of what he has, and we come to the last poem of the series:

悵恨獨策還	*Dejected, I return alone, staff in hand,*
崎嶇歷榛曲	*walking on a rugged road through the thickets.*
山澗清且淺	*The mountain brook is clear and shallow,*
遇以濯吾足	*where I wash my feet.*
漉我新熟酒	*Straining some new wine,*
隻雞招近局	*with a chicken I invite my neighbors.*
日入室中闇	*The sun goes down, the room gets dark,*
荊薪代明燭	*firewood replaces bright candles.*
歡來苦夕短	*Growing cheerful, we suffer from the brevity of the evening;*
已復至天旭	*once again, it is already dawning.*

The fifth poem starts with yet another homecoming, one imbued with melancholy, in sharp contrast with the homecoming in the first poem of the series. The abrupt beginning reminds us that we have to read this poem in the context of the others so as to make narrative sense. We don't know why he returns home alone; the youngsters have disappeared. Maybe he has left the ruins earlier than they did, unable to bear the melancholy sight.

On his way back, he encounters a brook, in which he washes his feet. Commentators point out a literary source for this couplet, which is the song sung by the fisherman in *Chuci*: "When the water of Canglang is clear, it is good for washing my cap strings; when the water of Canglang is muddy, it is good for washing my feet."[28] The implication, according to Eastern Han commentator Wang Yi (ca. second century), is that one should engage in public service or withdraw to be a hermit according to the circumstances. Cap strings are part of official attire. This song also appears in *Mencius* as a common proverb, but a different moral is embedded in it: what the water is used for depends on the nature of the water, and so Confucius admonishes his students to better themselves so as to gain the respect of others.[29] Davis thinks it might mean that even if it would be proper for Tao Yuanming to accept office, he did not want to do so.[30] Hightower suggests that by reversing the conditions of the song, the poet may be saying, "The mountain brook is clear (unlike the stream of political activity, which is too soiled for washing one's cap of office), but I can only bathe my feet in it, since I have no official's cap that might appropriately be washed in this pure water," though Hightower also concedes that this is no more than a reminder that here in the country the poet is "free at last from the contamination of official life."[31]

Like the beans in the third poem, this mountain brook is both "a real part of the scenery" and "a literary allusion,"[32] and what concerns us here is the act of the poet washing his feet in clear water—a gesture of physical and spiritual cleansing, even catharsis, after his depressing outing. This is indeed still the same poet who insists on a dust-free house, but, as we will see, he has been humbled by his most recent experience. Instead of looking at the village from afar, or meeting the villagers through chance encounters, he actively invites his neighbors over for dinner, persuading them with roast chicken (no more "rooster crowing on top of the mulberry tree" for the poet) and new brew, filling up his "empty chambers." Contrary to what some commentators think, it is not the companionship that is important to the poet's mood change, but it is his mood change that has brought the companionship. In other words, in the face of emptiness and nothingness, human happiness, at least for our poet, becomes an act of will. The English phrase "make merry" is realized quite literally here. And yet, amidst the very merriment that aims at dispelling thoughts of mortality, there is the shadow cast by the passage of time: it is already dawn, *again.* One thinks of the third poem, in which the poet has to rise very early in the morning to plant and plough, trying to wrestle a small victory from the devastating wilderness *(huang)* of time.

The verb in the eighth line, *dai* (to replace), is given a variant, *ji* 繼 (to succeed), in the 1192 edition: "The sun goes down, the room gets dark, / firewood succeeds bright candles." To "replace" the candles with firewood might indicate that the host is too poor to use candles for the night party; to succeed the candles with firewood, on the other hand, may simply mean that the night party lasts so long that all the candles burn out, and so they have to make do with the firewood—was it once a mulberry tree?—to light up the room. "Replace" is the universal choice, perhaps because Tao Yuanming looks best when presented in the light of an impoverished recluse. The real Tao Yuanming, however, has long been lost.

Another poem by Tao Yuanming, "Returning to My Former Residence" (Huan jiu ju), may be appended here as a sort of footnote to the "Return" series:

疇昔家上京　　*Some time ago I lived at Shangjing:*
六載去還歸　　*for six years I was in and out of town.*[33]
今日始復來　　*Only today did I come back for the first time,*
惻愴多所悲　　*sad to see so many things to grieve about;*
阡陌不移舊　　*paths in the fields have not changed,*
邑屋或時非　　*but some of the town houses are not quite the same.*
履歷周故居　　*I pace around my former home;*
鄰老罕復遺　　*few of the elderly neighbors still remain.*
步步尋往跡　　*Every footstep of mine traces the former tracks,*
有處特依依　　*at some places lingering with fondness.*
流幻百年中　　*Ah, this flowing illusion of one hundred years—*
寒暑日相推　　*cold and heat pushing each other along every day.*[34]
常恐大化盡　　*I often fear exhausting the Great Transformation*
氣力不及衰　　*even before my strengths decline.*
廢置且莫念　　*Let us cast the thought aside, forget about it;*
一觴聊可揮　　*for the moment, I could use a cup of wine.*

In this poem, we see a very similar theme to that of the fourth of the "Return" series, except that the much altered place in this case was once the poet's own hometown. Houses—artificial constructions of human civilization—prove to be less lasting than the pathways in the fields, which, even when overgrown with weeds, have not been dislocated, but the occupants of the houses are the most transient of all: there is already nothing left of them.[35] The poet uses the same phrase, *yiyi* (affectionately, fondly), to describe his sojourn. Reflecting on the power of change and the illusory nature of human life, he also voices the same worries and fears about mortality. But here the irony is that, although he is depressed by the metamorphosis of his former residence, he is much more afraid that the cycle of transformations is coming to an end—a euphemism for death—even before he can reach a mature old age. While the poet bemoans change, it is this conflicting desire to have the Great Transformation go on that gives this otherwise ordinary poem its particular pathos.

"Pretty Much Being An Old Farmer"

In distress, drinking serves the excellent purpose of making many things seem not to matter as much. Beginning in the third century (the late Three Kingdoms and early Western Jin periods), the eccentric Seven Worthies of the Bamboo Grove in particular helped make drinking a fashionable pastime for the "high-minded," until it gradually went out of vogue in the fifth century.[36] Both the "Returning to Dwell in Gardens and Fields" series and "Returning to My Former Residence" end with drinking, and drinking requires one essential condition: grain. We remember the apocryphal anecdote about Tao Yuanming planting glutinous rice in the public fields when he was magistrate of Pengze. Quite contrary to his portrayal in the biographies, however, in his poetry Tao Yuanming was obsessed with management of his "rural affairs." He repeatedly spoke of the vital importance of material life; providing adequate food for himself and his family was a source of constant concern. Like a farmer, he was always worried about the crops and the harvest. In no other poem do his complicated feelings about his chosen way of life come out more clearly than in the one written in the fall of 410 on harvesting dry rice.[37] The opening line reiterates the theme of return, only to emphasize the origin of all things: food and clothing.

人生歸有道　　*Human life comes down to possessing the Way,*
衣食固其端　　*but food and clothing are indeed its beginning.*

Human life is envisioned as a road: food and clothing provide the point of departure for pursuit of the Way.

There is, however, a problem with this much-praised couplet. This could very well be an idealized version, even revision, of Tao Yuanming. If we follow the variant reading, we have:

人生歸有事　　*Human life comes down to having a vocation,*
衣食固無端　　*food and clothing are truly a limitless matter.*

Shi is a rich word. It means "a vocation," "an occupation," as in the *Shi ji* sentence "His profession [*shi*] was being a dog butcher."[38] It also means "accomplishments," as in the phrase *shiye*. The kind of deed implied by *shi* has an undeniably concrete and pragmatic dimension; the philosopher Xunzi (third century B.C.E.) distinguishes *shi* from *xing* (also "action" or "deed") on such a basis, saying that *shi* is "acting on considerations of legitimate profit" (zheng li er wei wei zhi shi),[39] and John Knoblock has appropriately translated *shi* in this case as "business." He explains, "'Business' consists of those activities involved in one's vocation, particularly among those whose life does not involve self-cultivation, namely, merchants, farmers, and traders."[40]

If we read the character coming after *you* (having, possessing) as *shi* instead of the conventionally accepted *you dao* (possessing the Way), then not only does the phrase make an interesting parallel with *wu duan* (limitless, having no beginning and no end) in the next line, but it also manifests an attitude towards life which is very different from that implied by the phrase *you dao*. If *you dao* embodies the Confucian teaching "A gentleman works on the Way, not on food" and "A gentleman is concerned with the Way, not with poverty,"[41] then *you shi* (having a pragmatic vocation, accomplishing something concrete) defies such teachings by advocating a more practical philosophy of life. Maybe not incidentally, there are two lines in "Return" which explicitly relate *you shi* with farming, and in particular with the western fields: "The peasants tell me that spring is here, / and they will have work to do [*you shi*] in the western fields."

Unlike many other textual variants in Tao editions, *dao* and *shi* are similar neither in shape nor in sound, and they also entail very different meanings. While *you dao* (possessing the Way) is much more conventional, and the combination of *gui you dao* (return to the Way) and *yi shi gu qi duan* (food and clothing are its beginning) is so much easier to grasp, we see a typical case in which a phrase with a simpler, more conventional meaning is used in place of one that creates difficulty in interpretation and presents Tao Yuanming as less high-sounding.

The next couplet contains a key term, *zi an* (lit., "self-peace"):

孰是都不營　　*Who can be secure and at peace*
而以求自安　　*if he does not work on these things?*

Ying is another word indicating utilitarian action aimed at practical benefits; translated here as "work on," it means "to build," "to construct," "to manage," and "to acquire profit in commercial ventures." We may consider an example from "Biographies of Virtuous Officials" in *The Song History*. When people tried to persuade Jiang Bingzhi (381–440) to "take care of the fields" (*ying tian*), Jiang Bingzhi said with a serious face, "How can a family earning an official salary compete with farmers for profit?"[42]

開春理常業　*In spring I engaged in my usual vocation,*
歲功聊可觀　*and now the annual yield is not too poor.*
晨出肆微勤　*At dawn I go out and exert myself a little,*[43]
日入負禾還　*at sunset I come back with the grain.*[44]

Kai chun (at the beginning of spring) has a variant: *chun shi* 春事 (spring affairs). As Six Dynasties poets did not yet have as strong objections to the repetition of the same word in one poem as later poets did, and since *shi* is so closely related to *ye*, which also means "vocation," "profession," and "pragmatic achievements," it is tempting to adopt the variant reading here. However, even if we do not choose this variant, this couplet is wrought with reverberations of *gong ye*, which usually refers to the kind of feats a man achieves in the political arena, not in the agricultural world, as *chang ye* (usual vocation) is echoed by *sui gong* (the harvest), an agrarian term which literally means "yearly attainments." Tao Yuanming is intensely concerned with *gong ye*, and his poems return to this concern in various ways, which we will discuss further in chapter five. For now, we should bear in mind that *chang ye* (usual vocation) is not a common concept when it comes to farming.

Tao Yuanming is trying to put farming on a par with the enterprises which people of his own world would understand as true accomplishments for a man. But as he goes on, the less savory aspect of farming, the price he has to pay for choosing such a way of life, comes up:

山中饒霜露　*Frosts and dews are heavy in the hills,*
風氣亦先寒　*even the air turns cold earlier.*
田家豈不苦　*How could a farmer's lot be anything but hard?*
弗穫辭此難　*Yet there is no way to avoid such hardship.*

He does not say *who* has no way to avoid such hardship: the farmers? himself? or both? As he, together with the farmers, is obviously suffering from the harsh elements in the hills, he seems to be identifying himself with *tian jia*, "the peasants" (lit., "farming households"). It is one thing, however, to say that he renounces his official career to become a farmer, and it is a different thing to say that he has no choice but to suffer a farmer's hardships. In fact, he does have a choice. While it is obvious that farmers have to plow, this being their livelihood, it is not immediately clear why he, Tao Yuanming, cannot spare himself.

Many commentators believe that the next couplet gives us a hint:

四體誠乃疲	*Though the four limbs are indeed exhausted,*
庶無異患干	*may there be no intrusion of uncommon disasters.*

The first two characters of the second line, *shu wu* ("may there be no"), also read *jiao wu* 交無 in the Su Shi edition. The two phrases are roughly synonymous, with *jiao* being used as an informal term in the Southern Dynasties.[45] The choice of the more commonplace *shu wu* instead of *jiao wu* is another example of opting for the more conventional and more easily comprehensible variant.

The real problem lies in the variant reading *shu* [or *jiao*] *wu yi wo huan* 庶 (交)無異我患, which, however, makes no easy sense ("I hope that there is not the catastrophe of *considering me strange or different*"). And yet, *yi wo* (consider me strange or different) would not have been a strange term to Tao Yuanming's aristocratic contemporaries, who were immersed in the Daoist classics. Let us look at a Zhuangzi story:

> Among the followers of Lao Dan (Laozi) there was one named Gengsang Chu, who had partially mastered Lao Dan's Way. He went north to live in the mountains of Weilei. His servants with bright and smart looks he drove away, and his concubines who were self-righteously good-hearted he kept at a distance from himself. He stuck with the homely, and employed the free-and-easy. In three years, Weilei enjoyed a great harvest.
>
> The people of Weilei said to each other, "When Master Gengsang first came, we all considered him strange. But now, if we calculate by the day, there does not seem to be enough; and yet if we calculate by the year, there is actually some left over. Perhaps he is a sage! Why don't we set up a statue of him as our master and make offerings to him as God of Earth and Grain?"
>
> When Master Gengsang heard of this, he faced south [in Lao Dan's direction] and was displeased. His disciples considered him strange. Master Gengsang said, "Disciples, why do you consider me strange?

Look: when spring air comes forth, hundreds of plants begin to grow; when autumn arrives, ten thousand fruits are fulfilled. Can spring and autumn be so without being prompted? It is the Way of Heaven that gets them going. I have heard that the perfect man lives like a corpse in a tiny room of three square feet, leaving the people wild and free and not knowing where they are heading. Now even the petty people of Weilei in their meddlesome ways want to make sacrifices to me as one of their worthies—am I to become the object of their attention? That is why I feel so uneasy, remembering Lao Dan's words."[46]

Gengsang Chu further talks about how the perfect man should be able to completely hide himself, while Yao and Shun, the sage emperors who made a point of revering the worthy and conferring honor on them, are the very ones who have corrupted the primal innocence of their people.

Looking at this parable, we see that the word *yi* 異, "to consider strange," appears three times, ending with Gengsang Chu's protesting, "Disciples, why do you consider me strange?" We notice that it is this very capacity to cause amazement, first among the people of Weilei and then among his disciples, that has greatly upset Gengsang Chu, for, in his better judgment, he realizes that by becoming the target of wonder, by "distinguishing" and "differentiating" himself (which is also *yi*), he has not perfectly put his teacher's words into practice. While the Perfect Man should embody the undifferentiation of the great Way, Gengsang Chu has only obtained a portion of the Master's wisdom.

Tao Yuanming is writing about a harvest, and, besides the perfunctory mentioning of "carrying back the grain" in the eighth line, this variant reading of line fourteen certainly pertains very well to the topic. The poet is saying that, although we have had a harvest, unlike in the case of Gengsang Chu, there is no need to worry about distinguishing and differentiating myself, and there is fortunately no one who "considers me strange." It is, after all, not that great a harvest. This has suddenly become a wonderfully rich line, characterized by Tao Yuanming's whimsical sense of humor, which he shows from time to time in his poetry.

The next few lines support such a reading:

盥濯息簷下　*Washing my hands and feet, I take a rest under the eaves,*
斗酒散[ ]顏　*a cup of wine relaxes the [ ] countenance.*[47]

遙遙沮溺心	*The hearts of Ju and Ni, so far away now,*
千載乃相關	*still concern me across a thousand years.*

"Ju and Ni" are Changju and Jieni, the two farmer recluses mentioned in *The Analects* as the antithesis of the chosen Way of Confucius. When Confucius, lost in the wilderness, sent his disciple Zilu to inquire after the ford, instead of giving him road directions, the two men, especially Jieni, taught Zilu a lesson: that the whole world is overwhelmed by disorder which is like surging tides, and since there is no way to change it, it is much better to withdraw from it altogether. Zilu told this to Confucius, who said with a sigh, "It is impossible to associate with birds and beasts. If I do not associate with human beings, with whom should I associate? If the world observed the Way [*you dao*], then I would not have to try and change it."[48]

Reading the story, we realize that "the hearts of Ju and Ni" may have many ramifications, but perhaps what concerns the poet can be found in another text by Tao Yuanming, which gives us a more explicit indication of what he finds so admirable in the two recluses:

> Far away from us are Ju and Ni,
> they plow the fields and enjoy themselves.
> When they come near birds, birds do not startle;
> mixing with beasts, they herd with them.[49]

Here the poet is responding directly to Confucius's statement that he must befriend human beings, not "birds and beasts" (i.e., not become a recluse and shun the crowd). But the notable thing is that Changju and Jieni are presented as distinctly Daoist figures who not only hide themselves in plowing when the world is in disorder but also hide themselves successfully, unlike the unfortunate Gengsang Chu, who merely mastered a portion of the Master's teachings and caused so much amazement.

The poem ends with a wish:

但願常如此	*I only hope it will go on like this,*
躬耕非所嘆	*and plowing is not what I sigh about.*

The last line presents a particular syntactical structure: when one sees "X *fei* [is not] Y" in classical Chinese, one usually expects to see a follow-up sentence,

"X is in fact Z." Here we are not given a follow-up line. We are left on our own, but I think we may safely interpret the preceding line now: "this" does not just refer to the life of a farmer; it points to the ability to go into perfect hiding among birds and beasts and—yes, peasants.

It is always interesting to trace the trajectory of a word, to see how people perceive it and use it differently over time. *Wei* 為, "to do," in ancient times was interchangeable with the word *wei* 偽, which Xunzi uses in the sense that it is a "conscious exertion" or an "acquired nature."[50] Qing commentator Hao Yixing (1755–1823) argues against Tang commentator Yang Jing's (ca. ninth century) gloss of *wei* as "faking" and "pretending." Hao Yixing says, "Anything that is not inborn in a man's nature but is made or done by man is called *wei* 偽 in *Xunzi*, which is why *wei* is composed of two parts: a 'human' radical and the character 'to do' [*wei*]."[51] Xunzi, on the basis of his theory that "human nature is evil," further says that Jie and Zhou, the two famous tyrants in Chinese history, are acting from *xing* (human nature), while Yao and Shun, the sage emperors, are acting in the sense of *wei* (conscious exertion). But Xunzi's definition of *wei* never became mainstream, which is why as early as the Tang, Yang Jing was already glossing *wei* as "counterfeiting." In certain contexts *wei* is understood as "false" and "hypocritical"—a definite pejorative word—and the close affinity between *wei* 偽 and *wei* 為 is often ignored.

In Tao Yuanming's preface to the poem "Composed Upon Having an Encounter" (You hui er zuo), we see such a phrase using *wei*: "pretty much being an old farmer" (po wei lao nong).[52] *Wei* is translated as "being" here, for, on the one hand, "to be" is one of the many meanings of *wei*, though *wei* primarily means "to do," "to perform an action"; on the other hand, there is no other way of rendering the complicated meaning of the Chinese word *zuo*, which is the more colloquial counterpart of *wei*, as in the phrase *zuo ren* (or alternatively, *wei ren*). *Zuo ren* is a common phrase, used frequently in daily life even today. Literally, it means "to be/act as a human being." The point lies in *zuo/wei*: a very active, performative "being," so much so that one "is" a human being by "acting as" one. It is this performative aspect of the verb *wei* that stands out in Tao Yuanming's phrase *po wei lao nong* (pretty much being an old farmer).

Indeed, "it is not that Tao Qian simply 'is' a Jin farmer; he *wants* to be a Jin farmer."[53] It is a desire that is born of a desire to be "the Perfect Man" (*zhiren*) who masters all of the Master's teachings, unlike Gengsang Chu, who "blows it." But the more Tao Yuanming tries to explain this in his poetry, the "worse" it gets and the more "distinguished and differentiated" he becomes from his fellow farmers—and yet the better, the more interesting, is his poetry. "Tao Qian's poetry is filled with contradictions, the contradictions that come from a sophisticated, self-conscious man who yearns to be unsophisticated and unself-conscious."[54] This, rather than the claims that Tao Yuanming's simplicity and genuineness best represent the best of Chinese civilization, is a surprisingly good evaluation of Chinese intellectual culture, an extremely self-conscious culture that hates self-consciousness so much that, conceptually, it regards the concept of self-consciousness as equal to hypocrisy—with no consideration for the fact that a self-conscious action is more complicated than simply "impersonating" and "counterfeiting." Of all the premodern Chinese critics on Tao Yuanming, though, we have to give credit to one person who utters Tao Yuanming's secret. This is Wang Fuzhi (1619–1692), the cranky old master of Ginger Studio. In his "Discussions to While Away the Days at Evening Hall" (Xitang yongri xulun), he says of Tao Yuanming's self-conscious poetry making:

> "At the evening of the day no clouds are in the sky, / And springtime breezes spread faint balminess." In your imagination you can see Magistrate Tao Yuanming's state of mind at that moment. One of those alchemists, with his concoctions of mercury and lead, could never write lines like that. Master Cheng [Cheng Hao, 1032–1085, a neo-Confucian philosopher] claimed that seeing Lianxi [Zhou Dunyi, 1017–1073, another neo-Confucian philosopher] for a whole month was like sitting in the spring breeze. No one but Master Cheng could have known Lianxi to be like this [i.e., the spring breeze]; no one but Magistrate Tao could have known himself to be like this [i.e., his state of mind "found some corresponding quality in the scene at hand" and so matched perfectly with the spring breeze].[55]

Chinese literary culture, except for small moments like this, is a very sophisticated and worldly culture that, in its sophistication and worldliness, longs for its own antithesis—and naively believes in those claims to naiveté. It is a Zhuangzi-ish longing, and just as fraught with internal conflicts as Zhuangzi's philosophy (which, for example, advocates the value of wordlessness with words and denounces the uselessness of language with language). Tao Yuanming desires to blend in with nature and with the peasants working around him, and yet he has to show us in his poetry how he has achieved this. In the preface to "Composed Upon Having An Encounter" he declares, "If I do not transmit [my experiences] now, what would the later-born have to know?"

This is a sentence that, together with the poem title, deliberately echoes *The Analects*, though in a "negative" way. Confucius once claimed that he wanted to stop speaking. Zigong, one of the most eloquent of his disciples, was alarmed: "If the Master does not speak, what do we, the little ones, have to transmit?"[56] The syntax of this question is what Tao Yuanming has based his own question on. In another section of *The Analects*, Confucius describes himself as a transmitter (of the old), not a maker or doer (*shu er bu zuo*).[57] Tao Yuanming departs from the Master in that he not only intends to continue speaking, but he wants to both *zuo* ("to compose" or "to make," as in the title of "Composed Upon Having An Encounter") and *shu* (to transmit). What he transmits is not "the old" but his own experience, which, however, he is well aware will become "the old" to the "later-born." Tao Yuanming, as we can see, is both a *zuozhe* (as a recluse and as an author) and a *shuzhe* (as a recorder and transmitter of his own life).

The twelfth-century critic Huang Che stressed that Tao Yuanming was different from a farmer in that the latter is simply happy while Tao Yuanming *knows* he is happy.[58] But looking closely, we are not so sure that they share the same kind of happiness at all. In the second poem of the two poems "Upon Thinking of the Ancient Farmers in Early Spring of the *Guimao* Year [403]" (Guimao sui shichun huai gu tian she), the poet espouses a unique notion of happiness.

先師有遺訓	*The ancient master has left a lesson:*
憂道不憂貧	*"Be concerned with the Way, not with poverty."*
瞻望邈難逮	*I look up to it—but it is far away and hard to reach:*
轉欲[ ]長勤	*turning around, I will [ ] constant toil instead.*

"A gentleman works on the Way, not on [getting] food. Even when he plows, he may find hunger in it [such as when there is a bad year]; but when he studies, he will find salary in it. A gentleman is therefore concerned with the Way, not with food."[59] But even when the Master is teaching about the importance of the Way, he has to appeal to the utilitarian, practical side of human nature by hinting that studying is much more reliable than plowing in securing financial support for a person. The poet singles out the last part of this section from *The Analects* with a repetition of the word *you* (to be concerned about, to be troubled and anxious about).

As Hightower says, the poet "pays his respects to this Confucian ideal of behavior and then turns his back on it."[60] His concern lies with poverty, not really with the Way (in the first poem, he excuses his engagement with the farmwork by saying he has no other way around starvation). The third character in the fourth line, here left untranslated, has several variants: "to be afflicted with" (*huan* 患), "to think of" (*si* 思), or "to be intent on" (*zhi* 志). To be "afflicted with lifelong toil"—in other words, to be concerned with poverty (*you pin*)—would be an explicit subversion of Confucius's words. *Zhi*, on the other hand, is a loaded word in the Chinese cultural tradition: it indicates a man's ambition or aspiration, often related to public life in the political world. Confucius says that a person should "be intent upon the Way" (*zhi yu dao*),[61] and to be intent upon lifelong toil—farmwork—is again quite a different choice from what the Master preaches.

秉耒[ ]時務	*Holding the plow, I [ ] the season's work,*
解顏勸農人	*relaxing my countenance, I encourage the farmers.*

The third character of the first line has been read by virtually every commentator as *huan* 歡, "to enjoy" or "to take pleasure in," and so the line goes, "I hold the plow and rejoice in the season's work."[62] The choice of *huan*, of course, serves to confirm the image of the poet as a happy plowman, but *li* 力 (to work hard at) in the Su Shi edition both echoes "toil" in the preceding line and helps explain the phrase in the next line, *jie yan* (to relax one's facial muscles and break into a smile). No matter which variant we choose, we notice that a change has emerged: just as the poet's countenance becomes relaxed, the poem is moving away from the *you* (worrisome) and *qin* (toilsome) aspect of farming.

Here we must take a side trip into the phrase *quan nongren* (to encourage the farmers). Hightower gives a speculation on the identity of the *nongren* (farmer or farmers), and decides that "one (or more) of his neighbors is helping him with his first effort at farming."[63] It is not impossible, but unlikely. Despite the scantiness of biographical material, Tao Yuanming was not a farmer who supported himself and his rather large family solely by virtue of his personal farming. For one thing, he owned land in several different places, and some of his farms were not close to his home. In the preceding poem, he talks about "hitching his wagon" and "setting out" to go to the "southern acres" (which could just be a general term for "farm" or "farming" and does not necessarily indicate the location of the fields). The "western fields" in the poem on harvesting dry rice seem to imply a specific location in the hills. In a poem written in 416 entitled "Harvesting in the Farmstead at Xiasun in the Eighth Month in the *Bingchen* Year" (Bingchen sui bayue zhong yu xiasun tian she huo), the place of harvest seems to be yet another piece of land owned by our poet, which is again situated in the hills and so far away from Tao Yuanming's home that he has to cross a lake and then sail on a stream to get there. Moreover, in this poem he mentions a "supervisor of the fields" (*si tian*), who is clearly the overseer of his distant farmstead (we think, for instance, of the overseer working for the absentee landlord—the Jia family—in the eighteenth-century novel *Dream of the Red Chamber*, who visits the Jias at the end of the year and brings them the annual yield). Tao Yuanming may very well have plowed in person, but it is almost certain that he owned more than one farmstead and had tenants working for him.

If *nongren* refers to the farmers working for him, then *quan nongren* presents us with a picture of a genial landlord exhorting his tenants by words and by action (i.e., participating in the labor himself). *Quan nong*, "urging the farmers," was a highly political and ritualized activity whose tradition had been long established by Tao Yuanming's time. It bore a great symbolic importance in the national policy. *Quan nong* was made an office as early as the Western Han. Throughout imperial China, *quan nong* was not only constantly practiced by officials such as commandery and county magistrates, but was also a familiar theme in poetry, fiction, and drama.[64]

Shu Xi (264?–305?), the Western Jin writer, wrote "*Fu* on Encouraging the Farmers" (Quan nong fu), of which only two fragments survive.[65] In Shu Xi's poetic exposition, *quan nong* is satirized as a bureaucratic ceremony. The local magistrate comes to villages during the harvest time (instead of the plowing season) and is treated to a great banquet of chicken, pork, and wine. As a result, he would lower the amount of taxes—an early example of tax evasion in China. "It is all because hot food soothes his belly, and wine entertains his stomach."[66] About a hundred years later, Tao Yuanming wrote a poem entitled "Quan nong." With the ideological weight of *quan nong* looming in the background, the poem is nonetheless characterized by Tao Yuanming's straight-faced humor and wit.

The poet's smiling encouragement of the farmers, therefore, is embedded in a rich tradition established in the political world as an essential part of the empire-building project. But the potentially weighty implication of farming is balanced, or eased, by something quite uncalled for—an attention to the beauty of the rural scene:

平疇交遠風	*The level fields commune with the breeze from afar:*
良苗亦懷新	*the fine shoots will also cherish a freshness.*

It is of course the breeze that comes from afar to the level fields, but to put the fields in the position of the subject makes it seem as if the fields have become the active agent, and all of a sudden, they are endowed with a liveliness, a life.

In the next line, the third character, *yi* (also), speaks for the poet: he is the one who "cherishes a freshness or newness"—in the first poem of this series, he tells us this is the first time he has come out to this farm—and in a surge of joy at the (imagined) refreshing pastoral scene, he transfers his feelings to the tender shoots waving in the breeze.

I say it is an "imagined" pastoral scene because in the same line we encounter an interesting problem. This is only early spring, and, according to the poet, the farmers are plowing. Between plowing and the shoots coming out, there is a considerable interval. As the poet has mentioned "holding the plow," it is not likely that he sees the fine sprouts at the same time. Could the poet be imagining the seeds underground, all containing (*huai*, "to harbor within") new life and anticipating sprouting? This would call to mind "Zai shan," the *Shi jing* poem on farming life in which the seeds are described as "containing vitality" (*shi han si huo*) and "one after another coming out from the ground" (*yi yi qi da*).[67] Or could the poet, as he looks at the still-barren fields, anticipate the time when all the seeds will already have sprouted? Such anticipation would lead to the next couplet, in which the poet moves from anticipation of the future to the joy of the present moment:

雖未量歲功	*Although the annual yield is not assessed yet,*
即事多所欣	*in the immediate situation there is much joy.*

Sui gong, "the annual yield," is the same term used in the poem discussed above: "In spring I engaged in my usual vocation, / and now the annual yield is not too poor." But here the poet tells us that he is not so much concerned with the crops; he is completely absorbed "in the immediate situation," the pleasure of the moment.

The first two characters in the second line, *ji shi*, are hard to translate. Depending on the linguistic context and the historical period in which it was used, it may be roughly translated as "regarding the immediate situation" or "prompted by the present occasion." It is a phrase that became increasingly common in classical Chinese prose from around the Three Kingdoms period on (the second to third centuries), and became extremely popular in poetry titles beginning in the Tang. But Tao Yuanming must be credited as the first person who ever used this phrase in poetry. *Ji shi* appears in his poetry twice: once in this poem, and again in a poem entitled "Written on the First Day of the Fifth Month, Matching a Poem by Secretary Dai" (Wuyue yi ri zuo he Dai zhubu). In each case, *ji shi* signifies being stirred or moved by the event taking place at the moment, what is happening then and there, the situation or the circumstances at hand. It is for this reason we cannot emphasize too much the "immediate" aspect of this phrase, which is reflected in Davis's translation of this line as "In the *immediate* work there are many joys" (my italics).[68]

Here we might want to ask a simple question: what is farming all about? A farmer would tell you it is about producing food, so it is all about the annual yield. But when the poet says, "Although the annual yield is not assessed yet, / in the immediate situation there is much joy," he is referring to some "other" side of farming which is not at all about the end product. Those two lines point back to the preceding couplet, in which the poet constructs an imagined scene of the tender shoots seeming to be dancing with joy. Everything indeed meets and merges with the "state of mind" (*xiong ci;* in Wang Fuzhi's terms) of the poet. At this moment, at least, he is not plowing—a man busy with plowing cannot see "the level fields" but only the small patch of soil he is working on underneath his feet. He who includes the level fields in his vision is gazing far and wide. As he does so, he feels happy, and he knows it. He not only knows it, he wants to tell us about it, expound on it, and make it into some sort of lesson. Most importantly, by finding "much joy" in the circumstances (which happen to be farming), he discovers an original way to rise above the Master's teaching "Be concerned with the Way, not with poverty." As the Yuan commentator Liu Lü (1317–1379) says, "Taking pleasure in the immediate situation like this, how could he be anxious about poverty?"[69] This capacity to take pleasure in the circumstances and in the process, without forgetting about the end product, and the awareness of possessing such a capacity are what distinguish Tao Yuanming from the farmer or the small-minded person, the antithesis of the *junzi* (aristocratic gentleman) implied in Confucius's words.

The poet then returns to Confucius:

耕者有時息	*From time to time the plowman takes a rest,*
行者無問津	*but no traveler comes to inquire about the ford.*

This couplet evokes the *Analects* story about Changju and Jieni, again in a "negative" fashion. While Changju and Jieni "plow on without stopping," our plowman (or plowmen) does take a break, and he seems to feel a bit empty for having encountered no one who comes to inquire about the ford. "If the poet is playing the role of Changju and Jieni," Hightower speculates, "he can only be glad no Confucius comes to bother him with impertinent questions."[70] But if he is indeed playing the role of Changju and Jieni, it would be very hard for him to be a Changju or a Jieni if there were no Confucius around. The very existence of Changju and Jieni requires the man who inquires about the ford. Or they would have to undertake the task of "transmitting" their own way of life, as Tao Yuanming is doing here.

日入/田人相與歸	*[ ] go home together,*
壺漿勞近鄰	*with a jug of wine toasting the close neighbors.*
長吟掩柴門	*Chanting poetry, I close the brushwood gate;*
聊為隴畝民	*for now, I will just be a man of dykes and fields.*

The last four lines turn out to be a wonderful ending to a poem reflecting on ancient farmers. The 1192 edition records a variant for the first two characters, which leaves us in doubt as to *who* go home in one another's company. *Ri ru* ("when the sun goes down") is the universal choice. Commentators either cite "The Song of Tossing Sticks" (Jirang ge), supposedly sung by an old man in the age of Emperor Yao:

> When the sun comes up, I work;
> when the sun goes down, I rest.
> I dig a well for drink,

I plow the fields for food.
What does the emperor's power have to do with me?[71]

or a Zhuangzi passage in which the recluse Shanjuan says to the sage Emperor Shun who wants to turn the empire over to him,

> When the sun comes up, I work; when the sun goes down, I rest. Wandering free and easy between heaven and earth, I feel complacent in my heart. What do I need a throne for?[72]

We might be able to relate either citation to the context of the poem and make much sense, and yet the other reading is very attractive:

田人相與歸	*The farmers go home together,*
壼漿勞近鄰	*with a jug of wine they toast their close neighbors.*
長吟掩柴門	*Chanting poetry, I close the brushwood gate;*
聊為隴畝民	*for now, I will just be a man of dykes and fields.*

Although the characters *ri ru* and *tian ren* look similar enough to warrant a copying error in the transmission of Tao Yuanming's poetry manuscripts, the editorial choice of *ri ru* (the sun goes down) again constitutes a conventional reading that either celebrates the recluse's lifestyle or emphasizes the (idealized) self-sufficiency of a farmer's existence. On the other hand, if we opt for *tian ren* (the farming people), we see a considerably different picture, which portrays the poet as a much more solitary figure: while the farmers go home together with one another and have drinks to dissipate their fatigue, the poet alone, chanting poetry to himself, shuts his gate against the world instead of mixing with them.[73] The last line reaffirms his difference from the farmers by using the phrase *liao wei*—"to be (a farmer) for now, for the time being," not to mention the "drawn-out chanting [of poetry]." *Liao* is an adverb indicating tentativeness, and *wei* is not simply "being," it is a performative "being" that involves much conscious action.

Again, this is just one possible reading in addition to the other possible reading that opts for the easier and more personable "sun going down" (*ri ru*). Significantly, the poem closes with the closing of the gate, a gesture of delineating an enclosed private space and turning one's back on the outside world—the world of farming and farmers. So far as we know, Tao Yuanming was the first person to use the image of gate-closing in poetry, an image that became a conventional hallmark of the life of a recluse.[74] Apart from the second poem of the "Return" series and the one under discussion, the beginning lines in "Composed and Presented to My Cousin Jingyuan in the Twelfth Month of the *Guimao* Year [403]" (Guimao sui shieryue zhong zuo yu congdi Jingyuan) read,

寢跡衡門下	*Hiding my traces behind the rustic door,*
邈與世相絕	*I sever my ties with the remote world.*
顧盼莫誰知	*I look around, but no one knows:*
荊扉晝常閉	*my brushwood gate often remains closed during the day.*

It is the same image of self-isolation, and yet it is also the same awareness of a world "out there" beyond that closed gate, the same self-contradictory emotions implied in the action of "looking around" and finding no one who "knows" and feeling compelled to write this experience down and present it to someone—ostensibly his cousin, but implicitly the "later-born." Closing one's gate is a gesture fraught with conflicting desires; the gate both separates the inner world from the outer and connects them.[75] The poet can open up the gate any time, perhaps to receive an elderly farmer who tries to persuade him to serve, as in the ninth poem of his "On Drinking" series; he can also go out of the gate again, and so he often does—either to serve again, to go on an outing to a local scenic spot, or to associate with friends (the number of poems he wrote to secretaries, clerks, administrators, magistrates, and so forth—though not farmers—should be enough to dispel any illusion that our poet was indeed isolated), or, as upon at least one occasion, to "beg for food."

Food & Words

"Begging for Food" (Qi shi) is an ostensibly easy poem, in the sense that the surface message is clear and there are not as many textual problems or corruptions as in a few of his notoriously obscure poems. The text is simple, straightforward, and outright plain. And yet there is something unusual about it. It is the first poem on the topic of "begging" in the Chinese literary tradition.

While in ancient texts "begging for food" usually illustrates how a worthy man can be driven to desperate measures and how he may eventually reinvent himself from his poverty-stricken state,[76] during the Jin begging seems to have acquired a certain cultural cachet and to have developed further into one aspect of the Eastern Jin cultivation of an unrestrained personality, variously described by such phrases as *fangda* or *kuangda* or simply *da*.[77] "Absence of restraint," initially fashionable in the late Three Kingdoms period and inspired by Lao-Zhuang philosophy, was a sort of intellectual and cultural counter-movement against the more straight-laced Confucianism in the social life of the upper class. It was perfected into an art by some of the Seven Worthies of the Bamboo Grove in the third century, continued to be practiced and admired by many throughout the Eastern Jin, and only began to lose its cultural cachet sometime in the fifth century. In *Shishuo xinyu*, we see the following story about Luo You:

> Luo You of Xiangyang possessed a great disposition, but in his youth many people considered him idiotic. He once went to someone's sacrifice to beg for some food. He arrived too early and the gate was not opened yet. The host went out to greet the spirits, and asked him why he was there at such an ungodly hour. He answered, "I heard you were going to make sacrifices, and I just want to beg for a meal." With those words he retired to the side of the gate and waited until dawn, withdrawing as soon as he got his meal, without the slightest look of embarrassment.[78]

Sun Sheng's (302–373) *The Chronicles of Jin* (Jin yangqiu) describes Luo You as a man who had enjoyed studying since youth and was free and unrestrained in his behavior.

> By nature he loved wine, and if he could have a drink, he would not care if the host was a gentleman or a commoner. He also liked to attend other people's sacrifices and beg for the leftover food. Regardless of whether it was a camp, an office, a tavern, or a shop, he never considered it shameful. Huan Wen [312–373] once chided him, saying, "You are really too much. If you need food, why don't you ask for it from me, instead of going to such lengths?" Luo You arrogantly dismissed him, saying, "If I beg for food from you, today I may get some, but tomorrow there might not be any." Huan Wen laughed loudly at that.[79]

Luo You seems to have been a Daoist-style gourmet obsessed with food, and the same section of *Shishuo xinyu* records another anecdote about his complete lack of embarrassment in obtaining a delicacy and his instant withdrawal upon satisfying himself.[80] We should note that in his mixture with all sorts of company for the sake of wine and his instant withdrawal upon the satisfaction of his palate, Luo You bears a remarkable similarity to Tao Yuanming as portrayed both in his "Biography of Master Five Willows" and in Tao Yuanming's official biographies. We also note that while begging for food may be something a person is compelled to do in extreme situations, it could also be, literally, a "tasteful matter" (*yunshi*) in a quirky gentleman. In the Southern Dynasties, begging for food (*qishi*) was also a religious activity: it was the way Buddhist monks acquired their daily sustenance, and it was mentioned many times in the writings of the period.[81]

Confucian texts are much more harsh regarding begging for food. *The Record of Rites* records the story of a man who died because he was too ashamed to accept "Hey you, come eat!" food (i.e., food that had been offered in an insulting manner).[82] Luo You's begging for the leftover food from other people's sacrificial offerings clearly echoes the story in *Mencius* about the man of Qi, though there is a profound difference between the two. The man of Qi went out every day and came home stuffed. His wife and concubine asked him whom he dined with, and he boasted that he dined with the rich and powerful. Since they never had any rich and powerful visitors, the curious wife one day followed him, and discovered that he had gone to someone making sacrifices and begged for the leftover food; if he did not eat his fill, he would go to another and do the same. The wife returned and told the concubine, and the two of them wept out of shame. Mencius commented that many people sought for riches and fame in the same shameful way as the man of Qi.[83] We note that although Luo You begged from all sorts of people, he did not beg from Huan Wen, his employer and the most powerful political figure of the age; and when Huan Wen invited him to do so, he dismissed him with a proud look. *Shishuo xinyu* also takes care to note that Luo You once rejected Huan Wen's brother Huan Huo's (320–377) dinner invitation in order to go to an assistant clerk's party. In recording and endorsing stories like this in the "Free and Unrestrained" section, *Shishuo xinyu* does not subvert but confirms the power hierarchy in the social life of the Eastern Jin.

Reading Tao Yuanming's poem about begging for food against this background, we will see that the poem presents us with something complex and hybrid.

飢來驅我出/去	*Hunger came and drove me out,*
不知竟何之	*I didn't quite know where I was going.*

In the first line of the poem, Tao Yuanming takes care to show us that he is begging, not as a quirky habit, but out of necessity. From behind his closed door, the poet is "driven" out, but he stands lost for a while, not knowing where he should turn. Hunger is a force that, vividly conveyed in the verb *qu* (to propel, to spur, as in riding a horse), takes control of his body regardless of his mind, so that even though he does not "know" where he is to go, his body is still compelled to leave the house.

Many commentators have debated the "actuality" of the event. Some of them believe it is just a figurative way of speaking, while others oppose this suggestion, but still try to "elevate" the act of begging by associating it with Tao Yuanming's loyalty to the Jin. There is nothing inside or outside the text that gives us any hint about the dating of this poem. What we do know is that "begging for food" does not necessarily mean that he wants just one meal; it might also involve a larger need for borrowing to help himself and his family through a bad year. In fact, although many readers, including Su Shi, have taken this poem to be about eating a full meal at the host's house, examining the poem closely we find no mention of "eating," only of drinking.

行行至斯里	*Walking on and on, I came to this neighborhood;*
叩門拙言辭	*knocking on a door, I was clumsy with words.*

Without knowing the background against which Tao Yuanming writes these lines, we would probably not quite "get it"; unlike the "unrestrained" Luo You, who had no problem with informing the host of what he wanted in plain words ("I just want to beg for a meal"), the poet lets us know that he fumbles with words when the host opens the door. *Zhuo* (clumsy) is what Tao Yuanming keeps calling himself, and here we know it comes from embarrassment over what he has to say.

主人解余意	*The host understood what I was after,*
遺贈豈虚來	*he gave it to me—I didn't come in vain.*

So he never says outright what he was after, and it is both a tacit understanding and a sensitive consideration for an embarrassed friend's feelings that prevents the host from inquiring, as did the person in the Luo You anecdote, "What are you doing here?"

The second line has an interesting variant reading: "he gave it to me, fulfilling my vain hope" (yi zeng fu xu qi). It indicates that the poet had not really expected such an easy response to his need; to the embarrassed suppliant, this is a happy surprise.

談諧終日夕	*We chatted and quipped all day and evening,*
觴至/舉輒傾杯	*drained our cups as soon as a* pitcher came / they were raised.
情欣新知歡	*Enrapt by the joy of a new friendship,*[84]
言詠遂賦詩	*we chanted and then composed poems.*

There is a touching innocence in these lines. When we take note of the order of things happening, we see that once the poet gets what he wants, without his having to ask out loud, he seems to have rid himself of a great burden and feels quite relaxed, and there is no more clumsy fumbling for words ("we chatted and quipped all day and evening"). But he does not stop at the overflowing of words, for the fluent, unimpeded speech is further transformed into poetry. It is a small triumph in classical Chinese poetry that begging for food and the writing of poetry became intertwined.

The third line is a little troublesome; scholars are all silent on how to interpret "new friendship" or "new acquaintance," and they also seem to have all taken the friendship between the host and the poet as newly formed, which I find rather strange. There is no indication that the poet did not know the host before he came to knock on his door; instead, the host's intuition about the poet's need and the familiarity between the two (as shown in their chatting and quipping) seems to point to a previous relationship. Unless we assume that the poet has randomly chosen a door to knock on and has begged for food from a stranger, which is unlikely, there are two possible ways of understanding the third line here: one is that the feelings now between him and his friend are more genial than "the joy of a new friendship"—which, as Gu Zhi (1885–1959) points out, is an allusion to the *Chuci* line "There is no joy / greater than that of a new friendship."[85] The other is that although the poet has known the host before, what transpires between them today has turned their acquaintance into something deeper. *Xiang zhi* (knowing each other) does not just refer to acquaintance—it is a "mutual knowing and understanding."

感子漂母意	*Grateful for your kindness like the washerwoman's,*
愧我非韓才	*I am only ashamed that I am no Han Xin.*

銜戢知何謝	*With a full heart, how should I ever thank you?*
冥報以相貽	*I will make you an offer from the world beyond.*

As the late Ming commentator Huang Wenhuan (*jinshi* degree, 1625) observes, it is easy to feel overjoyed at obtaining what one asks for and to forget about the initial embarrassment about begging.[86] But despite the jovial drinking, talking, and poetry chanting, the poet remembers what he is there for, and his keen awareness of his situation bursts into the last four lines. He first compares the host to the washerwoman who offered food to a poverty-stricken Han Xin (?–196 B.C.E.), who later became a great general and handsomely repaid the washerwoman. As the story goes, Han Xin thanked the washerwoman after he ate his full, saying, "I will certainly pay you back generously." The washerwoman answered angrily, "You are a big man, who yet cannot feed yourself. I take pity on you, a fine young scion; how can you think that I am expecting any return?"[87] If the host, like the washerwoman, does not expect any return, the indebted poet nevertheless shares Han Xin's desire to pay him back for his kindness. It is at this juncture that, almost as a second thought, he reflects on himself and is "ashamed" to realize that he does not have the talents of Han Xin (which is not an entirely bad thing, for Han Xin was eventually executed). His solution is to pay back—literally "give" back—"from the world beyond." This is a somewhat theatrical gesture, and some commentators quote the story of a grateful old man in the *Zuo zhuan* who repaid a kindness by knotting grass to trap his benefactor's enemy.[88] But Tao Yuanming is in fact saying, "Thank you so much for everything, although I don't think I can ever pay you back in this lifetime." It could be that the "talent" he feels he lacks is not just a military genius, but also a kind of political ambition.

Chen Zuoming (1623–1674) criticizes the last four lines as being "a little clumsy," while others feel that the expression of gratitude in the last line shows exactly "where [Tao Yuanming] is clumsy at words."[89] Perhaps. But the "clumsy" effect in some readers' eyes takes us back to Tao Yuanming not as a poet who drinks wine and pours out words, but as a very human person.

"Begging for Food" is a strange poem on many accounts. It is conventionally eccentric—a paradox true of all Jin eccentrics—in the sense that "begging for food" was after all considered an acceptable "unrestrained" mannerism in the Eastern Jin, as Huan Wen's chiding of and then tolerance for Luo You shows;[90] but it does go beyond conventional eccentricity by being "unconventionally eccentric," which is achieved by being simply human. The poem is also a rare combination of intense self-consciousness and perfectly controlled candidness. The poet remains a sober observer of himself from beginning to end; from his momentary loss of orientation upon coming out of his house, to his clumsy fumbling of words, to his immense relief upon the host's understanding, to the joyful, carefree drinking afterwards, to the chanting of poetry after drinking, and finally to a mixture of embarrassment and pride in his both exaggerated and humble promise. No other poem can better present Tao Yuanming at his sophisticated and complicated best. A simple, naive person could hardly write such a poem: if the poet completely identified with that clumsy, ashamed person, the poem would be filled with self-pity and rage; but if the poet kept himself too detached from the whole experience, the poem would indeed become "playful" or even "cynical," and thus emotionally shallow.[91] To be able to offer a pained and yet humorous portrait of a person begging for food, to reveal the complexity of human nature without being confined to the stylized quest for eccentricity and Lao-Zhuang "unrestraint" (*kuangda*) or Confucian condemnation of compromising personal dignity by begging for food in hunger, is a feat rarely achieved in the Eastern Jin, and perhaps in any time.

Eventually, this poem reveals Tao Yuanming's lifelong obsession—with food, with words, and with how these two things, both the essential sustenance of the life of a poet, are for him inseparably related.

4 Food, Death, & Narration

Death and narration seem to share a darkly close relationship. In Boccaccio's *Decameron*, vivid stories are set in the threatening narrative frame of the Great Plague, which casts its shadow over the merry tales. In the Chinese tradition, establishing oneself by words (*li yan*) is on a level with establishing virtue (*li de*) and establishing deeds (*li gong*)—"the three things that do not decay" (*san buxiu*).[1] Discourse, in the broadest sense of the word, is seen as a way of resisting mortality. In Tao Yuanming's poetic discourse the poet constantly returns to the essential substances of human life, which for Tao Yuanming are often intertwined: food, drink, and words.

Tao Yuanming was squarely situated in a continuous but also ever-changing literary tradition, and he was first of all a writer, not a philosopher or thinker. It is much more productive to ask how Tao Yuanming made use of poetic conventions than to engage in a debate about whether he was primarily a Confucian or a Daoist or a mixture of both. It is true that Tao Yuanming's poetry and prose are filled with allusions to *The Analects*, and they are also rich with echoes of the Daoist classics, such as *Zhuangzi*, *Laozi*, and even the later *Liezi*.[2] But the references appear as poetic images or as phrases coming in handy when the right occasion or mood calls; they do not necessarily form a systematic structure of philosophical thought. A poem is, after all, not a treatise. Tao Yuanming writes both in the literary tradition and in a contemporary cultural milieu, and it is his genius, which often is expressed as a kind of quirkiness, that gives a particular twist to his poetry, in which one can nonetheless always recognize thematic elements from earlier poetry and from current intellectual concerns.

Divisions into "poetic schools" are often more for convenience in mapping literary history than for describing a particular moment in literary historical reality, which is never neat and clear-cut. The influences of predecessors and contemporaries may frequently be revealed in small and indirect ways, and come out in strange metamorphoses, especially in the works of an innovative poet. Tao Yuanming shares his contemporaries' penchant for the supernatural, but his interest in the poetic past—the poetry of the Jian'an (196–220) and the Western Jin periods—is unique in his age (it would be Xie Lingyun's task to bring the Jian'an poetic world to the public's attention again, by his poem series "Imitations of *The Collection of Ye*" [Ni Ye zhong ji]). This leads to Tao Yuanming's particular version of "the poetry of roaming immortals" (*youxian shi*), which is realized not in seeking immortals through the usual means—such as visiting famous mountains, taking a magic drug, or practicing breathing techniques—but rather in the experiences of reading, reflecting, and exercising literary imagination. Invariably, such experiences are associated with another essential element in Tao Yuanming's poetry—food and drink.

Obtaining Immortality

"Drinking Alone during Incessant Rain" (or, "No Visitors during Incessant Rain and I Drink Alone" [Lianyu renjue duyin]) is a good place to begin. The title of the poem is an interesting one: the "incessant rain" is a peculiar occasion, whose significance would be obvious to Tao Yuanming's contemporaries. "Suffering from the rain" (*kuyu*) was already an established topic by Tao Yuanming's time; Ruan Yu (165?–212), Fu Xuan (217–278), and Lu Ji all wrote about it.[3] Zhang Xie's (?–307) poem on the topic was singled out by the famous sixth-century critic Zhong Rong (?–518?) as among the best five-character poems in the tradition.[4] Zhong Rong's praise was probably influenced by Jiang Yan, who, in his "Thirty Poems of Miscellaneous Forms" (Zati shi sanshi shou), picked this poem as representative of Zhang Xie's style and did an imitation of it.[5] Tao Yuanming himself has a poem, "Hanging Clouds" (Tingyun), in which the poet laments that the rain has turned the level land to rivers and separated him from his friend(s): "Quietly I stay on the eastern porch, / cherishing spring wine by myself."

But the rain in "Hanging Clouds" is, after all, "seasonal rain" (*shiyu;* that is, spring rain), which helps the trees in the poet's garden grow ("The trees in the eastern garden— / their branches are blooming"). Despite the poet's loneliness and his longing for an absent friend, there is in Tao Yuanming's version a sense of ease and leisure, and in the last stanza the weather seems to be clearing up, with birds again chirping on the boughs of the trees. The tone is, however, very different in "Drinking Alone during Incessant Rain."[6]

Relatively little Jin poetry has survived, but from what we do have, we see that no one before Tao Yuanming had written about "drinking alone," during incessant rain or otherwise. For one thing, people shared the same poetic vocabulary, the same set of poetic images, and adopted the same turns of phrase according to the occasion and topic, and the occasions and topics themselves were a limited set. For another thing, drinking is a communal event—a public banquet, an informal gathering of friends, a harvest ritual, or an outing. As such, it strengthens the bonds among members of a community and plays an essential part in a feast, which is often an effective means of consolidating, or displaying, political power. As Shen Yue, the eminent fifth-century writer, says in a commentary on "The Seven Worthies [of the Bamboo Grove]" (Qixian lun): "The function of wine is not for drinking alone; one needs company to fulfill its pleasure."[7]

We see conventional poetic elements at work in "Drinking Alone during Incessant Rain." Drinking and feasting are often associated with thoughts of mortality and death and hence with pursuit of immortality in Jian'an poetry and the anonymous "ancient poems." But this poem, compared with Tao Yuanming's famous series "On Drinking," is particularly successful in sketching the portrait of a person who drinks himself tipsy and feels "high." The human truth peeping out from beneath the poetic conventions, combined with an ingenious use of *Zhuangzi* (which we will discuss later), is what makes this poem outstanding in Tao Yuanming's corpus.

運生會歸盡	*The cycle of life will revert to its end;*
終古謂之然	*people from all times have said so.*
世間有松喬	*Red Pine and Prince Qiao existed in the world,*[8]
于今定何聞	*and yet what do we hear about them now?*[9]

What is remarkable about this poem is that there is not one word about rain. Authors generally adhered to the topics announced by the titles of their poems, and Tao Yuanming's silence about the rain is rather unusual. The poet, so to speak, goes directly to the point, and begins the poem with a reflection on the emptiness of promises of immortality. This is very much within the conventional bounds of feasting and drinking poetry, in which an exhortation to seize the day and make merry is often linked with, and in fact seen as a consequence of, the vanity of seeking immortality.[10] The difference here is that after expressing doubts about the existence of immortals, the poet learns that drinking itself may be a way of reaching the immortals:

故老贈余酒 *An old fellow gave me this gift of wine—*
乃言飲得仙 *he actually said drinking makes an immortal out of a man.*

Nai, the first word in the second line, is an expression that indicates surprise and disbelief. That wine should lead to immortality or longevity is indeed counter to common sense. Xi Kang advises against drinking not only in his "Discourse on Nurturing Life" (Yangsheng lun) but also in his poem "Replacing the Song of Qiuhu" (Dai Qiuhu ge shi), which states that "wine and sex make a man wither."[11] The poem recapitulates Laozi's view that one should dispel wisdom and forsake learning, seeking peace in "dark silence" (*xuanmo*). The last two stanzas take off in the predictable direction of the poet desiring to become an immortal: "I wish to ride the clouds, along with Prince Qiao, / and roam the eight limits of the earth, / transcending the Five Mountains, / in an instant traveling millions of miles." Xi Kang's poem echoes many of the Jian'an poems on the subject of seeking immortality, and Tao Yuanming's account of his drinking experience (which is definitely forbidden to serious immortality-seekers) tropes on the vocabulary of roaming with immortals with a tongue-in-cheek tone:

試酌百情遠 *I take my first cup: a hundred cares fade away;*
重觴忽忘天 *the second cup is down: all of a sudden I forget Heaven.*

Wang Shumin is right here in correcting Ding Fubao, who glosses *baiqing yuan* (lit., "a hundred feelings become distant") as "a hundred feelings gather in my heart."[12] Wang Shumin cites the remark of Wang Yun (330–384) that "wine is just the thing to make every man naturally remote from the world." In the same section of *Shishuo xinyu*, Wang Hui (ca. mid-fourth century) said something similar: "Wine is just the thing which naturally draws a man up and sets him in a transcendent place."[13]

Forgetting Heaven is an unmistakable reference to *Zhuangzi*: "To forget things of the world and to forget Heaven are called 'forgetting oneself.' Of the one who forgets about oneself we say that he has entered Heaven."[14] In other words, a person who is oblivious of the world, of Heaven, and most of all of himself would merge with Nature and become one with Heaven. In Tao Yuanming's poem, "entering Heaven" is realized literally, as the poet, in a tipsy state, feels that his spirit can easily reach the eight limits of the earth (as the speaker in Xi Kang's poem yearns to do) on the back of an imaginary crane (or swan, as the variant has it), the magic carrier of immortals. When the "old fellow" says drinking makes an immortal of a man, he is not lying, except that the "heaven" the drinker enters seems to be located within himself, and this miniature "heavenly journey," squarely situated in the tradition of *Chuci* and Han writer Sima Xiangru's (179–117 B.C.E.) "*Fu* on the Great One" (Daren fu),[15] is humorously brought about by the inebriating effect of alcohol:

天豈去此哉/天際去此幾	How can Heaven be far away from here? / How far is Heaven from here?
任真無所先	*—so long as one follows natural impulses,* *and takes that as the priority.*
雲鶴/鴻有奇翼	*The* crane / swan *of cloud with marvelous* *wings*[16]
八表須臾還	*can reach the eight limits of the earth* *and return in an instant.*

The variant line "How far is Heaven from here?" could be taken as a real question, and certainly does not sound as confident and affirmative as the rhetorical question, "How can Heaven be far from here?" The extra "advantage" of choosing the latter is that it has the question word *zai* at the end, which makes the line sound prosaic, in the sense that it has a stylized naturalness of tone.

Wang Shumin scoffs at Gu Zhi and Ding Fubao for relating the "crane" couplet to being an immortal, for, he argues, Tao Yuanming already discredits immortals at the beginning of this poem; he explains the crane couplet as a metaphor for "the free rolling and unrolling of the poet's mind."[17] It is certainly true that the roaming of the crane is the poet's mind travel, and yet

Wang Shumin's interpretation seems to have missed the humor in Tao Yuanming's wry description of his rather peculiar means of obtaining immortality.

Ren zhen, the phrase we have seen in Xiao Tong's biography of Tao Yuanming, means "to follow one's natural impulses." *Zhen* (genuineness, naturalness) is an important concept in *Zhuangzi* (and not mentioned even once in *The Analects*), and *ren zhen* is a phrase that, although not appearing in *Zhuangzi* itself, has been used in Guo Xiang's (253?–312) influential annotation of *Zhuangzi.*[18] By the Tang, when Cheng Xuanying (ca. mid-seventh century) glossed *Zhuangzi, ren zhen* had already become a very common phrase. In chapter six of *Zhuangzi,* "The Great Master," Zhuangzi gives a detailed explanation of what a *zhenren* (genuine man) is.[19] In Zhuangzi's view, he is the ultimate Daoist sage, the Perfect Man (*zhiren*). One characteristic of the genuine man, according to Zhuangzi, is that his heart forgets. In the same chapter, a fictional dialogue between Confucius and his student Yan Hui also demonstrates the virtue of "forgetting." This *Zhuangzi* chapter (cited below) is, as we will see, the subtext of Tao Yuanming's whole poem:

> Yan Hui said, "I have improved!"
> Confucius said, "What do you mean?"
> "I have forgotten benevolence and righteousness."
> "Good, but you are not there yet."
> Another day he saw Confucius again, and said, "I have improved."
> "What do you mean?"
> "I have forgotten rites and music."
> "Good, but you are not there yet."
> Another day he saw Confucius again, and said, "I have improved."
> "What do you mean?"
> "I just sat down and forgot."
>
> Confucius, startled, said, "What do you mean by sitting down and forgetting?"
>
> Yan Hui said, "I became oblivious of my limbs, and drove out my perceptions. Once I transcend my body and dispose of my mind, I am one and the same with the great Thoroughfare. This is what I mean by sitting down and forgetting."
>
> Confucius said, "When you become one and the same with things, you have no preferences; when you have gone through the transforma-

tion, you have no inflexibility. How truly worthy you are! I would like to follow you."[20]

As Yan Hui happily reports back to Confucius the stages of his spiritual improvement, we notice that on the last occasion, he simply says he has "forgotten," without specifying *what* he has forgotten, as he had in the first two cases. This is indeed an improvement. He does explain his "forgetting," which involves destroying and eliminating (a figurative way of saying "forgetting") body (physical desires) and mind (cognitive facility). "The great Thoroughfare" (*da Tong*) refers to the Way, which is compared to a straight, unobstructed road: if one is identical with it, one will not have likes or dislikes but will treat all things equally, and if one participates in the great Transformation, one will not get stuck.

Only in forgetting can one become one with Nature and participate freely in its transformation. We may now better understand the abrupt turn taken in Tao Yuanming's poem:

自/顧我抱茲獨	*Ever since I harbored this solitude,*
僶俛四十年	*struggling hard, it has been forty years.*
形骸久已化	*My form and body were transformed long ago, /*
形體憑化遷	*My form and* body follow the transformation, /
形神久已死	*My form and* spirit were dead long ago,
心在/在心復何言	*but* the mind is still here / it is in my mind
	and what more is there to say?

The poet finally brings us back to the other part of the title: drinking *alone*. We should keep in mind that the crane transporting the poet to the eight limits of the earth has carried him back to where he is. When he returns, he reflects on his situation and remembers his solitude that has lasted for forty years. While Tao Yuanming is the first poet to continually take stock of his years in his poetry (how many years have passed since I did this or that), the juxtaposition of *babiao* (the eight limits of the earth) and *sishinian* (forty years) collapses the temporal and spatial dimensions into one single locale, a locale within the bounds of the mortal world, limited by space and, more importantly, time.

The enumeration of years surprises us. The title of the poem is "Drinking Alone during Incessant Rain," and the variant version makes it clear that the poet's "loneliness" is imposed on him by the bad weather, but his having been solitary for forty years shows us a different picture: a solitude that has been consciously chosen, not passively endured. *Bao*, here translated as "harbor," also means "to embrace," a verb indicating a voluntary action.

Wang Shumin quite rightly glosses *bao zi du* (harbor this solitude) with a quotation from another poem by Tao Yuanming, "Encountering a Fire in the Sixth Month of the Year *Wushen* [408]" (Wushen sui liuyuezhong yu huo): "Ever since I bound my hair and harbored this solitude, / all of a sudden, some forty years have passed."[21] When we look closely at these two poems, one about fire and one about water, we notice that even their concerns are reminiscent of one another: "This form and its traces will follow the Transformation, / but the numinous abode will remain constant." The numinous abode refers to the mind, which stays the same even as the outer form of the body is changed beyond recognition. The same conclusion is drawn at the end of the rain poem, if we adhere to the last couplet in the text proper.

This, of course, recalls the Daoist classics again, among which a remark from *Zhuangzi* 22, "Knowledge Wandered North" (Zhi bei you), is particularly relevant: "In antiquity, people changed on the outside but not on the inside; nowadays, people change on the inside but not on the outside. He who changes with things is identical to him who does not change."[22] Since all things are in constant transformation, only by going along with change and not resisting it may a person stay unchanged—that is, he remains undisturbed and peaceful deep inside, being harmonious with the pace of nature. The Han Daoist work *Huainanzi* echoes this idea: "The person who has obtained the Way will be changed outwardly, but remains unchanged inwardly."[23] As Zhuangzi puts it, "His physical form undergoes change, and his mind is changed as well. Wouldn't you call that the saddest thing of all?"[24]

The thought of "solitude" prompts the poet to reflect on his state of being for the past forty years, during which he has always been "alone" (*du*), and then on his changed external appearance; he is, after all, no immortal like Red Pine or Prince Qiao, and nothing can bring about "the outward transformation" better than the passage of forty years—a long time in a mere mortal's lifespan. We think of "The Great Master" again, a particularly poetic chapter in *Zhuangzi* to which Tao Yuanming comes back again and again for images, phrases, and inspiration.

> Zisi, Ziyu, Zili, and Zilai, the four of them, fell upon talking to one another. "Who can look upon nothingness as one's head, life as one's

back, death as one's buttocks, and know that life and death, existence and nonexistence, are but one, I will befriend him." The four of them looked at each other and smiled. Their hearts had no disharmony, and they became friends. After a while, Ziyu was sick, and Zisi went to see him. Ziyu said, "Great indeed, that Creator! He is making me all crooked like this!" A lump grew out of his back, his five vital organs were all on top, his chin was hidden in his navel, his shoulders were higher than his head, his hair-bun pointing toward the sky; in his body the energies of *yin* and *yang* were all messed up. But his mind remained peaceful and undisturbed. Staggering to the well, he looked at his reflection in the water, saying, "Oy, oy. That Creator—he is making me all crooked like this!"[25]

In Ziyu, we see the shadow of our poet Tao Yuanming, who, after his house has been burned by fire (as recorded in his poem "Encountering a Fire"), comforts himself by saying that despite the destruction of the outward appearance—be it the house for the body or the house of the body—his mind, the spirit's abode, alone remains "peaceful" (*du xian*). Here, in the rain poem, he is affirming the same truth; besides the exhortation to eat, drink, make merry, and seize the day, the poem provides an alternative to the vanity of seeking immortality.

If we read through "The Great Master" to its end, we will find the following section:

> Ziyu befriended Zisang, and it was raining for ten days. Ziyu said to himself, "Zisang may be having a hard time." He wrapped up some food and took it to his friend. When he was at Zisang's door, he heard a voice like singing and yet like crying, and a zither being struck: "Is it father, is it mother? Is it heaven, or is it man?" It was as if the voice were being overwhelmed and the singer's feelings were too much for his words, which came out hurriedly.
>
> Ziyu went in and said, "Why is your song like this?"
>
> Zisang said, "I am contemplating what has driven me to such extremities, but I don't get it. My father and mother certainly don't want me to be poor like this. Heaven covers everyone, with no partiality; Earth holds everyone up, with no partiality. So how could it be Heaven and Earth that have picked me out for such poverty? I look for the one who has done this but cannot find him. Then to be at the very extreme—surely, it must be the working of Fate."[26]

Zisang, the friend of Ziyu, is trapped inside by incessant rain, as is our poet. He is singing to a zither. Reflecting on his condition (extreme poverty), he realizes that he is not being singled out by Heaven and Earth for harsh treatment—everything is just as it should be, the workings of Fate. The fatalistic conclusion is less important than the fact that Zisang, in his extreme situation, still has a friend to visit him, a friend who cares about him and takes food to him, knowing that continuous rain, like continuous snow, will trap people at home; for those who do not have much grain stored at home, it is indeed a bad time.

There was a long poetic tradition that taunted and scorned people who stored things up and did not use and spend them while they could. Starting from the *Shi jing* poem "Hawthorn on the Mountain" (Shan you shu), we hear the voice urging people to consume what they have, for when a person dies, others will take what he has left unspent and go on enjoying it.[27] The "Rain" poem starts with the statement that all life will inevitably come to an end, moves to a careful calculation of what has gone and what is still here (the forty years versus the solitude, the bodily form versus the heart/mind), and closes with a declaration of the exhaustion of words: "What more is there to say?" While those who seek immortality must learn to conserve their vital essence and energy (*jing qi*), their breath, their saliva, and their semen, our poet proves just as shrewd in calculating what he has to spend in order to gain.[28] The elderly fellow who presents him with the wine promises him that "drinking will help a man obtain immortality" (*de xian*), but the kind of "immortality" obtained through such unconventional means is likewise unusual—it is a sort of spiritual freedom, a moment of enlightenment that enables the poet to soberly recognize that the most valuable possession, despite what he has used up, he still has in store.[29]

The last couplet of the rain poem, however, has some intriguing textual variants:

形骸久已化	*My form and body were transformed long ago, /*
形體憑化遷	*My form and* body follow the transformation, /
形神久已死	*My form and* spirit were dead long ago,
心在/在心復何言	*but* the mind is still here / it is in my mind *and what more is there to say?*

Xing hai and *xing ti* (form and body) are more or less interchangeable, but *Xing shen jiu yi si* (My form and spirit were dead long ago) is a very different claim. Here *xing* (form) probably should not be taken to refer to one's physical body; instead it might imply outward appearance, recalling a line from the second *Zhuangzi* chapter: "Can the outer form really be made like deadwood and can the mind really be made like cold ashes?"[30] This description is of Master Ziqi of Nanguo, who has just "lost the me" (*sang wo*); in other words, he has achieved the state of "forgetting himself," which is manifested in his "deadwood-like" outer form (*xing*). This, however, would make the last line "the mind is still here" a bit enigmatic, which is perhaps why it also has a variant reading: *zai xin,* "it is all in the mind," or "it all depends on the mind." And yet, this reading has never been seriously considered by any commentator. The usual connotation of the phrase *xing shen* is "body and spirit," which had become standard usage in the Eastern Jin, and the Zhuangzi association it might have evoked for Tao Yuanming's contemporaries would have sounded "unnatural" to later ears.

What's in a Name?

"Drinking Alone during Incessant Rain" is a poem based on a text or texts; its novelty is born of an ingenious combination and twist of familiar motifs and conventional images. It is interwoven throughout with echoes of *Zhuangzi,* and the poet's reading experiences figure prominently in what he writes. "An Excursion to Xie Brook" (You Xiechuan) is another of Tao Yuanming's quasi-*youxian shi* (poems of roaming immortals), and again it is intertwined with textual traditions and the poet's fascination with the written word. There is much debate about the first lines of the preface and of the poem, each of which contains a variant concerning the date of composition. In my translation, I will simply list the variant readings as they are.

Many of Tao Yuanming's poems have prefaces explaining the occasion for the writing of the poem. By Tao Yuanming's time, this had become a common practice. In 400, the year before Tao Yuanming went on the outing to Xie Brook described in the poem (that is, if we opt for the *xinchou* date), a group of about thirty Buddhist monks, supposedly led by the venerable Hui Yuan, went for an outing to Stone Gate Ravine Mountain on the northern part of Mount Lu (the South Mountain named in Tao Yuanming's preface). They wrote the famous "Preface and Poem on a Journey to Stone Gate" (You Shimen shi bing xu).[31] The other two well-known precedents for "literary outings" are Shi Chong's (249–300) party at Golden Valley (Jin Gu) and Wang Xizhi's (ca. 303–ca. 361) gathering at Lanting).[32] Both have left poems and prefaces (although there is doubt concerning the authorship of Wang Xizhi's preface); the practice of listing the name, age, and official title of everyone in the party in order to commemorate the occasion began with Shi Chong. Shi Chong relates that there was music being played at the party, and Wang Xizhi, in an apparent response to that, says in his preface that although "we had none of the magnificent sounds of strings and flutes, a cup of wine and then a poem were enough to express our innermost feelings."[33] Shi Chong and Wang Xizhi both describe the natural environment of and the reasons for their gatherings: Shi Chong and his friends were seeing General Wang Xu off to Chang'an, while Wang Xizhi and his friends met on the day of the Bathing Festival (the third day of the third month). In Tao Yuanming's case, the outing was neither for celebration of a festival nor for seeing a friend off (in fact it was carried out on a rather odd day—the fifth day of the first month). It seems to have been purely spontaneous:

> On the fifth day of the first month of the *xinchou* year [401] / the *xinyou* year [421], the weather was fine and clear, and all things of nature were peaceful and pleasant. Along with two or three neighbors, I went for an excursion to Xie Brook. Facing the long-flowing stream, we gazed at the Tiered Wall Hill in the distance. Bream and carp leaped out of the water, their scales shining in the sunset; gulls flew back and forth, riding on the mild air. That South Mountain [i.e., Mount Lu]—its name is truly old now, so it has no further need to be sighed over. As for Tiered Wall, it rises out of water all alone, with nothing around it; and when I think of the numinous mountain far away, I find something charming and lovely about its name. It was not enough just to look toward it with pleasure, and so we composed poetry together. Grieved by the passage of days and months, lamenting that our years are not staying for us, we each wrote down our age and native town, in order to commemorate this occasion.[34]

The "numinous mountain" or "soul mountain" (*lingshan*) refers to Mount Kunlun, populated, according to Chinese mythology, by immortals. Cengcheng, the Tiered Wall, is said to be the top level of Mount Kunlun.[35] It is often used in reference to Mount Kunlun, the immortals' paradise, as in the Stone Gate poem: "Lifting our robes, we long for the carriages of cloud; / gazing at the cliffs, we think of the Tiered Wall." Here it seems that the little hill arising out of the stream (Xie Brook itself?) is named Tiered Wall, and it is this name that arouses Tao Yuanming's fancy.[36] This turns out to be the most noticeable thing about Tao Yuanming's preface: he loves a place not because—or not only because—it is beautiful but because it has a great name, a name that evokes the legendary mountain inscribed in texts, including *The Classic of Mountains and Seas, The Biography of King Mu [of Zhou]* (Mu tianzi zhuan), and all the "unusual books" we know that Tao Yuanming was fond of reading.

開歲倏五十/日	*The year opens— suddenly* I am turning fifty / five days have passed,[37]
吾生行歸休	*and my life—it is coming to an end.*
念之動中懷	*When I think of it, my heart is touched;*
及辰/晨為茲游	*as the* time / morning *arrives, I go on this excursion.*

The reason for this excursion, not mentioned in the preface, is disclosed at the beginning of the poem: it is the thought of death that has prompted the poet. *You* is a rather loaded word, often indicating the kind of fantastic heavenly journey conducted in the *Chuci* tradition (such as in "Far Roaming" [Yuanyou])—a pursuit of immortals and immortality.[38] Tao Yuanming's poem presents a much more modest version of roaming:

氣和天惟/候澄	*The air is mild, the sky clear,*
班坐依遠流	*we sit together along the far-flowing stream.*
弱湍馳文魴	*Patterned breams dash in weak rapids,*
閒谷矯鳴鷗	*from the quiet valley soars a crying gull.*
迥澤散游目	*Casting our wandering eyes across vast waves,*
緬然睇曾丘	*we gaze at Tiered Wall Hill in the distance:*
雖微九重秀	*although it does not reach the lofty height of nine folds,*
顧瞻無匹儔	*nothing in sight is its match.*

Tao Yuanming has combined two different literary traditions. One is the tradition of gathering and partying in a relatively domesticated natural setting, as in the feast poems in the Jian'an period or in the more recent poetry of Shi Chong and Wang Xizhi. The other is the tradition of journeying far, either touring the universe in the more archaic *Chuci* tradition or paying a visit to a lofty mountain, as in Sun Chuo's (314–371) literary exposition on wandering to Tiantai Mountain (an imaginary journey) or the Buddhist monks' roaming over Stone Gate Mountain, both occurring in Tao Yuanming's own age. Tao Yuanming's "ascent" of the hill is purely optical; it is his eyes, instead of his body, that are roaming (*san you mu*), and he gazes at the hill from afar, just as he looks toward South Mountain from his own backyard. Although he realizes that it is not the real magic mountain—"nine folds" being the standard descriptive term for the Tiered Wall of Mount Kunlun, famous for its lofty height[39]—he is content that nothing within *his* sight is its match.

On the other hand, *wen fang* (patterned bream) evokes an entirely different atmosphere, as it is a remote echo of the mythical *Chuci* tradition. It is in "The Earl of Yellow River" (He bo) of the "Nine Songs" that we first encounter the term "patterned fish." The Yellow River's earl would ride on the white turtle and chase after those colorful fish, sporting by the river's isles. Later on, the "patterned fish" appear in Cao Zhi's "*Fu* on the Goddess of Luo River" (Luoshen fu), in which they leap out of the water, acting as a sort of a guard to the carriage of the river goddess.[40] As brief as it is, there is a touch of the fantastic, whimsical tone of the "Nine Songs" here.

提壺接賓侶	*Raising the flask, I offer it to my guests and companions;*
引滿更獻酬	*cups are filled, and we urge each other to drink—*
未知從今去	*who knows whether after this day,*
當復如此不	*we will ever be able to do this again?*
中觴縱遙情	*During the second round of drinking, we let our feelings roam far and free,*
忘彼千載憂	*and forget those cares of a thousand years.*
且極今朝樂	*Let us enjoy today's pleasures to the full,*
明日非所求	*as for tomorrow—it is not what we pursue.*[41]

This is the familiar motif of feast poetry or drinking poetry—guests or companions are always urged to eat and drink and enjoy the present to the full, for no one knows "whether we will ever be able to do this again." What is of interest is the line "During the second round of drinking, we let our feelings roam far and free." "Second round of drinking" is *zhongshang*, literally "the middle cup."[42] We think of Tao Yuanming's rain poem, in which he delineates the stages of drinking (and again we see the need to "forget," in forgetting the cares of a thousand years). Wang Xizhi says in his "Lanting" poem, "Three cups of wine would dissolve Heaven's law" (San shang jie tian xing).[43]

As Huang Wenhuan points out, “The feelings at the first cup are still under restraint, and are not uninhibited yet. As the feast carries on, in the middle of drinking, the power of wine gradually increases and the feelings are gradually let go . . . As what is close disappears, what is distant will emerge.”[44]

As the poet lets his feelings roam “far and free,” we see a strange sort of *youxian* poetry. It starts with a contemplation of a name (*ming*), whose “immortal associations” excite the poet much more than the reality (*shi*), and in fact prompt him to write these lines (he declines to sing of South Mountain only because its *name* is “truly ancient”). Because the hill has a name identical with that of one of the most sacred mountains in myth, even if it does not quite match the splendors of the legendary peaks of Mount Kunlun, it is peerless “in the eyes” of the poet—literally, as he says it is the most outstanding hill within his sight. Faint echoes of the archaic, fantastic, exotic landscape of the *Chuci* may be heard; however, what we have here is not vigorous traveling and seeking but a tour of the eye—both physical and spiritual.

Sometimes a drinking party may occur in an unlikely place. In Tao Yuanming’s collection there is a poem entitled “Partying under the Cypress Trees at the Zhou Family Graves” (Zhuren gongyou Zhou jia mubai xia):

今日天氣佳　　*Today’s weather is fair—*
清吹與鳴彈/蟬　　*there are shrill reed pipes and* zither / singing cicadas.
慼彼柏下人　　*Touched by those under the cypresses,*
安得不為懽　　*how can we not make merry?*
清歌散/發新聲　　*Clear songs spread new tunes,*
綠/時酒開芳顏　　Green / seasonal *wine relaxes youthful faces.*
未知明日事　　*Not yet knowing what will happen tomorrow,*
余襟良以殫　　*I have quite used up my feelings.*

As Gu Zhi dutifully points out, the thirteenth of “Nineteen Old Poems” has these lines that are very much reminiscent of Tao Yuanming’s poem:

驅車上東門　　*Driving my cart out Upper Eastern Gate,*
遙望郭北墓　　*I gaze at the tombs to the north of the city.*
白楊何蕭蕭　　*How the poplars rustle in the wind!*
松栢夾廣路　　*Pines and cypresses line the wide road.*
下有陳死人　　*Underneath there are people who are long gone,*

杳杳即長暮	*far, far away they went into the endless night.*
潛寐黃泉下	*Lying hidden under Yellow Springs,*
千載永不寤	*for a thousand years they do not wake up.*
	......
服食求神仙	*Taking elixirs and seeking immortality—*
多為藥所誤	*many have been misled by the magic pills.*
不如飲美酒	*Better yet to drink the good wine,*
被服紈與素	*and wear your clothes of fine silk.*[45]

We see in these lines the image of "long dead people" buried under pines and cypresses, and the "wide road," which, though good for a ride, inevitably leads to death.

I agree with Hightower that "whether the Chou Family graves belonged to the descendants of Chou Fang [260–320], friend of T'ao Ch'ien's ancestor T'ao K'an and connection by marriage of the T'ao family (as T'ao Shu suggested), is neither provable nor of much importance to a reading of this poem."[46] It is one of the many "feast poems" that, in paraphrasing, tell but a rather banal truth: if we do not make merry while we may, death will catch up with us. Such a carpe-diem theme is, indeed, commonplace and universal, with feasting again inextricably intertwined with mortality. But we do not read poetry for its "thought"; we read it for the pleasure offered by the words.

"Partying under the Cypress Trees" starts with "today" and ends with an unknown "tomorrow." The poem closes with the word *dan* (to exhaust, use up, or finish). The "exhaustion" of pleasure is implicitly contrasted with the preceding line, in which the poet tells us about his lack of knowledge of the future; that is, although his feelings of today have reached their zenith, the unknown "tomorrow" offers a counter move, and the little poem is delicately balanced between these two states—the small, intimate, tangible pleasures of today, and the vast, dark strangeness of an unknown future. Wang Fuzhi, the astute seventeenth-century literary scholar, comments that "at the poet's brush tip, there is a reserved force (*liu shi*, 'a momentum put in check')."[47]

The poem also plays with the phrase "under the cypress trees." It was customary for the ancient Chinese to plant pine and cypress trees beside a grave mound, a tradition continued in many regions until today. "Those under the cypresses" in the third line of the poem refers to the dead and buried. To play music, sing, and drink under the cypress trees beside a family graveyard, however, was not customary, then or now. Except for the "grave mounds" passage, this poem presents us with a conventionally joyful feast scene: the shrill reed pipes, the clear songs, the green wine echoing the color of the cypress trees, and the youthful faces (*fangyan*, lit., "fragrant faces") flushed red from the effects of the alcohol, which no doubt match the wild flowers blooming around the grave mounds. But in the midst of the rather noisy affair comes a dark note: they, the party goers, are also "those under the cypresses," as clearly indicated by the very title of the poem. It is a jarring note, quiet but insistent, stealing into the party music.

Maybe it is true that the Zhous were Tao Yuanming's relatives by marriage (as Tao Shu suggested), which gave him a sort of privilege to intrude into the family cemetery with friends, a band, and wine. But soon after, they will pass into silence as well, just like the others "under the cypresses." The surrounding stillness makes the noise made by the intruders pardonable.

Reading into the Dark

Tao Yuanming's thirteen poems "On Reading *The Classic of Mountains and Seas*" (Du Shanhai jing) are unusual in classical Chinese literary history in several ways. They are the first series of poems written on the topic of reading. Although many *yongshi* poems (poems on history) written before Tao Yuanming's time respond to the poet's reading of works of history, they do not present a framework within which the reading experience is explicitly embedded in the poems as it is here; that is, Tao Yuanming's series of poems is unique in that the first poem establishes a setting for the poet's reading—a sort of "summarizing" description of the time, place, and occasion. He not only tells us what he reads and what he thinks of his readings but also portrays in great detail the physical experience of reading itself.

The poet is not reading historical writings; instead, what he reads and sings of is an "unusual book," the sort of work that Yan Yanzhi, in his elegy for Tao Yuanming, said Tao Yuanming has always been fond of. Despite the title, in the opening poem Tao mentions two volumes as his summer reading: *The Classic of Mountains and Seas* and *The Biography of King Mu*. The latter was discovered by a grave-robber in a tomb in 281, only about a century before Tao Yuanming wrote these poems. It is an account of King Mu of Zhou's (956–918 B.C.E.) grand tours, including his journey to Mount Kunlun and his meeting with the Queen Mother of the West (Xiwangmu). *The Classic of*

Mountains and Seas is a work of mythical geography. Divided into five sections, it describes the Chinese heartland as a central territory surrounded by the four seas and a "great wilderness" extending beyond the seashores. These farflung regions are filled with fanciful mountains and waters, strange people, weird birds, and grotesque beasts, not to mention extraordinary plants and minerals. Scholars still cannot determine the work's date, but we know that it was already in existence in the Western Han.[48] Guo Pu (276–324), the Western Jin luminary famous for his *youxian* poems, wrote "Appraisals of the Illustrations of *The Classic of Mountains and Seas*" (Shanhai jing tu zan), which is still extant. Zhang Jun (307–346) did another set of appraisals, which has already been lost except for one piece preserved by the Tang encyclopedia *Primer for Study* (Chuxue ji). Since Tao Yuanming mentions browsing through "the pictures of mountains and seas," this has led some scholars to conclude that he must have been reading Guo Pu's appraisals along with the illustrations; we do not know this.

This series of poems is also unusual in that it forms a clear line of progression—not in the sense of narrative development or of a reading following the order of the book as we now have it (in fact, the poems often seem to pick out details in the book randomly, regardless of the book's internal order, and the details have no inherent connection to one another), but in the sense that it is a miniature Chinese epic on seeking immortals (*youxian*) and spiritual wanderings (*yuanyou*) in which we can still hear the distinct echoes of literary conventions, a strange medieval Chinese version of *Paradise Lost.* From a carefree land of immortals infused with bright light, the poet reads on to the feats of heroes who are half-god, half-man, and then to the dark world of mortals, characterized by betrayal, murder, and starvation. It is a series of poems that begins with an emphasis on pleasure, and ends with the discovery of sorrow and fear.

Finally, this series of poems keeps returning to food and drink. While mere mortals have to struggle for food and drink every day, the immortals have no such mundane worries. Food and drink are, therefore, the ultimate difference between an immortal's life and a mortal's.

孟夏草木長	*In early summer the plants grow,*
繞屋樹扶疏	*all around my house, trees spread branches.*
眾鳥欣有托	*Flocks of birds are happy to find shelter,*
吾亦愛吾廬	*as for me, I too love my home.*

既耕亦已種　*Having plowed, having sown,*
且還讀我書　*now I come back to my readings.*[49]

The poet begins with an affirmation of his love of home. The first couplet reminds one of another of his poems, the sixth of "On Impoverished Gentlemen" (Yong pinshi): "Zhongwei loved living in isolation, / all around his house grew wild weeds." Zhang Zhongwei (ca. first century) was an Eastern Han recluse, and Tao Yuanming praises him for his poetic talent: "Hiding away, he cut off his social ties, / and was skilled in writing poetry." But the trees and grasses surrounding Tao Yuanming's own house have a distinctly different "flavor" from the "weeds" (*hao peng*); they are "good plants," creating a home for the birds, and a refuge for the poet. As summer heat is imminent, their shade provides extra comfort.

What is noticeable here is that the poet delineates a clearly defined space, protected from the outside world, for his reading experience—both in spatial terms and in temporal terms. Reading is portrayed as an activity carried out in the time period set aside after the pragmatic concerns of plowing and sowing have been tended to: it is both leisure and pleasure.

窮巷隔深轍　*This isolated lane keeps away deep ruts,*
頗回故人車　*and quite turns back the carriages of old friends.*
歡言酌春酒　*Cheerfully I pour myself some spring wine,*
摘我園中蔬　*and pick some greens from my own garden.*
微雨從東來　*Drizzling rain comes from the east,*
好風與之俱　*in the company of a pleasant breeze.*

"This isolated lane" (*qiong xiang*) echoes the "living in isolation" (*qiong ju*) of Zhang Zhongwei. Deep ruts are left by big carriages, and big carriages are the means of transportation for the rich and famous. The next line, "quite turns back the carriages of old friends," is a euphemistic way of saying that old friends rarely visit. But if there seems to be a little bitterness in this line, the next few lines quickly dispel it. We might note the poet's repeated use of the word *wu* or *wo* here as the possessive pronoun "my." It appears with the house ("my house"), the books ("my books"), the garden, and the greens ("the greens in my garden"); there is no mistaking the poet's emphasis on a contentment that is self-contained, self-sufficient. Cutting off social ties, as in the case of Zhang Zhongwei, is considered more a blessing than a reason for grievance. While in nature everything seems to have its company (the birds being "a flock," and even the rain being "accompanied" by a breeze), the poet is alone, in an out-of-the-way lane with no friends visiting him. But he does not seem to mind; he has books to keep him company (as Mencius said, "to seek friends among the ancients") and, as he tells us later, he is happily absorbed in a spiritual journey.

In these lines we also see the physical aspect of the poet's reading—surrounded by summer trees, with a pleasant breeze as well as a misty rain, and accompanied by spring wine and fresh garden vegetables. The motif of food and drink appears for the first time, and will recur.

泛覽周王傳/典　*Browsing through the* biography / canon *of the Zhou king,*
流觀山海圖　*skimming the pictures of mountains and seas,*
俯仰終宇宙　*in one instant I reach the limits of the universe—*
不樂復何如　*if not happy [in this], what would I do?*

The attitude towards reading is consistent with that expressed in "The Biography of Master Five Willows": "He likes reading, but does not seek hard to understand; and yet, whenever he comprehends the concept, he becomes so happy that he forgets to eat."

Several premodern critics have noticed the word *le,* "happiness." They eagerly seize upon it as an expression of Tao Yuanming's Confucian leaning that he has truly mastered Confucius and Yan Hui's secret to personal happiness and fulfillment despite hardship in outer circumstances.[50] But "happiness" is framed negatively and in an interesting question: "If not happy [in this], what would I do?" His happiness is due to the fact that he has "reached the limits of the universe." This is the grand gesture of the Great One in the Han poetic exposition, or the cosmic traveler of the *Chuci* tradition. This is also the gesture of a person who embarks on a heavenly voyage into far space in the *youxian* poems. And indeed, the journey begins:

玉堂/臺凌霞秀　*In the Jade* Hall / Terrace *towering above the rosy clouds,*
王母怡/積妙顏　*the Queen Mother* looks pleased with / gathers *her marvelous countenance.*
天地共俱生　*She was born with Heaven and Earth—*
不知幾何年　*how old is she? No one knows.*[51]

靈化無窮已	*Ceaseless are her numinous metamorphoses;*
館宇非一山	*her lodgings are not limited to a single mountain.*[52]
高酣發新謠	*High and tipsy, she bursts forth into new songs;*
寧效俗中言	*never would her words imitate the worldly crowd.*

The Queen Mother of the West was an ancient Chinese deity, and Tao Yuanming again displays his wry sense of humor when he refers to her countenance as "marvelous" (*miao*). *Miao* means "wondrous" and does not necessarily indicate beauty.[53] To use "marvelous" to describe the Queen Mother as depicted in *The Classic of the Mountains and Seas* cannot but evoke a smile from the knowing reader. The Queen Mother appears in the *Classic of Mountains and Seas* three times, most notably in "The Classic of the Western Mountains" (Xishan jing): "Jade Mountain is where the Queen Mother of the West dwells. The Queen Mother of the West looks like a human being, but has a leopard's tail, tiger's teeth, and is good at whistling. In her tangled hair, she wears a hairpin. She is in charge of the Plague and the Five Destructions." Then, in "The Classic of the North within the Seas" (Hainei bei jing), we see another brief description: "The Queen Mother of the West leans on a short table and wears a jade hairpin. To the south there are three Blue Birds, who fetch food for the Queen Mother. They are to the north of Mount Kunlun." "The Classic of the Great Wilderness in the West" (Dahuang xi jing) says, "[On Mount Kunlun] There is a human being, wearing a hairpin, with tiger's teeth and a leopard's tail, living in a cave. Its name is the Queen Mother of the West."[54] Thus, in all three places the description of the Queen Mother's appearance seems to be quite consistent: she is not "beautiful," at least not from any human perspective, and "marvelous" is a humorously euphemistic way of referring to her.[55] The variant *ji* (to accumulate, to gather) in the second line of Tao Yuanming's poem is intriguing. We mentioned before the Daoist passion for "storing things up," and that she gathers her countenance may be another way of saying that her physical transformations are endless (the fifth line of the poem), from the beastly shape to courteous host to beautiful middle-aged goddess.

The last couplet alludes to her meeting with King Mu. At the feast, the Queen Mother of the West sang a song for the Son of Heaven:

> The white clouds are in the sky,
> mountains and hills rise up on their own.

The road is far and distant,
mounds and rivers lie in between.
I hope you will not die,
and will be able to come again.[56]

As an immortal, the Queen Mother can afford to be blunt; the expression of her good will is phrased in negative terms—"Do not die!"—instead of the more common and more graceful "I wish you a long life," and the distance between herself and the king is described as long and perilous. The Son of Heaven replies with a promise to return in three years, but this promise is, noticeably, a political statement: only by governing well can the king hope to see the Queen Mother again, just as in "*Fu* on Gaotang" (Gaotang fu), in which the Chu king's wish to meet with the goddess of Wu Mountain is also contingent on his political performance. The king plays a role both as ruler and as head shaman.[57]

It is interesting to note that the Queen Mother, not particularly an outstanding deity in *The Classic of Mountains and Seas* despite her later popularity in medieval Daoism, takes precedence in Tao Yuanming's poetic series.[58] In addition to her immortality, her endless transformations, and her many residences, all of which she shares in common with many gods and goddesses, two unique characteristics of the Queen Mother of the West stand out: her inebriation, and her composition of new songs. These remind us of Tao Yuanming: with his spring wine and his garden greens, he may be enjoying the state of being "high and tipsy" right now, and the high praise of the Queen Mother's versifying—that her songs are not at all like worldly words—is no less an expectation he sets for himself. In his imagination, it may very well be Tao Yuanming, not the Zhou king, who is meeting with the Queen Mother. The illusion, however, is quick to dissipate in the next poem:

迢遞槐江嶺	*How high and towering, that Huai River Peak,*
是為玄圃丘	*it is the hill where the Mysterious Garden is.*[59]
西南望崑墟	*It gazes towards Kunlun in the southwest—*[60]
光氣難與儔	*there the radiant aura is hard to match.*
亭亭明玕照	*Brilliantly shines the bright jade;*
洛洛清淫流	*the limpid Jasper Stream flowing down.*
恨不及周穆	*I regret not catching up with King Mu of Zhou,*
托乘一來游	*entrusting myself to his carriage for a visit.*

In "The Classic of the Western Mountains" there is a description of Huai River Peak: "Huai River Mountain . . . contains much jadeite, gold, and jade. . . . It is in fact the Flat Garden of the Heavenly Emperor. . . . It faces towards Kunlun in the south, where one can see blazing light and radiant aura. . . . There the limpid Jasper Stream flows down."[61] Guo Pu explains that the Flat Garden is the Mysterious Garden.[62] The one striking thing about this poem is its luminosity; the Mysterious Garden is intensely bright, both from its own glowing jewel stones and the clear Jasper Stream, and from the radiant light shining forth from Mount Kunlun in the distance.

The last couplet contains a double entendre. King Mu has a famous set of horses—the Eight Handsome Steeds. He also has Zaofu, the legendary driver. While on the surface the poet seems to be expressing his regret about not being King Mu's contemporary or not being as fortunate as King Mu, the implication is also that he is not fast enough to literally "catch up with" the king's speedy carriage. The unbridgeable distance between himself and the ancient king is both temporal and spatial. In the joy of reading and mind traveling, we begin to hear discontent. The next poem in the series opens with a question:

丹木生何許	*The cinnabar tree—where does it grow?*
迺在峚山陽	*There on the sunny slope of Mount Mi.*
黃花復朱實	*Yellow flowers, red berries:*
食之壽命長	*eating it prolongs a person's life.*
白玉凝素液	*Milky juice congealed of white jade,*
瑾瑜發奇光	*lustrous gemstones emit a wondrous light.*
豈伊君子寶	*It is not just the gentleman's treasure—*
見重我軒黃/皇	*it was prized by our Yellow Emperor.*

This poem is based on another section from "The Classic of the Western Mountains":

> Mount Mi has many cinnabar trees, which have round leaves and red stems, yellow flowers and red berries tasting like sweetmeats. If one eats from these, one does not feel hungry. From this mountain the Cinnabar River flows westward into Millet Marsh where there is much white jade. In the Cinnabar River flows a jade jelly, whose source is hot and bubbly, and the Yellow Emperor drank from it. A black jade is formed here. The jade jelly flows out and waters the cinnabar trees. When the cinnabar trees

were five years old, the Five Colors became clearly defined and the Five Tastes became aromatic. The Yellow Emperor then took the jade blossoms of Mount Mi and planted them on the sunny slope of Bell Mountain. From them grow *jin* and *yu*, both among the best of jades, being hard and of a fine texture, smooth to the touch and emitting a moist glow. Five colors are emitted from them, and their harmony assuages those who are tough. All spirits and gods between Heaven and Earth take them as food. A gentleman wears them to ward off the inauspicious.[63]

As Hightower observes, "The fruit [of the cinnabar trees] is a cure for hunger, but not an aid to the Long Life. Kuo P'u, however, quotes a source to prove that a single draft of white jade juice will make a man immortal, and it was this on which the Yellow Emperor feasted."[64] Guo Pu also wrote an appraisal of the jade jelly, in which he reconfirms that the Yellow Emperor ate it and ascended to heaven.[65] If in the second poem the mention of the Queen Mother's drinking resonates with the spring wine in the opening poem, then the motif of food appears here as an echo of the poet's garden vegetables. Compared to these divine foodstuffs that confer immortality, the fresh produce from the poet's own garden seems to have been outshone.

The food and drink motif continues in the next poem:

翩翩三青鳥	*Lightly flying are the three Blue Birds—*
毛色奇/甚可憐	*the color of their feathers is* wondrously / quite *charming.*
朝為王母使	*They are emissaries of the Queen Mother in the morning;*
暮歸三危山	*at dusk they return to Three Perils Mountain.*[66]
我欲因此鳥	*I would like to, through these birds,*
具向王母言	*tell the Queen Mother the following words:*
在世無所須/願	*in this world I* need / wish for *nothing*
惟酒與長年 / 惟願此長年	but wine and a long lifespan. / but only this long lifespan.

Because the birds' job is to fetch food for the Queen Mother, who is also fond of drinking (as shown in the second poem), the poet thinks of asking her for wine, and the Yellow Emperor's food of immortality in the preceding poem seems to have led to his wish for longevity. Rather than becoming an immortal like the Yellow Emperor, the poet is merely asking for a long life "in this world." If a person's wishes are an indicator of his dissatisfactions, the poet is revealing more and more discontent. Unlike the Queen Mother, mortals not only have to die, but when they are alive, they have no food-and-wine transporters to serve their needs. They have to plow and plant (what the poet claims he does in the opening poem), sweat and suffer; such are the consequences of living in the mortal world.

In the final couplet we have two variant readings. To "need" something and to "wish for" something are, of course, different. The alternative last line does not contain the request for wine, and the word "this" (*ci*) in "this long lifespan" is rather enigmatic. Perhaps for this reason, it remains a variant reading.

In the next poem we have a sort of interlude, when the pace of the poetic series slows down into a leisurely stroll:

逍遙蕪皋上	*Taking a leisurely stroll on Wugao Hill,*
杳然望扶木	*I gaze at the faraway Fusang Tree:*[67]
洪柯百萬尋	*its huge branches extend tens of millions of yards,*
森散覆暘谷	*spreading all over Hot Spring Valley.*[68]
靈人侍丹池	*The numinous being waits upon Cinnabar Pool;*
朝朝為日浴	*every morning she bathes the sun.*[69]
神景一登天	*Once the Divine Radiance ascends to heaven,*
何幽不見燭	*what darkness would not be illuminated!*

In Chinese mythology, Fusang is a huge mulberry tree from which the sun arises. Underneath the tree is Hot Spring Valley (Yang Gu), where the sun bathes. Huang Wenhuan is being his usual imaginative self as he focuses on the word *wu* (lit., "overgrown") in the first line. He feels that a place that is overgrown easily gets dark and is difficult to illuminate. The only problem is that the character *wu* appears as *wu* 無 (there is not) in *The Classic of Mountains and Seas* (the two characters are exchangeable homophones), and in fact Wugao Hill "has no grass or trees, and is very windy."[70]

Huang Wenhuan's suggestion does, however, draw our attention to the imagery of plant growth and barrenness in this poem. The barren mountain on which the poet stands forms a sharp contrast with the setting of his home, the physical environment of his reading. All around his house, early summer trees are spreading their leaves and branches. And yet, the poet does not direct his gaze to his hometown; his eyes are drawn to the Fusang tree in the distance, and the giant tree of cosmic proportion again eclipses the familiar pleasures of the poet's country home. Towering above Hot Spring Valley, it is home to the sun, the Divine Radiance and the source of light. The poet is so dazzled by this grand picture that he asks, once the sun rises, what darkness would not be illumined?

Hightower is right in stating that the poem is "infused with a sense of awe at these cosmic goings-on."[71] The key to understanding each poem in this series is, however, to think of each as part of a whole that forms a cosmic journey not unlike that in the *youxian* or *yuanyou* tradition, and yet unique in that it is a voyage undertaken in the imagination aroused by reading, a voyage from light to darkness, from marveling to lamentation. This is the inverse of the usual heavenly journey, as in "Far Roaming" or "*Fu* on the Great One," which begins with the lament over mortality and the confinement of the mundane realm, and comes at last to a world of light, an ecstatic state in which one is oblivious of all distinctions. Throughout the first part of the poetic series (that is, in the first seven poems), we often see a tension between the pleasant, intimate, but nevertheless commonplace home setting and the wonders of the cosmic tour. In this particular poem about the sun and its home, it is the huge legendary tree that stands out and strikes us as forming a sharp contrast with the shorter and much more tame trees around his house.

The image of the tree extends into the next poem:

粲粲三珠樹	*Splendid is the Triple Pearl Tree,*
寄生赤水陰	*growing on the southern bank of the Red River.*
亭亭凌風桂	*The Cinnamon, straight and tall, soars in the wind,*
八榦共成林	*its eight trunks forming a grove.*
靈鳳撫雲舞	*Among the clouds dances a numinous phoenix,*
神鸞調玉音	*a divine simurgh harmonizes the jade music.*
雖非世上寶	*Although they are not prized by the common world,*
爰得王母/子心	*they have captured the heart of* the Queen Mother / the Prince.

The Triple Pearl Tree looking like a bright comet, the Cinnamon whose eight trunks are so huge that together they form a forest, and the dancing phoenix and simurgh are all from different parts of *The Classic of Mountains and Seas*.[72] Together they form a world marked by prosperity and harmony. This poem, being the sixth of the twelve poems on the process of reading proper (not including the opening poem, which sets up a narrative frame as in a poetic exposition), is the culminating point of the bright side of the immortal land. After this poem, everything begins to decline.

自古皆有沒	*Since antiquity there is death for all,*
何人得靈長	*which person can live forever,*
不死復不老	*never passing away, never aging,*
萬歲如平常	*ten thousand years like a common day?*
赤泉給我飲	*Red Spring would then provide me with drink,*
員丘足我糧	*Round Hill replenish my food store—*[73]
方與三辰游	*wandering in the company of the Three Stars,*
壽考豈渠央	*my lifespan would never come to an end.*

In the discourse on immortal lands, the first couplet of the poem—a rhetorical question—comes as an abrupt, unpleasant surprise, with which we start our descent into the world of death, darkness, and decay. The rest of the poem should actually be read as part of the rhetorical question; it is fanciful thinking, no longer "real" as the immortal land is real.

Once again, we see the essential importance of food and drink. Huang Wenhuan is right in saying that "if one tires oneself out with obtaining clothing and food, then longevity means nothing but suffering."[74] But the worry about food and drink is not limited to mortals; the half-human, half-divine hero Kuafu, a Herculean figure, was destroyed by his great thirst:

夸父誕宏志	*Kuafu got this extravagant idea into his head:*
乃與日競走	*to run a race with the Sun.*
俱至虞淵下	*They reached the Yu Abyss together,*
似若無勝負	*as though there were no win, nor loss.*
神力既殊妙	*Marvelous and extraordinary was his divine power,*
傾河焉足有	*emptying the rivers was not enough to quench his thirst.*
餘跡寄鄧林	*Deng Grove is his remaining trace—*
功竟在身後	*his accomplishments were fulfilled after his death.*

Tao Yuanming tells the story of Kuafu quite well here, except for one point that needs to be clarified: Kuafu drank the Yellow and Wei rivers empty, but it was not enough for him, so he headed toward the Great Marsh in the north, and died of thirst on the way, his castaway staff metamorphosing into Deng Grove, which some say is a grove of peach trees.[75]

The awe at the sun's ascent in the sixth poem is transformed into amazement at Kuafu's extraordinary aspiration. To run a race with the sun is symbolic of the conquest of time, as is the desire to suspend darkness by "catching up" with the source of light. Kuafu's only limitation lies in his great need for drink. The third couplet of this poem—"emptying the rivers was not enough to quench his thirst"—again returns to Tao Yuanming's concern with *zu*—"what is enough." It reminds us of the eighth of Tao Yuanming's "Unclassified Poems":

> How can I expect to exceed a full belly?
> I only wish to eat my fill of grain,
> to have enough coarse cloth for the winter,
> and netted hemp to cope with the summer sun.

The first line in this stanza is a reference to the saying in *Zhuangzi*, "When a mole drinks from a river, all it takes is but a bellyful."[76] Kuafu was not being greedy when he was emptying the two great rivers—he was merely seeking what was "enough" for him. It seems that his vast capacity is his fatal flaw, and yet without it he would never be able to run the race, as such a capacity is only proportional to his magnificent "divine power."

The poet regards Deng Grove as the fulfillment of Kuafu's accomplishments (*gong*), which is a little enigmatic. The Qing scholar Chen Zuoming says, "What kind of posthumous accomplishment is this? His aspiration does not perish with him; maybe this is what is meant by his accomplishments."[77] Yuan Ke, the modern scholar of Chinese mythology, offers a more attractive suggestion: that the peach grove will help later generations to quench their thirst in their pursuit of light.[78] But of course peach trees can also ward off evil, especially wandering ghosts, hence the custom of setting the statues of "door gods" made of peach wood by the gate of a house on New Year's Eve.[79]

Many Chinese critics, obsessed with finding political references in a poet's works, desperately attempt to relate this poem to particular political situations in Tao Yuanming's time. They compare Kuafu to Liu Yu, who overthrew the Eastern Jin, or to Sima Xiuzhi, the general who fought against Liu Yu and escaped to the north, or to Tao Yuanming himself, who, like Kuafu who could not catch the sun, could not help restore the Jin royal house.[80] The problem with identifying Kuafu with Liu Yu the "usurper" is that the poem shows obvious admiration for Kuafu;[81] and if one identifies Kuafu with Sima Xiuzhi, then

Liu Yu would become the sun he wants to beat in the race, and it would be inappropriate to compare a usurper to "the sun"—the symbol of a monarch. As for vaguely identifying Kuafu with Tao Yuanming himself, it seems the best solution if one has to pin Kuafu down as referring to a single person; but to compare Kuafu's race with the sun to overthrowing Liu Yu is a rather suspicious undertaking for the reason already stated above. There is, moreover, no indication whatsoever of when Tao Yuanming wrote these poems, and a known date would be the necessary basis for any political interpretation.

The image of Kuafu, a tragic hero and giant whose aspiration proves even larger than himself and eventually consumes him, is reflected in an unlikely figure, the opposite of Kuafu in terms of size and strength, a descendent, like Kuafu, of the Fiery Emperor:[82]

精衛銜微木/石	*The Jingwei bird carries tiny* twigs / pebbles *in her mouth*
將以填滄海	*in order to fill up the vast sea.*
形夭無千歲	*Her form perished, enjoying no thousand-year life,*
猛志故常在	*but her fierce aspiration would always remain.*
同物既無慮	*Participating in the world of things leaves no worry,*
化去何復/不復悔	*so* why should she regret this transformation? / she does not regret this transformation.
徒設/役/使在昔心	*In vain she* cherishes / labors *the heart of old,*
良晨詎可待	*when can she expect the fine morning* *to ever dawn for her again?*

According to "The Classic of the Northern Mountains" (Beishan jing), Nüwa, the young daughter of the Fiery Emperor, drowned in the Eastern Sea and turned into a bird called Jingwei; swearing to take revenge on the sea, she transported twigs and pebbles from Western Mountain in an effort to fill up the sea.[83]

This poem is complicated by the existence of several variant characters. The third line was emended by the Northern Song scholar Zeng Hong (ca. early twelfth century) as "Xingtian brandished the battle-ax and shield" (Xingtian wu ganqi 刑天舞干戚). The 1192 edition of Tao Yuanming's collection appends Zeng Hong's short discussion at the end of this poetic series:

> I suspected that this second couplet did not make sense in the context, so I looked things up in *The Classic of Mountains and Seas*, in which it is

said that Xingtian is the name of a beast and it loves to dance around with a battle-ax and shield in its mouth. Therefore I know this line has to be *Xingtian wu ganqi*, which then corresponds to the next line, "fierce aspiration would always remain." The five characters are all wrong because the forms of the graphs look similar, which is not at all uncommon. When there was a chance, I told my friends Cen Rang [courtesy name Yanxiu] and Chao Yongzhi [courtesy name Zhidao]; the two of them clapped their hands in amazement.[84] They quickly fetched their own Tao Yuanming collections and corrected the error accordingly. Hence I think of Song Xuanxian's words: "Collating a book is like wiping dust off a table: just as you are wiping, the dust is already there again." This indeed is no lie.

My relative as well as my friend Fan Yuanxi sent me an edition of Tao Yuanming's collection printed by the magistrate of Yiyang. Moved by his love of antiquity and his learned elegance, I wrote this out for him. By Zeng Hong of Linhan, on the fifteenth day of the seventh month in the sixth year of the Xuanhe reign [1124].

In fact, there was no need for Zeng Hong to emend the characters *xing yao* to Xingtian; in some editions of *The Classic of Mountains and Seas*, Xingtian, which means "severed head," appears as Xingyao, which means "mutilated form."[85] Both are valid in relation to the story, in which the Heavenly Emperor (Yuan Ke thinks it is the Yellow Emperor) cut off the head of his competitor and buried it in Changyang Mountain. This competitor then used his nipples as his eyes and his navel as his mouth, brandishing his battle-ax and shield and dancing around. He is given the name Xingyao or Xingtian.[86]

The process of the birth of a variant is sometimes much more interesting than the variant itself. Zeng Hong's short appendix aroused much discussion among later scholars. As early as the Southern Song, Zhou Bida (1126–1204) had already argued that *xing yao* makes perfect sense in the context as referring to the youthful death of Nüwa, and his argument has since gained many supporters.[87] We do not know how Tao Yuanming's readers before Zeng Hong understood the second couplet, but ever since he raised the Xingtian suggestion, this headless god has become an integral part of this poem. In the early twentieth century, Lu Xun (1881–1936), who is considered the father of modern Chinese literature, in a cantankerous essay attacking a contemporary scholar and writer, Shi Zhecun (1905–2003), and giving a by-the-way lengthy discussion on modern anthologies of classical literature, singled out the first two couplets of this poem (with Zeng Hong's emended line) as an indication of the often-neglected "fierce side" of Tao Yuanming. Lu Xun's point is that some anthologies, in order to present a more unified image of Tao Yuanming as an easygoing recluse, tend to leave out those pieces that conflict with such an image. In another essay written around the same time, Lu Xun said of Tao Yuanming, "Exactly because Tao Qian was not all 'serenity,' he was a great poet."[88] Lu Xun became a literary icon in the socialist regime, and his remarks were cited frequently by twentieth-century Tao Yuanming scholars—especially mainland scholars influenced by Marxism—as proof that Tao Yuanming had the soul of a brave soldier. Xingtian was regarded as a member of the oppressed class, who rose up against his oppressor (always vaguely referred to as the Heavenly Emperor instead of the Yellow Emperor) and fought on despite a severed head. There is, however, no need at all to bring Xingtian into this poem. Zhou Bida was right in saying that the poem makes perfect sense even if we stick to the heroine Nüwa.

The real interpretative problem lies in the third couplet. Partially depending upon whether one takes *xing yao* as the name of the headless god or as a noun-verb phrase, the third couplet of the poem can be interpreted in several ways.[89] I choose to understand *tong wu* as "being one with the things of the world," which refers to the young girl's metamorphosis into a bird. A similar usage of *tong* can be found in the third of Tao Yuanming's "Bearers' Songs": "Entrusting my body to the mountains and being one with them" (Tuo ti tong shan e). The first line thus means that once she became a "thing" or a creature of nature (*wu*), there would be no more human cares. The final couplet of the poem says that despite Jingwei's resolve to take revenge, "the fine morning"—or the time when she can fulfill her desire—will never come. The reason for such a reading is simple: it is the least contrived, and it is not colored with political ideologies, whether loyalist sentiments or a proletarian rebellion.

Many scholars and critics have sided with Lu Xun and regarded this poem as showing tough-mindedness, an admiration for strong willpower, on the part of the poet Tao Yuanming. It is true that both Kuafu and Jingwei are heroes of will, but one should not forget to read the poems in a larger context; they are part of a prolonged contemplation on death and immortality, transformation, and what endures after transformation. They also represent the transitional phase in the overall structure of the poetic series. Kuafu and Jingwei are not immortals like the Queen Mother of the West; they not only die but die with unsatisfied desires. From the happy birds singing on the branches around the poet's house to the three Blue Birds transporting food for the Queen Mother to Jingwei, a pretty little bird with a colorful head, white beak, and red claws, we witness a gradual increase of discontent. In the next poem, we will come to some truly vicious and monstrous birds:

巨猾/危肆威暴	*The great* crafty one / Wei *indulged in violence;*
欽鵶違帝旨	*Qinpi disobeyed the Emperor's command.*
窫窳強能變	*Yayu was powerful enough to metamorphose,*
祖江遂獨死	*but Zujiang fell victim and died alone.*[90]
明明上天鑒	*Clear and bright is Heaven's mirror:*
為惡不可履	*one should not do evil deeds.*
長枯固已劇	*Eternal withering is harsh enough;*[91]
鵔鶚豈足恃	*how can one depend upon being transformed into birds?*

Metamorphoses continue in this poem. The poem describes the sad fate of the victims: after being murdered, the stronger one lost its only human characteristic ("a human face") and was transformed into a sinister creature that eats people; the other was simply dead. Though the bad are punished, there is no remedy for what they have done. And despite their execution, the murderers—Gu and Qinpi—have also turned into birds, just like their victim, and just like Jingwei. This makes the poem more complicated than a simply didactic poem about divine punishment for evildoers.

By now, of the immortal land of dazzling light in the first part of the poetic series, there is only the "clear and bright" mirror of Heaven left.

The next poem revolves around more images of birds:

鴟鴸見城邑	*When the* zhu *bird is seen in a city,*
其國有放士	*there will be a gentleman banished from the land.*[92]
念彼/昔懷王/玉世/母	*I think* during King Huai's reign / at the time of cherishing the jade,
亦得數來止	*it must have appeared several times.*
青丘有奇鳥	*There is a marvelous bird at Blue Hill,*[93]
自言獨見爾	*who says that it alone can see.*

本為迷者生	*It is born to help those who are lost,*
不以喻君子	*not to enlighten the princely man.*

The bad association with the appearance of evil birds in the preceding poem has led to a reflection on another kind of inauspicious bird, the *zhu* bird, whose appearance in a place foretells the banishment of worthy gentlemen. It seems to have provoked the poet to think of King Huai of Chu (r. 328–299 B.C.E.) and the minister he banished, the poet Qu Yuan, although, as Hightower says, "It is interesting to see how precarious a hold King Huai and Ch'ü Yuan have in the poem," as the third line is filled with variants.[94]

Indeed, if we choose to read *huai yu* (cherishing the jade), this line could very well refer to the story about He's Jade. A man named Bian He discovered a precious jade in the rough and presented it to the King of Chu, but the jade expert claimed it was no more than a common stone. The king had Bian He's left foot cut off as a punishment. When the next king succeeded to the throne, Bian He again presented the jade in the rough, and again was accused of deceiving the king, who had his right foot cut off. When the next king succeeded to the throne, Bian He took his jade in his arms and wept for three days and three nights. The king heard of this and sent an envoy to ask him why he cried so bitterly. He answered that it was not because of his mutilated body, but because an honest man was mistaken for a swindler, and a beautiful jade was mistaken for a stone. The king had his jade expert work on the jade in the rough, and he found the gem within.[95]

Bian He's story has henceforth become the standard allusion to a talented and upright person whose true worth, symbolized by the precious jade, is unrecognized by his ruler and the world at large. If we read *huai yu*, the "banished gentleman" in the second line of the poem would then be a reference to Bian He, who had been driven away from the king's court "several times." The variant reading of the sixth line, "who says that it alone can see the texture of the jade" (zi yan du jian li 自言獨見理), would also make much more sense in such a context: *li* is the very verb used for working on the jade in the rough; as a noun, it also means the texture of jade. The bird of Blue Hill could recognize the jade in the rough, and would have been able to prevent the dismissal of Bian He if its cries had been heard by the Chu kings.

Yet another intriguing textual variant in the third line evokes the Queen Mother of the West. There is no story about the Queen Mother and the *zhu* bird in *The Classic of Mountains and Seas* or in any other source we have, and yet, since we know that the *Classic of Mountains and Seas* we have may not be the same as the one read by Tao Yuanming, we cannot help wondering whether there is something we have missed and will never recover. Variants are often born because people want to "make sense of" an otherwise incomprehensible text, as in the case of Zeng Hong and the Jingwei poem; but we must also bear in mind how much we do not know and will perhaps never know, and make our choices on the premise that we are aware they are but compromises.

One question remains: the bird of Blue Hill is supposed to be able to clarify a confused person's mind ("It is born to help those who are lost"), but how can one listen to its call if he is already confused? Warnings may go unheard, and bad omens abound. The series "On Reading *The Classic of Mountains and Seas*" ends on a forlorn note. In the last poem, we are brought back to the theme of food and drink—or the lack of it:

巖巖顯朝市	*Tall and stern, the minister illuminates the court and market:*
帝者慎用才	*a ruler must be ever cautious in making an appointment.*
何以廢共鯀	*Why were Gong and Gun destroyed?*
重華為之來	*It was Chonghua who had it so.*[96]
仲父獻誠言	*His godfather offered him sincere words,*
姜公乃見猜	*but Duke Jiang showed distrust;*[97]
臨沒告飢渴	*on his deathbed the duke complained of hunger and thirst—*
當復何及哉	*that, alas, was too late!*

The last poem opens with an allusion to a *Shi jing* poem:

> Lofty is South Mountain:
> its rocks piled up high.
> Luminous is our minister,
> all people are looking up to you.[98]

This *Shi jing* piece is a satire of the minister who has failed in his duty. Jobs badly done lead to punishment, but if the ruler had exercised more caution in making appointments, then he would have been spared much grief. That the focus of Tao Yuanming's poem is on the judgment of the ruler instead of on the failure of the minister is clear when we come to the third and fourth couplets, which make a reference to Duke Huan of Qi.

The Classic of Mountains and Seas describes a creature of "human face and snake body, as big as a carriage wheel, and having two heads." It wears "purple clothes and a red hat." Its name is Yanwei. "If a human monarch captures and eats it, he will become a world leader."[99] Guo Pu's annotation of this paragraph states that this is the very creature once seen by Duke Huan of Qi (the "Duke Jiang" in Tao Yuanming's poem).[100] Guo Pu also refers the reader to a *Zhuangzi* story. In that story, Duke Huan went out hunting in a marsh, with Guan Zhong (ca. seventh century B.C.E.), the elderly minister he respectfully addressed as "Second Father" (rendered as "godfather"), as his driver. Then Duke Huan saw a phantom spirit. He grasped Guan Zhong's hand and asked him, "Did you just see that?" Guan Zhong said he saw nothing. Duke Huan returned from the hunting trip and fell ill. Finally a person called Huangzi Gao'ao stepped forward and told Duke Huan that no phantom spirit could hurt him if he did not hurt himself. But seeing that Duke Huan insisted on knowing whether spirits existed, Huangzi Gao'ao said to the duke that what he saw was in fact a creature called the Wei Snake, which was a good omen, for whoever got to see the Wei Snake would become a great leader. Upon hearing this, the duke's illness went away without his notice.[101] This *Zhuangzi* story, better than anything, exposes the psychological nature of the duke's illness and is an ironic comment on the duke's lack of wise judgment in disbelieving Guan Zhong's level-headed words and allowing a phantom to make him sick.

The story about Duke Huan and Guan Zhong unanimously cited by commentators in glossing this poem has one thing in common with the Wei Snake anecdote: Duke Huan chose not to listen to Guan Zhong. In this story, Duke Huan used his own favorites against Guan Zhong's deathbed counsel. Soon after, his favorites started a civil war, and Duke Huan was shut up in a palace room. A woman crept in through a hole in the wall to see him. The duke said, "I am hungry and want something to eat; I am thirsty and want something to drink. But I can get neither. What happened?" The woman told him. He sighed, saying that he would be too ashamed to see Guan Zhong. He then covered his face with his sleeves and died.[102]

The theme of food and drink thus returns in the series of poems on reading, but darkly, in the form of hunger and thirst. The cosmic journey that has led the poet to the splendid land of immortals finally takes him back into the human realm, and closes with the death of a human monarch, who was once a great leader among the lords, but made a bad mistake in his old age and fell to a pitiful end. The choice of the verb for death in the last couplet, *mo*, is also used for describing the sinking of the sun. In our poet's little country home surrounded by trees and birds, it must be getting dark as well.

The Map of Cultural Imagination & the Flaming Words

In a cosmic journey carried out in reading, places are marked by words. This imaginary, fantastic territory is just beyond the humble country home and garden where Tao Yuanming reads quietly and alone; and yet it is in that familiar domestic space, mundane but comfortable, limiting but secure, that our poet can begin his free and boundless voyage of the mind. Both Tao Yuanming and Xie Lingyun loved reading, and for both of them, reading was a way of comprehending and measuring the physical reality they lived in. Although Xie Lingyun has a reputation for having been a much more active traveler and explorer, Tao Yuanming was no less fascinated with "places." It is just that his places existed through reading, and on a cultural map.

"To Chief of Staff Yang" was presumably written in 417. Earlier that year, Liu Yu had defeated Qin, a northern dynasty, and temporarily recovered the ancient Han capital Chang'an. According to its short preface, the poem was presented to Chief of Staff Yang before he left for Chang'an as an emissary:

愚生三季後	*My ignorant self was born after the end of the Three Dynasties;*
慨然念黃虞	*much stirred, I long for the age of the great emperors.*
得知千載外	*To learn about what happened a thousand years ago,*
正賴古人書	*we can only rely on the books of the ancients.*
賢聖留餘跡	*Worthies and sages have left remaining traces—*
事事在中都	*everything they did, they did in the central capital.*
豈忘游心目	*Is it that I have neglected to let my heart and eyes roam?*
關河不可踰	*But passes and rivers are impossible to cross.*
九域甫已一	*As soon as the nine regions become one,*
逝將理舟輿	*I will surely prepare my boat and carriage.*
聞君當先邁	*But I heard you will go first—*
負痾不獲俱	*and I, being sick, cannot keep you company.*

The poem begins with impasses, both temporal and spatial: the poet was born too late for the age of the great kings, and he had been prevented from visiting the sites because of the division between north and south. Now that the land is united, he still cannot go because of his failing health. The only thing that connects him with the remote past and distant regions is reading—the books of the ancients. Instead of natural geography or the current political situation, the poet's concern is concentrated on the four recluses he has read about:

路若經商山	*If you pass by Shang Mountain,*[103]
為我少躊躇	*please linger there awhile for my sake;*
多謝綺與甪	*convey my regards to Qi and Lu,*
精爽今何如	*and see how their spirit is now.*
紫芝誰復採	*Who would again gather the purple mushrooms?*
深谷久/又應蕪	*The deep valley must have been* long / once more *deserted.*
駟馬無貰患	*Four-horse carriages cannot escape from trouble;*
貧賤有交娛	*the poor and humble have their own pleasures—*
清謠結心曲	*this clear song echoes in my inner being,*
人乖運見疏	*but we are of different ages, and our times are unlike.*
擁懷累代下	*Harboring feelings many generations later,*
言盡意不舒	*I exhaust my words, but my intention is not fully expressed.*

The poet asks his friend to linger for a while at Shang Mountain and inquire after the four recluses. The inquiry after their "spirit" leads to further quests for the recluses' "remaining traces," for only through "traces" (*ji*) can the spirit be revealed.

This echoes the earlier couplet:

賢聖留餘跡	*Worthies and sages have left remaining traces—*
事事在中都	*everything they did, they did in the central capital.*

It is useful to remember that *shi* (something that happens or is done), compared with *wu* (also meaning "thing"), emphasizes activity or acting. As Tang Yijie states, to distinguish between *wu* and *shi* means to distinguish between a trace (*ji*) and that which leaves a trace (*suoyi ji*) in the metaphysical discourse of the period.[104] In the above couplet, we could regard *shi* as a measure word, and so *shishi* means "each and every [remaining trace];"

but in the meantime, it is hard not to hear the echo of *shi* as "deed" (in contrast with the traces left by deeds). The deeds of the ancients are, of course, long gone, except for the traces which Guo Xiang, the famous commentator of *Zhuangzi*, contemptuously refers to as "things of the past" that are not worth admiring and holding onto.[105] For Guo Xiang, even "poetry and rites are old traces left by the former kings."[106] But for Tao Yuanming, traces are ever important in recognizing that which leaves traces: "To learn about what happened a thousand years ago, / we can only rely on the books of the ancients."

There is, however, not much left of the four recluses on Shang Mountain; as the purple mushrooms remain unpicked and the valley becomes overgrown, it seems that their traces are as much obliterated as their spirit, that which left traces. Thus the poet's request—to convey his regards to the recluses on Shang Mountain—is accompanied by a curious sense of emptiness: if the spirit of the four recluses, long dead, has dissipated and is nowhere to be found, then the mountain is equally vacant, deprived of the four men who once wandered on it. Shang Mountain is now nothing but a depleted husk, with its occupants—the spirit of the mountain—gone.

The only thing the poet can hold on to is a song—something handed down from "the books of the ancients": "The clear song echoes in my inner being." It is the song attributed to the Four White-heads of Shang Mountain:

> Hazy is the lofty mountain,
> its deep valleys twisting and turning.
> Bright and shiny are the purple mushrooms;
> they can cure a person of hunger.
> The age of the sage emperors is far;
> to whom can we return?
> A four-horse carriage with a high canopy—
> it brings with it great worry.
> Better than being rich and powerful and fearful of people,
> it is to be poor and humble and do what one pleases.[107]

The song is embedded in this couplet: "Four-horse carriages cannot escape from trouble; / the poor and humble have their own pleasures." But other than that, the distance between the Four White-heads and our poet is unbridgeable—not just the physical distance, but also the distance of time. Moreover, if in their song the four recluses were already lamenting over the remoteness of "the age of the sage emperors" ("The age of the sage emperors is far, / to whom can we return?"), then the poet's own longing for the Golden Age expressed at the very beginning of this poem is further undercut by his separation from the four recluses. Acutely feeling the double alienation, the poet closes the poem with a statement that proves exactly the opposite of the ending of the poem on partying under the cypress trees in the Zhou family cemetery: here the poet claims that although his words are finished, his "intent" is far from being exhausted.

Commentators, in discussing this poem, usually look to the hermit aspect of the Four White-heads. They tend to see Tao Yuanming's reference to the four recluses as a sign of his criticism of Liu Yu, the general who was to become the founding emperor of the Liu-Song. But there is something else about the four recluses that no commentator mentions: that they did come away from the mountain at the invitation of the Crown Prince (known posthumously as Emperor Hui, r. 195–188 B.C.E.), and that they were instrumental—unwittingly or not—in one prince's ascent to the throne and the other prince's murder.[108]

Tao Yuanming's contemporaries were not unaware of the inconsistency in the Four White-heads' behavior. About twenty years before Tao Yuanming wrote this poem, the Four White-heads of Shang Mountain had once been a topic of debate between none other than Huan Xuan—later the usurper of the Jin throne—and Yin Zhongkan (?–399), who was then governor of Jingzhou.[109] In the early 390s, Huan Xuan wrote a treatise, "On the Four White-heads" (Sihao lun), and sent it to Yin Zhongkan. In the treatise Huan Xuan criticizes the Four White-heads for coming out to serve the Crown Prince and his mother, Empress Lü. He argues that to take sides in partisan struggles is not a good way of preserving one's life and certainly does not befit a recluse. In his reply, Yin Zhongkan defends the Four White-heads by saying that Huan Xuan has failed to understand the intention of the benevolent men: their primary concern was not "the rise and fall of a single person" but the peace of the country. If a civil war should ensue from the power struggle between the Crown Prince and his younger brother, then it is the people who would suffer. In serving the Crown Prince and so stabilizing the throne, the four recluses secured peace for the country, by which they also secured peace for themselves. If Yin Zhongkan's view were to be further elaborated, we might say that for a benevolent man, the rise and fall of a dynasty is likewise less important than the peace and prosperity of a country.

Nowhere is the power of "the books of the ancients" more manifest than in this poem, "Composed and Presented to My Cousin Jingyuan in the Twelfth Month of the *Guimao* Year [403]":

寢跡衡門下	*Hiding my traces behind the rustic door,*
邈與世相絕	*I sever my ties with the remote world.*
顧盼莫誰知	*I look around, but no one knows:*
荊扉晝常閉	*my brushwood gate often remains closed during the day.*
淒淒歲暮風	*Chilly is the wind at the year's end;*
翳翳經日/夕雪	*concealing everything, the snow falls all* day / night.
傾耳無希聲	*I strain my ears to listen: there is not even the most attenuated sound;*[110]
在目皓/浩已結/潔	*but there before my eyes—an expanse of* congealed / pure *white.*
勁氣侵襟袖	*The sharp air invades my sleeves and lapels,*
簞瓢謝屢設	*dishes and pots decline my frequent calls.*
蕭索空宇中	*Lonely and desolate, in this empty house—*
了無一可悅	*not a single thing pleases me.*
歷覽千載書	*Reading through the books of a thousand years,*
時時見遺烈	*time and again, I see blazing deeds.*
高操非所攀	*Those noble standards I do not aspire to reach;*
謬/深得固窮節	by some cosmic error, *I have accomplished "firmness in adversity."*[111] / to a high degree *I have accomplished "firmness in adversity."*
平津苟不由	*If the good ford cannot be followed,*
栖遲詎為拙	*then who could call this hermit life "clumsy"?*[112]
寄意一言外	*I lodge my intent beyond these words—*
茲契誰能別	*the understanding between us, who could discern?*

The image of a recluse surrounded by snow would remind any contemporary reader of the famous story of Yuan An (?–92), whom Tao Yuanming praises in the fifth of his poetic series "On Impoverished Gentlemen."[113] Even the opening couplets of the two poems bear a similarity, as in both cases Tao Yuanming uses the word *miao* (remotely), and there is mention of the gate:

袁安門積雪	*By Yuan An's gate, snow piled up high;*
邈然不可干	*remaining aloof, he could not be disturbed.*[114]

A wonderful touch is added to the beginning couplet of this poem, when we associate the poet's "concealment of traces" (*qin ji*) with the fall of the snow, which covers everything up:

> Chilly is the wind at the year's end;
> concealing everything, the snow falls all *day / night.*
> I strain my ears to listen: there is not even the most attenuated sound;
> but there before my eyes—an expanse of *congealed / pure* white.

This is the snow scene seen by a person who keeps his door shut all day—never hearing a thing in his room; when he chances to go out, he is stunned by a world cloaked in white.

Although he tries to keep inside, there is this unwelcome visitor: the "sharp air" that "invades" his sleeves and lapels—openings in his clothes.

"Dishes and pots" are not entirely empty, but they do not have enough either, which is why they decline being "frequently" taken out to be put on a table. This phrase, *dan piao*, is reminiscent of the *Analects* passage, "With one basket of food and one ladle of water in a shabby lane, others could hardly bear the sorrows brought by such hardship, but Hui never lost his joy."[115] The poet, however, is not like Yan Hui, as he confesses to his cousin:

> Lonely and desolate, in this empty house—
> not a single thing pleases me.

"Empty house" reminds us of the *xushi*—"empty chambers"—in the "Return" series, but the tone is drastically different. What changes the tone is the cold brought by snow and hunger, and when the house is empty of furnishings, it feels even colder.

The poet is nevertheless capable of humor; in the last couplets, he claims that he has achieved "firmness in adversity," the virtue of a gentleman, by mistake. Interestingly, there is a variant for this phrase; the 1192 edition has *shen de guqiong jie* ("I have to a high degree accomplished 'firmness in adversity'"), which is followed by many subsequent editions. Modern editors often choose *miu de guqiong jie* ("by some cosmic error, I have accomplished 'firmness in adversity'") because they believe it is a humble expression. It may be, but it is also a darkly humorous one. It is explained by the next couplet, "If the good ford cannot be followed, / then who could call this hermit life 'clumsy'?" That is, the poet feels that he has been compelled to "hold firm in adversity" by circumstances. If the world were less chaotic, he would certainly come out and serve; but given the current political situation (Huan Xuan had just claimed the throne in the eleventh month of the same year, and civil war was tearing apart the country), to be a hermit would seem the best choice.

The snow has been falling for a whole day, and it is getting dark. In this cold darkness, the remaining comfort is, again, the books of the ancients:

> Reading through the books of a thousand years,
> time and again, I see blazing deeds.

The original meaning of *lie* in the last phrase of the second line (*yi lie*) is "the fierce burning of a fire"; its derived meaning is "light," "brilliance," and "prominence," from which derives yet another meaning: "feats" and "accomplishments." I have taken some liberty in translating *yi lie* as "blazing deeds," but I believe it is a proper translation. When the pleasant summer reading environment is transformed into winter snow, when there are no spring wine and fresh greens to fill the pots and dishes, it turns out that blazing words recording blazing deeds are the only flames to light up the darkness of a thousand years and bring warmth to the cold house.

5 Becoming A Vessel

And, strange to tell, among that Earthen Lot
Some could articulate, while others not:
And suddenly one more impatient cried—
"Who is the Potter, pray, and who the Pot?"

Then said another—"Surely not in vain
My Substance from the common Earth was ta'en.
That He who subtly wrought me into Shape
Should stamp me back to common Earth again."

—Omar Khayyám

Despite the efforts of some scholars to portray Tao Yuanming as a person deeply at odds with the world he lived in, in many ways, Tao Yuanming was very much a product of his age, an age that was dominated intellectually by "arcane learning" (*xuanxue*). *Xuanxue*, a strain of Daoist thought, was relentlessly attacked by Confucian moralists throughout imperial China, for it was seen as responsible for the collapse of the Western Jin under the invasion of the northern non-Chinese people. This is better evidence of the vanity of Confucian moralists regarding their own political importance than sound historical analysis. Nor was *xuanxue* a monolithic entity, unchanged in the two hundred years of the third and fourth centuries. Beginning with He Yan and Wang Bi, the two scholars living in the first half of the third century who annotated *Laozi* and *Zhuangzi*, respectively, *xuanxue* had developed and transformed in the hands of the Seven Worthies of the Bamboo Grove, most notably Xiang Xiu (227?–280), Xi Kang, Ruan Ji, and then Pei Wei (263–300) and Guo Xiang. We should keep in mind that these *xuanxue* figures were familiar with the Confucian classics, in particular *The Analects*, and both He Yan and Wang Bi had also written annotations of

The Analects in addition to their metaphysical works. Guo Xiang was instrumental in bringing together the two concepts—the Doctrine of Names (Ming Jiao), that is, Confucianism, and naturalness or be-of-itself-ness (*ziran*)—and reconciling them; the new concept he expounded was *neisheng waiwang* (a sage within and a king without). In other words, the "genuine being" praised by Zhuangzi does not, in Guo Xiang's view, have to exist in any transcendental realm; an emperor who resides in a palace and rules a kingdom may easily be the Perfect Man; the Doctrine of Names and the "arcane learning" of the Lao-Zhuang philosophers are not necessarily in conflict. While Guo Xiang raised the status of Confucius to an even higher plane than Zhuangzi himself, he was, in fact, explaining Confucian thought in such a way as to suit his own purposes. His theory derived from the *Zhuangzi* but also represented a transformation of the *Zhuangzi*, and was something distinctly Guo Xiang's own.[1] Guo Xiang's theory, embodied in his commentary on the *Zhuangzi*, gained immense influence in the Eastern Jin. It was against such an active but mixed intellectual background that Tao Yuanming lived and wrote.

Tao Yuanming, as we said before, was primarily a poet, not a philosopher or thinker. While we can clearly discern contemporary philosophical issues in his poetry, it may be more productive to approach his poetry as poetry rather than as philosophical discourse, which it is not and never aspired to be. Tao Yuanming's poems nevertheless return time and again to certain images, certain obsessions; it is in these images and obsessions that his deepest concerns are revealed, concerns that resonate with the concerns of an age.

In ancient Chinese philosophical texts, the vessel (*qi*) is a prominent image. The power of creation is often referred to as the Great Pottery Wheel (Da Jun, Hong Jun, or simply Tao Jun), which is eternally turning and making useful vessels out of common earth. A statement from *The Classic of Changes* best reveals the secondary nature of a "vessel": "What precedes physical form is called the Way; what ensues from physical form is called the vessel [i.e., the thing of the phenomenal world]."[2] In Laozi's philosophical discourse, the "vessel" is the product of the corrupted world, for the Way is undifferentiated and unnamed, an "uncarved block," and "when the uncarved block shatters it becomes vessels."[3] It is when the Way takes leave of "nothingness" and enters the realm of "existence" that the shapes of vessels are formed and that the vessels obtain their names—hence Confucianism, which deals with the social world, is called "the Doctrine of Names." In *The Analects*, however, Confucius once said, "A gentleman is not a vessel."[4] In other words, a gentleman should not be capable of fulfilling only one particular function, but should be, so to speak, a "comprehensive talent" (*tong cai*).

Confucius could not, however, avoid using "vessel" as a metaphor to refer to those who are "useful." In another passage of *The Analects*, the disciple Zigong asked the Master what he thought of him. Confucius said, "You are a vessel." Dissatisfied, Zigong continued questioning, "But what sort of a vessel?" Confucius said, "A sacrificial vessel, adorned with precious jade."[5] As James Legge (1815–1897) notes, while the master did not grant to Zigong that he was a gentleman (*junzi*), "he made him 'a vessel of honor,' valuable and fit for use on high occasions"—in fact, one of the highest.[6]

From Zigong's question, we realize that vessels are hierarchically divided, and sometimes the simplest way of evaluating a vessel is to look at its capacity for containing things. Just as "use" (*yong*) may be large or small, so are vessels. Once in *The Analects* Confucius refers to Guan Zhong, the minister of Duke Huan of Qi, as "a small vessel."[7] When it comes to contemporary ministers, Confucius is even more contemptuous: "Pooh! They are mere peck-measure men—not worth being taken into account."[8] In other words, they are "small vessels."

Vessels are made for practical use as containers. In this particular function, the image of the vessel acquires a symbolic significance: a vessel is the product of the physical, phenomenal world of being (*you*), but in order for the vessel to properly serve the need, it has to keep an empty space inside—a space of "non-being" (*wu* or *kong*). As Laozi says in *Dao de jing*, "When you knead clay to make a vessel, the nothingness within enables you to have the use of the vessel."[9] The paradoxical use of nothingness or uselessness is an important concept in *Zhuangzi* as well, and it is demonstrated in several ways. On one hand, "uselessness" is important in preserving life. The huge serrated oak, ignored by the carpenter because its timber is good for nothing ("Make a boat out of it and it'll sink; make a coffin out of it and it'll rot in no time; make a vessel out of it and it'll break soon"), lives a long life precisely because it is not one of those "useful" trees that are cut down in order to be used.[10] On the other hand, the "uselessness" of a big thing may also be due to the fact that people fail to perceive what such a big thing is good for. Huizi tells Zhuangzi that he has a gourd which is useless because it is too large: trying to make it into a water container, he finds it too heavy to be lifted up; trying to make it into a dipper, he finds it too clumsy to be wielded. Deciding it is a worthless thing, he smashes it to pieces. Zhuangzi replies that Huizi is simply "not very good at using large things." If he had had the gourd, he would have made it into a boat and taken a voyage in it on rivers and lakes.[11] In the end, Zhuangzi, just like Laozi, is keen on arguing that uselessness and usefulness are complementary and mutually dependent ("Only when a person knows about uselessness can you talk to him about usefulness") and the figure of a vessel, a container, is perfect for expounding the "usefulness of uselessness."[12] But if it is paramount for a vessel to have an empty space of nothingness to be of use and worth, then what if the vessel remains empty—with nothing to contain? Is this "uselessness" still considered "useful" in some way, or valuable at all?

The Shame of Emptiness

"Living at Leisure on the Ninth Day" (Jiuri xianju) is one of the greatest of Tao Yuanming's poems. Like many of his poems, it has a short preface narrating the occasion on which the poem was composed. This preface is a curious piece of prose:

余閒居, 愛重九之名.	*I live in leisure, and love the name of Double Ninth.*
秋菊盈園,	*Autumn chrysanthemum blossoms fill the garden,*
而持醪靡由/時醪靡至.	*and yet* there is no way to hold a cup of wine / the seasonal wine does not come.
空服九華,	*Eating the flowers of the ninth month just by themselves,*
寄懷于言.	*I lodge my feelings in these words.*

The Double Ninth, the ninth day of the ninth month, was a festival.[13] On this day, it was customary for people to take chrysanthemum wine as a way of promoting longevity.[14] His garden is filled with the autumn blossoms, but he has no wine, so Tao Yuanming is swallowing the flowers all by themselves (*kong fu jiu hua*, which could also mean "take the chrysanthemum blossoms in vain"). The word *kong* (lit., "empty") forms a contrast—a tension—with the word *ying* ("full"), the garden being *full* of flowers.

The opening sentence has a literary echo. Cao Pi once said in a letter, "The world all cherishes its name [i.e., the Double Ninth, the name of the festival, "nine," punning with "long-lasting," which is also *jiu*], for people think it is in line with 'permanence.'"[15] But this is not the first time that Tao Yuanming tells us of his fondness for a name. What seems a little odd is the logical connection between "living in leisure" and "loving the name of the Double Ninth." At first glance, these two clauses bear no relation to each other: the poet is living in leisure—*xian* referring to his retirement from office with plenty of free time on his hands, and implying a sense of peace and serenity—but what does it have to do with "my love of the name of the Double Ninth" indeed?

世短意恆多	*Our span is short, desires are many;*
斯人樂久生	*so mankind delights in living long.*
日月依辰至	*With star signs the day and month arrive,*
舉俗愛其名	*and all, by custom, love today's name.*
露淒暄風息	*The dews are cool, sultry winds cease,*
氣澈天象明	*the air is crisp, the heavens' bodies bright.*
往燕無遺影	*No shadows remain from departed swallows,*
來雁有餘聲	*but sounds aplenty from wild geese coming.*
酒能祛百慮	*Wine has the power to drive away cares;*
菊解制頹齡	*chrysanthemums curb declining years.*
如何蓬廬士	*How can a man in a cottage of thatch*
空視時運傾	*do nothing but watch seasons sink toward an end?*
塵爵恥虛罍	*My dusty cup shames the empty jar,*[16]
寒華徒自榮	*these cold-weather flowers blossom in vain.*
斂襟獨閑謠	*I pull my gown close, sing calmly alone,*
緬焉起深情	*then, lost in my musings, deep feelings rise.*
栖遲固多娛	*The quiet life indeed has many joys,*
淹留豈無成	*there is something achieved in just lingering on.*[17]

There is a quiet pathos in the first couplet: if our lifespan is short, then "living long" can only be relative; there is no way to satisfy the many desires in such a short lifespan, in any case. A variant line complicates the opening statement in a more pessimistic manner:

世短意恆多	*Our span is short, desires are many;*
斯人樂有生	*and yet mankind delights in life.*

The next couplet is almost an exact parallel with the preceding one in terms of sense, in that the second line opposes and is almost a defiant gesture towards the first:

日月依辰至　　*With star signs the day and month arrive,*
舉俗愛其名　　*and all, by custom, love today's name.*

The first line reveals the indifference of the cosmos to human activities: day and month arrive almost mechanically, and have nothing to do with what we are or are not partial to. And yet, everyone loves the name of the Double Ninth—a love born of self-love, the desire for "living long." What differentiates the poet from the crowd (*jusu*) is his awareness of the self-delusional nature of the fondness for a mere name; what distinguishes him is that despite his knowledge of the indifference of the universe, instead of becoming cynical and turning his back on it, he is still capable of joining the crowd in feeling fond of the manmade name.

The next couplet presents an autumn scene: the world is cooler, calmer, brighter, and more transparent. It is a season of few illusions. The going of the swallows and the coming of the wild geese form an ever-recurring cycle—unlike the world of men, nature is never depleted.

It is in autumn, after the sultry wind dies down, that a person sobers up, a hundred cares beset him, and he seeks to drown them in wine. "Wine has the power to drive away cares," but our poet is out of wine. In the next line, the positive statement that "chrysanthemums curb declining years" is changed by a variant into one that is more expressive of human wish and desire than of the actual state of things: "chrysanthemums *are for the sake of* [*wei* 為] curbing declining years." The verb "curb" (*zhi*) indicates how much strength is required in exercising control, and shows the power of what is being curbed. Indeed, what is striking in this and the next couplets is the image of collapse and breakdown: "*declining* [*tui*] years" and "seasons *sinking* [*qing*] to an end" both remind one of the crumbling of a mountain, an avalanche that is beyond human power to prevent. The chrysanthemum flowers seem to be terribly fragile in resisting such large-scale disintegration, and the question "How can a man in a cottage of thatch / do nothing but watch seasons sink toward an end?" takes on poignancy because it has no ready answer. The poet feels that he has disappointed the flowers; they are blossoming in vain (*tuzi rong*)—like the man who lives in leisure and does nothing but watch time pass by.

The poet draws our eye to himself now, as he pulls his gown close—unlike the "cold-weather flowers," the man feels chilly—and his singing is characterized again by the word *xian*: leisurely, peacefully, with much time on his hands. And we notice that he is not only alone but is self-conscious of his being alone. He is also the only person in this poem who is not paired off with somebody or something else: swallows are followed by wild geese; wine cup accompanied by wine jar; the flowers filling the garden have one another.

The conclusion sounds like a defense of himself against some imagined criticism—criticism of this leisurely life in retirement, this humming and chanting, sitting and watching, which seem to be a waste of time. He emphasizes that this quiet life "indeed" has many joys; and yet in case these small pleasures appear offensive to a serious person, he quickly adds the last line to affirm their value, although it is a curiously negative affirmation, framed by a rhetorical question, which literally reads: "How can one say that nothing is achieved in just lingering on?" What exactly is achieved, the poet does not say.

While in the world of nature chrysanthemum flowers replace the summer blossoms and the wild geese fill up the blank left by the departing swallows, a sense of emptiness dominates the poet's house as well as his state of mind. The wine jar is ashamed by the wine cup because, instead of providing it with wine, it has allowed dust to gather in the cup, which clearly indicates that it is not just on this particular day that the cup is out of wine, but that this emptiness has been going on for quite a while. The provision of wine is of course the responsibility of the master of the house: that the wine has run out for a long time can only mean that the master is not doing very well economically, which would be a direct consequence of his living a life in retirement. If the wine jar feels ashamed in front of the dusty cup, then how is the master of the house supposed to feel in front of his empty wine jar?

Laozi does say this: "The Way is empty; yet use it—for the longest time it is inexhaustible [*jiu bu ying*]."[18] And yet, the famous "leaning vessel" in the temple of Duke Huan of Lu, though overturning when filled to the brim, would slant towards one side when empty. It is only when the water level is just right that it stands upright.[19] The master of the house stoically pulls his robe around himself—a sign that no wine helps him dispel the chill—and declares that there is something accomplished after all in just "lingering on." But perhaps exactly because the ending of the poem is so rhetorical and argumentative, it loses some of its strength; the image that stands out in this poem is that of the wine vessel, feeling acutely the embarrassment of being empty inside, and useless.

A Completed Vessel & the Way of Flowers

In modern Chinese, one of the most common phrases a parent would use on a child who does not "make something of himself or herself" is *bu chengqi* (literally, "you are not turning into a vessel"). For someone who does not show much promise in his or her early years, one unfailing consolation is Laozi's saying "The great vessel is completed late" (*Da qi wan cheng*).[20] The anxiety to "become a vessel" (*chengqi*), and hence be "useful," is not unique to the Chinese culture, but the question is *what*, after all, is considered a *chengqi*, a completed vessel? Does *qi* have, so to speak, one shape and one form?

The Daoist philosophers certainly have an ambiguous attitude about "complete" (*cheng*). A finished vessel is the product of a corrupted world. "The potter says, 'I am good at throwing clay. The round ones fit the compass; the square ones fit the T square.' . . . To shatter the uncarved block and make vessels out of it, this is the crime of the craftsman; to destroy the Way and Attainment and make 'benevolence and righteousness' out of it, this is the fault of sages."[21]

In the second chapter of *Zhuangzi*, "A Discourse on All Things Being on the Same Level" (Qiwu lun), the philosopher uses the musician Zhaowen's playing of the zither to illustrate his viewpoint of "accomplishment" or "taking complete form" (*cheng*): "There *is* something taking complete form and attenuating—Zhao Wen playing on his zither. There is *nothing* taking complete form and attenuating—Zhao Wen *not* playing on his zither."[22] Guo Xiang elucidates the meaning of these two enigmatic sentences by saying that there exist innumerable sounds in the universe, and even those skilled in music playing would leave some sounds out: "Those who manifest sounds will end up leaving sounds out; those who do not manifest sounds will end up preserving sounds intact."[23] This, he states, is what is meant by "desiring to take complete form and yet attenuating it" and "taking no complete form and having no attenuation." The eminent modern scholar of ancient philosophy Feng Youlan (1895–1990), when explaining Guo Xiang, cites Tao Yuanming's well-known "zither without strings" as an example.[24]

Zhaowen's son continues his father's profession, but "to the end of his life he brought nothing to complete form" (*zhongshen wucheng*). It is almost as an afterthought that Zhuangzi muses thus:

> In a case like this, can we call it "reaching the complete form?" If so, even I [who have not reached complete form] may be said to have reached complete form. Or in a case like this, are we not able to call it "reaching complete form," for there is nothing that has reached complete form in things and myself?[25]

In Zhuangzi's view, only by staying incomplete can one avoid *kui*, "attenuation"—that is the true accomplishment. This is perhaps the only way in which we can understand what Tao Yuanming means by "there is something achieved in just lingering on." But the poet does not come to this conclusion easily; more often than not, we see him lament over the fact that he has not achieved anything in his life. In "The Blossoming Tree" (Rong mu), a poem about midlife crisis, the man looks at a tree in bloom and reflects on his career. The poem has a short preface:

榮木, 念將老也.	*"The Blossoming Tree" reflects on approaching old age.*
日月推遷,	*Days and months propel each other along,*
已復有夏.	*and it is high summer again.*
總角聞道,	*I heard of the Way when I was a young boy;*
白首無成.	*now I have white hairs on my head, and I have brought nothing to complete form.*

The opening sentence may be a surprise, for one does not spontaneously associate a blossoming tree with old age. It is only later that we discover that the blossoming tree is one whose flowers bloom in the morning and fade at evening. Gu Zhi thinks it is a *mujin*, a shrub althea or rose of Sharon.[26] "Hearing of the Way" (*wen dao*) comes from a remark by Confucius: "If one hears of the Way in the morning, it would be alright to die at evening."[27] On the basis that "hearing of the Way" is not an easy matter for an adult, not to mention for a young boy, Jiang Xun (1610–?) and Wen Runeng (1748–1811) believe the phrase *wen dao* is simply another way of referring to *zhi xue* (putting one's mind to studying), which comes from another passage of *The Analects.* In this passage Confucius relates the stages he went through in self-cultivation, beginning with the statement, "I put my mind to studying since the age of fifteen." In his preface, Tao Yuanming takes a step further than Confucius's motto: he implies that it is not enough for a man to hear of the Way; he has to achieve something.

Confucius's statement forms a contrast with the image of the rose of Sharon; its flowers bloom in the morning and wither at night, which is reminiscent of a man's hearing of the Way and passing away within the same day. The image of the flowering tree not only gives this poem a title but is also an invested symbolic presence, creating a tension-wrought space for the expression of the poet's thoughts:

采采榮木　　*Splendid is the blossoming tree,*
結根于茲　　*which takes root in this place.*
晨耀其華　　*In the morning it shows off its flowers,*
夕已喪之　　*toward dusk it already loses them.*
人生若寄　　*Human life is like a visit:*
憔悴有時　　*there comes a time for withering and fading.*
靜言孔念　　*I reflect on this, quietly but hard,*
中心悵而　　*and my heart feels sadness.*

It would be easy to compare the fast-fading flowers to fast-fading human life, and yet, the tree itself "takes root in this place." Human life, on the other hand, is merely *ji*, "a guest's stay."

采采榮木　　*Splendid is the blossoming tree,*
于茲托根　　*which takes root in this place.*
繁華朝起　　*Luxurious flowers come forth in the morning;*
慨暮不存　　*by evening nothing is left.*
貞脆由人　　*To be steadfast or fragile depends on the person,*
禍福無門　　*for good fortune or bad, there is no gate.*[28]
匪道曷依　　*What to be attached to, if not the Way?*
匪善奚敦　　*What to strive for, if not the good?*

"Steadfastness" (*zhen*) and "fragility" (*cui*) are words habitually descriptive of two different plants: the pine and the mushroom. The pine tree weathers the winter, while the mushroom dies in a short period of time.[29] Their lifespans are determined by their different natures. What is unique about human beings, however, is that they have free will: they can choose the quality of their lives—whether to remain steadfast or become fragile. And, unlike the blossoming tree, man's efforts could bear fruits, which would grant immortality to his name, if not to his physical body. Confucius said, "There are those who sprout but do not flower; there are those who flower but do not bear fruits."[30] This remark was almost certainly in Tao Yuanming's mind when he wrote this poem, for soon afterwards, he quotes another passage from the same section of *The Analects:*

嗟予小子	*Alas, as for me, a later-born,*
稟茲固陋	*I am endowed with an unpolished nature.*
徂年既流	*The passing years have flowed away,*
業不增舊	*and my accomplishments—they do not increase.*
志彼不舍	*Intent upon the fact of "not ceasing"*
安此日富	*and instead resting in "growing richer every day"*[31]—
我之懷矣	*ah, I have these feelings within,*
怛焉內疚	*filled with anxiety and guilt.*

In the fifth line, some modern editions have chosen *wang* 忘 (to forget), a suggested variant character in Tang Han's edition, instead of *zhi* 志 (to be intent upon). This is obviously an attempt to make this line consistent with the next, so that the couplet is taken to mean that the poet has forgotten about the unceasing passage of time and indulges himself in daily drinking. And yet, as Lu Qinli suggests, the poet is in fact intending an ironic contrast here: although always bearing in mind the fact of "not ceasing," yet, being weak, I indulge in drinking every day.[32] How to interpret "not ceasing" is another problem. While many agree it is an allusion, Tang Han believes it is an allusion to the *Xunzi* passage in the chapter "Exhortation of Learning" (Quanxue): "A great steed cannot exceed ten steps at one leap, but a poor nag covers a thousand miles in ten days, because it does not cease. If one carves something and leaves it aside, then even a rotten piece of wood cannot be broken; but if one keeps at it and does not cease, then even bronze and stone can be carved."[33] But since this poem is so rich in echoes of *The Analects*, particularly section nine, I think it is likely that "not ceasing" is instead a reference to the famous statement "Confucius said on the bank of a river: 'What has gone past us is just like this—it does not cease for day or night.'"[34] "Not ceasing" would then be a reference to time's flow. This also accounts for the usage of the verb "flow" in describing the passage of time in the third line.[35]

Hightower makes an insightful comment on this stanza: "He [the poet] may intend a further contrast with the flowering tree, for his is no rich endowment, and he should have worked hard to improve himself."[36] The point is that the poet has taken a further turn in the comparison of a human being to the flowering tree: although it is up to a person to choose steadfastness or fragility, he is still limited by natural endowments—not in the sense of moral quality, but in the sense of intellectual capacity. The poet admits that he is not born a "refined" type, and so, in order to excel, he has to increase his "achievements" (*ye*) and make them richer than before.

Moreover, a tree does not have to "work hard" to produce flowers or fruits, but a human being must. A tree is renewed every spring and a new burst of energy is expressed in its luxuriant flowering; but a man's life is different—a one-time thing, it is not renewable like a tree, and yet, in contrast with the fast-fading flowers that do not bear fruits, it is capable of accumulating capital, *ye*. It is perhaps not accidental that both Fu Yi (?–90 B.C.E.) and the Eastern Jin poet Zhang Hua (232–300), whose poems of "self-exhortation" are clearly Tao Yuanming's models, used the idea of farming in describing a person's accumulation of learning and good deeds, and later in this chapter we will see how Tao indeed calculates, measures, and takes stock like a farmer.[37]

That the poet feels that his moral or intellectual capital has not increased is ironically contrasted with a false sense of accumulation as a result of daily drinking and befuddled thinking.

先師遺訓	*The former teacher has left a lesson,*
余豈云墜	*how can I afford to neglect it?*
四十無聞	*"If at forty a man is unheard of by the world,*
斯不足畏	*then he is not worthy of awe."*[38]
脂我名車	*I shall grease my famed carriage,*
策我名驥	*and whip up my famed steed:*
千里雖遙	*even though a thousand miles is far indeed,*
孰敢不至	*how do I dare not reach my aim?*

Although the last stanza is generally understood as a sort of New Year's resolution, there are a few questions that remain. What does the poet mean by *famed* carriage and horses? Does that mean his capacities?[39] (In the *Xunzi* passage on exhortation of learning, the poor nag and the fast horse certainly refer to different inborn talents.) What, after all, is the point of his expected arrival in the last line? Thinking back to the preface of this poem, we might say that the poet is describing the pursuit of the Way he "heard of" when he was young, and that he has made the pursuit literal by mentioning his horse and carriage and giving an estimate of the distance (a thousand miles). And he has indeed come a long way from the blossoming tree, the poem's title; while the tree can afford to simply entrust itself to nature to accomplish its work, a human being must strive and seek to find.

Because of the poet's unambiguous reference to Confucius's teaching that a man who reaches forty and yet has not achieved anything is not worthy of much awe, commentators have naturally taken this poem to have been written before the poet reached that fatal age. Davis cautions readers not to take the last stanza too literally, for the poem seems to him "a product of a mood."[40] It might very well be, but then all poems are no more than "products of a mood." What we do notice about this poem is that it is quite incongruous with Tao Yuanming's poems on drinking, and that his conclusion from observing the fading flowers is exactly the opposite of carpe-diem poetry. But we know that, while the flowers bloom and fade within the same day, they are merely following their natural impulses (*ren zhen*); in that they do not make conscious efforts to "improve" themselves and do not harm their true nature, they seem to embody the Way itself. Who knows but perhaps these flowers die in the evening because they have already "heard of the Way."

Taking Stock

Tao Yuanming, like the rest of us, lives in a differentiated world. He is good at accumulating and taking stock in a true farmer's way, as in the following poem, the first poem of the series "Matching a Poem by Secretary Guo" (He Guo zhubu):

譪譪堂前/北林	*Dense is the grove* in front of / to the north of *my hall—*
中夏貯清陰	*in midsummer it stores cool shades.*
凱風因時來	*The gentle south wind comes with the season,*
回飆開我襟	*its whirling gusts blow open my robe.*
息交游閒業	*Breaking with social contacts, I enjoy leisure activities;*
臥起弄書琴	*lying around, or sitting up, I play with zither and books.*
園蔬有餘滋	*Of garden vegetables there is a surplus,*
舊穀猶儲今	*last year's grain is still in storage.*

營己良有極	*Providing for oneself does have a limit,*
過足非所欽	*more than enough is not my desire.*
舂/春秫作美酒	Crushing rice / Using spring rice *to brew some great ale,*
酒熟吾自斟	*I'll pour it myself when it is done.*
弱子戲我側/前	*My little child plays* by my side / in front of me,
學語未成音	*learning to talk, though not quite making the sounds right yet.*
此事真復樂	*This is something genuine and enjoyable,*
聊用忘華簪	*which helps me, for the moment, forget the official's cap.*
遙遙望白雲	*Gazing into the distance at the white clouds,*
懷古一何深	*how much do I yearn for ages past!*

This poem opens with the image of abundance and ends with that of yearning. The concept of storage appears from the very beginning: that the cool shade may be "stored" is a striking expression. We can imagine that as time passes by and high summer approaches, the leaves grow larger and thicker and seem to be saving up an increasing amount of shade. Then we move on to the garden greens, the grain, and the ale: there is not only "enough" of everything, there is in fact "more than enough," which is exactly what the poet declares that he does not desire. Even the poet himself has a duplicate image—his son, playing beside him and emulating his speech (*xue yu*). It is indeed a picture of almost perfect contentment. Reading and playing his zither in this environment, the poet claims that he is enjoying *xianye*, literally, "a leisurely vocation." *You*, "to enjoy or roam in," reminds one of the *Analects* passage: "Confucius said, 'One should set one's mind upon pursuing the Way, rely on attainment in the Good, feel attached to Benevolence, and enjoy the arts.'"[41] By "arts" we believe he means the Six Arts: rites, music, archery, charioteering, writing, and arithmetic. We can see how Tao Yuanming's "zither and books" easily fit here. However, when Confucius uses the word *you* (to roam), there is a sense of enjoyment and recreation implied—certainly not of the same seriousness as, for instance, the pursuit of the Way—and to refer to "zither and books" as *ye*, a vocation, is not common.

When there is *ye*, we know there is accretion and amassing (*ye* is both "amassing" and "what is amassed"); and when there is accretion and amassing, there will also be a day when the *ye* is considered *cheng*, "maturing into ripeness," "accomplished." In this poem, we see much accumulated and much accomplished, including the ale; the only thing "unachieved" (*wei cheng*) is the child, who is still small and literally "weak" (*ruo*), and is trying to learn how to talk. But *wei cheng* literally means "not accomplished yet," which points to the future, when the child will have mastered all his pronunciations and will make perfect sounds.

Then comes the following couplet:

> This is something genuine and enjoyable,[42]
> which helps me, for the moment, forget the official's cap.

Declaring one has forgotten something is another way of asserting its existence. Besides the self-sufficient world of the poet, we are suddenly presented with a different world—the world of politics, fame, and power—with its different set of values. It is a jarring note. And yet, the poem could have stopped here without further ado; it would still have been perfect, affirming the precious worth of the recluse's chosen life. But the poet goes on:

> Gazing into the distance at the white clouds,
> how much do I yearn for ages past!

Gu Zhi is right in pointing out that the last couplet is an allusion to the *Zhuangzi* passage. Commentators usually only cite the relevant sentences, without quoting the whole story—which, however, forms a basis for a proper understanding of the ending of this poem:

> Yao visited Hua. The border guard of Hua said, "Ah—here comes a sage. Please allow me to offer prayers for the sage. I wish the sage a long life."
>
> Yao said, "No, thanks."
>
> "I wish the sage riches."
>
> Yao said, "No, thanks."
>
> "I wish the sage many sons."
>
> Yao said, "No, thanks."
>
> The border guard said, "A long life, riches, and many sons, these are what people all want. You alone don't want them. Why?"

Yao said, "Many sons mean many worries. Riches mean many troubles. A long life means many shames. These three things are not what nourish virtue, which is why I reject them."

The guard said, "At first I thought you were a sage, but now you turn out to be a mere gentleman. Heaven gives birth to myriad people and it surely will give them jobs. If the many sons all have jobs, what is there for you to worry about? If you have riches, then you share them with others—what trouble can there be? As for a sage, he lives like a quail [which stays in the wilderness and does not have a constant home]; he eats like a fledgling [depending on its mother to feed it whatever she finds]; he travels like a bird that does not leave a trace. When the world has the Way, he prospers with it; when the world is without the Way, he cultivates his virtue and lives in leisure. After a thousand years, when he is tired of the world, he leaves it behind and becomes an immortal. Riding the white clouds, he arrives at the dwelling place of gods. The three worries you mentioned do not touch him, and his life is unharmed—how can there be any shame?"

The border guard then left Yao. Yao followed him, saying, "May I ask . . ."

The guard said, "Go away!"[43]

Many things in Tao Yuanming's poem echo this story: his affluence, his life in leisure (*xian*), and his progeny, which reflect the wishes of the border guard for a sage. But there is one thing that profoundly differentiates our poet from the true sage: when he gazes at the distant white clouds, he knows it is impossible for him to ride them towards the dwelling place of the gods. In "Return" the poet says, "Riches and power are not my desires, and the dwelling place of the gods cannot be expected." The two lines contain two different statements, which are often mistakenly confused as being on the same level: he does not desire "riches and power," but he does desire the dwelling place of the gods—which is, however, unobtainable. The sentiment is similar in the poem presented to Secretary Guo: when the poet looks towards the white clouds, what stirs in his heart is a deep longing for the transcendent realm of the immortals that is tightly interwoven with a craving for a temporal dimension equally out of reach. The poem about taking stock and recounting "riches" and self-sufficiency in a domestic space surrounded by plentiful cool shade in midsummer and backed up with abundant material provisions and containing the seeds of the family's future is complicated by a final note of pining and discontent.

The Sadness of the Purple Mallows

With the singular exception of Wang Fuzhi, the seventeenth-century critic, commentators have long tried to ruin one of the best poems of Tao Yuanming, the one simply entitled "Matching the Poem of Clerk Hu, and to Be Shown to Sheriff Gu" (He Hu xicao shi Gu zeicao). Some afflict it with tortuous political interpretations and absurd allegorical readings; some dismiss it as "flat and bland," supporting this judgment with the clumsy evidence that "many anthologies neglect to include it." Wang Fuzhi alone accords it the highest praise, although, like many Chinese commentators, he never gives his statement a full explanation: "It is vast and expansive, profound and dense. Those who emulate Tao Yuanming—how could they ever see its boundaries?"[44] It is indeed all that, but first of all, it is a poem about emptiness and lacking—the eternal want of fullness and completion (*cheng*):

蕤賓五月中	*In the fifth month, with warmth returning,*
清朝起南颸	*a south wind rises on one clear morning:*
不駛亦不遲	*neither too vigorous nor too weak,*
飄飄吹我衣	*it gently blows my robe about.*
重雲蔽白日	*Layered clouds conceal the white sun,*
閒雨紛微微	*drizzly and misty falls a leisurely rain.*
流目視西園	*My roving eye turns toward the western garden—*
曄曄榮紫葵	*there glow the purple mallows in full radiance.*
于今甚可愛	*They are indeed so lovely now,*
奈何當復衰	*but soon enough they will fade again.*
感物願及時	*Touched by things, I wish to catch my time,*
每恨靡所揮	*yet I always regret there is never a drop in the cup.*
悠悠待秋稼	*Slowly I await the autumn harvest, still far away;*
寥落將賒遲	*by then things will fall and wither, and it will be too late.*
逸想不可淹	*These racing thoughts cannot be checked,*
猖狂獨長悲	*wildly, alone, this vast sadness continues.*

The poem has a promising opening, but the south wind on this fine morning in the fifth month will eventually turn out to be the only "just right" thing in the poem, although in praising it, the poet has to use two negations—"neither too vigorous nor too weak." The rise of the south wind marks an upbeat mood for this fine day in a lovely season, but then everything diminishes and declines from the initial moment of perfection.

> Layered clouds conceal the white sun,
> drizzly and misty falls a leisurely rain.

The pleasure of the south wind is replaced by a rain shower, and the clear morning soon darkened by clouds. The fine scene never stays long, and this is only the first disappointment.

> My roving eye turns toward the western garden—
> there glow the purple mallows in full radiance.

This would be another upbeat move: although human beings may feel constrained by the rain, the world of nature welcomes it and is enjoying it. The glow of the purple mallows—an important vegetable for the Chinese people from early antiquity to the middle period—reminds one of the foodstuff of the Four White-heads. In their song, they use the same phrase, *yeye* (shining), to describe the magic "purple mushrooms."

And yet, while nature is rejoicing in the present, almost out of perversity the poet thinks of the future, and the poem is given another turn:

> They are indeed so lovely now,
> but soon enough they will fade again.

It is not just the "fading" but "fading *again*" that catches our attention: the cycle of nature always repeats itself, but that luxury is not for humankind. It is perhaps for this reason that the poet wants to enjoy life while he can, but again he is prevented from doing so:

> Touched by things, I wish to catch my time,
> yet I always regret there is never a drop in the cup.

Literally, the second line reads "I always regret there is nothing I can toss from my cup." The verb *hui*, "to toss away," refers to shaking out residue liquid, including dregs in the ale. The poet is saying that his drinking vessel is perpetually empty, perhaps filled with dust.

As Hightower notes, "Of its five other occurrences in Tao Yuanming's poems, the word *hui* is combined with a word for wine cup in four of them."[45] Gu Zhi may be the only one who argues that here *hui* should be glossed as *fen*, "to strive." That the irrevocable passage of time provokes the poet not to the determination to strive, as in the piece on the blossoming tree, but to the decision to make merry and enjoy life is evidenced by the next couplet:

> Slowly I await the autumn harvest, still far away:
> by then things will wither and fall, and it will be too late.

The reason the poet has to wait for the autumn harvest is that by then he will have the grain to make new ale. This, in the dismaying, downward motion of the preceding couplet lamenting the lack of ale, seems to be holding out some hope, which is, however, soon shattered: autumn is still far away, and, more importantly, autumn is the season of withering and falling—the mallows will be gone, and the pleasant early summer scene will be nowhere to be found. The human world is imperfect, and will remain so always:

> These racing thoughts cannot be checked,
> wildly, alone, this vast sadness continues.

In a poem about the limitations and restrictions of the human world, the poet finally emphasizes another impossibility: that of stopping desires and dreams, no matter how wild they are.

We remember that this poem was written in reply to Clerk Hu and to be shown to Sheriff Gu—there are two people in the poem's title, and yet the poet claims he dwells in this vast sadness "alone." Though we know nothing about those two people now, they were alive and real for the poet. Their silent presence adds to the sense of poignancy.

Coda

Tao Yuanming perhaps was the first poet to consider "writing" as a sort of vocation (*ye*), although this comes only from a variant reading. The sixth poem in the series "On Impoverished Gentlemen" sings of one of his favorite recluses, Zhang Zhongwei, with whom the poet seems to most perfectly identify himself:

仲蔚爱窮居	*Zhongwei loved living in isolation,*
繞宅生蒿蓬	*all around his house grew wild weeds.*
翳然絕交游	*Hiding away, he cut off his social ties,*
賦詩頗能工	*and was skilled in writing poetry.*
舉世無知者	*There was nobody who knew him,*
止有一劉龔	*except one—that Liu Gong.*
此士胡獨然	*How could this gentleman act this way?*
實由罕所同	*—indeed few things he could share with others.*
介焉安其業	*He was aloof and felt content in his vocation,*
所樂非窮通	*his delights lying not in good fortunes or bad.*[46]
人事固已拙	*As I am clumsy in human affairs,*
聊得長相從	*I would like to just follow him, always.*

Zhang Zhongwei, the Eastern Han recluse who "was good at composition and fond of poetry and poetic expositions," is quite different from the other "impoverished gentlemen" praised in this poetic series; while the others either accepted poverty with a stoic resignation or avoided riches obtained through unrighteous means, Zhang Zhongwei actively embraced this lonely life because he "loved" the isolation and because he took pleasure in things other than riches and power. Although the poet never explicitly says so, it appears that what Zhang Zhongwei delighted in, as well as the "vocation" in which he was content, was composing poetry. Tao Yuanming refers to Zhang's writing of poetry as "skilled" (*gong*)—a term implying conscious craftsmanship, polishing, and refinement, which figure prominently in later poetics.

It is interesting, therefore, to note that there is a variant line for "He was aloof and felt content in his vocation," which reads, "Forsaking the roots, he pursued the branches" (*Qi ben an qi mo* 棄本案其末). It is easy to see that the third and fourth characters, *an qi* 案其, are homophonous with *an qi* 安其, but otherwise these two lines have little in common; in fact, they indicate two very different value judgments. "Roots" and "branches" are a figurative way of saying the essential and the superfluous; in Confucian discourse, moral cultivation and a political career are the "basics," while the arts—what Confucius says a person should do with a sense of leisure and ease—are nonfundamental.

Zhang Zhongwei's indulgence in writing poetry in isolation, surrounded by weeds and bushes, would certainly be regarded as pursuing the inessential by a Confucian, but we can also understand it as tongue-in-cheek irony, a judgment handed out according to the "common" standard but not necessarily reflecting Tao Yuanming's own true opinions. In other words, Tao may accept that what Zhang Zhongwei worked on was mere "inessentials," but he thought of it as admirable because, after all, he found contentment in what he was doing and was not swayed by exterior circumstances. As he himself is "clumsy" in human affairs, he wishes to follow in Zhang Zhongwei's footsteps.

But the poet is not so fortunate:

少年罕人事	*In my early youth, I engaged in few human affairs;*
游好在六經	*my pleasures lay in the Six Classics.*
行行向不惑	*Gradually, I am marching towards forty;*
淹留遂無成	*lingering on without achieving anything.*
竟抱固窮節	*I ended up embracing the principle of "firmness in adversity,"*
飢寒飽所更	*and ate my full of hunger and cold.*
敝廬交悲風	*Desolate winds blow at this wretched house,*
荒草沒前庭	*weeds grow wild and conceal the front yard.*
被褐守長夜	*Tossing a piece of coarse clothing over my shoulders, I sit the long night out;*
晨雞不肯鳴	*the rooster will not crow in the morning.*
孟公不在茲	*There is no Menggong [Liu Gong's courtesy name] here for me—*
終以翳吾情	*in the end, my feelings are obscured, overgrown.*[47]

The one striking image emerging in this poem is that of concealment: a person of talent and passion being hidden under layers of coverings. His front yard is overgrown with weeds, a sign of receiving few visitors. The expression "wearing coarse clothing and holding jade within" comes from *Dao de jing;* it is a figurative way of describing a sage who lives incognito, his wisdom unknown to the world.[48] Here our poet makes the coarse clothing literal, though it still serves to remind us of what is hidden underneath. He also lives in a shabby house shaken by winds. Eventually, darkness cloaks everything, and in his long wait for the dawn, he feels that it is because the rooster refuses to crow that the day does not break. *Yi* (to cover up, to hide) seems to be one of Tao

Yuanming's favorite words. He uses it to describe the snow in the poem presented to his cousin Jingyuan, he uses it to describe Zhang Zhongwei's isolated life, and here he uses the same word to describe his feelings, his state of mind: unlike Zhang Zhongwei, there is no one who knows and understands him.

The latter half of the poem bears a sharp contrast with the opening of the poem. In his youth, the poet seems to have deliberately sought out isolation, for then he finds his pleasures in the Six Classics—*The Classic of Poetry, The Classic of Documents, The Rites, The Classic of Music, The Classic of Changes,* and *The Spring and Autumn Annals*;[49] but now, this lonely life, which is threatening to be engulfed by the shabby house, the weeds, the coarse clothing, the long, dark night, and finally the absence of an understanding friend, takes on a taste of bitterness. The second couplet is particularly gloomy: he is approaching the age of forty, after which Confucius says that a man, if still unknown, would be unworthy of respect and awe. The fourth line is a complete reversal of the defiant ending of the "Ninth Day" poem: "Isn't there something achieved in just lingering on?" The sense of *wucheng*, "having achieved nothing," underlies the whole poem. The poet becomes a piece of vessel uncompleted, unfulfilled, useless, and deserted, a vessel containing nothing substantial. What he holds on to underneath his coarse clothing is not jade, but the empty "principle of firmness in adversity"; what he dines on and even manages to eat his fill is not food, but "hunger and cold." There is not even a person like Liu Gong to admire him for "accomplishing something by achieving nothing."

If we still recall the short preface to the poetic series "On Drinking," we realize that the poet has in fact asked an old friend (or friends) to copy out all of the poems he claims he has written down when drunk. The poem is, paradoxically, a loud statement about being concealed; like a courtyard full of wild weeds, the poet fears he will eventually be "overgrown."

6 Hard Evidence: Reading a Stone

The Buddhist monk, holding the stone in his hand,
said with a smile, "Your body may be numinous,
but you don't have any practical value yet.
So we must carve a few characters on you
and make everyone who sees you become aware
that you are really an extraordinary thing."

—*Dream of the Red Chamber*
(or *Story of the Stone*)

The act of reading lies at the heart of hermeneutics. To read is to interpret. Interpretation is not just about understanding something, be it a literary work, a cultural object, or a life situation; it is essentially about giving meaning.

But what is meaning? What does "meaning" mean? Meaning is the way in which human beings negotiate with the world, and it is not stable. Historically and culturally conditioned, meaning is a constantly shifting ground, changing radically, appearing and disappearing. Therefore, the act of reading almost invariably points back to the reader's self. As we read the process of reading, we are also reading people who are engaged in the act of reading. This chapter is about reading a place, or more precisely, reading a stone. At one level, it is about how words, produced by a poet, reinvent the poet and reproduce a place.

The Song-period prefecture of Nankang, supposed to be Tao Yuanming's hometown, is not only the place where one of the rare Southern Song editions of Tao Yuanming's collection was printed but also the site where the poet's physical traces are claimed to have been discovered. The word "trace" (*ji*), a loaded term in the recluse tradition, is made literal in the Drunken Stone (Zuishi), a rock that, according to a fourteenth-century traveler, has preserved the body shape of Tao Yuanming. As time goes by, the physical preservation of the poet's body becomes curiously fragmented, although a part of Tao Yuanming is always there, whether in the form of a full body, or of a segment of his body, or of some sort of bodily ejection. As we peruse the various records produced in the prefecture of Nankang and those about it, especially those concerning the famous Drunken Stone, we realize that Nankang, with all its famous ancient sites (*guji*), has become an intersection point where literary, cultural, and political meanings converge; it turns out to be an eloquent locale on the cultural map of China. Even as we read, our reading continues to participate in recreating this space.

At another level, this chapter is about gullibility and the desire for a good story. People love their poets, and they love to hear the poet's life story. In the case of Tao Yuanming, famed for his love of wine and yet so elusive in his sketchy biographies, it almost seems imperative for later generations to pin him down in a physical time and place; the former impulse is manifested in the passion for a detailed chronology of Tao Yuanming's life, while the latter becomes the basis for the story of the Drunken Stone. We will never know exactly how the story originated—it might have been started by the excitable imagination of one of the locals, or by the inquisitive mind of a passing traveler. It may very well have begun as an oral account, but once it was written down, it assumed a protean textual life of its own.

In this chapter we will also look at the entanglements of memory and the confusion of human perception and perspective. A description of a place is produced either from the memory of previous readings of other texts or from the memory of an empirical experience. But memory slips, and words tangle up. Eyewitness accounts often contradict one another; travelogues frequently disagree. Inscriptions on a stone appear and then disappear, either chiseled off to leave room for fresh inscriptions, or fading away at the mercy of the elements. Our stone even literally reproduces: there are at least two Drunken Stones on record, not to mention a Drunken Stone Junior (Xiao Zuishi). On an April day in 1928, Hu Shi (1891–1962), one of the founders of the May Fourth Movement, visited Mount Lu. In his travel diary, he vehemently denounces the many "fake ancient sites" on this mountain, arguing that "boundless faith is an incurable laziness and the enemy of intellectual thought," a cultural "disease" that has led many people to take fake sites for real without investigating the sources. But a thunderstorm stopped him from going to the Drunken

Stone when he was about a mile away from it, and he jotted down in his notes that, according to a previous travelogue, the Drunken Stone had vanished and could no longer be found anywhere. Hu Shi's statement about the disappearance of the Drunken Stone has since been rejected by others.[1]

No doubt the Drunken Stone has been where it is for many millennia. We may be certain that its actual age can be roughly determined by a geologist, but its cultural age is both shorter and less ambiguous. Having remained just another one of the numerous faceless and nameless rocks in a small valley of Mount Lu, the Drunken Stone started to gain a name and an identity in the ninth century, five hundred years after Tao Yuanming's death. It has been written on and about ever since. As soon as it was singled out and left the realm of undifferentiation, it entered history and was endowed with a past. Like the stone in the famous eighteenth-century novel *Story of the Stone* (better known as *Dream of the Red Chamber*), it loses its innocence and falls into the world of red dust—the realm of mortality, flux, and inscription.

To get to this stone, we first need to situate ourselves in the manner of a Chinese tourist guide—or "record of a mountain," as it is called. Like a traditional Chinese landscape painting, such a description often seems oddly two-dimensional. To the south of Mount Lu there is a Buddhist temple, Guizong Temple (Guizong Si), an important landmark which is said to have been founded in the sixth year of the Xiankang reign (340) of Emperor Cheng of Jin (r. 325–342). As the legend goes, when Wang Xizhi, arguably the most famous Chinese calligrapher of all time, served as the governor of Jiangzhou, he frequented Mount Lu and loved its scenery. After he retired, he had a house built by the side of Mount Lu. It happened that a Buddhist monk, Buddhayaśas (or Fotuoyeshe) came to Mount Lu, and Wang Xizhi admired him so much that he turned his house into a temple and offered it to the monk. The story, however, is completely apocryphal. According to the biography of Buddhayaśas in Liang monk Hui Jiao's (497–554) *Biographies of Eminent Monks* (Gaoseng zhuan), he never set foot in the south, and the year he finished translating *Vinaya of the Four Categories of the Dharmagupta Sect* (Dharmaguptavinaya) in Chang'an was 410, some seventy years after Guizong Temple was said to have been established.[2]

A few miles to the west of Guizong Temple is supposed to be Lili, the elusive "Chestnut Village." In all four of Tao Yuanming's official biographies, Lili is perfunctorily mentioned as a halfway stopping point on Tao Yuanming's excursion to Mount Lu, where Tao Yuanming's old friends waylaid him with wine and brought him together with the then Jiangzhou governor Wang Hong. Its exact location is very vague, but the phrasing in the biographies makes it sufficiently clear that even in the problematic biographies Lili had nothing to do with Tao Yuanming's hometown.[3] Of the famous Tang poets, both Li Bai and Bai Juyi explicitly associated Lili with Tao Yuanming's home.[4] In the preface to a poem entitled "Visiting Master Tao Yuanming's Former Residence," written in 816, Bai Juyi states,

> I have always admired Tao Yuanming's personality. In the past, when I was living in leisure by the Wei River, I had written "Sixteen Poems in Imitation of Tao Qian's Style." Now during a tour of Mount Lu, I went through Chaisang and passed by Lili. Thinking of the man, I paid a visit to the site of his former residence. Unable to keep silent, I again composed a poem.

The poem contains the following couplet: "Chaisang, the ancient village; / Lili, the hills and streams of old."[5] And yet, the wording of Bai's preface and poem does not identify Tao Yuanming's former residence as Lili.

The monumental geographical work of the Northern Song, *The Account of the Realm in the Taiping Era* (Taiping huanyu ji) by Yue Shi (930–1007), supposedly makes reference to Lili and the Drunken Stone: "Sushan Yuan is to the south of the mountain. In the ravine there is the 'Drunken Stone' of Master Tao. . . . Sang Mountain is near Lili Yuan. Tao Qian was a native of this place."[6]

This cursory statement is not entirely clear on several accounts. Is Sushan Yuan an error in transcription and in fact the same as Lili Yuan? The Chinese character for *su* 粟 looks close enough to *li* 栗 to cause confusion for the copyist, and a widely circulated and much-praised Qing edition of *The Account of the Realm* indeed has "Lili Yuan is to the south of the mountain" instead.[7] Moreover, is Sang Mountain the same as Chaisang Mountain?[8] But much more problematic, even compromising, is the circulation history of *The Account of the Realm* itself. As early as the Ming Dynasty, one already could not find any Song edition of *The Account of the Realm* in China, and all late Ming/early Qing editions were incomplete. The copy in the Jigu ge collection of the great late-Ming book collector Mao Jin lacked eleven *juan* all together, among which was *juan* 111, the very section on Jiangzhou, the Nankang military prefecture, and the Drunken Stone. Eight *juan* are missing from other early Qing editions, including *juan* 4 and then *juans* 111 through 119. The *Siku quanshu* edition, from which our quotation is drawn, claims it has supplemented the missing sections by referring to an edition owned by the famous Qing book collector Wang Qishu (1728–1799). Although Wang's edition also lacks *juans* 113 through 119, at the end of each volume of this edition is appended one page of collations and corrections by an unknown hand, and the *Siku quanshu* editors have made generous use of these appendixes. Other major editions in the Qing, most notably the Wan Tinglan edition (1793) and the acclaimed Jinling shuju edition (1882), often include texts written up by later people in an effort to "fill in blanks," as evidenced by a rare Southern Song edition of *The Account of the Realm* discovered by the famous historical geographer Yang Shoujing (1839–1915) in Japan in 1880. Though still incomplete, this Southern Song edition became an important source for edition comparison and collation.[9]

The Imperial Encyclopedia of the Taiping Era (Taiping yulan) (comp. 984) relates Lili to Tao Yuanming in a more explicit way. Quoting from a record of Xunyang of unknown authorship and date, it says,

> Tao Qian's Lili now has a flat rock like a whetstone; its length and width are more than ten feet. It is said that Master Jingjie lay down on it when he was drunk. It is on the south side of Mount Lu.[10]

It is interesting to notice the turn of phrase "Tao Qian's Lili," which is very different from the statement "Tao Qian is a native of this place," for Lili is now seen as belonging to Tao Qian, and it is the poet, not the place, who has become a point of reference.

About a hundred years later, in the fifth year of the Xining reign (1072) of Emperor Shenzong of Song (r. 1068–1086), Chen Shunyu (courtesy name Lingju, ?–1077) was demoted to Nankang military prefecture as a supervisor of the salt and liquor tax. Like many demoted court officials, he engaged in active exploration of the local landscape—in this case, Mount Lu. He soon became a good friend of the local luminary Liu Huan (1000–1080), a native of Nankang who had passed the *jinshi* examination in the same year (1030) as the famous Northern Song politician and literary virtuoso Ouyang Xiu and had withdrawn to Mount Lu to be a recluse in 1051.[11] The two of them would often be seen touring Mount Lu riding on yellow oxen. The fruit of such tours was *A Record of Mount Lu* (Lushan ji), for which Liu Huan wrote a preface.[12] As befitting his official duty of supervising Nankang's liquor tax, Chen Shunyu took special note of the Drunken Stone. In *A Record of Mount Lu*, he explicitly identified Lili, Chestnut Village, as the place where Tao Yuanming once lived:

> One passes by Lili Yuan, where there is Magistrate Tao's Drunken Stone. Magistrate Tao's name was Qian and his courtesy name Yuanliang or Yuanming. In the third year of the Yixi reign [407], he served as the magistrate of Pengze. Then he said, "How can I bend my back and bow to some country bumpkin for the sake of five pecks of rice!" So he resigned from his post and composed "Return." Both *The Jin History* and *The Histories of the Southern Dynasties* contain his biography. At Lili, where he lived, there is a large stone between two hills. From it one looks up and can see the waterfall. It is flat and wide, and can hold more than ten people. Yuanliang indulged himself in wine, and so it is called Drunken Stone.[13]

Towards the end of *A Record of Mount Lu*, Chen Shunyu relates how, when he first toured Mount Lu and asked about "the rise and fall of pagodas and temples as well as the names of streams and stones," no one could enlighten his ignorance; and those who did try to answer his questions often made mistakes. He was left to his own devices. He thereupon diligently consulted historical maps and previous geographical records. *A Record of Mount Lu* is claimed to be a discriminating work whose statements have been substantiated by both textual accounts and empirical knowledge. "For all those sites that have fallen into obscurity or are overgrown with vegetation and become unknowable, I simply leave them unrecorded."[14] Nature, when too much (overgrown with vegetation) and devoid of human inscription, becomes "unknowable," and whatever is unknowable fails to find its way into textual record—and ceases to exist.

Chen Shunyu is affirming to his reader the truthfulness of what he set down in this book. But we already know that Chen Shunyu's words are not to be trusted. The story of the Eighteen Worthies of the White Lotus Society related in *A Record of Mount Lu*, for instance, is one of the accounts that have already been proved factitious. And yet, it is the affirmation of the veracity of the work that matters in the later tradition, and Chestnut Village, a place that appeared almost by accident in the Tao Yuanming biographies and whose location was vague enough to be anywhere in the vast Mount Lu area, from this point on is identified as Tao Yuanming's hometown, located in clear reference to other recognizable landmarks, and characterized by the Drunken Stone.

Chen Shunyu also wrote a poem to celebrate the Drunken Stone:

聒聒飛泉清繞石	*A bubbling waterfall surrounds the stone;*
悠悠天幕翠鋪空	*vast and distant, the sky stretches like an azure curtain.*
是非分付千鍾里	*Right and wrong—all entrusted to a thousand cups of wine;*
日月消磨一醉中	*sun and moon—worn away in one drunkenness.*
柳絮狂飄荒徑畔	*Willow catkins drift at will by the deserted path,*
菊花仍在舊籬東	*chrysanthemum flowers are still blooming to the east of the old hedge.*
水聲山色年年好	*The water sound and hill color remain enchanting year after year—*
堪使遊人恥素風	*enough to make the traveler feel ashamed by the master's pure ways.*[15]

As we read this poem, we recognize the allusion in the third couplet to the "five willows" in Tao Yuanming's fictional autobiography and his famous lines in the fifth of the "On Drinking" series—"Picking chrysanthemum flowers by the eastern hedge, / I gaze at South Mountain in the distance." The allusion thereby reconfirms the homestead of the poet as being the locale of the Drunken Stone.

Chen Shunyu was not the first person who composed a poem on the Drunken Stone. There are three Drunken Stone poems from the Tang, although their sources are shadowy and questionable. First there is a quatrain attributed to Zhang Gu (fl. 850), preserved in the Ming local gazetteer *Zhengde Gazetteer of Nankang Prefecture* (Zhengde Nankang fuzhi; comp. 1506–1522), which contains no allusion to Tao Yuanming.[16] Then there is a poem entitled "Written on Tao Qian's Drunken Stone" (Shu Tao Qian Zuishi), attributed to Wang Zhenbai (*jinshi* between 894 and 898).[17] Then there is another rather hyperbolic panegyric, entitled "On Tao Yuanming's Drunken Stone" (Ti Tao Yuanming Zuishi), supposedly by an obscure late Tang poet named Chen Guang.[18] The phrasing shows some remarkable similarity to that of Chen Shunyu's poem:

片石露寒色	*A piece of stone exposes its cold color—*
先生遺素風	*the Master has left behind his pure ways.*

醉眠芳草合	*As he slept in drunkenness, fragrant grass grew around him;*
吟起白雲空	*rising up, he chanted poetry; white clouds turned empty.*
道出乾坤外	*His way extends beyond heaven and earth;*
聲齊日月中	*his name equals the sun and moon.*
我知彭澤後	*But after my understanding of the Pengze magistrate—*
千載與誰同	*who else would be able to share with him in a thousand years?*

Despite the awkwardness of such a theatrical eulogy, we can detect efforts to equate the Drunken Stone with something visible and physical in the transmission of the otherwise intangible "pure ways" left behind by the Master, to locate the Drunken Stone in reference to a moral universe, to heaven and earth, sun and moon. The poet also tries to situate himself in this larger spatial and temporal context: he envisions himself at the middle point of the continuation of the Master's "pure ways," heading into a future extending for another millenium. He is the understanding friend of Tao Yuanming, who can both gaze back with admiration at the Master's achievements and look forward longingly to future generations and hope for someone who can "share" (*tong*) with them. This is the only way to fight back against the threat of the enclosing fragrant grass.

All three pre-Song poems date from the mid- to late ninth century to early tenth century. If they are authentic, then we may be reasonably certain that the story of the Drunken Stone, at least in written record, originated from that period. But it seems that only in the Northern Song did the stone and its environs begin to be inscribed.

Why do people want to carve their writings on stones and cliffs in a landscape? To put it simply, "By incorporating a text into the environment, the traveler sought to participate enduringly in the totality of the scene," even though at the same time "the text altered the scene by shaping the perceptions of later travelers and guiding those who sought to follow in the footsteps of earlier talents."[19] People also inscribe in order to tame the otherness of a place, and to transform it into a recognizable sign on a cultural map. But the inscriptions of men remain under the power of nature; words on stones tend to erode due to centuries of exposure to the elements, and so fall into obscurity. Sometimes they are chiseled away to leave room for new inscriptions. As avid travelers record those words in their travel accounts or diaries, errors occur due to careless copying or imperfect memory. So we are faced with different versions of what is or was carved at a certain place, unable to decide which is to be believed or which is to be discarded. The Drunken Stone has been inscribed to ensure a sense of spatial orientation and personal immortality, but as we shall see, the inscriptions are ever changing, and the Drunken Stone, now a sign of human frailty and culpability, is in constant flux.

The earliest dated inscription on the Drunken Stone was made by a man called Zhou Xingxian and others who visited the stone in 1049.[20] *The Record of Mount Lu* of Mao Deqi, eighteenth-century magistrate of Xingzi County, followed Sang Qiao's (?–1564) *Record of Mount Lu* (Lushan jishi; comp. 1561) and recorded two groups of travelers who left their names on the cliff beside the stone: "Ouyang Guohua and Li Shenghua visited together in the [character missing] year of the Huangyou reign [1049–1054]"; and "Wu Liang from Sanqu and Xu [character missing] from Chanlin, of the Song, in the third year of the Yuanyou reign [1088], drank at the Drunken Stone of Yuanming."[21]

In 1933, Wu Zongci (1879–?), when compiling his comprehensive *Record of Mount Lu*, fills in some of the missing characters. According to Wu Zongci, it was in the third year of the Huangyou reign (1051) that Ouyang Guohua and Li Shenghua paid their visit; he also noted that Sang Qiao had missed the name of a third friend, Han Zigao, after Li Shenghua. Since Mao Deqi's *Record of Mount Lu* had equally missed Han Zigao, we cannot help wondering if Mao Deqi had simply copied out Sang Qiao without exploring the Drunken Stone in person. As stone engravings tend to grow unclear as time passes by, we also wonder how Sang Qiao or Mao Deqi could not have recognized the character "*san*" (third) when each was writing his *Record of Mount Lu* a little more than two hundred years before Wu Zongci. A contesting record is *A Short Account of Mount Lu* (Lushan xiaozhi), compiled by a native of Xunyang called Cai Ying (who gave himself the appellation "The Flower Recluse of Mount Lu" [Kuang Lu hua yin]) and dated 1824. In this work (which the author claims "does not add or take away even one single character" in recording the landscape inscriptions), we see that the first inscription quoted above likewise does not contain the name "Han Zigao"; as for the second inscription, the word order is slightly different from the previous records: instead of "Wu Liang Chanlin Xu" it has "Wu Liangchan Xu Lin."[22]

Chen Shunyu's contemporary, Cheng Shimeng (1009–1086), an extremely capable official who once had also served as prefect of Nankang, left a rather lame quatrain on the stone, extolling its noble sensibilities and further contributing to the humanization of the landscape:

萬仞峰前一水旁	*In front of a ten-thousand-foot peak, by a single stream,*
晨光翠色助清涼	*morning light and azure color nurture its clear coolness.*
誰知片石多情甚	*Who would know that a slab of stone had so many feelings—*
曾送淵明入醉鄉	*it once sent Yuanming into the realm of drunkenness.*

The poem does not appear under Cheng Shimeng in *Quan Song shi*, though it is contained in Mao Deqi's *Record of Mount Lu*. But the modern annotator of Mao's work, Xu Xinjie, adds a note explaining that the attribution is misleading: the engraved text on the stone shows that the poem was actually written by Wang Kui (991–1072), a *jinshi* of 1019.[23] The problem is not entirely resolved when we refer to Wu Zongci's *Record of Mount Lu* of the Republican era. According to Wu's observation, only the seven characters of the first line are still recognizable, and then Wu notes that on the Drunken Stone there is a three-character inscription (*shu Zuishi,* which means "written on the Drunken Stone") by Wang Kui.[24] As we can see from the picture of the inscriptions on the Drunken Stone, the space is rather crowded, and the two inscriptions may simply be very close side by side, which leads to the confusion.

But the most famous inscription on the Drunken Stone, as well as the largest, is supposedly by the eminent neo-Confucian philosopher Zhu Xi (1130–1200). In 1179, the sixth year of the Chunxi reign of Emperor Xiaozong of the Southern Song, Zhu Xi served as prefect in the Nankang military prefecture (Nankang jun). His term of service ended in 1181. Although three years is not a long time, Zhu Xi kept himself busy and managed to accomplish a great deal in fulfilling his administrative and cultural duties. The things he did included sending one letter after another to the emperor, petitioning for exemption of tax for Nankang on account of the bad drought the area had suffered in 1179, writing to a local god and asking for rain, and repairing the tomb of Liu Huan and building a small pavilion in front of the tomb, naming the pavilion Stalwart Virtue (Zhuang Jie), a phrase from Ouyang Xiu's poem written upon seeing Liu Huan off to go into early retirement to Mount Lu. In a typical move in what Linda Walton terms the "neo-Confucian construction of sacred space," he also reestablished and brought to a soaring new height the famous White

Deer Grotto Academy (Bailu Dong Shuyuan), a neo-Confucian site at Mount Lu that was to exert its influence for many centuries to come.[25] Finally, during his days of leisure, he built a small vacation house for himself in the Mount Lu area, his familiarity with which is evidenced in his many poems composed during this period on the various Mount Lu scenic spots. He would invite his friends there every once in a while, and hold drinking parties. This small vacation house was located right by the side of the Drunken Stone, and he named it after the title of Tao Yuanming's famous literary exposition: Villa of Return (Guiqulai Guan).

One of Zhu Xi's fourteen poems on Mount Lu written in response to the poet You Mao (1127–1194) is devoted to the Drunken Stone and the little house close by:

予生千載後 *I am born a thousand years later,*
尚友千載前 *and yet I befriend people who lived a thousand years ago.*[26]
每尋高士傳 *Every time I peruse the biographies of noble recluses,*
獨嘆淵明賢 *I sigh at the worthiness of Yuanming alone.*[27]
及此逢醉石 *Coming to this place, I encounter the Drunken Stone,*
謂言公所眠 *people tell me the Master once slept on it;*
況復巖壑古 *not to mention the ancientness of the cliff and the ravine:*
飄渺藏風煙 *the hiding place for sweeping wind and hazy mist.*
仰看喬木陰 *Looking up at the shades of tall trees,*
俯聽橫飛泉 *I then bend down to listen to the waterfall.*
景物自清絕 *The scenery here is of itself so luminous,*
優游可忘年 *lingering here one could forget old age.*
結廬倚蒼峭 *Building a hut to lean against the dark green cliff,*
舉觴酹潺湲 *I hold up my wine cup, offering a toast to the rippling water.*
臨風一長嘯 *Giving a long whistling along the wind,*
亂以歸來篇 *I shall end with the piece of writing on return.*

Like Chen Guang, Zhu Xi also attempts to locate himself in history. The first line starts from Tao Yuanming's viewpoint, so that Zhu Xi sees himself as born too late (almost a thousand years later than the poet he admires), then the second line switches back to the present, and Mencius's well-known saying about befriending the ancients is realized in the act of reading—the reading of a text that is specially sought out (*xun*, here translated as "peruse"). Interestingly, the poet's discovery of the Drunken Stone seems to be less of a conscious effort:

he "encounters" it as if by chance. It, however, helps him locate the physical trace of the person he had only read about. Though the person is absent, the cliff and ravine are just as "ancient," and in their company he claims he will forget about his own creeping old age—an allusion to Confucius's saying that he was a person who (in pursuit of knowledge and/or the Way) forgot that old age was coming upon him.[28] In the next couplet, Zhu Xi takes the place of the ancient poet: having built a hut by the Drunken Stone, he now drinks to the waterfall and will probably lie down on the Drunken Stone himself. The poem ends with another text, the prose piece composed by Tao Yuanming expressing happiness over his withdrawal from the public world. For Zhu Xi, the Villa of Return is a temporary withdrawal only, but it can still be a gesture, signifying an ultimate aim. More importantly, the Villa of Return fills in the empty spot left by the absent poet. While it is doubtful that Tao Yuanming ever set foot on this particular part of the mountain at all, let alone lay himself down on the piece of large flat rock dubbed the Drunken Stone, Zhu Xi's building of the Villa of Return beside the stone somehow verifies and even provides a sense of the physical presence of Tao Yuanming, helping turn this place into a *ji*, "trace or site," a space rich with man-made meaning.

But Zhu Xi did not inscribe anything on the stone—not just yet. This event in fact took place after he left Nankang. In a colophon to the stone inscription Zhu Xi explained everything, and it is included in his collection of works, under the title "A Colophon to the Poem on Lili by Yan Lugong" (Ba Yan Lugong Lili shi).[29] Yan Lugong refers to Yan Zhenqing (709–784), a Tang minister and famous calligrapher who died a martyr at the hands of a rebellious general. The poem, which survives in part, praises Tao Yuanming's loyalist sentiments. On an autumn day in 1191, Zhu Xi, moved by the persistent request of a friend, wrote out the poem for him to be carved on stone, and appended the following colophon:

> The above is the poem on Lili by Yan, Duke Wenzhong of Lu County of the Tang. It may be seen in Chen Lingju's *A Record of Mount Lu*, but the complete poem cannot be obtained. Even so, to read it is enough for one to recognize the hearts of the two masters and understand the principles of ruler and minister. Lili is about fifty miles to the northwest of the seat of the Nankang military prefecture. In the valley there is a huge stone, and it is said that when Master Tao was drunk, he would sleep on it. I once visited there and felt a sadness, so I had the Villa of Return built by

> its side. Throughout the year I would often persuade my friends to pay a visit. When we enjoyed the forest and the stream, and held up wine cups for a toast, I always chanted this poem to them. A native of this land, Mr. Chen Zhengchen, Retainer Clerk of Lingling, heard the poem, and it seemed that he was touched deeply inside. He asked me to write it out in big script and have it carved on the stone. After I left the commandery, his request became even more insistent. Thus I wrote it out and sent it to him. On the *renwu* day of the seventh month, in the autumn of the *xinchou* year of the Chunxi reign [1181], by Zhu Xi [Zhonghui] of Xin'an.[30]

Presumably, Yan Zhenqing's poem, written out in Zhu Xi's hand, was engraved on none other than the Drunken Stone, but if it was, it has long vanished. What we can still see today on the Drunken Stone are four large characters, Villa of Return (Guiqulai Guan), reputed to have been written by Zhu Xi himself.

To carve something on stone is an immortalizing act. And yet, not only is the stone text of Yan Zhenqing's fragmentary poem nowhere to be seen, but when Zeng Ji, an ardent follower of Zhu Xi and a serious-minded official, came to Nankang as prefect ten years after Zhu Xi left in 1191, he discovered, to his consternation, that many of Zhu Xi's cultural construction projects had already fallen into decay. Zeng Ji immediately set out to repair and rebuild; in almost everything that we know he did, he was literally following in Zhu Xi's footsteps, and his aim was clearly to continue the tradition established by Zhu Xi in making Nankang a cultural space.

The first thing he did was to fix up the Pavilion of Stalwart Virtue, a shrine Zhu Xi had devoted to Liu Huan, the close friend of Chen Shunyu. Even though no more than a decade had gone by, "there was nothing left from the gate, the wall, or the pavilion plaque."[31] Zeng Ji built a new gate, a new wall, and planted some trees around the site. He then wrote to Zhu Xi, asking him for "a word to commemorate this event, so that the later-born would know about the heartfelt intention of the two of us and hence never become lax in their respect for the worthy and their admiration of virtue."[32] Zhu Xi, obviously pleased by the request, consented, and hence "An Account of the Pavilion of Stalwart Virtue" (Zhuang Jie Ting ji), written in the fifth month of 1192.

But Zeng Ji had gone one step further than Zhu Xi: on a day off from his administrative duties, he managed to find the site of Liu Huan's former residence. Lamenting over the desolate state into which it had fallen, he decided to restore the house, and, most importantly, he took care to reconstruct every hall, pavilion, terrace, and pond mentioned in the writings of Liu Huan and his son Liu Shu. Then he wrote Zhu Xi, again asking for an account, this time sending along a drawing of the reconstructed house and garden. Zhu Xi was duly impressed. It happened that someone had just given him a painting of Chen Shunyu riding on his ox, so he passed this painting on to Zeng Ji for him to hang in the newly restored residence of Liu Huan, together with "An Account of the Hall of Icy Jade" (Bingyu Tang ji).

Zeng Ji did not stop there. He conscientiously followed the example set by Zhu Xi, the grand master, and recreated everything Zhu Xi did in a more literal and more literary fashion. In the winter of 1192, he authorized the printing of a new edition of Tao Yuanming's works. Unlike other editions, this edition is not divided by *juan* but simply by genres—the first part of the collection being poetry, and the second part prose. Zeng Ji began his colophon by acknowledging the achievements of his predecessors: "Yuanming's collection is widely circulated in the world. The details regarding its collation and organization can be found in the 'private note' of Song Xuanhui and the commentary of Yang Xiuzhi of the Northern Qi."[33]

For Zeng Ji, the strength of his edition lies not in the collation or organization of the materials but in the authenticity of its place of origin, as it was printed in Tao Yuanming's home region; but the authority of place is subject to the power of time, and the constant transformations of the physical landscape forever threaten to remove the traces left by the poet:

> Nankang is where Yuanming used to stay. Lili and Shangjing are no more than twenty miles from each other. Time brought about so many changes that they were no longer recognizable. Only the Drunken Stone still lay in the mist of the wilderness, among grass and trees, by turbulent currents. Luxuriant vegetation concealed it, and there was no human trace in this spot.
>
> When Huiweng [i.e., Zhu Xi] presided over the prefecture, he first succeeded in cutting away the wild vegetation and establishing a path, erecting a pavilion at the top of the mountain, so that people who lived outside the public eye and who rose above the crowd could pay a visit to this place, stroke the stone, and, touched by the past, feel nostalgia for ancient times. But if they asked to look at Tao Yuanming's collection, and if we did not have it, would not this place be found wanting then?

As Lili and Shangjing, two places mentioned in relation to the poet, have become obscure, the Drunken Stone turns out to be the only visible trace left by Tao Yuanming, the archetypal recluse. This single trace proves vital to the memory of the poet, for, when wild vegetation covers it up, it fails to draw any "human trace" (*renji*). Nature is threatening to take over and would conceal the poet's trails entirely but for the efforts of Zhu Xi: he not only opened a path for visitors, but also literally installed a place—a pavilion for visitors to stop by and in which to linger for a moment. The verb chosen by Zeng Ji here is, interestingly, *zhi*, literally, "to *plant* a pavilion": the force of the verb lies in its metaphoric association with nature, and in the junction of the artificial and the natural. The pavilion *planted* thus becomes a new landmark, serving to mark the Drunken Stone as well as commemorate Tao Yuanming's hometown region. It was because of this pavilion, according to Zeng Ji, that there were visitors again, and that the visitors got a chance to contemplate the stone and think of the past—and, says Zeng Ji, ask for the collection of Tao Yuanming. Without the pavilion, there would have been no trace of the stone; without the stone, there would have been no memory of the past; without the memory of the past, already inscribed in the landscape, there would have been no inquiry about Tao Yuanming's writings. To print a new edition of the collection of Tao Yuanming's works becomes an act that fills up the gaping hole left in the cultural history of Nankang. From recreating physical places from the written word to reproducing the printed word from physical places, Zeng Ji shows us the complicated interconnections between art and life.

As the Drunken Stone gained fame, the fame of Lili faded, and seems to have disappeared from local memory by the twelfth century. Zhou Bida toured Mount Lu twice in 1167 and noted in the account of his second visit, *The Second Account of Mount Lu* (Lushan houlu), "I looked for Chestnut Village and the Drunken Stone. Local people simply said, 'If you go on from here, you'll find a Master Tao Cliff, but there is no such place as Chestnut Village.'"[34] The statement was repeated by a 1935 *New Guide to Mount Lu* (Lushan xin daoyou).[35]

The fascinating thing about Lili is that, at first, people felt that they could legitimately claim that the Drunken Stone had indeed served as a couch for Tao Yuanming because they had found it in Lili; but as the Drunken Stone became more and more prominent, it was used as a reference point to determine where the more and more shadowy ancient Chestnut Village was. In

Qing local luminary Cai Ying's *A Short Account of Mount Lu*, for instance, the ancient place name Lili Yuan was mentioned again, but it was reported to be "beside the Drunken Stone, and in the Drunken Stone Ravine."[36] Lili, which started out as a textual place, ends up as a textual place and lives on in textual records and the reader's imagination; visitors coming to this part of Mount Lu to pay homage to Tao Yuanming continue to ask about Lili and look for Lili, and, as a matter of fact, Lili occupies a spot on a modern-day Mount Lu map. And yet, I suspect that Lili has never really existed—or, more precisely, that its physical being as a geographical location was produced by text. Words create reality, and life imitates art.

Zhou Bida did, however, finally find the Drunken Stone, although the Drunken Stone he found now had a new imprint:

> Looking up, one can see the flying cascade washing down a huge stone, which forms quite an extraordinary sight. The stone has a hollow spot, which, according to popular legend, is the impression left by Master Tao Yuanming's head. They [i.e., the monks] also pointed out some trace that looks like that of a tiger, but the story is too absurd.

The assumption is that Tao Yuanming lay down there so often that the pressure of his head made a hollow spot in the hard surface of the stone. But what is so absurd about the story of the tiger's trace, Zhou Bida never says. The cliff above the Drunken Stone is named Tiger Claw Cliff (Huzhao Yai), and so there may be some connection between the name of the cliff and the story about the tiger's trace.[37] But we cannot help thinking of the Tiger Stream—another famous "ancient site" (*guji*) on Mount Lu associated with Tao Yuanming, which is, in Hu Shi's terms, a "fake." As the legend goes, Hui Yuan, the great fourth-century monk residing at the Donglin Temple of Mount Lu, made a rule that he would never walk across Tiger Stream when he saw off guests. But one night, carried away by his conversation with the Daoist Lu Xiujing (406–477) and Tao Yuanming, he unwittingly violated his own rule: at this point, the resident tiger by Tiger Stream began roaring as if warning the Buddhist master of his transgression, and the three friends started laughing. The story about Hui Yuan's not crossing Tiger Stream was recorded in Hui Jiao's *Biographies of Eminent Monks* and was widely known in the Tang,[38] but adding the element of Lu Xiujing and Tao Yuanming to the story seems to have occurred much later, perhaps in the late Tang.[39] In any case, the story of the three friends laughing has been refuted as apocryphal as early as in the Southern Song by Lou Yue (1137–1213), as Lu Xiujing was only ten when Hui Yuan died, and he did not come to Mount Lu until about twenty years after the death of Tao Yuanming.[40] But the love of myth overcomes the desire for truth, and, as Davis says, the Tiger Stream legend "was an established tradition" from the Northern Song and "has remained to this day."[41] It is tempting to associate the trace of the tiger on the Drunken Stone with the roaring tiger by Tiger Stream. Although one place is situated to the south of the mountain and one to the north, physical distance, like the temporal span, does not matter much in the need for a charming story.

The imprint made by Tao Yuanming's body on the stone grows deeper and larger in the fourteenth century. Another Nankang magistrate, Wang Wei (1321–1372), records in his *Record of My Travels* (Jingxing ji):

> I passed by the Drunken Stone shrine, Tao Jingjie's former residence, situated at Lili. The shrine has been deserted, and there is only a huge stone stretching in the ravine. On the stone one can vaguely detect the shape of a reclining person. It is said that Jingjie lay down on this stone when he was drunk. Some say that the peaks to the south of the temple are what the line "I catch sight of South Mountain in the distance" refers to.

The Drunken Stone shrine (Zuishi guan) is a Daoist temple erected on the site of Zhu Xi's Villa of Return sometime between the thirteenth and fourteenth centuries.[42] It seems to have declined quickly. But the Drunken Stone endures, and gains more "traces," thanks to the fertile imaginations of its visitors.

The stone impression undergoes a strange transformation in the sixteenth century. Sang Qiao, in his 1561 *Record of Mount Lu*, draws a quotation from *The Histories of the Southern Dynasties*: "After the Master gave up his post and came back, he would often go to Mount Lu in a sedan chair. When he was drunk, he would lie down on a stone. Even today we can see the traces of his ear and of his vomit after drinking on the stone."[43] Tao Yuanming's body shape inscribed on the stone becomes curiously fragmented, and it is notable that the ear and the mouth, the two organs receiving and giving sound, are the ones leaving traces for the later-born to see. The only problem is that nowhere in *The Histories of the Southern Dynasties* can this quotation be found.[44]

Sang Qiao's quotation is nonetheless repeated by many others. Wang Siren (1575–1646), the famous late-Ming writer known for his boisterous sense of humor, thus writes about his encounter with the Drunken Stone in his "Travel Account of Mount Lu" (You Lushan ji):

> South Mountain caught sight of in the distance is an overgrown lump. About three miles from Lili is the site of the Villa of Return, but now it belongs to a mountain farmer. There is a ravine, a small cascade, and a pool underneath with a large stone jutting out. Mr. Tao lay here every time he got drunk, and the traces of his vomit are still quite new. An anonymous poem is carved on the stone: "Yuanming got drunk on this stone, / this stone also got drunk on Yuanming. / For a thousand years no one understands, / —the mountain is lofty, the wind and moon clear." I almost want to break the stone into pieces with a bludgeon.[45]

What have been left on the stone—vomit traces and the poetic text—are both bodily emissions, but they lead to very different responses. The theatrical gesture of smashing the stone with a bludgeon recalls Lin Xiangru, who threatened to dash the much-coveted jade disk in front of a greedy King of Qin; it also reminds the reader of a grief-stricken Huang Tingjian's desire to shatter the rock loved and lost by his best friend, the then deceased Su Shi. Wang Siren does not try very hard to conceal his distaste for the quatrain inscribed on the stone, and here lies the irony: while the vomit traces of a great poet inspire reverence, a (bad) poem by an admirer makes Wang Siren want to destroy the stone on which the text is carved. The question is, since the anonymous poet believes that the stone also got drunk on Tao Yuanming, whose vomit was it, after all?

Wang Siren resolves the doubt in his own quatrain on the Drunken Stone:

淵明一吐後	*Ever since Yuanming vomited on it once,*
茲石遂千秋	*this stone became immortal.*
石在淵明去	*The stone is here, but Yuanming gone,*
聲餘澗水流	*the only remaining sound—water flowing in the ravine.*[46]

Poems about the Drunken Stone are generally mediocre at best, but even awful poems can be somewhat redeemed if they are short and not carved on rocks, and so Wang Siren's quatrain succeeds. Throwing up after drinking is hardly poetic, except perhaps in the classical Chinese literary tradition, and yet, I think it is more than mere perversity that makes one feel endeared to the Drunken Stone only upon reading about the vomit traces in Wang Siren's travel account and poem. In the first two lines of the poem, the word play is more obvious in the Chinese original: "one vomit" (*yi tu*) forms a parallel with the "a thousand years" (*qian qiu*), and the contrast between the fragile human act and the immortality of the stone is further enriched as it is precisely the former that leads to the latter. Wang Siren is obviously not thinking of the physical endurance of the stone when he considers its "immortality," but the physical endurance comes into play in the third line, in which the poet reminds the reader that the stone survives the person who grants it eternal fame, as much as great writings survive the writer. Moreover, time eliminates signs of any indecorous and messy human response to drunkenness, no matter whether it is the awful headache from a bad hangover, or the retching sound of throwing up after getting drunk; indeed, the only remaining sound is that of the cascade pouring into the pool, clean mountain water making its innocent splashing noises to the stony trace of the Master's ear. The human element is smoothed out and what remains of the experience of drunkenness may be safely lyrical.

Nonetheless, it is that mortal experience—getting drunk—that gives the Drunken Stone its name, its life, its immortality. Wang Siren's imagination, wayward as usual, preserves for us the humanity of Tao Yuanming by constructing a very unsentimental moment in the poet's life, by inscribing in stone the messy physical aspect of drunkenness as well as the vulnerability of the mortal body. More than any carving on the stone, this little poem represents a small triumph of words—perhaps the only quatrain in Chinese literary tradition that makes vomiting almost poetic.

In 1719, Mao Deqi, the magistrate of Xingzi County, under whose jurisdiction Mount Lu now stood, compiled a fifteen-*juan Record of Mount Lu*. In the fourth *juan*, he repeats Sang Qiao's *Histories of the Southern Dynasties* quotation; he also emulates Sang Qiao's practice in recording the four quatrains carved on the Drunken Stone, the first being identical with the one seen by Wang Siren. The contemporary editor and annotator Xu Xinjie explains that the third and fourth poems are absent; instead, there is a different third quatrain on the stone. Xu Xinjie also notes a mistake in copying or transmission of the stone text in the second quatrain.[47] But Xu Xinjie's own version is not error-proof either: comparing the third quatrain appended in a commentary in the 1991 Xu Xinjie edition with a photograph of the Drunken Stone taken in 1983, we see that Xu Xinjie's edition has taken the character *ri* 日 (day) for *shi* 時 (hour or time).[48] Even as one is busy correcting inaccuracies in transmission, new ones are being born.

What further complicates the matter is Huang Zongxi's claim in his 1660 *Travel Account of Mount Lu* (Kuang Lu you lu). The emphasis of this travel account is, in a modern annotator's words, "not on description of scenery, but on evidentiary scholarship and recording events."[49] Huang Zongxi says about the Drunken Stone, "I climbed onto its top, and saw an inscription left on the *shangsi* day of the ninth year of the Zhizheng reign [1349], but the other inscriptions are unrecognizable."[50] Can we trust Huang Zongxi, who claims in his preface that he has written the travel account so that "later travelers would not be blinded by worthless chaff"?[51] If so, what about the quatrain seen by Wang Siren not so long ago, or the other carvings recorded by Mao Deqi, Wu Zongci, and Xu Xinjie throughout the centuries? Is Huang Zongxi being careless, or is he exaggerating the lack of clarity of the stone texts? Or are the inscriptions on the stone redone by people who are anxious to recover what has been recorded by "previous worthies" in their travel accounts, people who, like Zeng Ji, are reluctant to leave anything "missing" from their local scenic spot and are determined to have reality accord perfectly with the writings? We do not know. What we do know is that the Drunken Stone inscriptions are always in flux, and accounts of them never completely agree with one another. The power of time and the human liability for faults and inaccuracies prove much stronger than the desire to stabilize and unify.

Towards the end of the eighteenth century, the Drunken Stone had long been firmly established as a landmark for the ancient Lili.[52] Cao Longshu, a native of Nankang motivated by a strong sense of local pride, traveled around in pursuit of the various "sites" left by Tao Yuanming, and "proved" each by quoting lines from Tao Yuanming's own writings. He stated that the area of the Drunken Stone was not only the ancient Lili ("The Drunken Stone is at Lili: from Song and Qi to Song and Yuan, in every dynasty there is some factual record, so one may suppose that there is no mistake in this statement"), but, he argued, as did the Song/Yuan editor Li Gonghuan, it must have also been the "south village" Tao Yuanming moved to, supposedly after his house was burned down in 408. Apparently unaware of the fact that Lu Xiujing did not come to Mount Lu until after Tao Yuanming's death, Cao Longshu says that since this area is so close to Mount Yujing, where the Daoist Lu Xiujing once lived, Lu Xiujing must have been among the "simple-hearted people" (*suxinren*) Tao Yuanming talks about in his poem "On Moving" (Yi ju).[53] In Cao Longshu's confident statement, backed up by his constant reference to empirical experiences (asking an old farmer, checking out a place in person, and so forth), we see again the desire to weave together elements of various legends—as well as those picked up from the poet's own writings—into a seamless whole.

The legend surrounding the Drunken Stone continues to grow into the twenty-first century. Gu Zhi, the eminent modern Tao Yuanming scholar, points out a second Drunken Stone located in the Mount Yujing area, on a little hill by Nine Peaks Bridge (Jiufeng Qiao).[54] Gu Zhi's observation is closely associated with his conviction that Yujing must have been the Shangjing where Tao Yuanming once lived and about which he wrote.[55] According to Gu Zhi, "When the lake water is full, the stone is right in the middle of the lake. The local people say that Tao Yuanming once lay on this stone in drunkenness and looked at Kaixian Cascade, which perfectly fits how Zhu Xi describes it in *Remarks of Master Zhu* (Zhuzi yulu)." Gu Zhi does not refute outright Chen Shunyu's designation of the Drunken Stone to the south of Mount Lu, but he criticizes the accuracy of the size of the stone as recorded by Chen Shunyu, who is quoted by Gu Zhi as saying that dozens of people can all sit together on the stone. "I once climbed onto that stone," Gu Zhi contends, "and it is rather small and at most has room for two or three people." Gu Zhi's quotation of Chen Shunyu is not exactly precise; in Chen Shunyu's words, it is "more than ten people" (*shi yu ren*), not "dozens of people" (*shu shi ren*). But Gu Zhi grants that Tao Yuanming must have owned farming land near Chen Shunyu's Drunken Stone and so he must have visited this area as well. "He came here in the harvest season and walked around in the valley, lying down on this stone when he was drunk. This is why the later-born named it Drunken Stone. In summary, the Master would drink whenever he had wine, and the Drunken Stone must not be limited to one or two."[56]

Wu Zongci, the compiler of the 1933 *Record of Mount Lu*, is not baffled by the presence of two Drunken Stones either. He gives a detailed commentary:

> Cao Longshu was a native of Xingzi in the Jiaqing era of the Qing Dynasty. Since he wrote about the previous worthies of his hometown as a local resident, we may trust most of his words. I looked for the

> inscription "Sun Shines on Xiechuan" in the area of Mount Yujing, but could not find it.[57] I asked a Mr. Peng Chaojie [a native of Mount Yujing], who said, "I have lived here for seventy years and have heard of the inscription. The elders say that it was chiseled off by stone workers." I then asked him about other old sites, and he answered, "The Drunken Stone is by the lake." I went to see it the next day.

Empirical experiences—being a local, living at one place for seventy years—again play a major role in judging the credibility of a person's words, even though Cao Longshu does not seem to be a fine scholar by any account, and Mr. Peng may be no more than a village elder whose only advantage lies in his age and his identity as a local resident.[58]

> The stone is about three miles from Kaixian Temple, just as Gu Cengbing [Gu Zhi] said. It is about ten feet tall and thirteen feet wide. There is a hollow spot on top, which has just about enough room for one person to lie down. The northern side of this hollow spot is raised slightly and so is just right for putting down one's head. Beside the hollow spot there is a small hole, in which one may put tea stuff and books. Lying down there, one can see Yellow Rock Cascade and Horse Tail Cascade, again fitting perfectly Gu's words and local legend. Thereupon I think to myself, even though this is the Drunken Stone, still we cannot say that what Chen Shunyu records as "the large stone between the two peaks that has room enough for dozens of people" is absolutely not the Drunken Stone. Master Tao was a recluse hiding himself in the wine; he could get drunk anywhere, and so he could have lain down anywhere.

Indeed, following the footsteps of Sang Qiao and Mao Deqi, Wu Zongci also remarks on yet another stone not too far from the Drunken Stone area. This stone is located to the west of Yellow Dragon Hill, near the site of a former architectural structure that some say is the former residence of Tao Yuanming and others say is a shrine to Tao Yuanming established since the Song Dynasty. To the southeast of this site there is a "chess-board stone," which probably gains its name because of its flatness. The inscription on this stone is perhaps one of the earliest left in Mount Lu, for a date is given: "Written on the first day of the ninth month of the first year of the Yuanjia reign" (Yuanjia yuan nian jiuyue yiri shu). Yuanjia is the reign title of Emperor Wen of the Liu

Song, and the first year of the Yuanjia reign was 424, three years prior to Tao Yuanming's decease. But nothing compares to the content of the inscription for its perfectly unconscious ironic nature. The four large characters carved on it are "naturalness born of heaven" (*tiansheng ziran*). On a smaller rock right beside this chess-board stone one can find another inscription of three characters: "Drunken Stone Junior" (Xiao Zuishi).[59] The Drunken Stone not only perpetuates but also proliferates.

Wu Zongci continues, "After two thousand years, if we must prove one stone right and another stone wrong, it would be a little too literal-minded. The humors of the ancients should be comprehended intuitively."[60] "Intuitive comprehension" (*yihui*) of ancient people's "humors" (*fengqu*) is an important concept in Chinese hermeneutics. It implies a direct communication with the mind of the ancients, an intuitive understanding of the most intrinsic psychological activities of the ancients. It excludes from consideration any sense of historical limitations: we are seen as existing in the same dimension of time and space as the ancients; there is no barrier between the two parties caused by different historical circumstances or social and cultural conditions. The Drunken Stone seems to be the perfect illustration of Wu Zongci's statement: a huge, heavy rock, it is stable, almost permanent (at least to human perception); it has no layers of depth but only a surface that is being inscribed, read, and stroked, and all meanings converge on this surface, which remains the same from the time of the ancients to the later-born. Preserving something tangible of the great poet, either by once-intimate contact with the poet's body or by visible impressions the poet's body is believed to have left, the stone offers a physical locus which helps the later-born to "pin down" the elusive Tao Yuanming, who is always ramifying into numerous variants, always just evading the most strenuous and thorough efforts to date his life and works. In this sense, the creation of the Drunken Stone parallels the editorial attempt to eliminate the prolific "textual errors" regarded as afflicting and corrupting Tao Yuanming editions in the Northern Song. In the end, the body of the poet becomes a readable text as well, although it changes and fragments and at one time even takes the form of bodily ejection, just like the poet's writings themselves, which are invariably taken as outer manifestations of the poet's inner being, the exterior traces of his mind (*xinji*).

But there is more to the Drunken Stone than its surface. When we trace back to the beginning of the story of the Drunken Stone and follow the path of its development, working through all the additions or erasures of the traces left on it, we realize that the story is not just about reading a rock but also about the manufacturing of meaning. It is about how a nameless rock in the middle of nowhere obtains an identity, a name, by being literally stamped with a poet's physical self, and so transforms a nowhere into a somewhere on the cultural map of China. The story is also about how words generate words, and then more words, and endow nature with meaning and significance. The story of the Drunken Stone is thus an allegory, not just of Tao Yuanming's writings, but of all writings.

Conclusion

Earlier work on Tao Yuanming has tended to accept the Song image of the poet, interpreting poems to confirm this image. By contrast, we have seen the fluidity of the medieval Chinese textual world and how its materials were historically reconfigured for later purposes. Central to our argument are the problems of manuscript culture, the proliferation of variant texts that survived into the Song Dynasty. In the early Song variorum editions and in scholars' notes on editorial practices, we can clearly see how the desire for a particular fixed image of the poet transformed a potentially more various and complex figure into an icon of strongly held Song values; Tao Yuanming's texts were edited and shaped to confirm that Song-intuited image of the person. Indeed, "Tao Yuanming" has long become a text collectively authored by generations of readers who were at the same time scribes, editors, commentators, and anthologists. In the detritus of contested and excluded variants, we may see traces of a less serene and timeless Tao Yuanming, who directly addressed the intellectual issues of his day.

It is vital to remember that this "less serene and timeless Tao Yuanming" is by no means the definitive version. It is only one possibility among many, a possibility that came to be deliberately neglected. The reason for singling out "this version" is that by doing so we may better recognize the motives and desires implied in choosing another version and making it the authoritative one. In other words, no early variant has a more privileged position over the others, and the Tao Yuanming who "gazes" (*wang*) at the mountain is neither more or less "genuine" nor more historically verifiable than the Tao Yuanming who "catches sight of" (*jian*) the mountain. This is perhaps the most difficult thing to accept: we do not now and never will have access to the original version of the text and to the poet who chose one word or another. Instead of attempting to replace one definitive Tao Yuanming with another, I am proposing multiple Tao Yuanmings. As Bernard Cerquiglini wryly asks, "It is hard enough to get used to the idea that there might be more than one *Chanson de Roland*, all of them authentic. But does one have to put up with, for example, several true *Percevals* by Chrétien de Troyes—the most famous romance of the European Middle Ages?"[1]

With this study of Tao Yuanming, I wish to bring attention not only to the profound textual instability of early and medieval China but also to the world beyond it. Texts are altered, truncated, and rewritten. Even authorship changes; names are appended to works that "look like" someone's writings or removed from those that do not "fit in" with an author's perceived style or personality. The "definitive editions" passed on to us, mediated by the editing of Ming and Qing scholars, must be recognized for what they truly are: the products of layers upon layers of emendations that more often than not are ideological decisions. Copying texts by hand was, moreover, practiced throughout imperial China, despite the spread of printing. While it is generally true that people were more conscious of faithful transmission when dealing with Confucian classics and highbrow literature, they felt much less compunction about fiddling with "lower" literary forms, such as vernacular fiction. Li Qing (1602–1683) records that a scribe even made changes to government documents to be sent to the Hanlin Academy for future history writing. Profoundly troubled to find that the sources for the historical record had been altered, Li Qing asked the scribe who had authorized those additions and deletions; the scribe answered, "It was me, your humble servant, sir."[2] Attention to the problems of manuscript culture is useful not only in examining earlier texts, but may also prove immensely valuable in reconsidering late imperial fiction and drama as well as the ways in which modern scholarship has used the evidence. The native Chinese tradition, with its patriarchal and hierarchical quest for a neat family tree of editions and manuscript copies of a given work, continued and still continues, easily merging with nineteenth-century European philological practice. This older version of philology was described by Cerquiglini as "a bourgeois, paternalist, and hygienist system of thought about the family; it cherishes filiation, tracks down adulterers, and is afraid of contamination."[3]

Tao Yuanming proves an excellent case in the study of manuscript culture not only because his collection is one of the few pre-Tang collections that have survived to us more or less intact (in contrast with many other Six Dynasties poets whose works had dispersed and been lost over the centuries and were only collected together again much later by the Ming editors from various sources, such as encyclopedias), but more importantly, because Tao Yuanming has become a cultural icon, to an extent that few other poets can match. During the imperial period Tao Yuanming was held up as a noble recluse and a loyal subject; twentieth-century Chinese scholarship on Tao Yuanming often lays great stress on how the perceived personal qualities of the poet constitute an essential "Chineseness." This "Chineseness" itself, however, is an imaginary construct born of nationalism. In many cases, to speak of the so-called "uniqueness of the Chinese experience" is only the consequence of the speaker's ignorance of other cultures and civilizations. By being too eager to define "China" against the Other (an equally imaginarily consolidated "West"), one risks reductionism; a cultural tradition that is vital, complex, full of internal conflicts, tensions, and different voices, and constantly changing and evolving is often reduced to a lifeless, changeless, monolithic thing called "traditional China." Much careful and deliberate dismantling of that image of "traditional China" is necessary, and it is here that we must turn back to an extremely useful tool whose significance far exceeds itself: philology.

There are several traditional Chinese branches of learning that may be considered as belonging to the sphere of philology: *banben xue* (edition studies), *jiaokan xue* (textual studies), and *xungu xue* (which is most properly "philology," as it is the study of words). All of these branches of learning are considered by many as reactionary, and even some of the scholars who are still working in these fields often feel apologetic for what they do. When I bring up philology here, however, I hope that the reader has already finished the major part of this book instead of "jumping to the conclusion," and so sufficiently understands that philology, instead of being irrelevant, dry, outdated, and reactionary, can bring about a revolution in what we do with traditional literature—it all depends on how we deploy it. Philology is, quite simply, a way of using the evidence and accepting the truth of where the evidence leads; those who make it into a tool for defending the iconic status of "canonical" authors and works are, quite frankly, abusing it.[4]

In the last work of the late Edward W. Said, *Humanism and Democratic Criticism*, a book passionately concerned with the fate of the humanities in the contemporary world, there is a chapter entitled "The Return to Philology." Said begins the chapter with the following statement: "Philology is just about the least with-it, least sexy, and most unmodern of any of the branches of learning associated with humanism, and it is the least likely to turn up in discussions about humanism's relevance to life at the beginning of the twenty-first century." He then goes on to defend philology as a discipline that "involves getting inside the process of language already going on in words and making it disclose what may be hidden or incomplete or masked or distorted in any text we may have before us," an "intellectually compelling discipline" which "needs *somehow* to be restored, reinvigorated, and made relevant to the humanistic enterprise" (my italics).[5] The question is, how? One of the things I have hoped to achieve in this book is to demonstrate, even in a small way, how we may use philological strategies such as edition studies and close reading to reexamine certain inherited "truths," as well as to question what it takes to make an idol, and why. Structures of power and authority are made of written and spoken words, and thus can only be understood and resisted with words.

To truly understand how the world works, we need to understand the cultures of which the world is composed; to truly understand cultures, we need to understand their histories; to truly understand histories, we need to understand what they are made of—largely words and texts, the results of censorship (often self-imposed), and generations of editing, emendation, and alteration. To understand the history of cultural phenomena as a process rather than a moment of origination is a means to see how history is still at work in the present; this makes it more difficult to wall off the past and claim a self-sufficient autonomy for the present. If we observe what is happening right now in the world, we may see something entirely new taking hold of our lives and at the same time may detect a familiar pattern of transformation in the history of human civilization. What I am speaking of is the Internet, which bears an interesting resemblance to manuscript culture.

When printing first flourished and replaced manuscript copies as the dominant mode of textual transmission, many people regarded it with apprehension and anxiety, if not downright hostility. Reading printed books, some alarmed Song scholars felt, was a serious threat to true learning. They argued that it completely changed a reader's relation with the text as compared to copying a text by hand. Of course, they were absolutely right. If textual instability is a central characteristic of manuscript culture, then print culture tries to fix things in several senses of the word: to repair and emend until the perfect edition is "reconstructed"—the one that "best reflects" the author's original intent, and to stabilize a text so that it becomes frozen, fixed, immutable, closed to outside intervention.

The Internet, however, makes things fluid again, and is extremely difficult to police. If the printed word is finite and authoritative, then the Internet has no authority, and it is admittedly much cheaper. (In Chinese cities and towns, "Internet bars" or *wangba* are spreading at an astonishing speed, where one can surf the Web at a very low cost). Compared to publishing by print, which is not yet for everyone, anyone who has access to the Internet may post a text on it and make his or her voice heard, and all the information posted on the Internet is rendered equally available, which again forms a contrast with book distribution and sale. Writings, when entered into the computer, are often excerpted, taken apart, fractured, and unattributed. To the horror of many an author, texts are running amok. The proprietorship of one's writings effectively established by print culture is falling apart on the Internet. Leah Marcus talks about the computerization of Shakespeare studies that is already taking place at some institutions, which enables readers to "become their own editors" and generate "myriad texts." "Soon those of us who choose to will—for better or worse—be able to construct our own editions of this and other plays on the computer screen and bring them almost instantly into the more stable medium of print via desktop publication."[6]

Internet publishing is of course not a simple replica of manuscript culture, but the two share a distinguishing trait: lack of authority and center. It is indeed no accident that the new textual criticism, represented by the works of scholars such as Jerome J. McGann, happened simultaneously with the spread of the computer technology.[7] In manuscript culture a text existed in a much more fluid and open form, so that a sixteen-year-old courtesan felt no diffidence in making emendations in the poetic text of Du Fu, already regarded as a major literary figure at the time, and her emendations were received with admiration. There is something immensely refreshing and liberating about such a story, which is so contrary to our accustomed notion of the author as a sacred genius, the canon as a hallowed, untouchable entity, and emendation as a right conferred by academic credentials. For a patriarchal culture emphasizing hierarchy, seniority, and male authority, this story comes as a surprise, but it effectively reminds us, once again, that classical Chinese culture was not a changeless, monolithic entity, and that our own conception of the text as a closed, finite form has a history often forgotten and yet much shorter than we think, whether in the West or the East.

In his famous metaphor, Song Shou compared collating to dust-sweeping. Although averse to dust in everyday life, I am rather fond of the idea of it, for it is, after all, our home. Tao Yuanming once asked us to "give oneself to the waves of the Great Transformation, / neither exultant nor with fear."[8] For him, as well as for his favorite philosopher, Zhuangzi, the "Great Transformation" is the only constant in human life.

Notes

Introduction

Unless otherwise noted, all translations are my own.

Ibn Hazm, *Ring of the Dove*, 50.

1. Ibn Hazm, *Ring of the Dove*, 48–50.

2. Dagenais, *Ethics of Reading in Manuscript Culture*, 17.

3. Guanxiu made a mistake here: the year of *xinchou* (881) was in fact the first year of the Zhonghe reign, and Emperor Xizong had changed reign titles twice since the Qianfu reign (874–879). Living in isolation in hiding, Guanxiu probably did not know what went on in the capital.

4. Guanxiu, "Shanju shi," in *Quan Tang shi*, 837.9425.

5. Gao Yanxiu, "Young Master Wei," in *Quan Tang wudai xiaoshuo*, 3.2085.

6. Cherniack, "Book Culture and Textual Transmission in Sung China," 73.

7. Ouyang Xiu, *Ouyang Xiu quanji*, 1189.

8. Ye Mengde, *Bishu luhua*, in *Song Yuan biji xiaoshuo daguan*, 3.2647.

9. *Ibid.*, 3.2985.

10. *The Sui History* (Sui shu) was compiled between 629 and 636, and *The Old Tang History* (Jiu Tang shu) was compiled between 941 and 945. The bibliography section (*jingji zhi*) of *The Sui History* records two manuscript copies of Tao Yuanming's collection: one in nine *juan* and one in six *juan* (35.1072). The bibliography section of *The Old Tang History* records a manuscript copy of Tao Yuanming's collection in five *juan* (47.2067). *The New Tang History* (Xin Tang shu), collaboratively compiled by Song Xiang's brother Song Qi (998–1061), Ouyang Xiu, and a number of others from 1044 to 1060, records a twenty-*juan* Tao Yuanming collection (60.1590).

11. Vice Director Yang is Yang Xiuzhi (509–582), who compiled a Tao Yuanming collection of ten *juan* after Xiao Tong. None of these early copies of

Tao Yuanming's works is extant, except for Xiao Tong's preface, his biography of Tao Yuanming, Yan Yanzhi's elegy, and Yang Xiuzhi's foreword.

12. Song Xiang's colophon first appeared in a printed edition of Tao Yuanming's collection which Song Xiang himself collated and edited. The edition is no longer extant except for his "note," which is often referred to as "Prime Minister Song's private note" (Song chengxiang siji) and is included in a number of later editions of the Tao Yuanming collection. For the most recent modern punctuated version, see Yuan Xingpei, *Tao Yuanming ji jianzhu*, 615.

13. *Song shihua quanbian*, 1.609.

14. Han Yu, *Han Yu quanji jiaozhu*, 18.

15. *Song shihua quanbian*, 1.789. The Du Fu line is from his poem "Respectfully Presented to the Assistant Director of the Left, the Senior Wei: Twenty-two Couplets" (Fengzeng Wei zuocheng zhang ershieryun) (*Du shi xiangzhu*, 73–80).

16. It is not immediately clear from the context whom one should "be afraid of," Wang Anshi or Huang Tingjian, but Liu Gongfu's ironic and disapproving attitude toward the creative editing style of Wang Anshi is quite clear (*Song Yuan biji xiaoshuo daguan*, 3.2939). The title of Du Fu's poem is "Visiting the Fengxian Temple at Longmen" (You Longmen Fengxian Si). There are about eight different versions for the second character of the line quoted in *Daoshan qinghua*. *Que* is now what most editions agree upon (*Du shi xiangzhu*, 1–2).

17. *Song shihua quanbian*, 1.612. Du Fu's line is taken from a poem entitled "A Drunken Song" (Zuishi ge) (*Du shi xiangzhu*, 174).

18. My calculation yields the result of one hundred and sixty-four notes for variants, barring the two pieces of prose included in Tang Han's edition.

19. Yuan Xingpei, *Tao Yuanming yanjiu*, 205–6.

20. *Ibid.*, 207–8.

21. Li Ruiliang, *Zhongguo gudai tushu liutong shi*, 406.

22. Ye Dehui, *Shulin qinghua*, 255–57.

23. *Jiaokan* means "collation." Having always been an important scholarly activity in imperial China, it reached a peak in the Qing.

24. Yao Boyue, *Huang Pilie pingzhuan*, 123.

25. See Chen Xianxing's preface to *Zhongguo guji gao chao jiao ben tulu* (An Illustrated Catalogue of Original Drafts, Manuscript Copies, and Collated Copies of Old Chinese Books), 9.

26. As Lucille Chia says, "the process of printing by facsimile woodcuts in

which the original handwritten copy is pasted face down on the block to be engraved made the bond between the manuscript and the final printed version far more intimate than was the case in Western typographic printing, in which both the text and image could diverge drastically from the manuscript original and did so increasingly with time" (*Printing for Profit*, 42). Both copyists and woodblock cutters could and did alter texts either consciously or by mistake or both.

27. For instance, Tao Yuanming's poems appear in elementary school textbooks, and a special program introducing him was broadcast as part of a TV series "The Five Thousand Years of China" (Zhongguo wuqian nian) on April 20 and 21, 1995.

28. Charles Yim-tze Kwong's book, *Tao Qian and the Chinese Poetic Tradition: The Quest for Cultural Identity*, embodies the essentialized view of Tao Yuanming as a transparent, "genuine" person and a "Chinese" cultural hero. Another case in point is Stephen Owen's essay "The Self's Perfect Mirror: Poetry as Autobiography," in *The Vitality of the Lyric Voice*, 71–102. The essay evokes much-heated responses, as Owen's attempt to see irony and complexities in the poetic persona of Tao Yuanming is construed as "character assassination." For instance, see Lin Wenyue's article "Koumen zhuo yanci" in *Zhonggu wenxue luncong*, 205–21. Her disagreement with Owen's reading is described by Zhong Youmin as a difference existing "between the Chinese Tao'ologist and American sinologist" (*Taoxue fazhan shi*, 457). What turns out to be even more interesting than the two different readings themselves is the deeper cultural message read into them and the contemporary identity politics embedded in these scholarly issues.

29. Marcus, *Unediting the Renaissance*, 26–27.

30. *Ibid.*, 30.

31. Shen Gua (ca. 1031–1095), *Xin jiaozheng Mengxi bitan*, 25.261. Zhu Bian, on the other hand, attributed the remark to Song Minqiu (*Song Yuan biji xiaoshuo daguan*, 3.2985).

1 Possession & Loss

Huang Tingjian quanji, 1.168.

1. This text is based on the fragment kept in *Classified Extracts from Literature* (Yiwen leiju), 65.1161. It is also based on the earliest extant handwritten copy of *Wen xuan* (*Tang chao Wen xuan jizhu huicun*, 1.470).

2. Wang Yao, *Tao Yuanming ji*, 63. Chrysanthemum flowers were thought to be an effective drug promoting health and longevity. Many pieces of prose and poetry on chrysanthemums from the medieval period emphasize their medicinal value more than anything else. Zhong Hui's (225–264) "*Fu* on Chrysanthemum Flowers" (Juhua fu) states that "those who take them will live a long life; those who eat them will communicate with gods" (Yan Kejun [1762–1843], *Quan sanguo wen*, 25.1188a). Chrysanthemums were often taken as an infusion in wine. See, for instance, Sun Chu's (218?–293) "*Fu* on Chrysanthemum Flowers" (Juhua fu) and Xin Xiao's (ca. the fourth century) "Encomium on Chrysanthemum Flowers" (Juhua song) (Yan Kejun, *Quan Jin wen*, 60.1801a, 144.2287b). In *Xijing zaji* (A Miscellaneous Record of the Western Capital), a work variously attributed to Liu Xin (53? B.C.E.–23 C.E.), Ge Hong (fl. 302–326), Xiao Ben (ob. 552), or even Wu Jun (469–520), a method of brewing the chrysanthemum wine with chrysanthemums and sticky rice was recorded (*Xijing zaji quanyi*, 3.106).

3. James R. Hightower (*Poetry of T'ao Ch'ien*, 131), following Wang Yao, notes that South Mountain may be "a prime symbol" of long life and cites a line from *Shi jing* (The Classic of Poetry), "Live as long as South Mountain," as a possible source of allusion (Wang Yao, *Tao Yuanming ji*, 63). For the *Shi jing* line, see *Maoshi zhengyi* in *Shisanjing zhushu* (Commentary and Subcommentary to the Thirteen Classics), compiled by Ruan Yuan (1764–1849), 913.331.

4. *Zhuangzi jishi*, 9.26.944; Burton Watson's translation, *Complete Works of Chuang Tzu*, 302.

5. Zhangye is in modern-day Gansu Province, in the far west of China; Youzhou is in modern-day Hebei, in the northeast.

6. The brothers Boyi and Shuqi protested against the Zhou conquest of the Shang and went to live on Shouyang Mountain, feeding on bracken. They eventually starved to death. The Yi River is where in the late Warring States period the Crown Prince of Yan saw off Jing Ke (?–227 B.C.E.), whom he sent to assassinate the King of Qin. See Sima Qian's (145?–87 B.C.E.) *Shi ji* (Records of the Historian), "The Biography of Boyi," and "The Biographies of the Assassins" (*Shi ji*, 61.2123, 86.2534).

7. The eighth poem in the series "In Imitation of Ancient Poems" (Nigu).

8. *Huainan honglie jijie*, 19.654; *Shuo yuan shuzheng*, 16.475. Zhuangzi lamented that he had nobody to talk to after Huishi died (*Zhuangzi*, 8.24.843).

9. Tang Yongtong, *Wei Jin xuanxue lungao*, 23–42.

10. From Wang Bi's *Zhouyi lueli* (General Remarks on *The Changes of the Zhou*) (*Zhouyi zhushu ji buzheng*, 9–10).

11. Stephen Owen's translation, *Readings in Chinese Literary Thought*, 33. Ouyang Jian (270?–300), in his essay "Language Giving Fullness of the Concept" (Yan jin yi lun), argues for the same case, but he also points out that the longstanding and commonly held belief is the opposite supposition (*Quan Jin wen*, 109.2084a).

12. That language and books are "the dregs of the ancients" and cannot truly reveal their essence and spirit is the argument of the story of wheelwright Bian (Lun Bian) (*Zhuangzi*, 5.13.490–91).

13. Liu Yiqing (403–44), *Shishuo xinyu jianshu*, 18.15.660–61.

14. *Ibid.*, 18.11.659.

15. *Ibid.*, 25.28.802. Ang Hill (appearing in a textually corrupted form as Yin Hill) is in modern-day Zhejiang Province.

16. Chaofu and Xu You both appear in Huangfu Mi's (215–82) *Gaoshi zhuan* (Biographies of High-minded Gentlemen). Upon hearing that the emperor wanted to abdicate the throne to him, Xu You felt his ears were sullied by the news and washed them in the river. When the "nest-dweller" saw it, he blamed Xu You for polluting the water (*Gaoshi zhuan*, 1.2a–3a).

17. *Gaoyi shamen zhuan* was written by Zhu Faji (ca. fourth century). It is cited in Liu Xiaobiao's (462–521) commentary to this anecdote (Liu Yiqing, *Shishuo xinyu jianshu*, 25.28.802).

18. *Jin shu* (The Jin History), 94.2460.

19. Jin poet Wang Kangju's poem "Opposing the Summons of the Recluse" (Fan zhaoyin shi) begins with these lines: "A lesser recluse hides in mountains or marshes; / a great recluse hides in court and market" (Lu Qinli, *Quan Jin shi*, 15.953).

20. "Those who visited Stone Gate" refers to a group of Buddhist monks who climbed Stone Gate Mountain in 400 and wrote poems (as well as a preface to the poems) celebrating their travel.

21. Yan Kejun, *Quan Song wen*, 20.2545–46. For a complete translation of Zong Bing's preface, see Susan Bush and Hsio-yen Shih, *Early Chinese Texts on Painting*, 36–38.

22. One thinks of the legendary Eastern Jin painter Gu Kaizhi (345?–407?), who, according to *Shishuo xinyu*, insists that the eyes are the most important part of a person in a figure painting, to the extent that he would ponder and reflect and leave the pupils unpainted for several years, because, he declares,

"The beauty and ugliness of the four limbs are not the 'point' of a portrait; the transmission of the spirit of a person and the portrayal of his likeness lie precisely in the pupils" (Liu Yiqing, *Shishuo xinyu jianshu,* 21.13.721).

23. *Song shihua quanbian,* 1.609.

24. *Ibid.,* 1.786.

25. *Ibid.,* 1.789.

26. For instance, Ma Yongqing (*jinshi* degree, 1109) says in *Lanzhenzi* that Su Shi's line "Blown by the dark wind from beyond sky, the sea stands up erect" was altered to "The sea is blown over by the dark wind from beyond sky" (*Song Yuan biji xiaoshuo daguan,* 3.3185). But an even more amusing instance is recorded in Shao Bowen's (1056–1134) *Shaoshi wenjian houlu*: Su Shi's grandson Zhonghu was once made to read one of Su Shi's poems aloud to him from a capital printed edition of Su Shi's collection as Su Shi wrote it down for someone who had asked for his calligraphy. As Zhonghu was reading, Su Shi suddenly put down the brush and stared at him angrily: "That you should say 'fragrant wine'!" Zhonghu was caught by surprise and trembled with fear for a long time before he realized that the printed edition had mistakenly used "fragrant wine" (*xianglao*) for "spring wine" (*chunlao*). "Fragrant" (*xiang*) and "spring" (*chun*) look similar graphically (*Song Yuan biji xiaoshuo daguan,* 2.1955).

27. "'Seeing South Mountain' is indeed marvelous. I don't know who on earth changed it to 'gazing at South Mountain'!" From *Wen xuan yuezhu,* annotated by Min Qihua (fl. 1628–1643), with critical notes by Sun Kuang (1542–1613), cited in *Tao Yuanming shiwen huiping* (subsequently referred to as *Huiping*), 169. Cheng Qianfan (1913–2000), an eminent modern scholar of classical Chinese poetry, strongly argues for the reading of *jian* on exactly the same ground as Su Shi and his followers. See *Gushi kaosuo,* 308–14.

28. *Song shihua quanbian,* 1.551.

29. *Ibid.,* 3.2440.

30. Shen Gua, *Xin jiaozheng Mengxi bitan,* 338. Also see *Song shihua quanbian,* 1.501.

31. Su Shi claims that "Shu printed editions with their large characters were all fine editions," and implies that he had seen the variant *jian* in one of those "fine editions" of Shu when he was young (*Song shihua quanbian,* 1.789). The region of Shu, modern-day Sichuan Province, was where Su Shi came from. It was a flourishing printing center in the ninth century.

32. Ye Mengde, *Shilin shihua.* See *Song shihua quanbian,* 3.2694. Although

the Chinese grammar does not make it absolutely clear it was Su Shi, rather than Zhao Delin, who effected the changes, Ye Mengde makes sure that we know it was Su Shi by adding that Su Shi also wrote two parallel couplets (one of which is a sort of proverb) at the end of the copy, which have nothing to do with Tao Yuanming's poetry. Ye Mengde wondered whether Su Shi had written them down because he was going to make use of them as materials for his poetry. But since he could not find these lines in Su Shi's poetry collection, he decided that the Master must have jotted them down randomly.

33. *Song shihua quanbian,* 2.1042–43. Du Fu's line is taken from his poem "Sending Off Commandant Cai Xilu When He Returns to Longyou; Also Sending to Secretary Gao the Thirty-fifth" (Song Cai Xilu duwei huan Longyou yin ji Gao sanshiwu shuji) (*Du shi xiangzhu,* 238). Guangling is the old name of Yangzhou, where Su Shi was magistrate, with Chao Buzhi serving under him for a brief period in 1092. In *Song shihua quanbian* the last sentence, from "Something like this" to "misleading," is included as part of Su Shi's remark.

34. *Song Shihua quanbian,* 1.213; Stephen Owen's translation, *Readings in Chinese Literary Thought,* 370.

35. *Song shihua quanbian,* 2.1017.

36. *Ibid.,* 2.954.

37. *Ibid.,* 2.948.

38. *Ibid.,* 2.1033.

39. *Ibid.,* 3.2388.

40. *Ibid.,* 3.3006.

41. Bai Juyi, *Bai Juyi ji jianjiao,* 306.

42. Wei Yingwu, *Wei Yingwu ji jiaozhu,* 316–17.

43. See Ge Lifang's *Yunyu yangqiu* in *Song shihua quanbian,* 8.8225-26. The ironic thing for Ge Lifang is, however, that his father, Ge Shengzhong (1072–1144), a great fan of Tao Yuanming and a careful reader of *Wen xuan,* obviously had taken *wang* for *jian* despite the opinion of Su Shi. Ge Shengzhong once built a pavilion and named it "Fundamental Truth" (Zhenyi). In a long poem celebrating the completion of the pavilion as well as praising Tao Yuanming, Ge Shengzhong wrote, "The autumn color by the eastern hedge is getting late; / I *gaze at* the green hills in the distance" (my italics; *Song shihua quanbian,* 3.2582–83).

44. Wei Yingwu, *Wei Yingwu ji jiaozhu,* 460.

45. The real Nine Glories Mountain is in modern-day Anhui Province.

46. Su Shi, *Su Shi shiji,* 6.2047–48.

47. Chao Buzhi, *Jilei ji*, 2.223. According to Su Shi's son Su Guo (1072–1123), the rock is only one foot tall. See his poem on the rock entitled "In the Collection of Li Zhengchen of Hukou There Is an Extraordinary Rock of About One Foot Long, with Nine Slender Peaks. Father Named It the Nine Glories Mountain in a Jug and Wrote a Poem to Commemorate It. He Ordered That I Write Another Poem After Him" (*Quan Song shi*, 23.15469). Guo Xiangzheng was a friend of Su Shi, a poet, and an active participant in the Northern Song culture of connoisseurship.

48. Egan, *Word, Image, and Deed in Su Shi's Life*, 157.

49. Su Shi, *Su Shi shiji*, 6.1940-42. Wang Jinqing is Wang Shen (ca. eleventh century), an art connoisseur and collector, the son-in-law of Emperor Yingzong of Song (r. 1064–1068). Su Shi proposed to exchange the rock for a Tang painting in Wang's collection, but Wang refused. Later Su Shi wrote another two poems revolving around the incident; at least three other friends, besides Wang Jinqing, joined in. One of the friends coveted both the painting and the rock, while another suggested the drastic solution that the painting be burned and the rock be smashed, so that none would be able to acquire them and subsequently would stop coveting them. See *Su Shi shiji*, 6.1945–48.

50. Su Shi, *Su Dongpo quanji*, 389–90. In the account he boasts of a change since his youth: that is, even if he still collected things, "I no longer cared when such things were taken by someone else." For a full English translation, see Owen, *Anthology of Chinese Literature*, 663–64.

51. There is debate as to who the General of Jianwei was—Liu Huaisu (367–407) or Liu Jingxuan (ca. early fifth century), but the identity of the general hardly matters to our understanding of the poem. Qian Creek is in modern Anhui Province.

52. The "righteous wind" is usually understood in the context of *The Classic of Changes*. Here it refers to the gentle spring wind that "furthers" the myriad things and helps them grow. *Yifeng* has a variant reading, *zaiyi*. If *zaiyi* is adopted, the line means that the myriad things reside harmoniously in the just, never severed from each other.

53. Many commentators have taken the first character of this line, *liang*, as signifying "truly" or "indeed." Here I follow one of the early meanings of *liang*, which is "to hold on to something."

54. *Analects* (*Lunyu zhushu* in *Shisanjing zhushu*), 9.81. A similar quotation can be found in *Zhuangzi jishi*, 9.28.982.

55. He Zhuo (1661–1722) and Tao Shu (1779–1839) are the only two pre-

modern scholars who give *guizhou* as the variant (Tao Shu, *Jingjie xiansheng ji*, 3.20). Of twentieth-century scholars, Lu Qinli, Yang Yong, and A. R. Davis form a minority group in adopting *hezhou*. But *guizhou* is the much more popular version. Gong Bin's opinion on this issue is fairly representative: "*Hezhou* does not make sense in the context. Therefore, we should follow the mainstream opinion and choose *guizhou*" (*Tao Yuanming ji jiaojian*, 189).

56. The character *shan* 山 (mountain) in this sentence might also be read *shan* with the water radical *shan* 汕, which means "fishnet."

57. *Zhuangzi jishi*, 3.6.243.

58. Huang Tingjian's poem is entitled "Matching Rhymes with Dongpo's 'Nine Glories in a Jug'" (Zhui he Dongpo "Huzhong Jiuhua") (*Huang Tingjian quanji*, 1.168–69). Stephen Owen gives an insightful reading of Su Shi's and Huang Tingjian's poems in *Traditional Chinese Poetry and Poetics*, 143–62.

59. The last we heard of Nine Glories Mountain in a Jug was in Zhu Yu's *Pingzhou ketan*, a collection of "random jottings" with a preface (now lost) dated the first year of the Xuanhe reign (1119): "In recent years the worth of a fist-size rock may rise so high that it could simply be priceless. Guo Xiangzheng, a native of Taiping, used to have a rock in his collection, which is about a foot wide, with nine small peaks and holes that look like ravines and valleys at the bottom. Ever since Dongpo named it Nine Glories Mountain in a Jug, it was heavily priced. I have heard that it is in the imperial collection now" (*Song Yuan biji xiaoshuo daguan*, 2.2322). The emperor, the ultimate *youlizhe* who became the last known owner of the much-coveted rock, was Huizong (r. 1101–1126), whose insatiable desire for collecting things, from antiques and art pieces to strange rocks and exotic flowers, is often held as responsible for the fall of the Northern Song. Fang Shao (1066–?), a contemporary of Su Shi, attempted to destroy the aura of the lost rock/mountain by pointing out its defect: "The rock kept in the possession of Li Zhengchen of Hukou, the one named Nine Glories Mountain in a Jug by Dongpo, I have never seen in person. And yet I once looked at the rubbing made by Zhengchen: although the nine peaks are arranged like an eagle's beak, they are not very craggy; besides, there is a white trace around the waist of the rock, as if it were bound by a silk cord—this is a disease of rocks. I don't know why Dongpo loved it so much that he wanted to purchase it with a hundred gold pieces. Wouldn't it be erring on the side of enthusiasm? I am afraid that a poet simply has too much brush power and so he often makes use of objects and phenomena to release his literary imagination in order to leave some extraordinary and strange spectacle for the

later-born" (*Bozhai bian*, 187). Like Chao Buzhi, Fang Shao understands that worth does not reside so much in the rock itself as in the poet's appreciation of it. In his account, Su Shi is restored to being the man of strength, *youlizhe*, the "extra power" of whose brush endows things of nature with charm and value.

60. Su Shi would often copy out a poem by Tao Yuanming and then write a colophon at the end. For instance, he writes in a colophon to the fifth poem of Tao Yuanming's "In Imitation of Ancient Poems" series: "On the twenty-first day of the second month of the second year of the Shaosheng reign [1095], I, Dongpo jushi, after drinking plenty of wine and having a full meal, sat in silence in the Studio of No Stray Thoughts, muddled and dazed as if falling asleep. Upon waking, I copied out one poem by Yuanming to show my son Guo" (*Song shihua quanbian,* 1.798). According to Shao Bowen, "Of all the ancients, Dongpo only copied the poetry of Tao Yuanming, Du Zimei [Du Fu], Li Taibai [Li Bai, 701–762], Han Tuizhi [Han Yu], and Liu Zihou [Liu Zongyuan, 773–819]" (*Song Yuan biji xiaoshuo daguan,* 2.1929). But this statement is an exaggeration. The anonymous author of *Daoshan qinghua* records that Su Shi loved the Tang poet Du Mu's (803–852) quatrain set "On Passing by Huaqing Palace" so much that "he himself claimed that he had written it thirty or forty times for people [who asked for his calligraphy]" (*Song Yuan biji xiaoshuo daguan,* 3.2932).

61. He Zhuo claims that he has collated his edition with "the original edition of the Xuanhe woodblock made of the wood of a date tree" ("Zhuben xulu" [Prefaces and Descriptions of Various Editions], 18, in Tao Shu's *Jingjie xiansheng ji*).

62. Liu Shengmu, *Changchu zhai suibi xubi sanbi sibi wubi*, 288.

63. Mao Yi's colophon is included in the various reprints of the Su Shi edition, which are discussed in detail in the bibliography.

64. Qian Qianyi, *Muzhai chuxue ji,* 85.1781–82.

65. First poem in the series "Eight Poems in Replacement of Prose Celebrating the Completion of the Tower of Crimson Cloud" (Jiangyun lou shangliang yi shi dai wen ba shou) (*Muzhai chuxue ji,* 20.738). Chen Yinke, one of the best-known twentieth-century Chinese historians, in fact says that "Muzhai owned two *youwu* all his life: one being the Song edition of *The Former and Latter Han Histories*, and the other being Hedong jun [Liu Shi]" (Chen Yinke, *Liu Rushi biezhuan*, 416).

66. Qian Zeng acquired a large number of whatever survived from Qian Qianyi's book collection after the fire of Crimson Cloud Tower. According to

Wang Shizhen (1634–1711), "Master Qian's book collection was the best in the south. After the fire of Crimson Cloud, he gave the rest of the Song editions to his grand-nephew Zeng [courtesy name Zunwang]. . . . After Master Qian passed away, Qian Zeng sold all of them to the Ji family of Taixing, and so Master Qian's book collection was all dispersed. I hear that the books have passed into the hands of the Xu family of Kunshan now" (Wang Shizhen, *Fen gan yuhua*, 4.91–92). Also see Tang Xuan's *Qing chu cangshujia Qian Zeng yanjiu*, 112–21.

67. See Zhang Hongwei's discussion of this in *Chuban wenhua shilun*, 196–97.

68. The story of the coveted Song edition did not end there. According to Qian Zeng's colophon on a Tao Yuanming collection in his possession, he and Gu Mei were as close as "brothers with different surnames," and so, seeing how much he "loved Tao Yuanming's collection," Gu Mei actually gave the edition back to Qian as "a present" (which almost certainly involved some sort of exchange, as was customary among book collectors). Then, between 1666 and 1667, Qian Zeng sold many of his Song editions to Ji Zhenyi (1630–1674), including this one. After Ji died, his book collection became dispersed, and Gu Mei bought the edition back and showed it to Qian Zeng—but this time, he did not give it to him as a present. The Tao Yuanming collection in Qian Zeng's collection on which he wrote this colophon was reportedly "a purchased facsimile of a Song edition done by a very good hand." See Qian Zeng's *Dushu minqiu ji*, 390–91.

69. Gu Zixiu's colophon is contained in Tang Han's edition, which was reprinted by Zhonghua Shuju of Beijing in 1987 (see bibliography).

70. Wu Qian gave an ambiguously phrased account regarding the reprint. According to Wu, "In the year of *xinchou* [1781], my friend Mr. Bao Yiwen obtained it [i.e., this edition] when he traveled to Wuqu (Suzhou). On his return trip he paid a visit to my lodge at Little Tong Tree Creek Mountain and showed it to me. The paper and ink are exquisite, and an ancient fragrance assailed the nose; it indeed is a fine edition printed in the Song. . . . Mr. Bao urged me to reprint it, so as to share it with people who have the same passion." This colophon is dated 1786. In the above account, Wu refrained from mentioning that Bao Yiwen gave the original Song edition to Zhang Yanchang out of ignorance; nor did he point out that his reprint was actually based on a copy of the original edition. By connecting the events of 1781 and 1786 together, he made it sound as if his reprint was directly from the original. This, of course, was intended to increase the value of his reprint as well as cover up

his embarrassment about having failed to recognize the Song edition when he first saw it. For Wu Qian's colophon, see "Zhuben xulu," 20–21, in Tao Shu's *Jingjie xiansheng ji.*

71. Fuxi was a legendary emperor of high antiquity.

72. *Quan Tang shi,* 815.9178.

73. *Jin shu,* 34.1020. Stephen Owen's translation in *Remembrances,* 23.

74. *Jin shu,* 34.1031.

75. Stephen Owen, *End of the Chinese "Middle Ages,"* 25.

2 "Who the Master Is, No One Knows"

Chunqiu Zuozhuan zhengyi, 15.255.

1. As mentioned before, Tao Dan, Tao Yuanming's uncle, was a much more resolute and "radical" recluse than Tao Yuanming, by all accounts. He lived in a cottage in the mountains, never got married, and only kept a white deer for company. If a relative or friend paid him a visit, he would escape to the other side of the ravine, where no one could approach him (*Jin shu,* 94.2460).

2. Davis, *T'ao Yüan-ming,* 1.1–2.

3. Both Kang-i Sun Chang and Stephen Owen have used this phrase "poetry as autobiography" in their discussions of Tao Yuanming's poetry. See Kang-i Sun Chang's *Six Dynasties Poetry,* 16–37; and Stephen Owen's "The Self's Perfect Mirror," in *Vitality of the Lyric Voice,* 71–102.

4. *Mengzi zhushu,* 10b.188.

5. From "The Great Preface to *The Classic of Poetry,*" *Maoshi zhengyi,* 1.13. Stephen Owen's translation (*Readings in Chinese Literary Thought,* 40).

6. *Mengzi zhushu,* 3a.55.

7. *Analects,* 1.6, 5.43.

8. "Shizhuan zhong de Tao Yuanming," 198.

9. The text quoted here is the version as recorded in Tao Yuanming's first official biography in *The Song History* compiled by Shen Yue between 487 and 488, about half a century after Tao Yuanming's death. There exist slight textual variations in other versions (*Song shu,* 93.2286).

10. "Master the Great Man is very old: his personal and courtesy names are not known. His narration of the beginning of heaven and earth and his descriptions of Shennong and the Yellow Emperor [legendary ancient emperors] are clear and illuminating, and no one knows how many years Master has

lived. He once stayed in the mountains of Sumen, hence people all consider him a man beyond worldly affairs and at ease" (Yan Kejun, *Quan sanguo wen,* 46.1315).

11. It is believed that the appearance of "Shenming" as Tao Yuanming's courtesy name in the *Nan shi* was a way of avoiding using Yuan in Yuanming, as the name of the founding emperor of the Tang was Li Yuan (*yuan* and *shen* share the same meaning—"profound" or "depth"). Since the *Nan shi* biography also contains "Yuanming" without changing *yuan* into *shen*, it is assumed that "Shenming" is the trace left from early copies of *Nan shi*, when it was still necessary to avoid using the character that was the personal name of the founding emperor.

12. This point was initially raised by Wu Renjie (*jinshi* degree, 1244), one of the first people to compile a chronology of Tao Yuanming's life. Since then, there has been much speculation concerning the mystery of Tao Yuanming's name(s). Zhu Ziqing once gave a summary of up to ten different theories in his essay "Tao Yuanming nianpu zhong zhi wenti" (*Zhu Ziqing gudian wenxue lunwenji*, 457–59).

13. Tao Yuanming's self-professed style of reading forms a contrast with *zhangju zhi xue*, the kind of painstaking annotation and explication of the Confucian or Daoist classics which was a prevailing scholarly practice in the Wei-Jin period. Yuan Can (421–478) wrote an autobiographical piece entitled "Biography of the Master of Wonderful Virtue" (Miaode xiansheng zhuan), which seems to have closely troped on Tao Yuanming's "Biography of Master Five Willows," and can at least provide a footnote to Tao Yuanming's statement about reading. Yuan Can states that the Master "from his childhood has been sickly, by nature is relaxed and lazy, and does not apply assiduous efforts to anything. As for the discourse of the nine schools and a hundred scholars, or the art of carving the dragon and discussing heaven, he knows about their general substance, but he does not use them to obtain personal fame" (Yan Kejun, *Quan Song wen,* 44.2682b). In other words, Yuan Can is saying that the Master's knowledge is extensive but nonspecialized, and it affords a personal diversion rather than a means of achieving reputation. "The art of carving the dragon and discussing heaven" refers to the Warring States rhetoricians Zou Shi and Zou Yan (ca. third century B.C.E.). See *Shi ji,* 74.2348. Such lack of assiduity in pursuing the *zhangju* type of exegesis may be traced back to the Han. Liang Hong (ca. first century), the famous Eastern Han recluse, was "very well read and extremely learned, but would not do the kind of scholar-

ship such as dividing lines into paragraphs and adding annotations" (*Hou Han shu*, 83.2765). This is considered a virtue in Lao-Zhuang thought. Tao Yuanming's contemporary, Zhang Zhan (ca. late fourth century), the very person who annotated *Liezi*, one of the classics of the Daoist philosophy, once wrote a teasing letter to Fan Ning (ca. late fourth century), a Confucian scholar, who suffered from eye problems, saying that the best way of preserving good eyesight is: "One, cut down reading; two, reduce laborious thinking and worrying; three, concentrate on looking inward; four, simplify outward looking; five, rise late in the morning; six, retire early at night" (*Quan Jin wen*, 138.2256). For an in-depth discussion of reading in Tao Yuanming's age, see Robert Ashmore's forthcoming book, *The Transport of Reading: Text and Understanding in the World of Tao Qian.*

14. Qianlou was an ancient recluse. The speech of his wife is recorded in Liu Xiang's (77–6 B.C.E.) *Lienü zhuan*, 52–53. This, however, might have been a later emendation: all editions of Tao Yuanming collections have "Qianlou once said" and only Zeng Ji's edition notes that one edition has "Qianlou's wife."

15. Wuhuai (No Worries) and Getian are two legendary lords of ancient times. Under their rule was the golden age of mankind.

16. *Analects*, 6.53, 11.98.

17. Qian Zhongshu, *Guan zhui bian*, 4.1228.

18. Alan J. Berkowitz translated Shen Yue's foreword in its entirety, and my translation, while mostly agreeing with his, shows some differences. See Berkowitz, *Patterns of Disengagement*, 178–81.

19. "Furry Elder" was a man who refused to take gold left on the road. When asked his name, he declined to answer (Huangfu Mi, *Gaoshi zhuan*, 4b).

20. The old man who hefted baskets was the recluse who put up Confucius's disciple Zilu overnight. When Zilu went back to seek him, he had left (*Analects*, 18.166).

21. *Song shu*, 93.2275–76.

22. *Laozi jiaoshi*, 25.101.

23. Berkowitz, *Patterns of Disengagement*, 137.

24. For example, the famous "bogus recluse" Huangfu Xizhi, the descendant of Huangfu Mi, was "hired" by the usurper Huan Xuan (369–404) to decline summons to official posts and to play the role of recluse, because each dynasty, Huan Xuan figured, had to have its own recluses (*Jin shu*, 99.2593–94). *Shishuo xinyu* records another story: "When Xu Xun lived in reclusion in a secluded cave to the south of Yongxing, he often received gifts from noble-

men from all over the country. Someone said to him, 'I have heard that the man of Qi Mountain [i.e., Xu You] did not seem to have behaved quite like this.' Xu Xun answered, 'Food wrapped up in rushes and contained in boxes is certainly lighter than the treasure of a throne?'" (Liu Yiqing, *Shishuo xinyu jianshu,* 18.13.660).

25. *Hou Han shu,* 83.2755. For a full translation, see Berkowitz, *Patterns of Disengagement,* 163–67.

26. Berkowitz, *Patterns of Disengagement,* 152.

27. Foucault, *Order of Things,* 144.

28. *Zhuangzi jishi,* 3.7.309.

29. *Bei shi,* 100.3433.

30. The translation is based on A. R. Davis's translation, with modifications (Davis, *T'ao Yüan-ming,* 2.170–74).

31. *Song shu,* 93.2286–90; Yan Kejun, *Quan Liang wen,* 20.3068–69; *Jin shu,* 94.2460–63; *Nan shi,* 75.1856–59.

32. See Liu Yiqing, *Shishuo xinyu jianshu,* 14.23.615. The ethnicity of Tao Kan (and hence of Tao Yuanming) is a point of debate. See Chen Yinke's article "*Wei shu* Sima Rui zhuan jiangdong minzu tiao shizheng ji tuilun," in *Jinmingguan conggao chubian,* 69–106. Also see Gu Zhi's article "Tao Kan ji Tao Yuanming shi Hanzu haishi Xizu ne?" in *Guangming Ribao,* 14 July 1957.

33. Liu Yiqing, *Shishuo xinyu jianshu,* 14.23.615. There are about a dozen anecdotes recorded in *Shishuo xinyu* that are related to Tao Kan, and they to a large extent reflect the Eastern Jin aristocrats' mixed attitude towards him: they both admired his military talent and felt somewhat contemptuous of his humble background as well as his pragmatic, down-to-earth personality. One story is about how Tao Kan had wanted to execute Yu Liang (289–340) for his failure as a minister, but Yu Liang, a nobleman from a well-known clan, won Tao Kan over with his elegant manners as well as his false humility and frugality. Yu Liang assumed humility to soothe Tao Kan's vanity (that a high-class nobleman would actually bow to him), and frugality to appeal to Tao Kan's thrifty, pragmatic instinct. Liu Yiqing had classified their encounter under three categories according to different narrative foci: "Appearance and Behavior," "Guile and Chicanery," and "Stinginess and Meanness" (Liu Yiqing, *Shishuo xinyu jianshu,* 14.23.615, 27.8.856, 29.8.875). For a complete English translation, see Richard Mather's *New Account of Tales of the World,* 312–13, 444–45, 457. Although Yu Liang is not presented in an exactly positive light in "Guile and Chicanery," Tao Kan does not come off well in all three records.

He is shown as vain, beguiled, and stingy, completely under the charm of the well-mannered and sophisticated Yu Liang, even though at the time Tao Kan had come to Yu Liang's aid, not vice versa. Tao Kan may very well have tolerated Yu Liang for political reasons, but in the world of *Shishuo xinyu*, a good story and witty repartee are much more important than social and political reality.

34. *Jin shu*, 66.1782.

35. Liu Yiqing, *Shishuo xinyu jianshu*, 19.19.690.

36. For instance, see *Hou Han shu*, 14.559; *Wei shu*, 7.156, 22.589.

37. Yan Zhitui, *Yanshi jiaxun jijie*, 1.4.47.

38. *Jin shu*, 66.1768; Liu Yiqing, *Shishuo xinyu jianshu*, 19.19.689.

39. *Jin shu*, 66.1768–79. See also Liu Yiqing, *Shishuo xinyu jianshu*, 3.16.178–79.

40. "To the Duke of Changsha" (Zeng Changsha gong) and "Charge to My Son" (Ming zi).

41. In many ways, Tao Yuanming's maternal grandfather, Meng Jia (ca. mid-fourth century), seems to have been closer to the kind of person admired by the Eastern Jin elite and after whom Tao Yuanming modeled his own image. Tao wrote a biography of Meng Jia, "Biography of His Excellency Meng, the Former Chief of Staff to the Zhengxi General of the Jin" (Jin gu Zhengxi dajiangjun zhangshi Meng fujun zhuan). For a complete English translation, see Davis, *T'ao Yüan-ming*, 1.201–6.

42. While scholars agree that *qin* ("parent" *or* "parents") should be understood as one parent only, there is some debate as to which parent it refers to, mother or father. According to Yan Yanzhi's elegy for Tao Yuanming, Tao began his official career as a result of his mother being old and his children young, which means Tao had a family in need of financial support (*Quan Song wen*, 38.2646b). Tao Yuanming's own statement in his elegy for his younger sister, Madame Cheng ("Ji Chengshi mei wen"), that their mother died when he was twelve and she was nine, however, is in direct contradiction to Yan Yanzhi's claim. This contradiction leads to Tang Han's explanation that the mother mentioned in Tao Yuanming's elegy on his sister was the birth mother of his sister, but not Tao Yuanming's own birth mother. This hypothesis is endorsed by Li Gonghuan and Tao Shu as well as many modern commentators. The flaw of this theory is that it fails to take into account Tao Yuanming's rather explicit assertion in his elegy: "Which person has no sibling? / And they are born from the same mother as well. / And yet the affection shared by you

and me / was a hundred times more than the common sibling love." This seems to indicate that Tao Yuanming and his sister were born of the same mother.

43. In the elegy he wrote for Tao Yuanming, Yan Yanzhi cites Tian Guo (fourth century B.C.E.) and Mao Yi (first century), two filial sons who chose to serve only as a way of providing for their parents, to explain Tao Yuanming's official career (*Quan Song wen,* 38.2646b). For Tian Guo's story, see *Hanshi waizhuan jianshu*, 7.589, and *Shuo yuan shuzheng,* 19.578. For Mao Yi's story, see *Dongguan Han ji,* 18.187. For detailed English translations of the *Hanshi waizhuan* and *Dongguan Han ji* passages, see Davis, *T'ao Yüan-ming,* 1.245.

44. Hightower, *Poetry of T'ao Ch'ien,* 268; Davis, *T'ao Yüan-ming,* 1.191.

45. For instance, in "Biographies of Recluses" in *Song shu*, Dai Yong (378–441) is described as "always frail and sickly"; Lei Cizong (386–448) in a letter to his children claimed that he "had always been frail and sickly since youth," and "had returned to the farming life in the fields, dwelt in the mountains, and drunk from the valley stream" (*Song shu,* 93.2276, 93.2293).

46. *Song shu,* 5.75.

47. "Zither and song" refers to taking up an official post, especially the office of a county magistrate. The source story is a passage in *The Analects,* 17.154. "Three-path," on the other hand, is an allusion to Jiang Xu, a first-century Han official who retired during Wang Mang's (45 B.C.E.–23 C.E.) usurpation (8–23 C.E.) and opened three paths leading to his hut, only associating with two other men who were also recluses. Xi Kang's *Gaoshi zhuan* refers to Jiang Xu. It is cited in *Taiping yulan* (comp. 984), 510.2450. In Tao Yuanming's literary exposition "Return," he states, "The three paths have become overgrown."

48. Yuan Xingpei, *Tao Yuanming yanjiu*, 317–20; Li Jinquan, *Tao Yuanming pingzhuan*, 76.

49. Tao Yuanming mentions an uncle named Tao Kui in his biography of Meng Jia, generally taken to be the same uncle as the one referred to here. But Tao Yuanming may have had more than one uncle, and it is unclear who this uncle was or what office he held. Yuan Xingpei, not wanting to believe that Tao Yuanming's uncle appointed him, suggests an emendation of the text, but the emendation does not have any textual basis in the various editions of Tao Yuanming collections (*Tao Yuanming ji jianzhu*, 467–68).

50. For instance, we have two letters written by Zhang Rong (444–497), one of them addressed to his uncle, demanding an office for the reason of

supporting his family (*Nan Qi shu,* 41.726–27). An earlier example is Ruan Ji, who asked to be commandant of infantry on account of the infantry's storage of good wine (Liu Yiqing, *Shishuo xinyu jianshu,* 23.5.729). Wang Hongzhi (365–427) asked to be magistrate of Wucheng because of the beautiful local scenery (*Song shu,* 93.2281).

51. "To My Sons: Yan and the Others" (Davis, *T'ao Yüan-ming,* 1.229).

52. *Ibid.,* 2.179.

53. Liu Yiqing, *Shishuo xinyu jianshu,* 23.5.729, 23.24.741.

54. *Song Yuan biji xiaoshuo daguan,* 3.3177.

55. *Wen xuan,* 45.2026.

56. Davis, *T'ao Yüan-ming,* 2.180.

57. Hong Mai, *Rongzhai suibi,* 819. "Discipline and restraint" and "going against myself" are quotations from Tao Yuanming's preface.

58. *Jin shu,* 66.1768–69.

59. This is an allusion to Liu Zhen's (courtesy name Gonggan, ?–217) letter to Cao Zhi (192–232) on Cao Zhi's treatment of Xing Yong (?–223), who had been appointed as Cao Zhi's household superintendent by his father Cao Cao (155–220). In the letter, Liu Zhen expressed concern over the fact that Cao Zhi showed more respect for Liu Zhen himself than for Xing Yong, which Liu Zhen felt was unfair as well as politically unwise: "I am worried that observers will say Your Highness is intimate with unworthy people, but lacks attentiveness to the worthy. . . . Bringing blame on one's superiors is no small offence: for this very reason I toss and turn in uneasiness" (*Sanguo zhi,* 12.383).

60. Zhang Ye (ca. 350–418) has a poem entitled "Answering Monk Hui Yuan's Poem on Visiting Mount Lu" (Fenghe Hui Yuan you Lushan shi) (*Quan Jin shi,* 14.938). The political interpretation of this poem dates this poem to the end of 418, which creates a conflict with the supposed authorship; as a result, Attendant Zhang is alternatively identified with Zhang Quan (359–423), a distant cousin of Zhang Ye and one of the "Eighteen Worthies of the Lotus Society." See Yuan Xingpei, *Tao Yuanming ji jianzhu,* 168–69. And yet, neither Zhang Ye nor Zhang Quan had served as attendant; it was an official title conferred on them by the court, but never accepted by the two confirmed recluses. Moreover, as far as we know, Zhang Quan seems to have only been mentioned in "Biographies of Eighteen High-minded Worthies" (Shiba gaoxian zhuan), which is also called "Biographies of the High-minded Worthies of the Lotus Society" (Lianshe gaoxian zhuan). This work is of uncertain date but is generally believed to have appeared somewhere between the ninth and

eleventh centuries. Its credibility is highly problematic, and the White Lotus Society almost certainly never existed. See Tang Yongtong's *Han Wei liang Jin nanbeichao fojiao shi*, 258–61.

61. In some of the Song printed editions of Tao Yuanming's collection, such as the Zeng Ji edition, there is a note appended to the preface to this poem identifying Chief of Staff Yang with Yang Songling (ca. late fourth century), but the note is clearly added later, either by a copyist or by the editor.

62. Liu Yiqing, *Shishuo xinyu jianshu,* 23.4.729, 23.12.733.

63. *Ibid.*, 23.38.749.

64. *Ibid.*, 23.41.752–53, 23.44.757–58.

65. *Song shu,* 42.1311–23.

66. Davis has a detailed note on Lili (Chestnut Village) (*T'ao Yüan-ming,* 2.181–82). We will return to Lili in chapter six.

67. *Taiping yulan,* 697.3239.

68. Liu Yiqing, *Shishuo xinyu jianshu,* 5.52.327.

69. *Song shu,* 73.1892.

70. Another recluse, Wang Hongzhi, a member of the Wang clan, died in the same year as Tao Yuanming and also at the age of sixty-three. Yan Yanzhi wrote to Wang's son to convey his condolences as well as express an interest in writing an elegy, which, however, was never completed. See *Song shu,* 93.2282–83.

71. Wang Guoying, "Shizhuan zhong de Tao Yuanming," 208.

72. Davis, *T'ao Yüan-ming,* 2.185. Tao mentions "zither and books" in various poems such as "Seasons Shift" (Shi yun), "In Reply to Aide Pang" (in four-character lines), and "Upon Passing through Qu'e," as well as his literary exposition "Return." About the inconsistency between Tao Yuanming's own claim and the biographies, also see Wang Guoying, *Gujin yinyi shiren zhi zong Tao Yuanming lunxi*, 97; her article "Shizhuan zhong de Tao Yuanming," 209–10; Qi Yishou, "Lun shizhuan zhong de Tao Yuanming shiji yu xingxiang," 138–41; and Chen Yiliang's *Tao Yuanming zhi renpin yu shipin*, 154–62.

73. *Yiwen leiju,* 23.424; *Songben Cefu yuangui,* 816.9709.

74. The major portion of the *Jin History* biography of Tao Yuanming basically ends at this point. One much later biographical account of Tao Yuanming, which is mostly identical with the *Jin History* biography, is found in "Biographies of Eighteen High-minded Worthies." The only difference it shows from the *Jin History* biography occurs at this juncture: "At the time,

Master Hui Yuan, along with the other worthies, started the Lotus Society, and he wrote a letter to summon Yuanming. Yuanming said, 'I will go if I am allowed to drink.' Hui Yuan agreed, so he went. But then he suddenly knitted his eyebrows and just left." This anecdote is spurious.

75. *Song shihua quanbian,* 1.779. The line cited by Su Shi is taken from Tao Yuanming's prose piece "In Sacrifice for Myself" (Zi ji wen).

76. Head cloth (*jin*) is usually made of linen and sometimes of fine silk and differs from a cap (*mao*). Wang Yao's suggestion that it refers to the kind of head cloth worn by Confucian scholars is anachronistic (*Tao Yuanming ji,* 70–71). A *jin* was once used by a commoner, as distinguished from the "hat" (*guan*) worn by officials, but by the end of the Eastern Han (the second century), it had already become a mark of casual elegance and continued to be so regarded throughout the Six Dynasties, and had nothing to do with Confucian scholars. See Zhu Dawei, *Wei Jin nanbeichao shehui shenghuo shi,* 77–78.

77. *Song shu,* 93.2280–81.

78. The poem has an alternative title: "To Be Shown to the Three Secretaries: Shi Zhou Xuzhi, Zu Qi, and Xie Jingyi" (Shi Zhou Xuzhi, Zu Qi, Xie Jingyi san lang). The names were most likely added by a copyist or an editor familiar with Xiao Tong's biography.

79. *Song shu,* 45.1373.

80. Lu Qinli argues strongly for Tao Yuanming's intense pride in his own family background (*Tao Yuanming ji,* 207–13).

81. Si Yue's commentary has subsequently been reprinted in many premodern editions. See Yuan Xingpei's *Tao Yuanming ji jianzhu,* 615–16.

82. See Tao Shu, *Jingjie xiansheng ji,* 3.2–7. Xie Bingde (1226–1289), for instance, believed that Tao Yuanming had "foreseen" the fall of the Jin ever since Liu Yu had risen to power at the beginning of the Yixi reign. Tao Shu maintains that Shen Yue must have had access to a now-lost collection of Tao Yuanming's works compiled by the poet himself in a chronological manner (*Jingjie xiansheng ji,* 3.9–12).

83. Zhu Ziqing, "Tao Yuanming nianpu zhong zhi wenti," 462.

84. *Ibid.*, 463.

85. Bai Juyi, *Bai Juyi ji jianjiao,* 1.362.

86. *Song shihua quanbian,* 8.8238.

87. The reference to "Lai's wife" occurs in Tao Yuanming's letter to his sons. Laolaizi's wife once dissuaded Laolaizi from serving the King of Chu (Liu

Xiang, *Lienü zhuan,* 2.55–56). Wang Guoying has a detailed discussion of this issue in her book *Gujin yinyi shiren zhi zong Tao Yuanming lunxi,* 325–50.

3 Lost Homesteads: Returning to Tao

1. *Song shihua quanbian,* 4.3544. According to Guo Shaoyu, there were two persons named Chen Shugu in the Song: one was the son of Chen Yaozi (*jinshi* degree, 1000), who died young; another was a *jinshi* in 1042. Both were very literary. There were likewise several Northern Song prime ministers surnamed Zhang. See Guo Shaoyu's "Tao ji kao bian," 708–9.

2. Gong Bin, for example, argues for *yun* since it was "frequently used in the evaluation of people in Wei and Jin." See *Tao Yuanming ji jiaojian,* 74, 76. Wang Shumin, for example, dismisses *yuan* as an error in copying or some shallow editor's emendation (*Tao Yuanming shi jian zheng gao,* 100).

3. *Jin shu,* 75.1968.

4. Ding Fubao, *Tao Yuanming shi jianzhu,* 48. For Dongfang Shuo's letter, see Yan Kejun, *Quan Han wen,* 25.265a. Yan Kejun did not give its source.

5. *Jin shu,* 75.1984.

6. *Jin shu,* 75.1985.

7. "Yancius" refers to Yan Hui, Confucius's favorite disciple.

8. Tao Yuanming makes a reference to "southern acres" (*nan mu*) in the first of the two poems "Upon Thinking of the Ancient Farmers in Early Spring of the *Guimao* Year" (Guimao sui shichun huai gu tian she). One commentator regards "southern acres" as some specific farming land owned by Tao Yuanming (Gong Bin, 74), but *nan mu* is in fact a conventional term often used in the *Shi jing* poems.

9. Translated by Francesca Bray, in Needham, *Science and Civilization in China,* VI.2.96.

10. *Ibid.,* 98. Bray grants that "the clearing of patches of forests up in the mountains where no landlords or officials went required no capital and comparatively little labor" (98). Bray also states that "shifting cultivation in China is generally a southern rather than a northern phenomenon," and that although shifting cultivation "was not entirely confined to tribal peoples," it seems that some southern tribes were the main practitioners, and that "the [Han] Chinese were not very good at shifting cultivation." It is tempting to relate shifting cultivation with the Tao Yuanming clan's non-Han ancestry. In another poem, "Answering a Poem by Liu Chaisang" (He Liu Chaisang), Tao

Yuanming again makes a reference to land clearance: "The new fields again need to be ploughed." *Yu* or *she* 畬, here simply translated as "ploughed," is a technical term, used to indicate shifting cultivation or one of the stages of shifting cultivation. See Needham, 96, 99.

11. *Jian* is a word for measuring house space, I believe originally designating the space between columns.

12. The ballad opens with this couplet: "Rooster crows on top of a tree, / dogs bark in a deep compound [or in a deep lane]" (Lu Qinli, *Quan Han shi,* 9.257–58).

13. *Laozi jiaoshi,* 309. The citation also appears in *Zhuangzi jishi,* 4.10.357.

14. "To His Wife, On Behalf of Gu Yanxian," no. 1 (Wei Gu Yanxian zeng fu) (Lu Qinli, *Quan Jin shi,* 5.682).

15. *Zhuangzi jishi,* 2.4.150–51.

16. In what we have of Eastern Jin poetry, the phrase "dusty thoughts" only appears once, that is, in the poem under discussion. All the prose pieces of the period in which it appears are, interestingly, Buddhist (indeed "dust" itself is a common Buddhist concept and figures in many Buddhist phrases, usually referring to the defilement of the material world). Tao Yuanming's contemporary, Xie Fu (late fourth century), in his preface to a Buddhist manual on breathing techniques, *The Ānāpānasmṛti Sutra* (Anban shouyi jing), says that "dusty thoughts may be checked by the stillness of meditation" (*Quan Jin wen,* 138.2259a). Hui Yuan, the most famous Southern monk of Tao Yuanming's day, used the term in his "Inscription on the Reflected Image of the Ten Thousand Buddhas" (Wan Fo ying ming; written in 413) (*Quan Jin wen,* 162.2403a). The third instance of the usage of this term may be found in a preface to "The Essential Principles of the Lotus Sutra" (Fahua zongyao), written by Hui Guan, a monk acquainted with Hui Yuan (*Quan Song wen,* 63.2777a). Although Tao Yuanming never explicitly referred to Hui Yuan or the doctrine of Buddhism in his writings, he shared the same intellectual ambiance, and some of the images and phrases in his poetry and prose become illuminated in a Buddhist context.

17. Wang Shumin, *Tao Yuanming shi jian zheng gao,* 108.

18. Owen, "The Self's Perfect Mirror," 84.

19. *Ibid.,* 85.

20. Lu Qinli understands "grass" as "clothes made of grass" (*cao yi*), a term that refers to the coarse clothes worn by impoverished people or by recluses (*Tao Yuanming ji,* 42).

21. Hightower mentions that hemp and mulberry are "crops that produce

fabrics, not food, and would not seem to be more susceptible to frost than garden crops" (*Poetry of T'ao Ch'ien*, 52). Hemp is in fact valued both for its use in making fabrics and for its oil-containing seeds. According to Needham, although hemp oil is not a very good cooking oil, it is excellent for oil lamps. Hemp can grow to six or eight meters high, and as an annual, will certainly die with the frost (*Science and Civilization in China*, VI.2.519).

22. Wang Shumin, *Tao Yuanming shi jian zheng gao*, 109; Owen, "The Self's Perfect Mirror," 85.

23. *Chuci zhangju buzhu*, 4.

24. *Song shihua quanbian*, 1.609.

25. The beans are more literary than empirical, a good example of how Tao Yuanming's reading experience becomes intertwined with his life experiences in producing poetry. Scholars have all noted the literary precedent for the opening lines; the song by Yang Yun (?–56 B.C.E.), Sima Qian's grandson, in his famous "A Reply to Sun Huizong" (Bao Sun Huizong shu): "I plough land at that south mountain, / but the weeds are not controlled. / I plant several acres of beans, / the beans wither and become stalks. / A man should make merry in life, / what time does he have to wait for riches and honor?" (*Quan Han wen*, 32.303a). The song reveals either a laissez-faire attitude or a profound sense of helplessness (the weeds cannot be controlled, and the beans will turn into dry stalks), which leads to the final statement about seizing the day. Yang Yun's letter was written when he was banished from court; it later cost him his life, as the emperor reportedly found it unrepentant and resentful, and Yang Yun was executed.

26. *Lang mang* is an ambiguous term. Here I follow Hightower in translating it as "deprived of" (*Poetry of T'ao Ch'ien*, 53–54). He Mengchun (1474–1536) glosses it as "expansive." See Tao Shu, *Jingjie xiansheng ji*, 2.8. Ding Fubao takes it to mean "unrestrained" (*Tao Yuanming shi jianzhu*, 50). Wang Shumin glosses *lang mang* as "neglect" (*Tao Yuanming shi jian zheng gao*, 112).

27. *Zhuangzi jishi*, 7.22.746.

28. From "Yufu" (The Fisherman), *Chuci zhangju buzhu*, 108.

29. *Mengzi zhushu*, 7a.128.

30. Davis, *T'ao Yüan-ming*, 2.40.

31. *Poetry of T'ao Ch'ien*, 55–56.

32. *Ibid.*, 55.

33. Shangjing has a variant, Shangjing 上荊. For the origin of this variant,

see Davis, *T'ao Yüan-ming,* 2.79. "Six years" reads alternatively as "ten years" in Zeng Ji's 1192 edition and the Tang Han edition. Shangjing has been taken to mean "the capital city" by some commentators—Deng Ansheng makes a strong argument for such a reading in his article "A New Interpretation of Tao Yuanming's Poem 'Returning to My Former Residence'" (Tao Yuanming "Huan jiu ju" shi jiqi shiji xintan)—but it could easily be the name of any town where Tao once lived. Since where and what Shangjing is does not really matter to the interpretation of the poem, I have simply kept the transliteration "Shangjing" in my translation. The only problem lies with the phrase "left and came back again" (*qu huan gui*) in the second line. Since the third line clearly indicates this "return" is the first since he moved away from his former residence, I take it that the period of six years, during which he came and went, refers to the duration of his former residence at Shangjing, not to the period of time that lapsed since he permanently left the place. See Hightower's explication in *Poetry of T'ao Ch'ien*, 116–17.

34. In a variant reading, we have *zhui* (pursue) instead of *tui* (to push along, to alternate): "Cold and heat *pursue* each other every day."

35. An item of "A Sequel to *In Search of the Supernatural: The Written Record*" (Soushen houji, also known as *Xu Soushen ji* or *Soushen xu ji*), a collection of stories attributed to Tao Yuanming, tells about Ding Lingwei, an immortal who came back to visit his hometown in the form of a crane and sang a song: "There is a bird, oh, a bird called Ding Lingwei, / he left home for a thousand years and came back today. / The town is as of old, but the people are no more, / why not leave here and strive to become an immortal / instead of residing among the massive graves for nothing" (*Soushen houji*, 1). While there are problems surrounding the authorship and circulation of editions of *Soushen houji* (and some sources attribute this anecdote to *Soushen ji*), the Ding Lingwei legend, as well as his song of return, must have been a familiar story in the Six Dynasties period. Interestingly, Tao Yuanming has a poem entitled "Drinking Alone during Incessant Rain," in which he says a friend has given him some wine, with the words that "drinking makes an immortal out of a man." He drinks the wine and discovers that wonderful feeling of relaxation, and a spiritual freedom not far from that of being an immortal: "The crane of cloud with marvelous wings / can reach the eight limits of the earth and return in an instant." Scholars often repudiate the authorship of *Soushen houji* on the ground that Tao Yuanming, being a "transcendental" person, would not have

been interested in "affairs of ghosts and gods," which to me seems to be quite a strange argument, considering Tao Yuanming's "love of unusual books" (a phrase from Yan Yanzhi's elegy) such as *The Classic of Mountains and Seas*. See Wang Zhizhong's *Han Wei liuchao xiaoshuo shi*, 89–90.

36. See Wang Yao's "Wenren yu jiu" (The Literati and the Wine) in *Zhonggu wenxueshilun*, 156–75. For many living during the Jin, drinking embodied a philosophical attitude associated with the popularity of Lao-Zhuang discourse, a self-conscious choice of a way of life.

37. The poem is entitled "Harvesting Dry Rice in the Western Fields in the Ninth Month of the Year *Gengxu*" (Gengxu sui jiuyue zhong yu xitian huo han dao). "Dry rice" reads "early rice" (*zao dao*) in all editions, but, just as Ding Fubao has noted, a harvest in October or even early November cannot be considered "early" (*Tao Yuanming shi jianzhu*, 108). Indeed, early rice is usually harvested in the seventh month. As Francesca Bray observes, with only a single stroke of the brush to distinguish *zao* from *han*, "the confusion often seems to be made in Chinese texts." Dry rice is usually grown in hillside fields where a water source is far, and this does accord with Tao Yuanming's description of the western fields as "in the mountains." The whole process of growing dry rice can be very labor-intensive, as pointed out by Bray, quoting from the sixth-century agricultural work *Qimin yaoshu* (Needham, *Science and Civilization in China*, VI.2.496–98).

38. *Shi ji*, 95.2651.

39. *Xunzi*, translated and annotated by John Knoblock, 3.127.

40. *Ibid.*, 3.122.

41. *Analects*, 15.140–41.

42. *Song shu*, 92.2270.

43. The Ming commentator Zhong Xing (1574–1625) considers this a "wonderfully modest" way of saying "working in the fields," but I suspect Tao Yuanming was not exactly being "modest" if we measure his work in the fields against a real farmer's (*Huiping*, 146).

44. There is a variant character for *he* (grain), which is *lei* 耒, a tilling tool, translated as "a plough". I follow the 1192 edition here. If we choose *lei*, this couplet would be still about the springtime plowing rather than a description of the harvest scene.

45. Xiao Daocheng (427–482), the first emperor of Qi, in a handwritten note to his favorite minister, Zhang Rong, says, "If you are to wear bad clothes [jiao er lanlü; lit., "If I cause you to wear bad clothes"], it would be damaging

to the reputation of the court" (*Nan Qi shu*, 41.727). Alternatively, *jiao* may be glossed as a borrowed character for *jiao* 徼, which is also exchangeable with *yao* 邀 (to seek, to invite).

46. *Zhuangzi jishi*, 8.23.769–71.

47. The penultimate character in this line has several variants, all of which make perfect sense and yet would lead to different interpretations of this line. The 1192 edition has *jin*, a character glossed by Lu Qinli as "cold and shivering" (85), which may well be a borrowed character for *jin* 凚. Wang Yunlu believes that this *jin* 凚, when glossed as "cold," is interchangeable with *jin* 矜, but the several examples Wang gives are problematic (*Han Wei liuchao shige yuyan lungao*, 236–37). In fact, *jin* 矜 is one of the variants listed by the 1192 edition, but even though *jin* 矜 may act as a borrowed character for 凚 or 噤 in certain phrases indicating cold (as in *jin zhan* 矜戰, "shivering with cold"), the basic meanings of *jin* 矜 have nothing to do with feeling cold. It means "proud and self-complacent" or "serious and somber" (sometimes with a shade of uptightness). Another textual variant, *jin* 襟, translated as "breast" (Hightower, *Poetry of Tao Ch'ien*, 121) or "heart" (Davis, *T'ao Yüan-ming*, 93), is preferred by almost all commentators. Yet another variant is *qu* 劬, "fatigued," "tired."

48. *Analects*, 18.165.

49. This is part of "Appraisals of Fan Paintings" (Shan shang hua zan), a series of "appraisals" of ancient hermits written in rhymed four-character lines.

50. *Xunzi*, 3.122. See Michael Puett's detailed discussions of this issue in "The Sage as Artisan: The Writings of Xunzi" in his book *The Ambivalence of Creation*, 64–73.

51. *Xunzi jijie*, 274.

52. *Lao nong*, "old farmer," echoes Confucius's criticism of Fan Chi, one of his disciples. Fan Chi asked to learn about plowing, and Confucius answered, "I am not as good at that as an old farmer [hence you are asking the wrong person]." He then asked to learn about gardening, and Confucius answered, "I am not as good at that as an old gardener." After Fan Chi left, Confucius called him a "small man"—the antithesis of a gentleman—for he should have, so Confucius thought, inquired about the way of governing (*Analects*, 13.116).

53. Stephen Owen, "The Self's Perfect Mirror," 76.

54. *Ibid.*, 83.

55. Stephen Owen's translation, with modifications (*Readings in Chinese

Literary Thought, 461). "Those alchemists" refers to the Eastern Jin "arcane poets" (*xuanyan shiren*).

56. To this Confucius answered, "What does Heaven have to say? Four seasons run their courses, and hundreds of things grow. What does Heaven have to say?" (*Analects*, 17.157).

57. *Analects*, 7.60.

58. *Song shihua quanbian*, 3.2377.

59. *Analects*, 15.140–41.

60. Hightower, *Poetry of T'ao Ch'ien*, 109.

61. *Analects*, 4.37, 7.60. In the first instance, Confucius said, "A gentleman who is intent upon the Way and yet feels ashamed of bad clothes and bad food is not worth conversing with."

62. Hightower, *Poetry of T'ao Ch'ien*, 108.

63. *Ibid.*, 109.

64. One of the notable examples is the late Ming drama *The Peony Pavilion* (Mudan ting) by Tang Xianzu (1550–1616), in which the eighth act is entitled "Quan nong." I sketched a history of *quan nong* as a literary theme in "The Tension between Fields and Garden: 'Encouraging the Farmers' in *The Peony Pavilion*," presented at the International Conference on Tang Xianzu and *Mudan ting*, held at Academia Sinica in Taibei, April 27–28, 2004.

65. Lien-sheng Yang translated the longer fragment in his article "Notes on the Economic History of the Chin Dynasty," 134.

66. *Quan Jin wen*, 87.1962b. Shu Xi's "*Fu* on Encouraging the Farmers" was regarded as "base and vulgar" by his contemporaries (*Jin shu*, 51.1428). The literary critic Liu Xie (ca. 465–522) notes that in Wei and Jin times comic works like Shu Xi's were abundant, and he criticizes them as "weedy words" (*Wenxin diaolong yizheng*, 3.15.535–36).

67. *Maoshi zhengyi*, 19.747–48.

68. Davis, *T'ao Yüan-ming*, 1.85. Donald Holzman, in using Hightower's translation ("The work itself brings me much joy"), focuses instead on the "work" part of the phrase, concluding that "Tao Qian is asking us to look on farming as a valid occupation for a 'superior man' [*junzi*]" and that he is "attempting to broaden the criteria for what is and is not suitable for a man of the ruling class." This interpretation is problematic: by depending on Hightower's English translation of this line, Holzman does not take into account the primary meaning of this phrase as "the immediate situation," and the "immediate situation" in this poem by Tao Yuanming, as I will show, involves

much more than "the work" of farming—one may even say that it has nothing to do with farming at all. On the other hand, being a "gentleman farmer" is essentially the coded behavior and ostentatious gesture of a recluse. When we look at "Biographies of Recluses" in official histories, we see numerous examples of recluses or would-be recluses claiming that farming, as an antithesis of serving, is a worthy thing to do. If farming had already become an admittedly suitable occupation for a man of the ruling class long before Tao Yuanming, why should Tao Yuanming's attribution of value to farming be considered something particularly "in response to the tremendous changes in thought and in social structure that have brought a new, 'mediaeval' era in Chinese history"? See Donald Holzman's paper "A Dialogue with the Ancients: Tao Qian's Interrogation of Confucius," in *Culture and Power in the Reconstitution of the Chinese Realm*, 89.

69. *Huiping*, 126.

70. Hightower, *Poetry of T'ao Ch'ien*, 110.

71. Lu Qinli, *Xian Qin shi*, 1.1–2. The old man sings this to defy an observer's praise of Emperor Yao's sagely rule.

72. *Zhuangzi jishi*, 9.28.966.

73. One is reminded of the Tang poet Wang Wei's "Farmsteads by the Wei River" (Weichuan tianjia), in which the poet observes the pastoral scene and "so long as he remains an observer, he can never fully enter the world on which he looks" (*Wang Youcheng ji jianzhu*, 37; Owen, *Anthology of Chinese Literature*, 387).

74. Closing the gate or the curtains often appeared in prose before Tao Yuanming, usually describing a hardworking scholar/hermit. In "Return," Tao Yuanming says that "although there is a gate, it is often closed." Tao Yuanming's illustrious contemporary Yan Yanzhi incorporates the image of gate-closing in "Answering Chamberlain Wang Sengda" (Zeng Wang taichang Sengda), in a line which bears a remarkable similarity to Tao Yuanming's line cited later in this section: "The village residence's gate is often closed in daylight" (*Quan Song shi*, 5.1232). A little later, in the hands of Shen Yue, the image of door-closing takes an interesting turn, as it signifies the privacy of a woman's boudoir, such as in his "Ballad of Encountering in A Narrow Lane" (Xiangfeng xialu jian) (*Quan Liang shi*, 6.1616). The final "gate-closing" is, of course, the closing of the "tomb-gate." In the third of Tao Yuanming's "Bearers' Songs" (Wan ge), we see these lines: "Once the dark chamber is closed, / for a thousand years there will be no more dawn."

75. The poet can open his gate any time and go out again, and so he does. Of the later-born, Wang Wei shows Tao Yuanming's influence by incorporating such an image time and again. See "Pleased by the Visit of Zu the Third, I Kept Him for the Night" (Xi Zusan zhi liusu) (*Wang Youcheng ji jianzhu*, 120). His poetry likewise shows that closing the gate does not need to mean a total negation of the outside world; instead, it provides the person within a convenient and unique observation point, from which the poet is free to observe the world without himself being observed. I am thinking of the poem entitled "Inspired by Dwelling in the Mountains" (Shanju jishi), whose first line is "In quiet solitude I close the brushwood gate." But the poet goes on to describe all kinds of things taking place in the outside world (*Wang Youcheng ji jianzhu*, 124).

76. The most famous pre-Han beggars include Chong'er, Wu Zixu, and Baili Xi. They endured much hardship, but eventually rose to power, just like Han Xin, the Western Han general mentioned in Tao Yuanming's poem.

77. *Shishuo xinyu* records the following anecdote: "When Ruan Hun grew up, his temperament and disposition were like his father's, and he too wanted to practice the way of unrestraint [*zuo da*]. Ruan Ji [Ruan Hun's father] said, 'Zhongrong [the courtesy name of Ruan Xian, Ruan Ji's nephew] is already doing it. You should not try that again'" (Liu Yiqing, *Shishuo xinyu jianshu*, 23.13.734). Although Dai Kui in his "Zhulin qixian lun" (On the Seven Worthies of the Bamboo Grove) says that Ruan Ji restricted Ruan Hun because Ruan Hun did not understand the reason why Ruan Ji was behaving in an unrestrained way (*wei da*), the point of the story is how *da* is more a mannerism, even a family business, than one's nature (temperament and disposition) (*Quan Jin wen*, 137.2252b).

78. Liu Yiqing, *Shishuo xinyu jianshu*, 23.41.752–53.

79. Huan Wen, a powerful minister in the mid-fourth century, was also the employer of Tao Yuanming's maternal grandfather Meng Jia (Liu Yiqing, *Shishuo xinyu jianshu*, 23.41.753).

80. Liu Yiqing, *Shishuo xinyu jianshu*, 23.44.757–58.

81. For the Buddhist practice of begging for food, see Richard Mather's article "The Bonze's Begging Bowl," 418–19.

82. *Li ji zhushu*, 10.196.

83. *Mengzi zhushu*, 8b.156.

84. For the last character of this line, Wang Shumin opts for the variant *quan* 勸 (to urge), so the line would read, "Delighted by the urging of the new friend." See *Tao Yuanming shi jian zheng gao*, 135.

85. From "Junior Master of Lifespans" (Shao si ming) of the "Nine Songs" (Jiu ge), *Chuci zhangju buzhu*, 43.

86. *Huiping*, 67.

87. *Shi ji*, 92.2609.

88. *Chunqiu Zuozhuan zhengyi*, Duke Xuan 15, 24.409.

89. *Huiping*, 68.

90. Although it is said that Huan Wen did not want to grant Luo You an official post initially because he felt Luo had gone too far, Luo You finally did get to be the magistrate of Xiangyang, and later was promoted to be prefect of Guangzhou and then of Yizhou.

91. Some commentators indeed have erred in calling the poem just that. See *Huiping*, 67–68.

4 Food, Death, & Narration

1. *Chunqiu Zuozhuan zhengyi*, Duke Xiang 24, 35.609.

2. According to Zhu Ziqing, in Gu Zhi's annotated edition of Tao Yuanming's poetry, Tao Yuanming refers to *Zhuangzi* forty-nine times and *Liezi* twenty-one times, and to *The Analects* thirty-seven times ("Taoshi de shendu," in *Zhu Ziqing gudian wenxue lunji*, 568).

3. *Quan Wei shi*, 3.381; *Quan Jin shi*, 1.571. Lu Ji's poem was entitled "Two Poems, Presented to Secretariat Gu Yanxian" (Zeng Shangshulang Gu Yanxian ershou), but they clearly belong to the *kuyu* type, as they express the poet's longing for his friend as he is isolated by the incessant rain (*Quan Jin shi*, 5.680–81).

4. *Quan Jin shi*, 7.747; Zhong Rong, *Shipin jizhu*, 346.

5. *Quan Liang shi*, 4.1574. There are also a number of Wei and Jin literary expositions or rhapsodies on the same topic. For instance, Pan Ni (ca. 251–311) wrote "*Fu* on Suffering from the Rain" (Kuyu fu) (*Quan Jin wen*, 94.1999a).

6. In this poem the poet does not talk about longing for a friend. The motif of drinking during rains and thinking of absent friends is picked up by the fifth century poet Bao Zhao (414?–466) in a poem entitled "Suffering from Rain" (*Quan Song shi*, 9.1306).

7. *Quan Liang wen*, 29.3117a.

8. Two Daoist immortals often mentioned together.

9. "Hear about" (*wen*) is the variant character for *jian* 間. I have chosen *he wen* rather than *he jian* (where are they) because *he jian* would conflict with *shijian*

(in the world) in the preceding line. Both *wen* and *jian* rhyme with *ran* (the ending rhyme word of the second line) in Middle Chinese, and they look similar.

10. For instance, the fifteenth of "Nineteen Old Poems," and a similar version of the *yuefu* song "West Gate" (Ximen xing): "The fools begrudge expenses / and will only earn mockery in later ages. / Prince Qiao, the immortal, / it is hard to match his span" (*Quan Han shi*, 12.333, 9.269).

11. *Quan sanguo wen*, 48.1324b; *Quan Wei shi*, 9.480.

12. Wang Shumin, *Tao Yuanming shi jian zheng gao*, 156.

13. Liu Yiqing, *Shishuo xinyu jianshu*, 23.35.748, 23.38.749; Mather's translation, *Tales of the World*, 389, 384.

14. *Zhuangzi jishi*, 5.12.428.

15. The heavenly journey is associated with both Chu shamanism and the Han Daoist practice of seeking immortality.

16. Birds often get confused in early manuscript tradition: crane, wild goose, duck, and swan (yellow, white, and black) are all variations and different realizations of "one poem." See Stephen Owen's discussion of this issue in relation to the *yuefu* poem "Prelude: O, When" in *The Making of Early Chinese Classical Poetry*. However, "crane" is unanimously chosen by later editors as the text proper, presumably because it is associated with immortals.

17. Wang Shumin, *Tao Yuanming shi jian zheng gao*, 157.

18. Gu Zhi cites Guo's commentary on chapter two: "For those who follow nature and forget about right and wrong, they are merely following their natural impulses" (*Tao Jingjie shi jian*, 301). Guo Xiang uses the exact phrase *ren zhen* in his commentary on chapters eleven, thirteen, and thirty-two.

19. *Zhuangzi jishi*, 3.6.226–34.

20. *Zhuangzi jishi*, 3.6.282–85.

21. Wang Shumin, *Tao Yuanming shi jian zheng gao*, 158.

22. *Zhuangzi jishi*, 7.22.765.

23. *Huainan honglie jijie*, 18.622.

24. *Zhuangzi jishi*, 1.2.56; Stephen Owen's translation, *Anthology of Chinese Literature*, 115.

25. *Zhuangzi jishi*, 3.6.258–59.

26. *Zhuangzi jishi*, 3.6.285–86.

27. *Maoshi zhengyi*, 611.217–18.

28. We may contrast the ending of Tao Yuanming's poem with the ending of Cao Pi's (187–226) poem "Composed by the Lotus Pond" (Furong chi zuo shi): "Human life is not like Red Pine and Prince Qiao— / who can obtain

immortality? / One had better roam around and please oneself, / preserving oneself and reaching a hundred-year span." We hear echoes of this in Tao Yuanming's poem, and the vanity of obtaining immortality leads directly to the decision to make merry, have a good time, and yet cherish and conserve one's life and live a natural lifespan (*Quan Wei shi,* 4.400).

29. Tao Yuanming has a poem, "On the Two Shus" (Yong er Shu), which is a *yongshi* poem (poem on history) based on the story of Shu Guang (first century B.C.E.) and his nephew Shu Shou, who were both teachers of the Crown Prince in the Western Han and retired from their posts, with honor, at the same time. They went home and spent all the gold the emperor and the Crown Prince had given them, giving feasts to friends and relatives. The poem is written in the tradition of the poem on the same topic by the Western Jin poet Zhang Xie, who emphasizes the value of not saving and conserving: "Distributing gold to take pleasure in the present; / at year's end they leave nothing in store" (*Quan Jin shi,* 7.745). Interestingly, in Tao Yuanming's version, we see two slightly changed lines: "Giving free rein to their desires, and taking pleasure in the remaining years, / they did not care about what would happen after death." The idea is similar, but the expression "the remaining years" (*yu nian*), together with the previous mention that they did not care about the glory they left behind—a "superfluous honor" (*yu rong*), characterizes Tao Yuanming's poem as more keenly aware of spending, consumption, worries about surplus, and leaving a different kind of legacy behind.

30. Stephen Owen's translation, *Anthology of Chinese Literature,* 113.

31. *Quan Jin shi,* 20.1085–86; Davis's translation, *T'ao Yüan-ming,* 1.52–54. Also see Strassberg, *Inscribed Landscapes,* 68–71.

32. *Quan Jin wen,* 33.1651a, 26.1609a–b. For the Shi Chong preface, see Wilhelm, "Shih Ch'ung and His *Chin-ku-yüan,*" 315–27. Wang Xizhi's "Preface to *Collected Poems from the Lanting*" is translated and included in Strassberg, *Inscribed Landscapes,* 65–66. Kang-i Sun Chang gives a detailed discussion of Tao Yuanming's echoing of and departure from Wang Xizhi's preface, and rightly points out the stylistic differences between Tao Yuanming's poem and Wang Xizhi's "Orchid Lanting" poems (*Six Dynasties Poetry,* 6–12).

33. Strassberg's translation (with modifications), *Inscribed Landscapes,* 66.

34. These last lines closely imitate Shi Chong's preface: "Moved by the impermanence of life, and fearing the imminence of decay, we list each and every one's official title, full name, and age" (*Quan Jin wen,* 33.1651a).

35. Li Daoyuan (?–527) writes in his *Annotations of the Classic of Rivers*: "There are three levels of Mount Kunlun: the lowest level is Fantong, also called Bantong; the next level is the Mysterious Garden, also named Langfeng; the top level is the Tiered Wall, also named Tianting (Heavenly Court); it is the abode of the Grand Emperor" (*Shuijing zhu*, 1).

36. I agree with Ding Fubao, who follows Zeng Guofan (1811–1872) in suggesting that Cengcheng, Tiered Wall, must be the name of a little hill at Xie Brook (*Tao Yuanming shi jianzhu*, 54). Davis argues that Cengcheng is a descriptive term for South Mountain (Mount Lu), which does not seem to fit the context, as Tao Yuanming has made a point of contrasting Cengcheng and South Mountain, particularly pointing out that Cengcheng "rises out of the water, with nothing around it" (Davis, *T'ao Yüan-ming*, 1.50–51).

37. Whether the variant should be "fifty," Tao Yuanming's age, or "five days," referring to the date of the outing, is a hotly debated point. Su Shi seems to have read "fifty." In his poem "Matching the Rhymes of Tao Yuanming's 'An Excursion to Xie Brook'" (He Tao You Xiechuan), the second couplet is: "Although I have passed Jingjie's age, / I may still go on the excursion of Xie Brook" (*Su Shi shiji*, 7.2318). Su Shi's son, Su Guo, named his garden the Little Xie Brook and wrote a poem about it. In the preface to that poem, Su Guo notes, "This year is the *xinchou* year [1121] again, and I am also turning fifty, so Yuanming and I were both born in the *renzi* year (352 and 1072)" (*Quan Song shi*, 23.15456). Ma Yongqing says in *Lanzhenzi* that an "old copy" of Tao Yuanming's collection from the Donglin Temple of Jiangzhou reads "five days," which he takes to be the correct version (*Song Yuan xiaoshuo biji daguan*, 3. 3135–36). Yuan Xingpei argues strongly for the reading of "*xinchou*" and "fifty," which he uses as major evidence for moving Tao Yuanming's year of birth from the conventional 365 to 352. See his article "Tao Yuanming xiangnian kaobian" in *Tao Yuanming yanjiu*, 218–27.

38. In the fourth century, the range of *you* also included less fantastic excursions—for instance, visits to famous mountains—though still ending in visions of immortals. Sun Chuo's "*Fu* on Wandering to the Tiantai Mountain" (You Tiantai shan fu) is a well-known example (*Quan Jin wen*, 61.1806a–b). See Richard Mather's "The Mystical Ascent of the T'ien-t'ai Mountains," 226–45.

39. "Heavenly Questions" (Tianwen): "Tiered Wall has nine folds— / how many miles high is it?" (*Chuci zhangju buzhu*, 54). I choose to interpret "nine folds" (or "nine layers") as descriptive of Tiered Wall instead of as the name of another peak of Mount Kunlun. I believe this better fits the context of *Huai-*

nanzi, in which the author gives the height of only one peak, not two: "Within [Mount Kunlun] there is the Tiered Wall Peak of nine folds, whose height measures eleven thousand miles, one hundred fourteen yards, two feet, and four inches" (*Huainan honglie jijie*, 4.133).

40. *Quan sanguo wen*, 13.1123a. In a fragment of Lu Ji's "Poem on Summoning the Recluse" (Zhaoyin shi), the image of "patterned fish" also appears (*Quan jin shi*, 5.692). Again, "summoning the recluse" is a theme located within the *Chuci* tradition.

41. The fifteenth of "Nineteen Old Poems": "Human life does not reach a hundred years, / and yet we always cherish cares for a thousand. . . . We should make merry at this very moment, / how can one wait for times to come?" (*Quan Han shi*, 12.333).

42. *Shang* has a variant, *chang* 腸, a borrowed character for "intestines" (*chang* 腸), and *zhong chang* means "in one's heart." The Su Shi edition and Tang Han edition both have *shang*.

43. *Quan Jin shi*, 13.896.

44. *Huiping*, 61.

45. *Quan Han shi*, 12.332.

46. Hightower, *Poetry of T'ao Ch'ien*, 64; Tao Shu, *Jingjie xiansheng ji*, 2.16. Zhou Fang (260–320), like the Taos, was a native of Xunyang; he married his daughter to Tao Kan's son, Tao Zhan. See *Jin shu*, 58.1579.

47. Wang Fuzhi, *Gushi pingxuan*, 201.

48. For a basic introduction to points of view surrounding the authorship and date of *The Classic of Mountains and Seas* and *The Biography of King Mu*, see Loewe, *Early Chinese Texts*, 357–67, 342–46.

49. There is a variant in this line: the first character, *qie* (for the moment, for now), as both *Wen xuan* (30.1392) and *Yiwen leiju* (55.991) have it, reads *shi* 時 (sometimes, from time to time) in all the Song editions. Wang Shumin glosses *shi* as *ji* 即 (and then), so that it better fits the context (*Tao Yuanming shi jian zheng gao*, 476–77). It is, however, a rather contrived reading of *shi*, and I choose to follow *Wen xuan* and *Yiwen leiju*.

50. The Qing critic Wu Song emphasizes that "happiness" is the key to understanding this poem; Wu Qi (1615–1675) says that "happiness" is the basis of this poem and equates this "happiness" with that of Confucius and of Yan Hui, who "never lost his happiness," even when living in a shabby lane with meager food (see *Analects*, 6.53). He even goes so far as to say that "Jingjie [Tao Yuanming] read *The Classic of Mountains and Seas* because he was happy; it

is not that he was happy because he was reading *The Classic of Mountains and Seas*" (*Huiping*, 292–93).

51. Zhuangzi mentions the Queen Mother in what seems to be Tao Yuanming's favorite chapter, "The Great Master" (Da zong shi): "The Queen Mother of the West obtained it [the Way] and took her residence on Mount Shaoguang: no one knows her beginning, no one knows her end" (*Zhuangzi jishi*, 3.6.247). As Hightower notes, the second couplet of this poem seems to be echoing this *Zhuangzi* passage rather than *The Classic of Mountains and Seas* (*Poetry of T'ao Ch'ien*, 233).

52. Guo Pu's commentary: "Although the Queen Mother of the West lives in her palace at Kunlun, she also has other residences and grottos. Her travels and stays are not limited to one single mountain" (*Shanhai jing jiaozhu*, 16.409).

53. Davis quotes Cheng Xuanying's annotation to the Zhuangzi passage cited above that the Queen Mother "smiles well" (*shan xiao*) (*Zhuangzi*, 3.6.250), and translates the second line of the poem as "The Queen Mother sets her wondrous features in a smile" (1.154). But I suspect that *shan xiao*, which in Middle Chinese was close in sound to *shan xiao* ("good at whistling") in the *Classic of Mountains and Seas* text, might have been either a scribe's or Cheng Xuanying's own error, due to the fact that by Cheng's time (the seventh century), the Queen Mother had already been transformed into a beautiful, amiable, somewhat middle-aged goddess in popular legend.

54. *Shanhai jing jiaozhu*, 2.50, 12.306, 16.407.

55. In *The Biography of King Mu*, the Queen Mother's physical appearance is not described, but she seems to observe human rites and, since she shares a feast with King Mu of Zhou and "exchanges poetry" with him, we suppose she cannot look too uncivilized. In *The Inner Biography of Emperor Wu of Han* (Han Wudi neizhuan), a work of uncertain date (scholars speculate that it was written between the third and fourth century), the Queen Mother of the West is transformed into a beautiful goddess, "wearing a robe of yellow brocade. . . . with flowers in her coiffure. . . . a little more than thirty years old, neither too tall nor too short . . . with a face matchless in the world." It could have been inspired by the newly unearthed *The Biography of King Mu*. See *Han Wei liuchao biji xiaoshuo daguan*, 142.

56. *Han Wei liuchao biji xiaoshuo daguan*, 14. The Queen Mother's song is entitled "The Ballad of White Cloud" (Baiyun yao) and is included, along with the king's reply, in Lu Qinli's *Xian Qin shi*, 3.35–36.

57. Yan Kejun, *Quan shanggu sandai wen*, 10.73a–74a.

58. For a detailed study of the Queen Mother of the West, see Suzanne E. Cahill's book study, *Transcendence and Divine Passion.*

59. *Tiaodi*, the beginning two words, usually means "far and distant," but when it is used to describe a mountain, it also means "tall." I have chosen to interpret the first line "vertically" instead of "horizontally," for Huai River Peak is presented as the hill where the Mysterious Garden is and from which one can see Kunlun in the distance, a point of view that emphasizes height rather than width.

60. Kunlun is four hundred miles to the southwest of Huai River Mountain (*Shanhai jing jiaozhu,* 2.47).

61. *Ibid.*, 2.45.

62. *Ibid.*, 2.46.

63. *Shanhai jing jiaozhu,* 2.41.

64. Hightower, *Poetry of T'ao Ch'ien*, 236. Huang Wenhuan has a long discussion about how the function of cinnabar trees watered by the jade jelly is not limited to curing hunger (*Huiping*, 297).

65. *Quan Jin wen,* 122.2160a.

66. See *Shanhai jing jiaozhu,* 2.54. The second character also reads *deng* 登 ("climb" or "ascend"), which is clearly an error.

67. "One comes to Wugao Hill; from there one sees the You Sea in the south and the Fu Tree in the east" (*Shanhai jing jiaozhu,* 4.112).

68. "Above Hot Spring Valley there is the Fusang Tree; it is where the ten suns bathe" (*Shanhai jing jiaozhu,* 4.260). The tree is said to be three hundred *li* tall (14.354).

69. Xihe, the wife of Emperor Jun (Di Jun), gave birth to ten suns, and she bathes the ten suns in the Sweetwater Abyss (Gan yuan) (15.381).

70. *Shanhai jing jiaozhu,* 4.112.

71. Hightower, *Poetry of T'ao Ch'ien*, 238.

72. "As a tree, [Triple Pearl Tree] is like a cypress, and its leaves are all pearls" (*Shanhai jing jiaozhu,* 6.192). The tree is also compared to a comet. "The Cinnamon Forest has eight trees; it is to the east of Panyu." Guo Pu adds an ingenious annotation: "Eight trees can form a forest—this tells you how big the trees are" (10.268–69). The dancing phoenix and singing simurgh are related to the Mountain of the Queen Mother (16.397). They are signs of peace and prosperity.

73. "The Undying People live to the east. They have dark complexions and live long lives—in fact, they do not die" (*Ibid.*, 6.196). Guo Pu's annotation

says: "There is a Round Hill, on which grows the Undying Tree. Eating from the tree makes a person live a long life. There is also a Red Spring, drinking from which makes a person never age" (6.197). Guo Pu's annotation may be based on Western Jin writer Zhang Hua's *Bowu zhi* (An Extensive Account of Things), which has a paragraph almost identical to Guo Pu's description, except for one extra sentence: "It [i.e., Round Hill] has many big snakes that harm people; it is impossible to live there." In Zhang Hua's version, no place is perfect (*Bowu zhi jiaozheng,* 1.13).

74. *Huiping,* 300.

75. "Kuafu ran a race with the sun. At sunset, he was thirsty, and drank from the Yellow River and the Wei River. It was not enough for him, so he went north to drink from the Great Marsh. Before he reached it, he died of thirst on the way. He cast away his staff, which was transformed into Deng Grove" (*Shanhai jing jiaozhu,* 8.238). "The Classic of the Great Wilderness in the North" (Dahuang bei jing) records a similar story, except that in this case Kuafu "caught up with the sun at Yu Valley" (17.427). Guo Pu annotates that "Yu Valley" is where the sun sets. "The Classic of the Middle Mountains" (Zhongshan jing) says there is a "peach grove" to the north of the Kuafu Mountain, which stretches three hundred miles. The Qing scholar Bi Yuan (1730–1797) believes this is Deng Grove (5.139–40).

76. *Zhuangzi jishi,* 1.1.24.

77. *Huiping,* 301.

78. Yuan Ke, *Zhongguo gudai shenhua,* 120–21. The peach grove is, of course, also reminiscent of Tao Yuanming's more famous prose piece, "The Record of Peach Blossom Spring" (Taohuayuan ji). The fisherman was lured into the utopia hidden in the mountains because he first entered into a large peach grove. This may in fact be the very reason why the name "Kuafu Mountain" is given to a hill at Yuanling (in modern-day Hu'nan Province), which neighbors Peach Spring County (Taoyuan) where some say Peach Blossom Spring was.

79. Wang Chong (27–97?) quotes a section (now lost) from *The Classic of Mountains and Seas,* relating the story of the two door gods carved out of peach wood (Wang Chong, *Lunheng* 22.65.938–39). Fu Xuan mentions this in "*Fu* on the Peach" (Tao fu) (*Quan Jin wen,* 1718). Zong Lin's (ca. sixth century) *An Account of the Seasonal Activities in Jing-Chu Region* (Jingchu suishi ji) records the custom (*Jingchu suishi ji yizhu,* 16).

80. See *Huiping,* 301–2; Wang Shumin, *Tao Yuanming shi jian zheng gao,* 488.

81. He Zhuo is the only reader who insists that the poem satirizes Kuafu's "kua" (boastfulness, exaggeration). He takes the last couplet not as the poet's appraisal of Kuafu but apparently as Kuafu's own wishful thinking. Such a view is not convincing (*Huiping*, 301).

82. Kuafu was the son of Xin, and Xin was the son of Houtu (*Shanhai jing jiaozhu*, 17.427). Houtu was a remote descendent of the Fiery Emperor (8.238). In the rather garbled system of kinship in Chinese mythology, some say that the Fiery Emperor was a half-brother of the Yellow Emperor.

83. *Shanhai jing jiaozhu*, 3.92.

84. Chao Yongzhi was the cousin of Chao Buzhi. See *Song shi*, 444.13112.

85. See Yuan Ke's annotation in *Shanhai jing jiaozhu*, 7.214.

86. *Ibid.*, 7.214.

87. See *Huiping*, 302–7.

88. The sixth and seventh of his essays "Drafts with Undecided Titles" (Ti wei ding cao) (*Luxun quanji*, 336, 344).

89. Lu Qinli takes the couplet to mean that both Jingwei and Xingyao were "living creatures" and so death was inevitable (*Tao Yuanming ji*, 138). This does not adequately explain the usage of "regret" in the second line. Hightower translates the couplet as "Alike in that they took no forethought, / Though transformed, they have no regrets." Also see his speculations on other possible interpretations (*Poetry of T'ao Ch'ien*, 241–43). Wang Shumin thinks that the troubling phrase *tong wu* in the first line means "before they are transformed" (i.e., before they die) (*Tao Yuanming shi jian zheng gao*, 490).

90. "Erfu's minister was called Wei. He conspired with Erfu and killed Yayu. The Emperor imprisoned him on Shushu Mountain. He chained his right foot and tied his hands behind his back with his hair, and bound him to a tree on the mountain" (*Shanhai jing jiaozhu*, 11.285). Qinpi conspired with Gu (a creature with a human face and dragon's body) and killed Zujiang at Mount Kunlun. The Emperor executed them. "Thereupon Qinpi turned into a huge osprey, which looks like a hawk, but with black stripes and a white head, a red beak and tiger claws; its cries sound like a wild goose" (2.42–43). "Yayu has a dragon's head and lives in the Ruo River. . . . [He] eats people." According to Guo Pu's annotation, "Yayu originally had had a human face and a snake's body; after being killed by Erfu's minister, he was transformed and became this [new] creature" (10.278).

91. Ding Fubao emends *ku* 枯 (withering) to a similar graph *gu* 梏 (chaining the hands), which would refer to Wei's imprisonment on Shufu Mountain

(*Tao Yuanming shi jianzhu*, 170). Wu Song, on the other hand, understands this line as referring to the murdered victims, Yayu and Zujiang (*Huiping*, 308).

92. "There is a bird that looks like an owl but has human hands, who cries like a quail, and whose name is *zhu*. It calls out its own name. When it is seen, there will be many gentlemen banished from the land" (*Shanhai jing jiaozhu*, 1.9). The original name in Tao Yuanming's poem, *zhou-e* 鵃鵝 (the *zhou* goose), is not seen in the present text of *The Classic of Mountains and Seas*, and has been emended by all commentators to *chi zhu* 鴟鴸 (the *zhu* bird that looks like an owl).

93. "Blue Hill . . . has a bird, whose shape is like a pigeon and whose cries sound like a ho-ho. Its name is *guan'guan*; wearing it [i.e., its feathers] prevents confusion" (*ibid.*, 1.6).

94. Hightower, *Poetry of T'ao Ch'ien*, 246. See the section on Qu Yuan in David Hawkes's introduction to *The Songs of the South*, 51–66.

95. *Hanfeizi jijie*, 66.

96. Gong is Gonggong, who, in a fight with Zhuanxu, knocked down Buzhou Mountain, which had been used as one of the pillars of heaven, and caused a great flood on earth. Guo Pu annotates that while trying to stop the flood, Yu killed Gonggong's minister Xiangliu (also called Xianggun) (*Shanhai jing jiaozhu*, 17.428, 8.233). As for Gun, he was killed because he stole the "resting soil" from the Heavenly God to stop the flood without having waited for God's command (*ibid.*, 18.472). Some say it was Shun (Chonghua) who asked to have Gun killed (*Shi ji*, 1.28).

97. "The godfather" refers to Guan Zhong, the worthy minister of the Kingdom of Qi in the Spring and Autumn period. He served Duke Huan of Qi (Qi Huangong).

98. *Maoshi zhengyi*, 12.393.

99. *Shanhai jing jiaozhu*, 16.456.

100. *Ibid.*, 16.457.

101. *Zhuangzi jishi*, 7.19.650–54.

102. *Hanfeizi jijie*, 52; *Shi ji*, 32.1493.

103. Shang Mountain is located in Shang County to the southeast of Chang'-an. Towards the end of the Qin Dynasty, four elderly men—Dongyuan gong, Qili Ji, Xia huang gong, and Luli xiansheng—lived in the mountain as recluses. The founding emperor of the Han (r. 206–195 B.C.E.) invited them out, but they refused. Later, however, they came out at the request of the Crown Prince, who invited them with "humble words and sumptuous gifts." When the

emperor saw that his son had such influence, he gave up the plan of deposing him in favor of the younger son (who was eventually murdered by Empress Lü, the Crown Prince's mother) (*Shi ji,* 55.2045–47). The four men are usually referred to as the Four White-heads of Shang Mountain (Shang shan si hao). See Alan Berkowitz's detailed account of the four recluses in *Patterns of Disengagement*, 64–80.

104. Tang Yijie, *Guo Xiang yu Wei Jin xuanxue,* 251.

105. *Zhuangzi jishi,* 4.10.344.

106. *Zhuangzi jishi,* 9.26.928. "Poetry" here refers to *The Classic of Poetry,* and "rites," *The Record of Rites.*

107. From Cui Qi's (ca. the first century) "A Eulogy to the Four White-heads" (Si hao song) (*Quan Han shi,* 1.90). See Berkowitz, *Patterns of Disengagement*, 68, note 12.

108. As Alan Berkowitz points out, the account of the Four White-heads in Huangfu Mi's *Gaoshi zhuan* makes no mention of their participation in the partisan struggles at the Han court (*Patterns of Disengagement*, 68–69). This would seem to be an attempt to cleanse the image of the Four White-heads of any "impure" aspect.

109. See *Jin shu,* 84.2196–97.

110. The phrase *xi sheng* is from Laozi's *Dao de jing*: "The great sound has the most attenuated sound" (Dayin xi sheng) (*Laozi jiaoshi,* 14.171).

111. *Analects,* 15.137: "Zilu asked angrily, 'Does a gentleman also encounter adversity?' Confucius answered, 'The gentleman is firm in adversity, while a small-minded man will simply go to pieces.'"

112. The poet is alluding to the story of "inquiring for the ford" in *The Analects.* In other words, if there is no ford to follow in a chaotic world, then it is better to lead a reclusive life.

113. After a snowstorm, the magistrate of Luoyang made an inspection tour. Everywhere he saw people coming out of their houses and sweeping the snow; there were also people begging for food. When he arrived at Yuan An's door, there was nobody. He thought Yuan An must have died, but when he broke into Yuan An's house, he found Yuan An lying in bed. When asked why he did not go out, he answered, "In such a great snowstorm, people are all hungry; it is not right to go visit and disturb others." The magistrate thought well of his answer and recommended him to the court. Cited in the commentary to "The Biography of Yuan An" in *Hou Han shu,* 45.1518, from a lost work, *Ru'nan xianxian zhuan* (Biographies of the Former Worthies of Ru'nan).

114. The first line in the 1192 edition has a textual variant for the third character: *kun* 困, so that the line reads, "Yuan An was *trapped* by the deep snow." Interestingly, if we choose this variant, then Yuan An's remaining in his house would become a compelled act instead of an act of free will.

115. *Analects,* 6.53.

5 Becoming a Vessel

Omar Khayyám, *Rubáiyát*, trans. Edward FitzGerald, 1st edition (London: Collins, 1953), 79.

1. Tang Yijie's *Guo Xiang yu Wei Jin xuanxue* gives an excellent analysis of *xuanxue* development from the third to fourth centuries. Also see Tang Yongtong, *Wei Jin xuanxue lungao*; and Liu Dajie, *Wei Jin sixiang lun*. For a recent English study of Guo Xiang, see Brook Ziporyn, *The Penumbra Unbound.*

2. *Zhou Yi zhengyi,* 7.158.

3. *Laozi,* 28.114; D. C. Lau's translation, *Tao te ching*, 86. Another passage from *Laozi* says, "I have three treasures, which I hold and cherish: . . . The third is known as not daring to take the lead in the empire. . . . Not daring to take the lead in the empire, one could afford to be lord over the vessels" (*Laozi,* 67.271; D. C. Lau, 129).

4. *Analects,* 2.18.

5. *Ibid.*, 5.41.

6. James Legge, *Chinese Classics*, 1.173.

7. *Ibid.*, 3.30. In several other places in *The Analects* Confucius praised or defended Guan Zhong when others criticized him (see 14.124, 126, and 127). There is much speculation as to why Confucius refers to Guan Zhong as a small vessel here. Some think it is because Guan Zhong assisted Duke Huan to become a leader among the lords but not yet a ruler capable of uniting the empire. See *Shi ji,* 62.2136; *Xin xu,* 4.113. Dong Zhongshu (179–104 B.C.E.) thinks it is because of Duke Huan's self-complacence (*Chunqiu fanlu,* 5.67–68). Yang Xiong says: "Someone asked, 'It was because of Guan Zhong that Qi achieved hegemony. If Guan Zhong was a small vessel, then what is a great vessel?' [I answered,] 'Isn't a great vessel like a carpenter's square? First put oneself in order, then put others in order; this is 'a great vessel'" (*Fa yan,* 9.297–98).

8. *Analects,* 13.118.

9. *Laozi,* 11.44.

10. *Zhuangzi,* 2.4.170–71.

11. *Ibid.*, 1.1.36–37.

12. *Ibid.*, 9.6.936.

13. See Davis, "Double Ninth Festival in Chinese Poetry," in *Wen-lin,* 45–64.

14. "On the ninth day of the ninth month, people. . . . drink chrysanthemum wine, which is said to bring longevity" (*Xijing zaji quanyi,* 3.106). According to Du Gongzhan's (ca. early seventh century) commentary on *Jingchu suishi ji,* "It is unknown when people began to hold a banquet on the ninth day of the ninth month, but the custom had never changed from Han to Song [i.e., the Liu Song]. Today even the northerners set great store by this festival" (Zong Lin, *Jingchu suishi ji yizhu,* 31.122).

15. "A Letter to Zhong Yao Written on the Ninth Day" (Jiuri yu Zhong Yao shu) (Yan Kejun, *Quan sanguo wen,* 7.1088b).

16. This is an allusion to a line from a *Shi jing* poem: "The emptiness of the pitcher / is the shame of the jar" (*Maoshi zhengyi,* 13.436).

17. Stephen Owen's translation, *Anthology of Chinese Literature,* 315.

18. *Laozi,* 4.18.

19. *Xunzi jijie,* 28.341.

20. *Laozi,* 41.171.

21. *Zhuangzi jishi,* 4.9.330–36.

22. *Ibid.*, 1.2.74. Stephen Owen's translation, *Anthology of Chinese Literature,* 117.

23. *Ibid.*, 1.2.76.

24. See *Zhuangzi jinzhu jinyi,* 67.

25. *Zhuangzi jishi,* 1.2.75; Stephen Owen's translation (with modifications), *Anthology of Chinese Literature,* 118.

26. Gu Zhi, *Tao Jingjie shi jian,* 254.

27. *Analects,* 2.16.

28. "For good fortune or bad, there is no gate; it arrives at the person's bidding" (*Chunqiu Zuozhuan zhengyi,* Duke Xiang 23, 35.605).

29. From Yin Zhongwen's (?–407) poem, "Composed at the Nine Wells of the Duke Huan at Nanzhou" (Nanzhou Huangong Jiujing zuo): "How to mark out the steadfast and the fragile? / Here are some words I leave for the pine and the mushroom." Li Shan's (?–689) commentary says, "The pine and the mushroom have different qualities, and so are the steadfast and the fragile different in nature" (Xiao Tong, *Wen xuan,* 22.1033).

30. *Analects,* 9.80.

31. "They are befuddled and ignorant, / once drunk, they think they are growing richer every day" (*Maoshi zhengyi,* 12.419).

32. Lu Qinli, *Tao Yuanming ji,* 17.

33. *Xunzi jijie,* 1.5.

34. *Analects,* 9.80.

35. As Davis said, it is also possible to believe that Tao Yuanming is "primarily" referring to Xunzi, but expects the reader to think of the well-known statement of Confucius as well (Davis, 1.18). It is noteworthy that Zhou Mi (1232–1308), in his *An Alternate Collection of Miscellaneous Notes from the Guixin Lane* (Guixin zashi bieji), records Liu Zai's (1166–1239) comment on this poem, which not only takes "not ceasing" as an allusion to Confucius's statement on the flowing water but also considers the allusion as the key to understanding this poem. It is interesting to note that in quoting the fifth and sixth lines, Zhou Mi provides yet another variant for the verb *zhi,* which is a homophonous character of *zhi,* but synonymous with *wang*: "I *discard* the fact of 'not ceasing'" (*Zhi bi bu she* 寘彼不捨) (*Song Yuan biji xiaoshuo daguan,* 6.5854).

36. Hightower, *Poetry of T'ao Ch'ien,* 21.

37. Fu Yi wrote "Poem on Self-inspiration" (Dizhi shi) (*Quan Jin shi,* 5.172–73); Zhang Hua, "Poem on Urging Myself" (Lizhi shi) (*Quan Jin shi,* 3.614–15).

38. "The later-born deserve our sense of awe, for how do we know the coming generations are not as good as the current one? But if a person, by forty or fifty, is still unheard of by the world, then he is not worthy of awe" (*Analects,* 9.80).

39. Lu Qinli is the only person who suggests that the "famed carriage" and "famed steed" should be understood as "carriage and steed of fame"—that is, a metaphorical way of saying that the poet is prepared to embark on a journey of seeking a great reputation in the political world (*Tao Yuanming ji,* 17).

40. Davis, *T'ao Yüan-ming,* 1.17.

41. *Analects,* 7.59.

42. Or, "This is something truly enjoyable."

43. *Zhuangzi jishi,* 5.12.420–23.

44. *Huiping,* 111–12.

45. Hightower, *Poetry of T'ao Ch'ien,* 92.

46. "Those who had obtained the Way in antiquity were always happy, no matter whether they encountered bad fortunes or good fortunes, because the

source of their happiness did not lie either in good fortunes or bad" (*Zhuangzi jishi*, 9.28.983).

47. This poem is the sixteenth of the "On Drinking" series.

48. *Laozi*, 70.281.

49. *The Classic of Music* is no longer extant.

6 Hard Evidence: Reading a Stone

Cao Xueqin, *Dream of the Red Chamber* (or *Story of the Stone*), chapter one.

1. *Lushan youji*, 71, 34.

2. *Gaoseng zhuan*, 65–67. Hu Shi gives a long and detailed argument against this theory (*Lushan youji*, 37–59).

3. Deng Ansheng discusses the inauthentic claims about Lili in section two of his article "Tao Yuanming liju bianzheng" (*Wenshi*, 173–83).

4. See Li Bai's poem "Playfully Presented to Magistrate Zheng of Liyang" (Xizeng Zheng Liyang) (*Li Bai quanji jiaozhu huishi jiping*, 1557–58). However, in this poem Lili has a variant, Lili 溧里.

5. *Bai Juyi ji jianjiao*, 362.

6. *Taiping huanyu ji*, 111.6a–7a; *Yingyin Wenyuan ge siku quanshu*, 470. 178–79.

7. That is, the Jinling Shuju 1882 edition. Davis has used this edition in his quotation. See Davis, *T'ao Yüan-ming*, 2.182.

8. Again, the Jinling Shuju edition of *Taiping huanyu ji* and another geographical work of the Southern Song, *Fine Scenes of the Regions* (Fangyu shenglan), have "Chaisang Shan." *Fangyu shenglan*, written by Zhu Mu (thirteenth century) and supplemented by his son Zhu Zhu (*jinshi*, 1256), contains the following item: "Mount Chaisang: ninety miles southwest of Dehua County. It is close to Lili Yuan. Tao Qian was a native of this place." *Fangyu shenglan* was first printed in 1239 and then reprinted with Zhu Zhu's supplements between 1266 and 1267 (*Fangyu shenglan*, 228).

9. *Songben Taiping huanyu ji*, 13–26. Unfortunately, the part of *juan* 111 which contains our citations is among the missing sections.

10. *Taiping yulan*, 41.6b.

11. Upon seeing Liu Huan off to Nankang, Ouyang Xiu wrote a poem, "Lofty Mount Lu" (Lushan gao zeng tongnian Liu Zhongyun gui Nankang),

to praise his retirement (*Ouyang Xiu quanji*, 1.35–36). Among Liu Huan's connections was another renowned political and cultural figure of his day, Sima Guang, who wrote a funerary inscription for his son Liu Shu (1032–1078). Liu Huan's friend Chen Shunyu's demotion won him admiration from Su Shi, who was also demoted for holding the same ideological views as Chen Shunyu. After Chen died, Su Shi wrote a sacrificial address to him, generously praising him as a "vessel worthy of a hundred people" (see *Su Dongpo quanji*, 1.415). Then, in 1093, Huang Tingjian, the best-known of the Su Shi group, was moved to write another funerary inscription for Liu Shu when Liu Shu's son relocated his father's tomb. Liu Huan, Liu Shu, Chen Shunyu, and their powerful connections added a great deal of cachet to their names as well as to Nankang, which was drawn upon by Zhu Xi about a hundred years later in his efforts to transform Nankang into a cultural space. This will be discussed in greater detail later.

12. See Wu Zongci's *Lushan zhi* (comp. 1933), 2.37.

13. *Lushan ji*, 50–51.

14. *Ibid.*, 80–81.

15. *Quan Song shi*, 403.4966. The text is slightly different in Li E's (1692–1752) *An Account of Incidents around Song Poetry* (Song shi jishi) and Mao Deqi's *Record of Mount Lu* (Lushan zhi, comp. 1719). The most remarkable variation occurs in the last line: instead of "enough to make the traveler feel ashamed by the master's pure ways," *Song shi jishi* has "still reminding the traveler of the master's pure ways" (shang shi youren xiang sufeng) (*Song shi jishi*, 1.422).

16. *Quan Tang shi bubian*, 2.1112.

17. *Quan Tang shi*, 885.10007.

18. *Quan Tang shi*, 886.10021.

19. Strassberg, *Inscribed Landscapes*, 5.

20. Wu Zongci, *Lushan zhi*, 2.591.

21. Mao Deqi, *Lushan zhi*, 122; Sang Qiao, *Lushan jishi*, 3.5a.

22. Langhuan bieguan edition, 12.12b–13b.

23. *Ibid.*, 122.

24. Wu, 2.590–91.

25. See Linda A. Walton's article "Southern Sung Academies and the Construction of Sacred Space," in *Landscape, Culture, and Power in Chinese Society*, 23–49.

26. This is an allusion to the famous Mencius passage: "A good *shih* in one small community will befriend the other good *shih* of that community. The

good *shih* of a single state will befriend the other good *shih* of that state. The good *shih* of the whole world will befriend the other good *shih* of the whole world. But if befriending the good *shih* of the whole world is not enough, then one may go on further to consider the ancients. Yet is it acceptable to recite their poems and read their books without knowing what kind of persons they were? Therefore one considers the age in which they lived. This is 'going on further to make friends'" (*Mengzi zhushu,* 10b.188; Stephen Owen's translation, *Readings in Chinese Literary Thought,* 34).

27. These two lines are adapted from the Tang poet Meng Haoran's (689–740) couplet from a poem entitled "Sending to My Old Friends of the Capital upon Returning to the South Garden in Midsummer" (Zhongxia gui Nanyuan ji jingyi jiuyou): "I once read the biographies of noble recluses, / and most admired the worthiness of summoned gentleman Tao" (*Meng Haoran ji jiaozhu,* 61). We might, however, notice that while Meng Haoran considered Tao Yuanming the most admirable (*zui*) of all recluses, Zhu Xi regarded Tao Yuanming as the one and only (*du*).

28. *Analects,* 7.62.

29. *Quan Tang shi,* 152.1583. In *Quan Tang shi,* the title of the poem is simply given as "On Tao Yuanming" (Yong Tao Yuanming), and Lili is nowhere mentioned in the poem.

30. *Zhu Wengong wenji,* 8.1478.

31. "An Account of the Pavilion of Stalwart Virtue" (*ibid.,* 8.1455).

32. *Ibid.,* 8.1455.

33. The "private note" refers to that written by Song Xiang. However, Song's posthumous title is Yuanxian, not Xuanhui.

34. *Zhou Yiguo wenzhong gong ji,* 169.6a–b.

35. *Lushan xin daoyou,* 37a.

36. *Lushan xiaozhi,* 12.13a.

37. Huang Zongxi (1610–1695) writes, "Above the Drunken Stone there is the Tiger Claw Cliff. Yigong [i.e., Zhou Bida] says that the stone has a hollow spot, which is said to be the trace left by Master Tao Yuanming's head; and he also mentions the story about the trace left by a tiger, which he dismisses as absurd. Thus it may be said that the tiger's claw and the Drunken Stone actually share one stone" (*Kuang Lu you lu,* 27a–b).

38. *Gaoseng zhuan,* 221. Wang Bo (650?–684?), Wang Wei, Meng Haoran, and Li Bai, for instance, all alluded to this story in their writings.

39. *A Desultory Record of the Cloud Immortal* (Yunxian sanlu), an early

tenth-century compilation of quotations from various sources, records three anecdotes about Tao Yuanming allegedly from "An Unofficial Biography of Yuanming" (Yuanming biezhuan). The sources of *Yunxian sanlu* are problematic, and even if "An Unofficial Biography of Yuanming" did exist once, it is hardly reliable. And yet, the anecdotes show that apocryphal stories about Tao Yuanming were circulating in the late Tang. The Tang monk Guanxiu wrote a poem on Hui Yuan's violation of rules by sending wine to Tao Yuanming and going beyond Tiger Stream for Lu Xiujing, but the two anecdotes are related as two separate things in the short preface to this poem, which does not mention Hui Yuan's seeing Tao Yuanming off (*Quan Tang shi*, 846.9420). Chen Shunyu noted the story of "three laughing friends" (see *Lushan ji*, 26–27). Su Shi's appraisal of a painting, "Three Laughing Friends" (San xiao tu) by Shi Ke (fl. ca. 965), is supposed to be about Hui Yuan, Lu Xiujing, and Tao Yuanming, although Su Shi's appraisal does not make it clear at all who are the three people laughing in the painting (*Su Dongpo quanji*, vol. 2, 303).

40. Colophon to Dongpo's "Appraisal of 'Three Laughing Friends'" (Lou Yue, *Gongkui ji*, 77.717).

41. Davis, *T'ao Yüan-ming*, 2.187.

42. Ouyang Xuan (1273–1357) wrote a letter on behalf of Heavenly Master Zhang (Zhang Tianshi) asking a Superintendent Lei to stay at the Drunken Stone shrine. It begins, "His drunkenness is not real drunkenness, but leaves traces on the stone in vain; should one return or not? The residence in the mountains has grown old. To give value to the famous sites of previous worthies, one has to rely on the great talents of the day." See Wu Zongci's *Lushan zhi*, 2.58.

43. *Lushan jishi*, 3.4b.

44. This pseudo-quotation from *The Histories of the Southern Dynasties* continues to be cited as authentic, by, among others, Mao Deqi, Wu Zongci, and a recent book on Mount Lu, *Lushan yu mingren*, 82.

45. *Wenfan xiaopin*, 339.

46. *Ibid.*, 132.

47. Sang Qiao's second quatrain is identical with Mao's and so contains the same error (*Lushan jishi*, 3.5b).

48. Mao Deqi, *Lushan zhi*, 122.

49. *Huang Zongxi shiwen xuan*, 228.

50. *Kuang Lu you lu*, 27a.

51. By "worthless chaff," Huang refers to the three things which he considers

sufficient to efface famous sites: "Vulgar people's travel accounts, foolish people's change of [place] names, and VIPs' inscriptions" (*Kuang Lu you lu*, 1a–b).

52. The belief has become so deeply rooted that Zhong Youmin, a contemporary scholar of Tao Yuanming, does not hesitate to assert that "Lili is at the foot of Mount Lu and is Master Tao Yuanming's hometown" (*Taoxue fazhan shi*, 464). Gu Zhi, on the other hand, insists that Lili is situated at Chucheng Xiang of Dehua County. He gives three reasons, the second of which is that in 1512, a flood in the Luzi Ban area of Chucheng Xiang flushed out a stele of unknown date, on which were carved these words: "The Old Hometown of Master Tao Jingjie." Li Mengyang (1473–1529), then the superintendent of education of Jiangxi, built a tomb for Tao Yuanming and established a shrine to him on the spot where the stele had surfaced. See Gu Zhi's *The Chronology of Tao Jingjie* (Tao Jingjie nianpu) in *Cengbing Tang wu-zhong*, 395. The fight over the hometown of Tao Yuanming (besides being a point of interest for Tao Yuanming scholars and admirers) is largely a matter between Xingzi and Dehua, two neighboring counties whose names, boundaries, and legislatures have shifted for centuries. It continues to this day. See, for instance, Deng Zhongbo's article "Tao Yuanming guli shuo" in *Jiangxi Shiyuan Xuebao*, 59–62; and Xu Xinjie's "Tao Yuanming guli bian" in *Jiujiang Shizhuan Xuebao*, 22–24.

53. Wu Zongci, *Lushan zhi*, 2.102.

54. Wu Zongci notes that it should be Nine Floods Bridge (Jiuhong Qiao) (*Lushan zhi*, 1.311).

55. Tao Yuanming's poem "Returning to My Former Residence" opens with the line: "Some time ago I lived at Shangjing" (see chapter three).

56. *Tao Jingjie nianpu*, in *Cengbing Tang wuzhong*, 426.

57. Cao Longshu claims that he found these characters carved on a stone cliff by the lake at the foot of Mount Yujing. He believes it proves that this was the very place written about in Tao Yuanming's poem "An Excursion to Xie Brook" (see chapter four) and thus proves beyond doubt that the Mount Yujing area was indeed where Tao Yuanming's residence was.

58. Wu Zongci's stand in the matter of the Drunken Stone is typical. Later, when discussing which is the real hometown of Tao Yuanming, he adopts a similar reconciliatory attitude: "Let me find a middle ground [i.e., amidst contending theories] and make a compromising statement. Yuanming lived in all three places: Shangjing, Lili (where the Drunken Stone is), and Chaisang. As for the precedence and duration of his stay in each place, if we only infer from

his biographies and writings, it would be too arbitrary, and much more so if we try to decide, after several thousand years, which was his former residence and which was not. Huang Lizhou [i.e., Huang Zongxi] comments on the Ink Pool of Right General Wang [i.e., Wang Xizhi, the famous calligrapher], saying that [even though it was not real] it was an ancient site after all. I think this is a very open-minded statement. I would say the same of the former residence of Tao" (Wu Zongci, *Lushan zhi,* 1.382).

59. Sang Qiao, *Lushan jishi,* 3.2a; Mao Deqi, *Lushan zhi,* 118; Wu Zongci, *Lushan zhi,* 2.591.

60. Wu Zongci, *Lushan zhi,* 1.311. He then adds his own observation that again derives authority from empirical experience: "Gu Zhi says that the Drunken Stone between the two peaks can only contain two or three people, which is not accurate. I have examined it: it has enough room for more than ten people."

Conclusion

1. Cerquiglini, *In Praise of the Variant,* 38.
2. Li Qing, *Sanyuan biji,* 18–19.
3. Cerquiglini, *In Praise of the Variant,* 49.
4. That would be the kind of philology Bernard Cerquiglini talks about, which "took [variance] to be merely a childhood disease, a guilty offhandedness of an early deficiency of scribal culture" (*In Praise of the Variant,* 21).
5. Said, *Humanism and Democratic Criticism,* 57, 59, 6.
6. Marcus, *Unediting the Renaissance,* 130.
7. For Jerome J. McGann's work, see *A Critique of Modern Textual Criticism.*
8. From Tao Yuanming's poem "Body, Shadow, and Spirit" (Xing ying shen).

Chinese Glossary

Anban shouyi jing 安般守意經

Bai Juyi 白居易 (Bai Letian 白樂天)
Baijing Lou 拜經樓
Baijing lou ben 拜經樓本
Baili Xi 百里奚
Bailu Dong Shuyuan 白鹿洞書院
Baiyun yao 白雲謠
banben xue 版本學
Bao Sun Huizong shu 報孫會宗書
Bao Tao Zhai 寶陶齋
Bao Tingbo 鮑廷博 (Bao Yiwen 鮑以文)
Bao Zhao 鮑照
Baohui Tang 寶繪堂
Beishan jing 北山經
Bi Yuan 畢沅
Bian He 卞和
Bingchen sui bayue zhong yu xiasun tian she huo 丙辰歲八月中於下潠田舍穫
Bingyu Tang ji 冰玉堂記
Bishu luhua 避暑錄話
Boya 伯牙
Boyi 伯夷
bu chengqi 不成器
Buzhou shan 不周山

Cai Qi 蔡啟 (Cai Juhou 蔡居厚, Cai Kuanfu 蔡寬夫)
Cai Ying 蔡瀛
Cao Cao 曹操
Cao Longshu 曹龍樹
Cao Pi 曹丕
Cao Zhi 曹植
Cen Rang 岑穰 (Cen Yanxiu 岑彥休)
Chaisang Shan 柴桑山
Changyang 常羊
Chao Buzhi 晁補之
Chao Yongzhi 晁詠之 (Chao Zhidao 晁之道)
Chaofu 巢父
Chen Congyi 陳從易
Chen Guang 陳光
Chen Kui 陳揆
Chen Li 陳澧
Chen Longzheng 陳龍正
Chen Shidao 陳師道
Chen Shugu 陳述古
Chen Shunyu 陳舜俞 (Chen Lingju 陳令舉)
Chen Xianxing 陳先行
Chen Xingzhen 陳杏珍
Chen Yaozi 陳堯咨
Chen Zuoming 陳祚明
cheng 成
Cheng Hao 程顥
Cheng Qianfan 程千帆
Cheng Shimeng 程師孟
Cheng Xuanying 成玄英

chengqi 成器
Chi Chao 郗超
Chong Zun 寵遵 (or Pang Zun 龐遵)
Chong'er 重耳
Chonghua 重華
Chucheng Xiang 楚城鄉
Chunming Fang 春明坊
Chunxi 淳熙
Chuxue ji 初學記
Cui Qi 崔琦

da 達
da jun 大鈞
Da Pang canjun 答龐参軍
da qi wan cheng 大器晚成
da tong 大通
Da zong shi 大宗師
Dahuang bei jing 大荒北經
Dahuang xi jing 大荒西經
Dai Kui 戴逵
Dai Qiuhu ge shi 代秋胡歌詩
Dai Yong 戴顒
Daoshan qinghua 道山清話
Daren fu 大人賦
Daren xiansheng zhuan 大人先生傳
Dayin xi sheng 大音希聲
de 得
Dehua Xian 德化縣
Di Jun 帝俊
Ding Fubao 丁福保
Ding Lingwei 丁令威
Dizhi shi 迪志詩
Dong Zhongshu 董仲舒
Dongfang Shuo 東方朔
Donglin si 東林寺
Dongting gong 洞庭公
Dongyuan gong 東園公
Du Fu 杜甫
Du Gongzhan 杜公瞻
Du Mu 杜牧
Du Shanhai jing shisan shou 讀山海經十三首
Du Yu 杜預
duo lei bei 墮淚碑
Duqing Tang ben 笃慶堂本
duyou 督郵

Fahua zongyao 法華宗要
Fan Chi 樊遲
Fan Ning 范寧
Fan Ye 范曄
Fan Yuanxi 范元羲
Fan zhaoyin shi 反招隱詩
Fang Shao 方勺
Fang Tao gong jiuzhai 訪陶公舊宅
fang zheng 方正
fangda 放達
Feng Youlan 馮友蘭
Fenghe Hui Yuan you Lushan shi 奉和慧遠游廬山詩
fengqu 風趣
Fengzeng Wei zuocheng zhang ershieryun 奉贈韋左丞丈二十二韻
Fotuoyeshe 佛陀耶舍
Fu Xuan 傅玄
Fu Yi 傅毅
Fu Yue 傅約
Furong chi zuo shi 芙蓉池作詩

Gan yuan 甘淵
Gao Yanxiu 高彥休
Gaotang fu 高唐賦
Gaoyi shamen zhuan 高逸沙門傳

Ge Hong 葛洪
Ge Lifang 葛立方
Ge Shengzhong 葛勝仲
geng 耕
Gengsang Chu 庚桑楚
Gengxu sui jiuyue zhong yu xitian huo han dao 庚戌歲九月中於西田穫旱稻
gong ye 功業
gonggeng 躬耕
Gonggong 共工
Gongxi shihua 鞏溪詩話
Gu 鼓
Gu Hao 顧皜
Gu Kaizhi 顧愷之
Gu Mei 顧湄 (Gu Yiren 顧伊人)
Gu Zhi 古直 (Gu Cengbing 古層冰)
Gu Zixiu 顧自修
guan 冠
Guan Zhong 管仲
Guanxiu 貫休
Gui yuan tian ju 歸園田居
Guimao sui shichun huai gu tian she 癸卯歲始春懷古田舍
Guimao sui shieryue zhong zuo yu congdi Jingyuan 癸卯歲十二月中作與從弟敬遠
Guiqulai ci 歸去來辭
Guiqulai Guan 歸去來館
Guixin zashi bieji 癸辛雜識別集
Guizong Si 歸宗寺
guji 古跡
Gun 鯀
Guo Pu 郭璞
Guo Shaoyu 郭紹虞
Guo Xiang 郭象
Guo Xiangzheng 郭祥正
guozu weirun 過足為潤
Guyi congshu 古逸叢書

Hainei bei jing 海內北經
Han Ju 韓駒 (Han Zicang 韓子蒼)
Han Wudi nei zhuan 漢武帝內傳
Han Xin 韓信
Han Yu 韓愈
Han Zigao 韓子高
Hanfen Lou 涵芬樓
Hao Yixing 郝懿行
He bo 河伯
He Guo zhubu 和郭主簿
He Hu xicao shi Gu zeicao 和胡西曹示顧賊曹
He Liu Chaisang 和劉柴桑
He Mengchun 何孟春
He Shao 何邵
He Tao he jian 和陶合箋
He Tao You Xiechuan 和陶游斜川
He Xianyi 何咸宜
He Yan 何晏
He Zhuo 何焯
hong jun 洪鈞
Hong Mai 洪邁
Houshan shihua 後山詩話
Houtu 后土
Hu Boji ben 胡伯薊本
Hu Fengdan 胡鳳丹
Hu Shi 胡適
Hu Zi 胡仔
Hua shanshui xu 畫山水序
huai yu 懷玉
Huainanzi 淮南子
huan 患
Huan Huo 桓豁
Huan jiu ju 還舊居

Huan Wen 桓溫
Huan Xuan 桓玄
huang 荒
Huang Che 黃徹
Huang Pilie 黃丕烈
Huang Tingjian 黃庭堅 (Huang Luzhi 黃魯直)
Huang Wenhuan 黃文煥
Huang Zongxi 黃宗羲
Huangfu Mi 皇甫謐
Huangfu Xizhi 皇甫希之
Huangzi Gao'ao 皇子告敖
hui 揮
Hui Guan 慧觀
Hui Hong 惠洪
Hui Jiao 慧皎
Hui Yuan 慧遠
Huiweng 晦翁
Huizi 惠子
Huizong 徽宗
Huzhao Yai 虎爪崖
Huzhong Jiuhua 壺中九華

ji 跡
Ji Chengshi mei wen 祭程氏妹文
ji shi 即事
Ji Zhenyi 季振宜
Jia Sixie 賈思勰
jian 見
jian ao 簡傲
Jiang Bingzhi 江秉之
Jiang Xu 蔣栩
Jiang Xun 蔣薰 (Jiang Danyai 蔣丹崖)
Jiang Xun ping ben 蔣薰評本
Jiang Yan 江淹
Jiangsu Shuju 江蘇書局
Jiangyun Lou 絳雲樓
Jiangyun lou shangliang yi shi dai wen ba shou 絳雲樓上梁以詩代文八首
Jianning 建寧
Jianzhu Tao Yuanming ji 箋注陶淵明集
jiao er lanlü 交爾藍縷
jiao wu 交無
jiaokan xue 校勘學
Jiaoran 皎然
Jiaqing 嘉慶
Jieni 桀溺
Jigu ge ben 汲古閣本
Jiming 雞鳴
jin 巾
Jin Chengdi 晉成帝
Jin Gu 金谷
Jin gu Zhengxi dajiangjun zhangshi Meng fujun zhuan 晉故征西大將軍長史孟府君傳
Jin yangjiu 晉陽秋
Jing Ke 荊軻
jing qi 精氣
Jingde 旌德
Jingji zhi 經籍志
Jingjie xiansheng ji 靖節先生集
Jingjie xiansheng nianpu kaoyi 靖節先生年譜考異
Jingxing ji 經行記
Jingzhou 荊州
Jinling Shuju 金陵書局
Jirang ge 擊壤歌
jiu 久
jiu 九
jiu bu ying 久不盈
Jiu ge 九歌

Jiufeng Qiao 九峰橋
Jiuhong Qiao 九洪橋
Jiuri xianju 九日閑居
Jiuri yu Zhong Yao shu 九日與鍾繇書
Juhua fu 菊花賦
Juhua song 菊花頌

kai huang 開荒
Kaixian 開先
Kang Sengyuan 康僧淵
kong 空
Kong Qun 孔群
Kuang Lu hua yin 匡廬花隱
kuangda 曠達
kuyu 苦雨
Kuyu fu 苦雨賦

Lai fu 萊婦
Lanting 蘭亭
Lanzhenzi 嬾真子
Lao Dan 老聃
Laolaizi 老萊子
Laozi 老子
Lei Cizong 雷次宗
leiji 羸疾
Lengzhai yehua 冷齋夜話
Li Bai 李白
Li Dashi 李大師
Li Daoyuan 酈道元
Li Gonghuan 李公煥
Li Gonghuan ben 李公煥本
Li ji 禮記
Li Mengyang 李夢陽
Li Qing 李清
Li sao 離騷
Li Shan 李善
Li Shimin 李世民
Li Tao Zhai 禮陶齋
Li Wenhan 李文韓
Li Xiang 李詳
Li Yanshou 李延壽
Li Zhengchen 李正臣
Liang Hong 梁鴻
Lianshe gaoxian zhuan 蓮社高賢傳
Lianyu duyin 連雨獨飲
Lianyu renjue duyin 連雨人絕獨飲
Liao cheng hua yi gui jin 聊乘化以歸盡
Liezi 列子
Lili 栗里
Lili Yuan 栗里源
Lin Xiangru 藺相如
lingshan 靈山
Liu Bin 劉邠 (Liu Gongfu 劉貢父)
Liu Chang 劉昶 (Liu Gongrong 劉公榮)
Liu Huaisu 劉懷肅
Liu Huan 劉渙
Liu Jingxuan 劉敬宣
Liu Kai 柳開
Liu Ling 劉伶
Liu Liu 劉柳
Liu Lü 劉履
Liu Shengmu 劉聲木
Liu Shi 柳是
liu shi 留勢
Liu Shu 劉恕
Liu Song 劉宋
Liu Xiaobiao 劉孝標
Liu Xiang 劉向
Liu Xie 劉勰
Liu Xin 劉歆
Liu Yilong 劉義隆

Liu Yimin 劉遺民
Liu Yiqing 劉義慶
Liu Yu 劉裕
Liu Zai 劉宰
Liu Zhen 劉楨 (Liu Gonggan 劉公幹)
Liu Zongyuan 柳宗元 (Liu Zihou 柳子厚)
Liuyi shihua 六一詩話
Lizhi shi 勵志詩
Lou Yue 樓鑰
lu 祿
Lu Ji 陸機
Lu Qinli 逯欽立
Lu Xiujing 陸修靜
Lu Xun 魯迅
luben 錄本
Luli xiansheng 甪里先生
Luling 廬陵
Lun Bian 輪扁
Luo Tingzhi 駱庭芝
Luo You 羅友
Luoshen fu 洛神賦
Lushan gao zeng tongnian Liu Zhongyun gui Nankang 廬山高贈同年劉中允歸南康
Lushan houlu 廬山後錄
Lushan jishi 廬山紀事
Lushan zhi 廬山志
Luzi Ban 鹿子阪

Ma Yongqing 馬永卿
mao 帽
Mao Deqi 毛德琦
Mao Jin 毛晉
Mao Yi 毛扆
Mao Yi 毛義
mei yi 每役
Meng Haoran 孟浩然
Meng Jia 孟嘉
Meng Tao Zhai 夢陶齋
Mengxi xubitan 夢溪續筆談
miao 妙
Miaode xiansheng zhuan 妙德先生傳
Min Qihua 閔齊華
ming 名
Ming xiang 明象
Ming zi 命子
mingjiao 名教
Mo Youzhi 莫友芝
Mo Youzhi ben 莫友芝本
Mu tianzi zhuan 穆天子傳
Mudan ting 牡丹亭
mujin 木堇/槿

Nankang jun 南康軍
Nanzhou Huangong Jiujing zuo 南州桓公九井作
neisheng waiwang 內聖外王
Nenggaizhai manlu 能改齋漫錄
Ni Ye zhong ji 擬鄴中集
Nigu 擬古
Ning Song Zhuren 佞宋主人
Nüwa 女娃

Ouyang Guohua Li Shenghua Huangyou [illegible] nian tongyou 歐陽國華李升華皇祐 [illegible] 年同遊
Ouyang Jian 歐陽建
Ouyang Xiu 歐陽修
Ouyang Xuan 歐陽玄

Pan Lei 潘耒
Pan Ni 潘尼

Pan Yue 潘岳
Pang Tongzhi 龐通之
Pei Wei 裴頠
Peng Cheng 彭乘
Pengze 彭澤
pin 娉
Pingzhou ketan 萍洲可談
Piping Tao Yuanming ji 批評陶淵明集
po wei lao nong 頗為老農

qi 器
Qi Huangong 齊桓公
Qi shi 乞食
Qian Jia xuepai 乾嘉學派
Qian Meixian 錢梅仙
Qian Qianyi 錢謙益
Qian Zeng 錢曾 (Qian Zunwang 錢遵王)
Qianfu 乾符
Qianlong 乾隆
Qianlou 黔婁
qile taotao 其樂陶陶
Qili Ji 綺里季
Qimin yaoshu 齊民要術
qin 親
qing tan 清談
Qiwu lun 齊物論
Qixian lun 七賢論
Qu Shaoji 瞿紹基
Qu Yong 瞿鏞
Qu Yuan 屈原
quan nong 勸農
Quan nong fu 勸農賦
Quanxue 勸學
Quwei jiuwen 曲洧舊聞

ren zhen 任真
renji 人跡
Rong mu 榮木
Ru'nan xianxian zhuan 汝南先賢傳
Ruan Hun 阮渾
Ruan Ji 阮籍
Ruan Xian 阮咸 (Ruan Zhongrong 阮仲容)
Ruan Yu 阮瑀
Ruan Yuan 阮元

san buxiu 三不朽
San shang jie tian xing 三觴解天刑
San xiao tu 三笑圖
Sang Qiao 桑喬
sang wo 喪我
shan 山
shan 汕
Shan shang hua zan 扇上畫贊
shan xiao 善嘯
shan xiao 善笑
Shan you shu 山有樞
shanben 善本
Shang shan si hao 商山四皓
shang shi youren xiang sufeng 尚使遊人想素風
Shanhai jing tu zan 山海經圖讚
Shanju jishi 山居即事
Shanju shi 山居詩
Shanjuan 善卷
Shao Bowen 邵伯溫
Shao hao qin shu 少好琴書
Shao lai hao shu or *shaonian lai hao shu* 少(年)來好書
Shao si ming 少司命
Shao xue qin shu 少學琴書
Shaoshi wenjian houlu 邵氏聞見後錄

Shaoxing ben 紹興本
Shen Gua 沈括
Shen Yue 沈約
Shengxian qunfu lu 聖賢群輔錄
shenming 神明
shi 事
shi 實
Shi Chong 石崇
shi han si huo 實函斯活
Shi jing 詩經
Shi Ke 石恪
shi yu ren 十余人
Shi yun 時運
Shi Zhecun 施蟄存
Shi Zhou Xuzhi, Zu Qi, Xie Jingyi san lang 示周續之祖企謝景夷三郎
Shi Zhou yuan Zu Xie 示周掾祖謝
Shi zuo Zhenjun canjun jing Qu'e 始作鎮軍參軍經曲阿
Shiba gaoxian zhuan 十八高賢傳
Shilin shihua 石林詩話
shiye 事業
shiyu 時雨
shu 述
shu er bu zuo 述而不作
Shu Guang 疏廣
Shu jiu 述酒
shu shi ren 數十人
Shu Shou 疏受
Shu Tao Qian Zuishi 書陶潛醉石
Shu Xi 束皙
shu Zuishi 書醉石
Shun 舜
Shuqi 叔齊
Si ba mu 四八目
Si hao song 四皓頌
si tian 司田
Si Yue 思悅
Si Yue ben 思悅本
Sihao lun 四皓論
Sima Guang 司馬光
Sima Qian 司馬遷
Sima Xiangru 司馬相如
Sima Xiuzhi 司馬休之
Song ben 宋本
Song ben zuo mou 宋本作某
Song Cai Xilu duwei huan Longyou yin ji Gao sanshiwu shuji 送蔡希魯都尉還隴右因寄高三十五書記
Song Gaozong 宋高宗
Song Luo 宋犖
Song Minqiu 宋敏求
Song Qi 宋祁
Song Shenzong 宋神宗
Song Shou 宋綬
Song Xiang 宋庠
Song Xiang ben 宋庠本
Song Xiaozong 宋孝宗
Su Guo 蘇過
Su Jun 蘇峻
Su Longmen 宿龍門
Su Shi 蘇軾 (Su Dongpo 蘇東坡, Dongpo jushi 東坡居士)
Su xie ben 蘇寫本
Su xie keben 蘇寫刻本
Suimu he Zhang changshi 歲暮和張常侍
Sun Chu 孫楚
Sun Chuo 孫綽
Sun Kuang 孫鑛
Sun Sheng 孫盛
suoyi ji 所以跡
Sushan Yuan 粟山源
suxinren 素心人

Tan Daoji 檀道濟
Tan Daoluan 檀道鸞
Tan Shao 檀韶
Tang Han 湯漢 (Tang Boji 湯伯紀)
Tang Han ben 湯漢本
Tang Xianzu 湯顯祖
Tang Yongtong 湯用彤
Tao Dan 陶淡
Tao Fan 陶範 (Tao Hunu 陶胡奴)
Tao fu 桃賦
Tao Fuxiang 陶福祥 (Ailu 愛廬)
Tao ji fawei 陶集發微
Tao Jingjie shihua 陶靖節詩話
Tao Jingjie shiji kaoyi 陶靖節詩集考異
Tao Jingjie xiansheng shizhu 陶靖節先生詩注
tao jun 陶鈞
Tao Kan 陶侃
Tao Kui 陶夔
Tao Lu 陶廬
Tao shi hui ping 陶詩彙評
Tao shi hui zhu 陶詩彙注
Tao shi xi yi 陶詩析義
Tao shi yan 陶詩衍
Tao Shu 陶澍
Tao Shu ben 陶澍本
Tao Tao Shi 陶陶室
Tao Yuanming 陶淵明 (Tao Qian 陶潛, also Tao Jingjie 陶靖節 and Tao Pengze 陶彭澤)
Tao Yuanming shiji 陶淵明詩集
Tao Zhan 陶瞻
Taohuayuan ji 桃花源記
Taoyuan 桃源
Ti Tao Yuanming Zuishi 題陶淵明醉石
Ti wei ding cao 題未定草
Tian Guo 田過
Tianjin tushuguan guben miji congshu 天津圖書館孤本秘籍叢書
tiansheng ziran 天生自然
Tianwen 天問
Tiaoxi yuyin conghua houji 苕溪漁隱叢話後集
Tiaoxi yuyin conghua qianji 苕溪漁隱叢話前集
Tieqin tongjian lou cangshumu 鐵琴銅劍樓藏書目
Tingyun 停雲
Tingzhai shihua 艇齋詩話
tong 同
tong cai 通才
Tong Han langzhong xianting nanwang qiujing 同韓郎中閑庭南望秋景
Tongcheng 桐城
Tongwen shanfang 同文山房
tui 推
tui 頹
Tuo ti tong shan e 托體同山阿

Wan Fo ying ming 萬佛影銘
Wan ge 挽歌
Wan Tinglan 萬廷蘭
wang 望
Wang Anshi 王安石 (Wang Jinggong 王荊公)
Wang Bi 王弼
Wang Bo 王勃
Wang Chong 王充
Wang Dao 王導
Wang Fuzhi 王夫之
Wang Guoying 王國瓔
Wang Hong 王弘

Wang Hongzhi 王弘之
Wang Houzhi 王厚之 (Zhongliang 仲良)
Wang Hui 王薈
Wang Huzhi 王胡之 (Wang Xiuling 王修齡)
Wang Ji 王績
Wang Kangju 王康琚
Wang Kui 王逵
Wang Mang 王莽
Wang Qishu 汪啟淑
Wang Shen 王詵 (Wang Jinqing 王晉卿)
Wang Siren 王思任
Wang Tanzhi 王坦之
Wang Wei 王維
Wang Wei 王褘
Wang Xizhi 王羲之
Wang Yao 王瑤
Wang Yi 王逸
Wang Yun 王蘊
Wang Zhenbai 王貞白
Wang Zhu 王洙 (Wang Yuanshu 王原叔)
wangba 網吧
wei da 為達
Wei Gu Yanxian zeng fu 為顧彥先贈婦
wei ji jiao bing 違己交病
wei ren 為人
Wei she 委蛇
Wei Yingwu 韋應物 (Wei Suzhou 韋蘇州)
Weichuan tianjia 渭川田家
wen 文
Wen Qiao 溫嶠
Wen Runeng 溫汝能
Wen Runeng ben 溫汝能本
Wen xuan 文選
Wen xuan yuezhu 文選瀹注
wen yi jin er yi you yu 文已盡而意有餘
wu 物
Wu Jun 吳均
Wu Qi 吳淇
Wu Qian 吳騫 (Wu Kuili 吳葵里)
Wu Renjie 吳仁傑
Wu Song 吳菘
Wu xiao zhuan 五孝傳
Wu Xiu 吳脩 (Wu Zixiu 吳子脩)
wu yi 無役
Wu Zeng 吳曾
Wu Zhantai 吳瞻泰
Wu Zhantai ben 吳瞻泰本
Wu Zhuo 吳焯
Wu Zixu 伍子胥
Wuliu xiansheng zhuan 五柳先生傳
Wushen sui liuyue zhong yu huo 戊申歲六月中遇火
Wuyue yi ri zuo he Dai zhubu 五月一日作和戴主簿

Xi gou 溪狗
Xi Kang 嵇康
Xiwangmu 西王母
Xi Zusan zhi liusu 喜祖三至留宿
Xia huang gong 夏黃公
xian 顯
Xianfeng 咸豐
Xiang Xiu 向秀
Xiangfeng xialu jian 相逢狹路間
Xiangliu 相柳 (or Xianggun 相繇)
Xiangyang 襄陽
xing yao or Xingyao 形夭

Xiankang 咸康
Xianqing fu 閑情賦
Xiao Ben 蕭賁
Xiao Daocheng 蕭道成
Xiao Tao Qian ti shi shiliu shou 效陶潛體詩十六首
Xiao Tong 蕭統
Xiao Tong ben 蕭統本
Xiao Zuishi 小醉石
Xie An 謝安
Xie Bingde 謝枋得
Xie Fu 謝敷
Xie Jingyi 謝景夷
Xie Lingyun 謝靈運 (Xie Kangle 謝康樂)
Xie Shang 謝尚 (Xie Renzu 謝仁祖)
Xihe 羲和
Xijing zaji 西京雜記
Ximen xing 西門行
xin 心
Xin Xiao 辛蕭
xing 興
xing 行
xing 性
Xing ying shen 形影神
Xing Yong 邢顒
Xingzi Xian 星子縣
Xining 熙寧
xinji 心跡
xiong ci 胸次
Xishan jing 西山經
Xitang yongri xulun 夕堂永日緒論
xiuzhen ben 袖珍本
Xizeng Zheng Liyang 戲贈鄭溧陽
Xu Jiaocen 徐椒岑
Xu Jin yangqiu 續晉陽秋
xu shi sheng bai 虛室生白
Xu Xun 許詢
Xu Yinfang 許印芳
Xu You 許由
xuan yan 玄言
Xuanhui 宣徽
xuanmo 玄默
xuanxue 玄學
xuanyan 玄言
xuanyan shiren 玄言詩人
xun 尋
xungu xue 訓詁學
Xunyang 尋陽 (or 潯陽)
Xunyang ji 潯陽記

yan 言
Yan Hui 顏回
Yan jin yi lun 言盡意論
Yan Na 嚴訥 (Yan Wenjing gong 嚴文靖公)
Yan Yanzhi 顏延之
Yan Zhan 嚴栴 (Yan Dexin 嚴德馨, Yue'an 約菴)
Yan Zhenqing 顏真卿
Yang Gu 暘谷
Yang Hu 羊祜
Yang Jing 楊倞
Yang Shi 楊時
Yang Shoujing 楊守敬
Yang Songling 羊松齡
Yang Xiong 揚雄
Yang Xiuzhi 陽休之 (Yang Zilie 陽子烈)
Yang Xiuzhi ben 陽休之本
Yang Yun 楊惲
Yangsheng lun 養生論
Yanwei 延維
Yao 堯

ye 業
Ye Mengde 葉夢得
yi 意
Yi ju 移居
yi yi qi da 驛驛其達
yi zeng fu xu qi 遺贈副虛期
yihui 意會
Yike 意可
yimin 逸民
Yimin zhuan 逸民傳
yin 隱
Yin Zhongkan 殷仲堪
Yin Zhongwen 殷仲文
ying li 營利
ying Song chao 影宋抄
ying tian 營田
Yinjiu 飲酒
yinshi 隱士
Yisi sui sanyue wei Jianwei canjun shi du jing Qianxi 乙巳歲三月為建威參軍使都經錢溪
yixing 一形
yong 用
Yong er Shu 詠二疏
Yong pinshi 詠貧士
Yong Tao Yuanming 詠陶淵明
yongshi 詠史
you dao 有道
You hui er zuo 有會而作
You Longmen Fengxian Si 游龍門奉先寺
You Lushan ji 游廬山記
You Mao 尤袤
you shi 有事
You Shimen shi bing xu 游石門詩并序
you Song Sanqu Wu Liang Chanlin Xu [illegible] Yuanyou san nian yin yu Yuanming zuishi 有宋三衢吳亮禪林徐 [illegible] 元祐三年飲于淵明醉石
You Tiantai shan fu 遊天台山賦
You Xiechuan 游斜川
youlizhe 有力者
youwu 尤物
youxian 游仙
youxian shi 游仙詩
Yu 禹
Yu Liang 庾亮
yu nian 餘年
yu rong 餘荣
Yu Xin 庾信 (Yu Yicheng 庾義城)
Yu zi Yan deng shu 與子儼等疏
yuan 願
Yuan An 袁安
Yuan Can 袁粲
Yuan shi Chu diao shi Pang zhubu Deng zhizhong 怨詩楚調示龐主簿鄧治中
Yuan Shu 袁淑
Yuanji Shuzhuang 沅記書莊
Yuan Xingpei 袁行霈
Yuanjia yuan nian jiuyue yiri shu 元嘉元年九月一日書
Yuanling 沅陵
Yuanming biezhuan 淵明別傳
Yuanxian 元憲
yuanyou 遠遊
Yue Shi 樂史
Yujing shan 玉京山
yun 韻
yunshi 韻事
Yunyu yangqiu 韻語陽秋
Yutang ben 玉堂本

Za shi 雜詩
Zai shan 載芟
Zaofu 造父
Zati shi sanshi shou 雜體詩三十首
Zeng Changsha gong 贈長沙公
Zeng congxiong juji 贈從兄車騎
Zeng Guofan 曾國藩
Zeng Hong 曾紘
Zeng Ji 曾集
Zeng Ji ben 曾集本
Zeng Jili 曾季貍
Zeng Shangshulang Gu Yanxian ershou 贈尚書郎顧彥先二首
Zeng Wang taichang Sengda 贈王太常僧達
Zeng Yang zhangshi 贈羊長史
Zhan 湛
Zhang Gu 張固
Zhang Hua 張華
Zhang Jun 張駿
Zhang Quan 張詮
Zhang Rong 張融
Zhang Tianshi 張天師
Zhang Xie 張協
Zhang Yanchang 張燕昌 (Zhang Qitang 張芑堂)
Zhang Ye 張野
Zhang Yinjia 張蔭嘉
Zhang Zhan 張湛
Zhang Zhongwei 張仲蔚
Zhang Zilie 張自烈
zhangju zhi xue 章句之學
Zhao Lingzhi 趙令畤 (Zhao Delin 趙德麟)
Zhaoming taizi 昭明太子
Zhaoming taizi ben 昭明太子本
Zhaowen Qu shi 昭文瞿氏
Zhaoyin shi 招隱詩
zhen 真
Zhen yin zhuan 真隱傳
zhenben 真本
Zheng li er wei wei zhi shi 正利而為謂之事
Zheng Xuan 鄭玄
Zhengde Nankang fuzhi 正德南康府誌
zhenren 真人
zhi 植
Zhi Daolin 支道林
zhi ren lun shi 知人論世
zhi yu dao 志於道
zhiren 至人
Zhizheng 至正
Zhong Hui 鍾會
Zhong Rong 鍾嶸
Zhong Xing 鍾惺
Zhong Ziqi 鍾子期
Zhongguo shanben guji shumu 中國善本古籍書目
Zhonghe 中和
Zhonghu 仲虎
Zhongshan jing 中山經
zhongshen wucheng 終身无成
Zhongxia gui Nanyuan ji jingyi jiuyou 仲夏歸南園寄京邑舊遊
Zhou Bida 周必大
Zhou Chun 周春
Zhou Dunyi 周敦頤 (Lianxi 濂溪)
Zhou Fang 周訪
Zhou Mi 周密
Zhou Wenkun 周文焜
Zhou Xingxian 周行先
Zhou Xuzhi 周續之
Zhouyi lueli 周易略例

Zhu Bian 朱弁
Zhu Faji 竺法濟
Zhu Yu 朱彧
Zhuang Jie 壯節
Zhuang Jie Ting ji 壯節亭記
Zhuang Zhou 莊周
Zhuanxu 顓頊
Zhuben xulu 諸本序錄
zhui 追
Zhui he Dongpo "Huzhong Jiuhua" 追和東坡壺中九華
Zhulin qixian lun 竹林七賢論
Zhuren gongyou Zhou jia mubai xia 諸人共游周家墓柏下
Zi ji wen 自祭文
zi wei shi Xi huang shang ren 自謂是羲皇上人
Zigong 子貢
ziran 自然
Zong Bing 宗炳
Zou Shi 鄒奭
Zou Yan 鄒衍
Zu Qi 祖企
zuben 祖本
Zuishi 醉石
Zuishi ge 醉時歌
Zuishi guan 醉石觀
zuo 做
zuo da 作達
zuo ren 做人
zuozhe 作者
zuyi wei jiu 足以為酒

Editions of Tao Yuanming's Collection

An Annotated List of Important Premodern Editions of Tao's Collection

Pre-Tang

There were at least five different manuscript copies of Tao Yuanming's collection before the Tang, none of which is still extant. Yang Xiuzhi (courtesy name Zilie) records a copy of eight *juan* with no preface and a copy of six *juan* including a preface by an unknown author and a table of contents. He describes them as "disorganized in terms of ordering, and not complete" (see Yuan Xingpei, *Tao Yuanming ji jianzhu*, 614).

There was a copy of eight *juan* compiled by Xiao Tong, and this copy is referred to as Xiao Tong's edition (Xiao Tong ben) or the Crown Prince Zhaoming's edition (Zhaoming Taizi ben). From this edition only Xiao Tong's preface, his Tao Yuanming biography, and Yan Yanzhi's elegy have survived. Yang Xiuzhi's comment on this copy is, "Although this edition lacks *The Biographies of Five Filial Pieties* [Wu xiao zhuan] and A *Category of Fours and Eights* [Si ba mu], its compilation follows an appropriate format and the works are put in good order." *Si ba mu* is also designated as *A Record of Sages, Worthies, and Their Various Assistants* (Shengxian qunfu lu). These two works are considered spurious by most modern scholars. We cannot be certain that Tao Yuanming must have written those two works, and yet there is not enough proof against it.

A copy of Tao Yuanming's collection was compiled by Yang Xiuzhi, consisting of ten *juan*, which is referred to as Yang Xiuzhi's edition (Yang Xiuzhi ben), whose foreword survives.

There was another copy in nine *juan*, as recorded by the bibliography section of *The Sui History* (Sui shu). *The Sui History* also notes that during the Liang there was a copy of six *juan*, with one *juan* being a table of contents. It might be the same one as described in Yang Xiuzhi's account.

Tang

During the Tang, there must have been numerous copies of Tao Yuanming's collection in circulation. *The Old Tang History* (Jiu Tang shu) and *The New Tang History* (Xin Tang shu) record two versions: one in five *juan* and one in twenty *juan*. Neither is extant.

Song

Two Northern Song editions deserve mentioning, although neither of them is extant. The first is Song Xiang's edition (Song Xiang ben), often simply referred to as "the Song edition" (Song ben). It is presumably a printed edition, which would have made it the earliest-known printed edition of Tao Yuanming's collection, but we cannot be certain about it. The only thing left from this edition is Song Xiang's colophon (referred to as his "private note"). Song Xiang's edition, although lost, is often used as a reference in other editions for marking down textual variants, in the form of "also as X in the Song edition" (Song ben zuo mou). It is a shadowy presence, and yet a powerful one, as many textual variants are preserved this way.

The second Northern Song edition is called Si Yue's edition (Si Yue ben), with a colophon dated 1066 (the year of Song Xiang's death). We know practically nothing about Si Yue, except that he was a monk at a temple of Tiger Hill in Suzhou (see the twelfth-century author Zeng Jili's *Tingzhai shihua* in *Song shihua quanbian,* 3.2632). This edition is interesting because of its two surviving sections: Si Yue's colophon, and a piece of commentary contending Shen Yue's statement about Tao Yuanming's loyalty to the Eastern Jin (see chapter two). He writes in the colophon, "Crown Prince Zhaoming's compilation [of Tao Yuanming's works] is quite old; moreover, in the process of transmission it has accumulated many mistakes as well as many omissions. Although later people tried to integrate and put things together, there has never been a complete and correct version. I have collected different versions and collated them." He praises Song Xiang's edition: "When it comes to filling in missing characters and resolving doubtful points, it has proved most helpful" (see Yuan Xingpei, *Tao Yuanming ji jianzhu*, 616).

The subsequent editions are all extant, either in the original, or as reprints, and are the most important editions in identifying early textual variants.

The printed edition in Su Shi's handwriting (Su xie keben or Su xie ben)

This edition and the much later Li Gonghuan edition are the only two editions that include an anonymous colophon dated the tenth year of the Shaoxing reign of the first emperor of the Southern Song (1140). Because of this, it has been suggested that this edition may be one and the same as the so-called Shaoxing edition (Shaoxing ben), which acquires its name from the colophon and is considered lost by some scholars (see Guo Shaoyu's *Tao ji kaobian*, 710–11). An original copy of this edition, if we may believe Mao Yi's words, had been in the collection of his maternal grandfather and then went to Qian Qianyi; it was eventually destroyed in the fire of Crimson Cloud Tower of 1649. Mao Yi seems to believe that it was written out by Su Shi himself (see chapter one). Mao Yi's copy, produced by his teacher Qian Meixian, was recopied and reprinted a number of times in the Qing.

In writing this book, I have consulted three reprints of the Su Shi edition, two from the Qing and one from the early Republic era. The first is the Duqing Tang edition (Duqing Tang ben) printed in 1864, currently in the collection of the Harvard-Yenching Library. This edition still avoids some of the Song taboo characters (the names of Song emperors and their ancestors), and is stamped with many seals, quite a few of which are the Mao family's. The second is Hu Boji's edition (Hu Boji ben), printed in 1879. It was written out in Hu Boji's hand, and has a colophon by Chen Li (1810–1882). Hu Boji was a native of Hu'nan, but the edition was printed in Guangdong, as testified by a note at the end of the last *juan* saying, "Collated by Fuxiang, a descendent of Pengze." Tao Fuxiang was a well-known nineteenth-century collator from Guangdong, whose studio name was Ailu. The third reprint was *Tao ji fawei*, printed by Yuanji Shuzhuang of Shanghai in 1918, and edited and with a preface by Gu Hao, written in the summer of 1917. This edition is based on the Su Shi edition, but clearly aspires to be a much more comprehensive collection in that it includes prefaces, colophons, commentaries, annotations, a list of editions beginning with the Li Gonghuan edition, and Tao Yuanming's chronology, as well as textual variants, from a variety of sources.

Zeng Ji's edition (Zeng Ji ben), or the 1192 edition

About Zeng Ji, much has been said in chapter six. Now we turn our attention to the edition he compiled, which proves most invaluable in the textual studies of Tao Yuanming. It does have the division of *juan*, but is divided into two parts: poetry and miscellaneous prose. The most important feature of this edition, and most useful for our purpose, is that it preserves by far the largest number of textual variants of Tao Yuanming's poetry. In all 126 poems (the poem "Peach Blossom Spring" being grouped with the prose record in the prose section), there are 591 places marked with variants, sometimes giving more than one variant character in one place. None of these variants appear in the Su Shi or Tang Han edition (see below). One interesting note is that the text proper in the Su Shi edition often gets recorded in Zeng Ji's edition as textual variant, which seems to suggest that Zeng Ji had consulted something like the Su Shi edition in compiling his edition, but did not use it as a base text.

This edition also has some extra materials, such as Huang Tingjian's remark on the poem "An Account of Ale," and Zeng Hong's comment on the line "Xingtian wu ganqi" (see chapter four). None of these appears in the Su Shi edition. Zeng Ji's edition may be seen as a precursor to the later critical editions with collected commentaries.

Zeng Ji's edition has several reprints. The one I consulted is an 1875 reprint in the collection of the Harvard-Yenching Library. It has a colophon by "Master Qu of Zhaowen" (Zhaowen Qu shi), which shows that this collection was once in the collection of the Qu family from Zhaowen (in Jiangsu Province). The Qu family was famous for their large book collection, started by Qu Shaoji (1772–1836) and continued by his son Qu Yong (1794–1836) and two more generations of descendents. The colophon was written by Qu Yong and included in his "Catalogue of the Book Collection of the Tower of Iron Lute and Bronze Sword" (Tieqin tongjian lou cangshumu). It compares Zeng Ji's edition with the "Jigu ge edition" (see below), claiming that even though they are not of one edition, they are both "completely different from the other common editions" in terms of their large number of textual variants.

The "Jigu ge edition" (Jigu ge ben)

Although this edition is dubbed the "Jigu ge edition," it probably dates from the Southern Song. It is now in the collection of the Chinese National Library (formerly the Beijing Library). According to Hashikawa Tokio, there are three late Qing reprints of this edition. One of them is in the collection of the Harvard-Yenching Library, which I consulted in writing this book.

This edition is one of those so-called pocket-treasure editions (*xiuzhen ben*) because of its miniature size. It is an 1876 reprint by Xu Jiaocen of Tongcheng (in Anhui Province) of the 1861 edition printed by Li Wenhan of Jingde (also in Anhui). It is also called Mo Youzhi's edition (Mo Youzhi ben) because it contains a colophon by Mo Youzhi (1811–1871). The most notable feature of this edition is that it contains a large number of variants. Of the 126 poems by Tao Yuanming, there are approximately 585 places marked with variants, six fewer than in Zeng Ji's edition. But this 1876 reprint is a complete collection of Tao Yuanming's works, while Zeng Ji's edition omits *The Biographies of Five Filial Pieties, A Category of Fours and Eights*, and the rhymed appraisals.

This reprint, like Zeng Ji's edition, avoids the Song taboo characters by omitting a stroke of the characters used in the names of Song emperors and their ancestors or the homophones of such characters, which helps scholars determine the date of an edition's first printing. If this 1876 reprint had indeed faithfully kept the appearance of its base edition (*zuben* 祖本), then the base edition might be dated to Song Gaozong's reign (1127–1163).

Tang Han's edition (Tang Han ben)

This edition has been handsomely reprinted in 1987 by Zhonghua Shuju of Beijing as *Annotated Poetry of Master Tao Jingjie* (Tao Jingjie xiansheng shizhu) (*Guyi congshu*, 3.32).

According to his biography in *Song shi*, Tang Han (courtesy name Boji; 1202–1272) was a well-known scholar who served in a series of official posts both at court and in the provinces (438.12975–79). Presumably printed in Jianning (in modern-day Fujian Province) around the mid-thirteenth century and entitled *Tao Jingjie xiansheng shizhu*, Tang Han's edition consists entirely of Tao Yuanming's poetry, except for the prose record of Peach Blossom Spring and "Return." It opens with Tang Han's preface dated 1241. Based on the names of the woodblock cutters (who were of Jianning) and Tang Han's chronology, Chen Xingzhen argues that Tang Han's edition, despite the 1241 preface, must have been printed much later, probably around the 1260s. However, another possibility is that after the first print run in 1241 or soon after, the edition was recut in the 1260s, as it is quite unusual that the actual printing date should come more than twenty years after the writing of the preface (see Chen Xingzhen's preface to the 1987 reprint).

Tang Han's edition is characterized by two things. First, of all the Southern Song editions listed here, it has the least number of variants. In most cases, it seems to have adopted the text proper in Zeng Ji's edition rather than the Su Shi edition, for whenever those two editions are at variance, Tang Han's edition follows Zeng Ji's version. Second, Tang Han's edition is notable for its inclusion of the editor's commentary, which primarily focuses on explicating the poet's intent, with a small number of philological notes. These notes are frequently inserted in a smaller font into the poems. Tang Han's main purpose is to stress Tao Yuanming's loyalty to the Jin dynasty and his refusal to serve the new Liu Song regime, and everything is read as political allegory. Tang Han's commentary represents the Southern Song emphasis on Tao Yuanming's morality and loyalism, which would exert a strong influence on later interpretations.

Song-Yuan

Li Gonghuan's edition (Li Gonghuan ben)

Nothing is known about Li Gonghuan, except that he was from Luling (in modern-day Jiangxi Province). He Mengchun claims he lived during the Yuan dynasty (1279–1367), though we do not know what this claim was based on (see Tao Shu's *Jingjie xiansheng ji, Zhuben xulu* 12).The Yuan being a rather short-lived dynasty, Li Gonghuan might have easily lived from the late Southern Song into the Yuan.

It is uncertain when the first Li Gonghuan edition was printed, and whether Li Gonghuan had a hand in the compilation of the whole book. Wu Zhuo (1676–1733), the Qing book collector who had a copy of Li Gonghuan's edition in his collection, wrote in his colophon dated 1714, "This collection had gathered together the commentaries by various gentlemen of the Song, and was printed by the government during the Chunyou reign [1241–1253]. It was called the Jade Hall edition [Yutang ben] at the time [Jade Hall referring to the Hanlin Academy or the elite literati in general]. But this current edition does not avoid the names of Song emperors as did the earlier Song printed edition, so it might be a Yuan reprint [of the original Song edition]" (cited in Hashikawa Tokio's study of the filiation of the editions of Tao Yuanming's collection, *Tô Shû hanpon genryû kô,* 22b). Guo Shaoyu speculates that the edition itself might have originated in the Southern Song and that Li Gonghuan simply reprinted the edition in the Yuan and added collected commentaries (*Tao ji kaobian,* 721–22).

Li Gonghuan's edition is entitled *An Annotated Collection of Tao Yuanming*

(Jianzhu Tao Yuanming ji). I have seen two facsimile copies of Li Gonghuan's edition. One is a Hanfen Lou *SBCK* edition reprinted by Shanghai's Shangwu Yinshuguan in the 1920s. It is described as a facsimile reprint of a Song edition. The other is a copy currently in the collection of the Zhejiang Library and described as a Yuan edition, reprinted by Shanghai Guji Chubanshe in *Xuxiu siku quanshu*, vol. 1304. The two editions are slightly different in their arrangement of materials.

Li Gonghuan's edition is almost completely devoid of textual variants. It is, however, the first edition we have with collected commentaries on Tao Yuanming and his writings. Although one can already see the beginning of such a tendency in Zeng Ji's edition, Li Gonghuan's edition goes much further. It also places commentaries on individual poems after each poem. These practices paved the way for later editions of Tao Yuanming's collection with "collected commentaries." Perhaps for this reason, Li Gonghuan's edition had been widely circulated and was used as a base edition for various reprints in the Ming.

Ming and Qing

The following list of Ming and Qing editions is by no means exhaustive. These editions are primarily useful for their commentaries. The number and substance of the textual variants contained therein usually do not exceed those of the Song editions. Many other Ming and Qing editions with critical notes, such as He Mengchun's *The Collection of Tao Jingjie* (Tao Jingjie ji), Zhang Zilie's (1597–1673) *A Critical Edition of Tao Yuanming's Collection* (Piping Tao Yuanming ji), and Huang Wenhuan's *An Analysis of the Meaning of Tao's Poetry* (Tao shi xi yi), are incorporated in *Tao Yuanming shiwen huiping* and *Tao Yuanming yanjiu ziliao huibian*, and so will not be listed here.

Chen Longzheng edition, Elaboration on Tao's Poems (Tao shi yan)

This edition was compiled by Chen Longzheng (1585–1645) in 1635, and printed in 1643. It is divided into two parts, the first consisting of a selection of Tao Yuanming's poems and prose pieces, with short critical notes, and the second of poems by poets from the Tang to the Ming who were considered to be writing in Tao Yuanming's tradition. The edition has a colophon written by Chen Longzheng's son, Chen Kui, in 1643. In the colophon, Chen Kui relates that his father suffered from "the greatest sorrow" when he was staying in the capital (given the date of the printing, this must have referred to the suicide of the last Ming emperor), and sent back this old compilation for Chen Kui to print.

This edition is currently in the collection of the Tianjin Library, and has been reprinted in *Tianjin tushuguan guben miji congshu* (vol. 16) in 1999.

Jiang Xun's critical edition (Jiang Xun ping ben)

This edition is entitled *Tao Yuanming's Poetry Collection* (Tao Yuanming shiji), and was reprinted several times in the Qing. The edition I consulted was reprinted by Tongwen shanfang during the Xianfeng reign (1821–1861). It opens with Jiang Xun's (courtesy name Danyai) preface dated 1672 and his nephew Zhou Wenkun's preface dated 1690. This edition includes comments on individual poems after each poem; Jiang Xun's own comments usually appear in the top margin of a page and occasionally between the lines, or listed at the end of a poem.

The publisher also inserted into the reprint Hu Fengdan's (1823–1890) *Remarks on Tao Jingjie's Poetry* (Tao Jingjie shihua) and *A Study of Textual Variants for Tao Jingjie's Poetry Collection* (Tao Jingjie shiji kaoyi).

Wu Zhantai's edition (Wu Zhantai ben)

Wu Zhantai (1657–1735) was a scholar and poetry critic. His edition is entitled *Collected Annotations of Tao Yuanming's Poetry* (Tao shi hui zhu), first printed in 1705. The edition I consulted is an 1896 reprint by Xu Yinfang (1832–1901).

Wen Runeng's edition (Wen Runeng ben)

Wen Runeng's edition consists of two volumes: *Collected Commentaries on Tao Yuanming's Poetry* (Tao shi hui ping) and *An Annotated Edition of Su Shi's Poems Matching Rhymes with Tao Yuanming's Poetry with Collected Commentaries* (He Tao he jian), each with a preface written by Wen Runeng in 1806. It was printed in Guangdong.

Tao Shu's edition (Tao Shu ben)

This edition is named *The Collection of Master Jingjie* (Jingjie xiansheng ji). It was compiled by Tao Shu and first printed in 1840, the year after his death, by his nephew in Nanjing. Tao Shu's edition has been reprinted many times since. The ones I have consulted are an 1883 reprint by Jiangsu Shuju and a 1973 reprint by Zhonghua Shuju of Hong Kong.

This edition includes a collection of general commentaries on Tao Yuanming and his writings. "A Study of Master Jingjie's Chronology" (Jingjie xiansheng nianpu kaoyi) is attached at the end. Tao Shu's edition clearly aspires to be comprehensive, and it is indeed so in terms of commentaries. He always notes down the source of a comment, which is a great improvement over Li Gonghuan's edition.

A SELECTED LIST OF MODERN EDITIONS OF TAO YUANMING'S COLLECTION

Ding Fubao 丁福保. *Tao Yuanming shi jianzhu* 陶淵明詩箋注. Reprint, Taibei: Yiwen Yinshuguan, 1964.

Fang Zushen 方祖燊. *Tao Qian shi jianzhu jiaozheng lunping* 陶潛詩箋注校證論評. Reprint, Taiwan: Lantai Shuju, 1977.

Gong Bin 龔斌. *Tao Yuanming ji jiaojian* 陶淵明集校箋. Shanghai: Shanghai Guji Chubanshe, 1996.

Gu Zhi 古直. *Tao Jingjie shi jian* 陶靖節詩箋. In *Cengbing Tang wuzhong* 層冰堂五種. Reprint, Taibei: Guoli Bianyiguan, 1984.

Guo Weisen 郭維森 and Bao Jingcheng 包景誠. *Tao Yuanming ji quanyi* 陶淵明集全譯. Guiyang: Guizhou Renmin Chubanshe, 1992.

Li Hua 李華. *Tao Yuanming shiwen shangxi ji* 陶淵明詩文賞析集. Sichuan: Bashu Shushe, 1988.

Lu Qinli 逯欽立. *Tao Yuanming ji* 陶淵明集. Beijing: Zhonghua Shuju, 1979.

Meng Erdong 孟二冬. *Tao Yuanming ji yizhu* 陶淵明集譯注. Changchun: Jilin Wenshi Chubanshe, 1996.

Sun Junxi 孫鈞錫. *Tao Yuanming ji jiaozhu* 陶淵明集校注. He'nan: Zhongzhou Guji, 1986.

Tang Manxian 唐滿先. *Tao Yuanming ji qianzhu* 陶淵明集淺注. Nanchang: Baihuazhou Wenyi Chubanshe, 1985.

Wang Mengbai 王孟白. *Tao Yuanming shiwen jiaojian* 陶淵明詩文校箋. Ha'erbin: Heilongjiang Renmin Chubanshe, 1985.

Wang Shaoying 汪紹楹, ed. *Soushen houji* 搜神後記. Beijing: Zhonghua Shuju, 1981.

Wang Shumin 王叔岷. *Tao Yuanming shi jian zheng gao* 陶淵明詩箋證稿. Taibei: Yiwen Yinshuguan, 1975.

Wang Yao 王瑤. *Tao Yuanming ji* 陶淵明集. Beijing: Zuojia Chubanshe, 1956.

Yang Yong 楊勇. *Tao Yuanming ji jiaojian* 陶淵明集校箋. Hong Kong: Wuxingji Shuju, 1971.

Yuan Xingpei 袁行霈. *Tao Yuanming ji jianzhu* 陶淵明集箋注. Beijing: Zhonghua Shuju, 2003.

A SELECTED LIST OF ENGLISH AND JAPANESE TRANSLATIONS WITH COMMENTARIES

Davis, A. R. *T'ao Yüan-ming, A.D. 365–427: His Works and Their Meaning.* 2 vols. Cambridge: Cambridge University Press, 1984.

Hightower, James Robert. *The Poetry of T'ao Ch'ien*. Oxford: Clarendon Press, 1970.

Shiba Rokurō 斯波六郎. *Tō Emmei shi chūyaku* 陶淵明詩注釋. Kyoto: Tōmon Shobō, 1951.

Suzuki Torao 鈴木虎雄. *Tō Emmei shi kai* 陶淵明詩解. Tokyo: Kōbundō, 1948.

Selected Bibliography

Ashmore, Robert. *The Transport of Reading: Text and Understanding in the World of Tao Qian*. Cambridge: Harvard University Asia Center Press, forthcoming.

Bai Juyi 白居易. *Bai Juyi ji jianjiao* 白居易集箋校. Edited by Zhu Jincheng 朱金城. Shanghai: Shanghai Guji Chubanshe, 1988.

Bei shi 北史. Compiled by Li Yanshou 李延壽. Beijing: Zhonghua shuju, 1974.

Berkowitz, Alan J. *Patterns of Disengagement: The Practice and Portrayal of Reclusion in Early Medieval China*. Stanford: Stanford University Press, 2000.

Bush, Susan, and Hsio-yen Shih, eds. *Early Chinese Texts on Painting*. Cambridge: Harvard University Press, 1985.

Cahill, Suzanne E. *Transcendence and Divine Passion: The Queen Mother of the West in Medieval China*. Stanford: Stanford University Press, 1993.

Cai Ying 蔡瀛. *Lushan xiaozhi* 廬山小志. Langhuan Bieguan 嫏嬛別館 edition, n.d.

Cerquiglini, Bernard. *In Praise of the Variant: A Critical History of Philology*. Baltimore: Johns Hopkins University Press, 1999.

Chang, Kang-i Sun. *Six Dynasties Poetry*. Princeton: Princeton University Press, 1986.

———. "The Unmasking of Tao Qian and the Indeterminacy of Interpretation." In *Chinese Aesthetics: The Orderings of Word, Image, and the World in the Six Dynasties*, edited by Zong-Qi Cai. Honolulu: University of Hawai'i Press, 2004.

Chao Buzhi 晁補之. *Jilei ji* 雞肋集. *SBCK* edition. Reprint, Taibei: Shangwu Yinshuguan, 1967.

Chen Shunyu 陳舜俞. *Lushan ji* 廬山記. Taibei: Guangwen Shuju, 1969.

Chen Xianxing 陳先行 et al., eds. *Zhongguo Guji gao chao jiao ben tulu* 中國古籍稿鈔校本圖錄. Shanghai: Shanghai Shudian Chubanshe, 2000.

Chen Yiliang 陳怡良. *Tao Yuanming zhi renpin yu shipin* 陶淵明之人品與詩品. Taibei: Wenjin Chubanshe, 1993.

Chen Yinke 陳寅恪. "*Wei shu* Sima Rui zhuan jiangdong minzu tiao shizheng ji tuilun" 魏書司馬睿傳江東民族條釋證及推論. In *Jinmingguan conggao chubian* 金明館叢稿初編, 69–106. Shanghai: Shanghai Guji Chubanshe, 1980.

———. *Liu Rushi biezhuan* 柳如是別傳.Reprint, Beijing: Sanlian Shudian, 2001.

Cheng Qianfan 程千帆. *Gushi kaosuo* 古詩考索. Shanghai: Shanghai Guji Chubanshe, 1984.

Cherniack, Susan. "Book Culture and Textual Transmission in Sung China." *Harvard Journal of Asiatic Studies* 54:1 (June 1994): 5–102.

Chia, Lucille. *Printing for Profit: The Commercial Publishers of Jianyang, Fujian (11th–17th Centuries)*. Cambridge: Harvard University Asia Center Press, 2003.

Chuci zhangju buzhu 楚辭章句補注. Taibei: Shijie Shuju, 1965.

Chunqiu Zuozhuan zhengyi 春秋左傳正義. Annotated by Du Yu 杜預, with a commentary by Kong Yingda 孔穎達. Reprint, Taibei: Yiwen Yinshuguan, 1955. See under *Shisanjing zhushu.*

Dagenais, John. *The Ethics of Reading in Manuscript Culture: Glossing the* Libro de buen amor. Princeton: Princeton University Press, 1994.

Davis, A. R. "The Double Ninth Festival in Chinese Poetry: A Study of Variations upon a Theme." In *Wen-lin: Studies in the Chinese Humanities*, edited by Chow Tse-tsung, 45–64. Madison: University of Wisconsin, 1968.

Deng Ansheng 鄧安生. "Tao Yuanming 'Huan jiu ju' shi jiqi shiji xintan" 陶淵明還舊居詩及其事跡新探. *Bohai Xuekan* 渤海學刊. April 1995: 42–47.

———."Tao Yuanming liju bianzheng" 陶淵明里居辨證. *Wenshi* 文史. 20 (September 1983): 173–83.

Deng Zhongbo 鄧鐘伯. "Tao Yuanming guli shuo" 陶淵明故里說. *Jiangxi Shiyuan Xuebao* 江西師院學報. February 1982: 59–62.

Dong Zhongshu 董仲舒. *Chunqiu fanlu* 春秋繁露. Taibei: Shijie Shuju, 1967.

Dongguan Han ji 東觀漢記. Compiled by Liu Zhen 劉珍 et al. *Siku quanshu* 四庫全書. Vol. 370. Taiwan: Shangwu Yinshuguan, 1983.

Du Fu 杜甫. *Du shi xiangzhu* 杜詩詳注. Annotated by Qiu Zhao'ao 仇兆鰲. Beijing: Zhonghua Shuju, 1979.

Egan, Ronald. *Word, Image, and Deed in Su Shi's Life*. Cambridge: Harvard University Press, 1994.

Fang Shao 方勺. *Bozhai bian* 泊宅編. Beijing: Zhonghua Shuju, 1991.

Feng Zhi 馮贄. *Yunxian sanlu* 雲仙散錄. Beijing: Zhonghua Shuju, 1998.

Foucault, Michel. *The Order of Things: An Archaeology of the Human Science.* New York: Vintage Books, 1973.

Gu Zhi 古直. *Tao Jingjie nianpu* 陶靖節年譜. In *Cengbing Tang wuzhong* 層冰堂五種. Taibei: Guoli Bianyiguan, 1984.

———. "Tao Kan ji Tao Yuanming shi Hanzu haishi Xizu ne" 陶侃及陶淵明是漢族還是溪族呢? *Guangming Ribao* 光明日報. July 14, 1957.

Guo Shaoyu 郭紹虞. "Tao ji kaobian" 陶集考辨. In *Tao Yuanming yanjiu* 陶淵明研究. Vol. 2, 695–757. Taibei: Jiusi Chubanshe, 1977.

Han Wei liuchao biji xiaoshuo daguan 漢魏六朝筆記小說大觀. Shanghai: Shanghai Guji Chubanshe, 1999.

Han Yu 韓愈. *Han Yu quanji jiaozhu* 韓愈全集校註. Chengdu: Sichuan Daxue Chubanshe, 1996.

Hanfeizi jijie 韓非子集解. Taibei: Shijie Shuju, 1969.

Hanshi waizhuan jianshu 韓詩外傳箋疏. Annotated by Qu Shouyuan 屈守元. Chengdu: Bashu Shushe, 1996.

Hashikawa Tokio 橋川時雄. *Tô Shû hanpon genryû kô* 陶集版本源流考. Beijing: Wenzitongmengshe, 1931.

Hawkes, David. *The Songs of the South: An Anthology of Ancient Chinese Poems by Qu Yuan and Other Poets*. London: Penguin Books, 1985.

Holzman, Donald. "A Dialogue with the Ancients: Tao Qian's Interrogation of Confucius." In *Culture and Power in the Reconstitution of the Chinese Realm, 200–600*, edited by Scott Pearce, Audrey Shapiro, and Patricia Ebrey. Cambridge: Harvard University Asia Center Press, 2001.

Hong Mai 洪邁. *Rongzhai suibi* 容齋隨筆. Shanghai: Shanghai Guji Chubanshe, 1978.

Hou Han shu 後漢書. Compiled by Fan Ye 范曄. Beijing: Zhonghua Shuju, 1965.

Hu Shi 胡適. *Lushan youji* 廬山遊記. Shanghai: Xinyue Shudian, 1928.

Huainan honglie jijie 淮南鴻烈集解. Beijing: Zhonghua Shuju, 1989.

Huang Tingjian 黃庭堅. *Huang Tingjian quanji* 黃庭堅全集. Chengdu: Sichuan Daxue Chubanshe, 2001.

Huang Zongxi 黃宗羲. *Kuang Lu you lu* 匡廬游錄. Taibei: Guangwen Shuju, 1968.

———. *Huang Zongxi shiwen xuan* 黃宗羲詩文選. Shanghai: Huadong Shifan Daxue Chubanshe, 1990.

Huangfu Mi 皇甫謐. *Gaoshi zhuan* 高士傳. *Sibu beiyao* edition. Shanghai: Zhonghua Shuju, 1934.

Hui Jiao 慧皎. *Gaoseng zhuan* 高僧傳. Annotated by Tang Yongtong. Beijing: Zhonghua Shuju, 1992.

Ibn Hazm. *The Ring of the Dove*. Translated by Anthony Arberry. London: Luzac Oriental, 1994.

Jin shu 晉書. Beijing: Zhonghua Shuju, 1974.

Jiu Tang shu 舊唐書. Beijing: Zhonghua Shuju, 1975.

Knechtges, David R. *Court Culture and Literature in Early China*. Ashgate Publishing Ltd., 2002.

Knechtges, David R., trans. *Wen xuan, or Selections of Refined Literature*. Vol. 1. Princeton: Princeton University Press, 1982.

———. *Wen xuan, or Selections of Refined Literature*. Vol. 2. Princeton: Princeton University Press, 1987.

———. *Wen xuan, or Selections of Refined Literature*. Vol. 3. Princeton: Princeton University Press, 1996.

Knoblock, John, trans. *Xunzi*. Stanford: Stanford University Press, 1994.

Kwong, Charles Yim-tze. *Tao Qian and the Chinese Poetic Tradition: The Quest for Cultural Identity*. Ann Arbor: University of Michigan Press, 1994.

Laozi jiaoshi 老子校釋. Annotated by Zhu Qianzhi 朱謙之. Beijing: Zhonghua Shuju, 1984.

Lau, D. C. trans. *Tao te ching*. London: Penguin Books, 1969.

Legge, James, trans. *The Chinese Classics*. Vol. 1. Reprint, Taibei: Jinxue Shuju, 1969.

Li Bai 李白. *Li Bai quanji jiaozhu huishi jiping* 李白全集校注彙釋集評. Tianjin: Baihua Wenyi Chubanshe, 1996.

Li Daoyuan 酈道元. *Shuijing zhu* 水經注. Taibei: Shijie Shuju, 1969.

Li E 厲鶚. *Song shi jishi* 宋詩紀事. Shanghai: Shanghai Guji, 1983.

Li ji zhushu 禮記注疏. Annotated by Zheng Xuan 鄭玄 with a commentary by Kong Yingda 孔穎達. Reprint, Taibei: Yiwen Yinshuguan, 1955. See under *Shisanjing zhushu*.

Li Jinquan 李錦全. *Tao Yuanming pingzhuan* 陶淵明評傳. Nanjing: Nanjing Daxue Chubanshe, 1998.

Li Qing 李清. *Sanyuan biji* 三垣筆記. Wuxing: Jiaye Tang 嘉業堂 edition, 1927.

Li Ruiliang 李瑞良. *Zhongguo gudai tushu liutong shi* 中國古代圖書流通史. Shanghai: Shanghai Renmin Chubanshe, 2000.

Lin Wenyue 林文月. "Koumen zhuo yanci: Shilun Tao Yuanming zhi xingxiang" 叩門拙言辭—試論陶淵明之形象. In *Zhonggu wenxue luncong* 中古文學論叢, 183–222. Taibei: Da'an Chubanshe, 1989.

Liu Dajie 劉大傑. *Wei Jin sixiang lun* 魏晉思想論. Shanghai: Shanghai Guji Chubanshe, 2000.

Liu Shengmu 劉聲木. *Changchu zhai suibi xubi sanbi sibi wubi* 萇楚齋隨筆續筆三筆四筆五筆. Beijing: Zhonghua Shuju, 1998.

Liu Xiang 劉向. *Lienü zhuan* 列女傳. Taiwan: Guangwen Shuju, 1979.

———. *Xin xu* 新序. Tianjin: Tianjin Guji Chubanshe, 1987.

Liu Xie 劉勰. *Wenxin diaolong yizheng* 文心雕龍義證. Annotated by Zhan Ying 詹鍈. Shanghai: Shanghai Guji Chubanshe, 1989.

Liu Yiqing 劉義慶. *Shishuo xinyu jianshu* 世說新語箋疏. Annotated by Yu Jiaxi 余嘉錫. Shanghai: Shanghai Guji Chubanshe, 1993.

Loewe, Michael. *Early Chinese Texts: A Bibliographical Guide*. Berkeley: University of California Press, 1993.

Lou Yue 樓玥. *Gongkui ji* 攻媿集. *SBBY* edition. Shanghai: Shangwu Yinshuguan, 1967.

Lu Qinli 逯欽立, ed. *Xian Qin Han Wei Jin Nanbeichao shi* 先秦漢魏晉南北朝詩. 3rd. ed. Beijing: Zhonghua Shuju, 1995.

Lu Xun 魯迅. *Luxun quanji* 魯迅全集. Beijing: Renmin Wenxue Chubanshe, 1957.

Lunyu zhushu 論語注疏. Annotated by He Yan 何晏, with a commentary by Xing Bing 邢昺. Reprint, Taibei: Yiwen Yinshuguan, 1955. See under *Shisanjing zhushu*.

Lushan xin daoyou 廬山新導遊. Jiangxi: Lushan Guanli Ju, 1935.

Lushan yu mingren 廬山與名人. Beijing: Lüyou Jiaoyu Chubanshe, 1997.

Mao Deqi 毛德琦. *Lushan zhi* 廬山志. Collated by Xu Xinjie 徐新傑. Jiangxi: Jiujiang Wenshi Weiyuanhui, 1991.

Maoshi zhengyi 毛詩正義. With commentaries by Mao Heng 毛亨, Zheng Xuan 鄭玄, and Kong Yingda 孔穎達. See under *Shisanjing zhushu*.

Marcus, Leah S. *Unediting the Renaissance: Shakespeare, Marlowe, Milton*. New York: Routledge, 1996.

Mather, Richard B. "The Bonze's Begging Bowl: Eating Practices in Buddhist Monasteries of Medieval India and China." *Journal of the American Oriental Society* 101:4 (October–December, 1981): 417–24.

———."The Mystical Ascent of the T'ien-t'ai Mountains: Sun Ch'o's *Yu T'ien-t'ai shan Fu*." *Monumenta Serica* 20 (1961): 226–45.

Mather, Richard B., trans. *A New Account of Tales of the World*. Minneapolis: University of Minnesota Press, 1976.

McGann, Jerome J. *A Critique of Modern Textual Criticism*. Reprint, with a foreword by D. C. Greetham; Charlottesville: University Press of Virginia, 1999. Originally published in 1983 by University of Chicago Press.

Meng Haoran 孟浩然. *Meng Haoran ji jiaozhu* 孟浩然集校注. Annotated by Xu Peng 徐鵬. Beijing: Renmin Wenxue Chubanshe, 1989.

Mengzi zhushu 孟子注疏. Annotated by Zhao Qi 趙岐 with a commentary by Sun Shi 孫奭. Taibei: Yiwen Yinshuguan, 1955 reprint. See under *Shisanjing zhushu*.

Nan Qi shu 南齊書. Compiled by Xiao Zixian 蕭子顯. Beijing: Zhonghua Shuju, 1972.

Nan shi 南史. Compiled by Li Yanshou 李延壽. Beijing: Zhonghua Shuju, 1975.

Needham, Joseph. *Science and Civilization in China*. Cambridge: Cambridge University Press, 1984.

Ouyang Xiu 歐陽修. *Ouyang Xiu quanji* 歐陽修全集. Taibei: Shijie Shuju, 1963.

Owen, Stephen, *The End of the Chinese "Middle Ages": Essays in Mid-Tang Literary Culture.* Stanford: Stanford University Press, 1996.

———. *The Making of Early Chinese Classical Poetry*. Cambridge: Harvard University Asia Center Press, forthcoming.

———. *Readings in Chinese Literary Thought*. Cambridge: Harvard Asia Center Press, 1992.

———. *Remembrances: The Experiences of the Past in Classical Chinese Literature*. Cambridge: Harvard University Press, 1986.

———. "The Self's Perfect Mirror: Poetry as Autobiography." In *The Vitality of the Lyric Voice: Shih Poetry from the Late Han to the T'ang.* Edited by Shuen-fu Lin and Stephen Owen, 71–102. Princeton: Princeton University Press, 1986.

———. *Traditional Chinese Poetry and Poetics: Omen of the World*. Madison: University of Wisconsin Press, 1985.

Owen, Stephen, ed. and trans. *An Anthology of Chinese Literature: Beginnings to 1911*. New York: W. W. Norton, 1996.

Puett, Michael James. *The Ambivalence of Creation: Debates Concerning Innovation and Artifice in Early China*. Stanford: Stanford University Press, 2001.

Qi Yishou 齊益壽. "Lun shizhuan zhong de Tao Yuanming shiji yu xingxiang" 論史傳中的陶淵明事跡與形象. In *Zheng Yinbai xiansheng bashi shouqing lunwenji* 鄭因百先生八十壽慶論文集, 109–59. Taipei: Taiwan Shangwu Yinshuguan, 1985.

Qian Qianyi 錢謙益. *Muzhai chuxue ji* 牧齋初學集. Shanghai: Shanghai Guji Chubanshe, 1985.

Qian Zeng 錢曾. *Dushu minqiu ji* 讀書敏求記. Facsimile reprint of 1728

Yangu Tang 延古堂 edition in *Xuxiu siku quanshu* 續修四庫全書. Vol. 923. Shanghai: Shanghai Guji Chubanshe, 1995–1999.

Qian Zhongshu 錢鍾書. *Guan zhui bian* 管錐編. Hong Kong: Zhonghua Shuju, 1980.

Quan Song shi 全宋詩. Beijing: Beijing Daxue Chubanshe, 1995.

Quan Tang shi 全唐詩. Beijing: Zhonghua Shuju, 1960.

Quan Tang shi bubian 全唐詩補編. Edited by Chen Shangjun 陳尚君. Beijing: Zhonghua Shuju, 1992.

Quan Tang wudai xiaoshuo 全唐五代小說. Edited by Li Shiren 李時人. Xi'an: Shanxi Renmin Chubanshe, 1998.

Said, Edward W. *Humanism and Democratic Criticism*. New York: Columbia University Press, 2004.

Sang Qiao 桑喬. *Lushan jishi* 廬山紀事. Reprinted in *Yuzhang congshu* 豫章叢書, 54–59. Nanchang: Tuilu, 1916.

Sanguo zhi 三國志. Compiled by Chen Shou 陳壽 and annotated by Pei Songzhi 裴松之. Beijing: Zhonghua Shuju, 1973.

Shanhai jing jiaozhu 山海經校注. Edited by Yuan Ke 袁珂. Shanghai: Shanghai Guji Chubanshe, 1980.

Shen Gua 沈括. *Xin jiaozheng Mengxi bitan* 新校正夢溪筆談. Annotated by Hu Daojing 胡道靜. Hong Kong: Zhonghua Shuju, 1978.

Shi ji 史記. Compiled by Sima Qian 司馬遷. Beijing: Zhonghua Shuju, 1964.

Shisanjing zhushu 十三經注疏. Compiled by Ruan Yuan 阮元. Reprint, Taibei: Yiwen Yinshuguan, 1955.

Shuo yuan shuzheng 說苑疏證. Shanghai: Huadong Shifan Daxue Chubanshe, 1985.

Song shi 宋史. Taibei: Dingwen Shuju, 1987.

Song shihua quanbian 宋詩話全編. Nanjing: Jiangsu Guji Chubanshe, 1998.

Song shu 宋書. Compiled by Shen Yue 沈約. Beijing: Zhonghua Shuju, 1974.

Song Yuan biji xiaoshuo daguan 宋元筆記小說大觀. Shanghai: Shanghai Guji Chubanshe, 2001.

Songben Cefu yuangui 宋本冊府元龜. Beijing: Zhonghua Shuju, 1989.

Songben Taiping huanyu ji 宋本太平寰宇記. Beijing: Zhonghua Shuju, 2000.

Strassberg, Richard E. *Inscribed Landscapes: Travel Writings from Imperial China*. Berkeley: University of California Press, 1994.

Su Shi 蘇軾. *Su Dongpo quanji* 蘇東坡全集. Taibei: Shijie Shuju, 1969.

———. *Su Shi shiji* 蘇軾詩集. Beijing: Zhonghua Shuju, 1982.

Sui shu 隋書. Beijing: Zhonghua Shuju, 1973.

Taiping huanyu ji 太平寰宇記. Compiled by Yue Shi 樂史. In *Yingyin Wenyuan ge siku quanshu* 景印文淵閣四庫全書. Vols. 469–70. Taiwan: Shangwu Yinshuguan, 1984.

Taiping yulan 太平御覽. Taiwan: Shangwu Yinshuguan, 1974.

Tang chao Wen xuan jizhu huicun 唐鈔文選集注匯存. Shanghai: Shanghai Guji Chubanshe, 2000.

Tang Xuan 湯絢. *Qing chu cangshujia Qian Zeng yanjiu* 清初藏書家錢曾研究. Taibei: Hanmei Tushu, 1991.

Tang Yijie 湯一介. *Guo Xiang yu Wei Jin xuanxue* 郭象與魏晉玄學. Beijing: Beijing Daxue Chubanshe, 2000.

Tang Yongtong 湯用彤. *Han Wei liang Jin nanbeichao fojiao shi* 漢魏兩晉南北朝佛教史. Beijing: Beijing Daxue Chubanshe, 1997.

———. *Wei Jin xuanxue lungao* 魏晉玄學論稿. Shanghai: Shanghai Guji, 2001.

Tao Yuanming shiwen huiping 陶淵明詩文彙評. Taibei: Zhonghua Shuju, 1969.

Tao Yuanming yanjiu ziliao huibian 陶淵明研究資料彙編. Edited by the Chinese Department of Beijing University and Beijing Normal University. Beijing: Zhonghua Shuju, 1962.

Walton, Linda A. "Southern Sung Academies and the Construction of Sacred Space." In *Landscape, Culture, and Power in Chinese Society*. Edited by Wen-hsin Yeh, 23–49. Berkeley: Institute of East Asia Studies, 1998.

Wang Bo 王勃. *Wang Zian ji zhu* 王子安集注. Shanghai: Shanghai Guji Chubanshe, 1995.

Wang Chong 王充. *Lunheng* 論衡. Beijing: Zhonghua Shuju, 1990.

Wang Fuzhi 王夫之. *Gushi pingxuan* 古詩評選. Beijing: Wenhua Yishu Chubanshe, 1997.

Wang Guoying 王國瓔. *Gujin yinyi shiren zhi zong Tao Yuanming lunxi* 古今隱逸詩人之宗陶淵明論析. Taibei: Yunchen Wenhua Gongsi, 1999.

———. "Shizhuan zhong de Tao Yuanming." *Taida Zhongwen Xuebao* 臺大中文學報. 12 (May 2000): 193–228.

Wang Shizhen 王士禛. *Fen gan yuhua* 分甘餘話. Beijing: Zhonghua Shuju, 1989.

Wang Siren 王思任. *Wenfan xiaopin* 文飯小品. Edited by Jiang Jinde 蔣金德. Changsha: Yuelu Shushe, 1989.

Wang Wei 王維. *Wang Youcheng ji jianzhu* 王右丞集箋注. Annotated by Zhao Diancheng 趙殿成. Hong Kong: Zhonghua Shuju, 1975.

Wang Yao 王瑤. *Zhonggu wenxueshilun* 中古文學史論. Beijing: Beijing Daxue Chubanshe, 1986.

Wang Yunlu 王雲路. *Han Wei liuchao shige yuyan lungao* 漢魏六朝詩歌語言論稿. Xi'an: Shanxi Renmin Jiaoyu Chubanshe, 1997.

Wang Zhizhong 王枝忠. *Han Wei liuchao xiaoshuo shi* 漢魏六朝小說史. Hangzhou: Zhejiang Guji Chubanshe, 1997.

Watson, Burton, trans. *The Complete Works of Chuang Tzu*. New York: Columbia University Press, 1968.

Wei shu 魏書. Compiled by Wei Shou 魏收. Beijing: Zhonghua Shuju, 1974.

Wei Yingwu 韋應物. *Wei Yingwu ji jiaozhu* 韋應物集校注. Shanghai: Shanghai Guji Chubanshe, 1998.

Wilhelm, Hellmut. "Shih Ch'ung and His *Chin-ku-yüan*." *Monumenta Serica* 18 (1959): 315–27.

Wu Zongci 吳宗慈. *Lushan zhi* 廬山志. Nanchang: Jiangxi Renmin Chubanshe, 1996.

Xiao Tong 蕭統. *Wen xuan* 文選. Shanghai: Shanghai Guji Chubanshe, 1986.

Xijing zaji quanyi 西京雜記全譯. Annotated by Cheng Lin 成林 and Cheng Zhangcan 程章燦. Guiyang: Guizhou Renmin Chubanshe, 1993.

Xin Tang shu 新唐書. Beijing: Zhonghua Shuju, 1975.

Xu Xinjie 徐新傑. "Tao Yuanming guli bian" 陶淵明故里辨. *Jiujiang Shizhuan Xuebao* 九江師專學報. January–February 1985: 22–24.

Xunzi jijie 荀子集解. Taibei: Shijie Shuju, 1969.

Yan Kejun 嚴可均, ed., *Quan shanggu sandai Qin Han sanguo liuchao wen* 全上古三代秦漢三國六朝文. Beijing: Zhonghua Shuju, 1996.

Yan Zhitui 顏之推. *Yanshi jiaxun jijie* 顏氏家訓集解. Edited by Wang Liqi 王利器. Shanghai: Shanghai Guji Chubanshe, 1980.

Yang, Lien-sheng 楊聯陞. "Notes on the Economic History of the Chin Dynasty." *Harvard Journal of Asiatic Studies* 9:2 (June 1946): 107–85.

Yang Xiong 揚雄. *Fa yan* 法言. Beijing: Zhonghua Shuju, 1987.

Yao Boyue 姚伯岳. *Huang Pilie pingzhuan* 黃丕烈評傳. Nanjing: Nanjing Daxue Chubanshe, 1998.

Ye Dehui 葉德輝. *Shulin qinghua* 書林清話. Edited by Zishi 紫石. Beijing: Yanshan Chubanshe, 1999.

Yiwen leiju 藝文類聚. Edited by Ouyang Xun 歐陽詢 et al. Taibei: Wenguang Chubanshe, 1974.

Yuan Ke 袁珂. *Zhongguo gudai shenhua* 中國古代神話. Beijing: Zhonghua Shuju, 1981.

Yuan Xingpei 袁行霈. *Tao Yuanming yanjiu* 陶淵明研究. Beijing: Beijing Daxue Chubanshe, 1997.

Zhang Hongwei 章宏偉. *Chuban wenhua shilun* 出版文化史論. Beijing: Huawen Chubanshe, 2002.

Zhang Hua 張華. *Bowu zhi jiaozheng* 博物志校證. Collated by Fan Ning 范寧. Beijing: Zhonghua Shuju, 1980.

Zhong Rong 鍾嶸. *Shipin jizhu* 詩品集注. Edited by Cao Xu 曹旭. Shanghai: Shanghai Guji Chubanshe, 1994.

Zhong Youmin 鍾優民. *Taoxue fazhan shi* 陶學發展史. Changchun: Jilin Jiaoyu Chubanshe, 2000.

Zhou Bida 周必大. *Zhou Yiguo wenzhong gong ji* 周益國文忠公集. Compiled by Ouyang Qi 歐陽棨. Jiangxi: Lushan Guanliju, 1935.

Zhou Yi zhengyi 周易正義. Annotated by Wang Bi 王弼 and Han Kangbo 韓康伯, with a commentary by Kong Yingda 孔穎達. Reprint, Taibei: Yiwen Yinshuguan, 1955. See under *Shisanjing zhushu*.

Zhouyi zhushu ji buzheng 周易注疏及補正. Taibei: Shijie Shuju, 1978.

Zhu Dawei 朱大渭 et al. *Wei Jin nanbeichao shehui shenghuo shi* 魏晉南北朝社會生活史. Beijing: Zhongguo Shehui Kexue Chubanshe, 1998.

Zhu Mu 祝穆 and Zhu Zhu 祝洙. *Fangyu shenglan* 方輿勝覽. Shanghai: Shanghai Guji, 1984.

Zhu Xi 朱熹. *Zhu Wengong wenji* 朱文公文集. *SBCK* edition. Shanghai: Shangwu Yinshuguan, 1967.

Zhu Ziqing 朱自清. "Taoshi de shendu" 陶詩的深度. In *Zhu Ziqing gudian wenxue lunwenji* 朱自清古典文學論文集, 567–75. Shanghai: Shanghai Guji Chubanshe, 1981.

———. "Tao Yuanming nianpu zhong zhi wenti" 陶淵明年譜中之問題. In *Zhu Ziqing gudian wenxue lunwenji* 朱自清古典文學論文集, 451–92. Shanghai: Shanghai Guji Chubanshe, 1981.

Zhuangzi jishi 莊子集釋. Edited by Guo Qingfan 郭慶藩 and Wang Xiaoyu 王孝鱼. Beijing: Zhonghua Shuju, 1961.

Zhuangzi jinzhu jinyi 莊子今注今譯. Annotated by Chen Guying 陳鼓應. Hong Kong: Zhonghua Shuju, 1990.

Ziporyn, Brook. *The Penumbra Unbound: The Neo-Taoist Philosophy of Guo Xiang*. Albany: State University of New York, 2003.

Zong Lin 宗懍. *Jingchu suishi ji yizhu* 荊楚歲時記譯注. Annotated by Tan Lin 譚麟. Hubei: Hubei Renmin Chubanshe, 1985.

Index

Acquisition. See *de*
The Analects, 62, 115, 118–19, 132, 172, 174–76, 182, 184, 187, 242n47, 251n52, 255n2, 265nn111–12, 266n7, 268n38. *See also* Confucius

Bai Juyi (Bai Letian), 35, 36, 92, 199
Baijing Lou, 50
Baili Xi, 254n76
Bailu Dong Shuyuan (White Deer Grotto Academy), 206
banben xue (study of editions), 16, 222
Bao Tao Zhai (Studio of Treasuring Tao), 52
Bao Tingbo (Bao Yiwen), 49–50, 236n70
Bao Zhao, 255n6
Baohui Tang, 40
Bei shi (The Histories of the Northern Dynasties), 68
Berkowitz, Alan, 64, 265n103, 265n108
Bi Yuan, 262n75
Bian He, 46–47, 164
Bishu luhua (Remarks Recorded While Avoiding the Heat; Ye Mengde), 9
Boccaccio, 132
Boya, 25–26
Boyi and Shuqi, 92, 229n6
Bozhai bian (Fang Shao), 234n59
Bray, Francesca, 99, 246n10, 250n37
Buddhayaśas (Fotuoyeshe), 198

Cai Qi (Cai Juhou), 10–12, 31, 105
Cai Ying, 204, 211
Cao Longshu, 215–17, 273n57
Cao Pi, 178, 256n28
Cao Zhi, 243n59, 145
Cefu yuangui, 87
Cen Rang (Cen Yanxiu), 161
Cengcheng (Tiered Wall), 143–46, 258nn35–36, 258n39
Cerquiglini, Bernard, 221, 274n4
Chaisang, 53–54, 68–69, 199, 273n58
Chang'an, 36, 143, 167, 198, 264n103
Changju and Jieni, 115, 123
Chao Buzhi, 33–36, 38–39, 44, 232n33, 235n59, 263n84
Chao Yongzhi (Chao Zhidao), 161, 263n84
Chaofu (Nest-Dweller), 28, 63, 66, 230n16
Chen Congyi, 34
Chen Guang, 202, 206
Chen Kui, 295–96
Chen Li, 291
Chen Longzheng, 295
Chen Shidao, 35
Chen Shugu's edition, 96
Chen Shunyu (also Chen Lingju), 200–202, 208–9, 216–17, 270n11, 272n39
Chen Xianxing, 17
Chen Xingzhen, 293
Chen Yinke, 235n65, 240n32
Chen Zuoming, 130, 159
Cheng, 6, 78–79, 241n42
Cheng Hao, 117
Cheng Qianfan, 231n27
Cheng Shimeng, 204–5
Cheng Xuanying, 137, 260n53
Cherniack, Susan, 9
Chi Chao, 27
Chia, Lucille, 227n26
Chong Zun (Pang Zun), 79–80
Chong'er, 254n76
Chuci, 107, 129, 136, 144–46, 151, 156, 259n40
Chunming Fang (Chunming Ward), 10

Chuxue ji (Primer for Study), 149
Confucianism, 98, 126, 175
Confucius, 42, 66, 89, 98–99, 108, 119, 175–76, 182–84, 186–87, 207; comment on passage of time, 268n35; comment on Yan Hui, 62, 259n50; criticism of Fan Chi, 251n52; dialogue with Yan Hui, 137–38; distrust of crafty words, 58; exchange with Zilu, 265n111; inquiring for the ford, 115, 123; on Guan Zhong, 176, 266n7; secret to happiness, 151; as a transmitter, 118
Cui Qi, 265n107

Dagenais, John, 4
Dai Kui, 27, 254n77
Dai Yong, 242n45
Dangtu, 38
Dao de jing (*or* Tao te ching; Laozi), 100–101, 132, 174, 194, 265n110, 266n3. *See also* Laozi
Daoshan qinghua (Pure Chat at Daoshan), 11, 235n60
Davis, A. R., 57, 77, 79, 86, 108, 122, 186, 212, 258n36, 268n35
de (acquisition), 19, 23, 26–27; obtain the concept and forget the words (*deyi wangyan*), 25, 53; of a rare edition of Tao Yuanming's collection, 44–52; of a rock, 38–40; Su Shi's obsession with, 39; of truth, 25
The Decameron (Boccaccio), 132
Ding Fubao, 98, 135–36, 248n26, 250n37, 258n36, 263n91
Ding Lingwei, 249n35
Doctrine of Names (Ming Jiao), 126, 175
Dong Zhongshu, 266n7
Dongfang Shuo, 98
Donglin Temple (Donglin Si), 211, 258n37
Double Ninth Festival, 53, 55, 86, 93, 177–79, 267n14
Dream of the Red Chamber (*or* Story of the Stone; Cao Xueqin), 120, 196, 198
Drunken Stone (Zuishi), 196–219,
Drunken Stone Junior (Xiao Zuishi), 197, 218
Du Fu, 9, 11, 18, 35, 224, 227nn15–17, 232n33; transcribing the poetry of, 8, 235n60; variants in poetry of, 11, 34
Du Gongzhan, 267n14
Du Mu, 235n60
Du Yu, 54–55
Duke Huan of Qi, 165–66, 176
Dunhuang, 7
duo lei bei (stele for shedding tears), 54
Duqing Tang ben (Duqing Tang edition), 291

Editing: mediating role of, 221, 223; metaphor for, 22; practice of Northern Song scholars, 9–12, 277n16; in production of manuscript copies, 8–9; of Tao Yuanming's collection, 11, 14–15, 20, 124, 218, 220
Egan, Ronald, 39
Eighteen Worthies of the White Lotus Society, 201, 243n60
Emperor An of Jin, 91
Emperor Gaozong of Song, 293
Emperor Hui of Han, 170
Emperor Huizong of Song, 234n59
Emperor Taizong of Tang, 68
Emperor Wen of Song. *See* Liu Yilong
Emperor Wu of Song. *See* Liu Yu

Fan Ning, 98–99, 239n13
Fan Ye, 65, 67, 79, 239n13, 265n113
Fang Shao, 234n59
Fangyu shenglan (Fine Scenes of the Regions; Zhu Mu and Zhu Zhu), 269n8
Fashen, 28
feast poetry, 134–35, 144–47
Feng Youlan, 181
Fu Xuan, 133, 262n79
Fu Yi, 185, 268n37
Fuxi, 50, 83

Gao Yanxiu, 8
Gaoseng zhuan (Biographies of Eminent Monks; Hui Jiao), 198, 211
Gaoshi zhuan (Biographies of High-

minded Gentlemen; Huangfu Mi), 65, 230n16, 265n18
Gaoshi zhuan (Biographies of High-minded Gentlemen; Xi Kang), 65, 242n47
"Gaotang fu" (*Fu* on Gaotang), 153
Gaoyi shamen zhuan (Biographies of Lofty and Reclusive Monks; Zhu Faji), 28, 230n17
Ge Hong, 229n2
Ge Lifang, 37, 92, 232n43
Ge Shengzhong, 232n43
Gengsang Chu, 113–16
Ginger Studio, 117
Gong Bin, 234n55, 246n2
Gongxi shihua (Remarks on Poetry at Gong Creek; Huang Che), 36
Gu Hao, 291
Gu Kaizhi, 230n22
Gu Mei (Gu Yiren), 47–48, 50, 236n68
Gu Zhi, 129, 136, 146, 182, 188, 192, 216–17
Gu Zixiu, 49–50
Guan Zhong, 166, 176, 264n97, 266n7
Guanxiu, 7–8, 226n3, 272n39
Guixin zashi bieji (Zhou Mi), 268n35
Guizong Temple, 198
Guo Pu, 149, 155; commentary on *Shanhai jing*, 154, 166, 260n52, 261nn72–73, 262n75, 263n90, 264n96
Guo Shaoyu, 246n1, 291, 294
Guo Xiang, 137, 169, 174–75, 181, 256n18
Guo Xiangzheng, 38, 233n47, 234n59

Han Ju (Han Zicang), 96
Han Wudi neizhuan, 260n55
Han Xin, 129–30, 254n76
Han Yu (Han Tuizhi), 9, 11, 35, 235n60
Hao Yixing, 116
Hashikawa Tokio, 292, 294
"He bo" (The Earl of Yellow River), 145
He Mengchun, 248n26, 294–95
He Yan, 98, 174
He Zhuo, 233n55, 235n61, 263n81
Hightower, James R., 108, 119, 123, 147, 155, 157, 164, 184, 192, 229n3, 247n21
Holzman, Donald, 252n68
Hong Mai, 79
Hou Han shu (The Latter Han History; Fan Ye), 65, 239n13, 265n113
Houshan shihua (Houshan's Remarks on Poetry; Chen Shidao), 35
Hu Boji ben (Hu Boji edition), 291
Hu Fengdan, 296
Hu Shi, 197–98, 211, 269n2
Hu Zi, 45, 96
"Hua shanshui xu" (Preface to a Painted Landscape; Zong Bing), 29–31
Huainanzi, 26, 139, 258n39
Huan Huo, 127
Huan Wen, 126–27, 130, 254n79, 255n90
Huan Xuan, 170, 173, 239n24
Huang Che, 36, 118
Huang Pilie (Ning Song Zhuren), 16–17, 51–52
Huang Tingjian (Huang Luzhi), 11, 32–33, 35–36, 44, 213, 227n16, 234n58; funerary inscription for Liu Shu, 270n11
Huang Wenhuan, 130, 146, 156, 158, 261n64, 295
Huang Zongxi (Huang Lizhou), 215, 271n37, 273n51, 274n58
Huangfu Mi, 65, 230n16, 239n24, 265n108
Huangfu Xizhi, 239n24
Hui Guan, 247n16
Hui Hong, 32
Hui Jiao, 198, 211
Hui Yuan, 88, 142, 211, 243n60, 245n74, 247n16, 272n39
Huishi (Huizi), 26, 176–77, 229n8
Hundun (Undifferentiated), 66
Huzhong jiuhua (Nine Glories Mountain in a Jug), 38–39, 44, 232n45, 233n47, 234n58–59

Ibn Hazm, 3–5
Internet, 21, 223–24

James Legge, 176
ji (trace), 63–64, 66, 168, 172, 196, 207
Ji Zhenyi, 236n68
Jia Sixie, 99, 250n37
Jian'an poetry, 133–35, 144
Jiang Bingzhi, 112

Jiang Xu, 242n47
Jiang Xun (Jiang Danyai), 182, 296
Jiang Xun ping ben (Jiang Xun's critical edition), 296
Jiang Yan, 96–97, 133
Jiangyun Lou (Tower of Crimson Cloud), 46–47, 235nn65–66
Jiangzhou (prefecture), 57, 71–73, 79, 81–82, 85, 89, 198–99
jiaokan xue (textual studies), 16, 222
Jiaoran, 53–55
Jigu ge, 46, 199
Jigu ge ben (Jigu ge edition), 14, 46, 292
"*Jiming*" (Cockcrow), 100
jin (head cloth), 245n76
Jin Gu (Golden Valley), 142
Jin shu (The Jin History), 60, 68–94 passim, 98, 201, 244n74
Jin yangqiu (The Chronicles of Jin; Sun Sheng), 126
Jing Ke, 229n6
Jingzhou (prefecture), 54, 170
"Jirang ge" (The Song of Tossing Sticks), 123
"Jiu ge" (Nine Songs), 145, 255n85
Jiu Tang shu (The Old Tang History), 10, 226n10, 290
John Knoblock, 111

Kang Sengyuan, 27–28
Kang-i Sun Chang, 237n3, 257n32
King Huai of Chu, 164
King Mu of Zhou, 144, 148, 152–54
Kong Qun, 78
Kuang Lu you lu (Travel Account of Mount Lu; Huang Zongxi), 215, 271n37, 273n51
Kunlun, Mount, 29–30, 143–54 passim, 258n35, 258n39
kuyu (suffering from the rain), 133–34, 255n3, 255nn5–6
Kwong, Charles Yim-tze, 228n28

Langfeng Peak, 30, 258n35
Lanting, 143
Lanzhenzi (Ma Yongqing), 78, 231n26, 258n37
Laolaizi, 245n87; wife of, 93, 245n87
Laozi (Lao Dan), 64, 100, 113–14, 135, 175–77, 180–81
Lei Cizong, 242n45
Lengzhai yehua (Night Chat of the Cold Studio; Hui Hong), 32
Li Bai (Li Taibai), 199, 235n60, 269n4, 271n38
Li Daoyuan, 258n35
Li Dashi, 68
Li E, 270n15
Li Gonghuan, 215
Li Gonghuan ben (Li Gonghuan's edition), 14, 241n42, 294–95
Li Mengyang, 273n52
Li Qing, 221
"Li sao" (Encountering Sorrow; Qu Yuan), 104
Li Shan, 267n29
Li Shimin (Emperor Taizong of Tang), 68
Li Tao Zhai, 50, 52
Li Wenhan, 293
Li Xiang, 70
Li Yanshou, 68
Li Zhengchen, 38, 233n47, 234n59
Liang Hong, 238n13
"Liangli zhuan" (Biographies of Virtuous Officials; Shen Yue), 112
"Lianshe gaoxian zhuan" (Biographies of the High-minded Worthies of the Lotus Society). *See* Shiba gaoxian zhuan
Liezi, 132, 239n13, 255n2
Lili (Chestnut Village), 81–82, 198–201, 207–15 passim, 269nn3–4, 271n29, 273n52
Lin Wenyue, 228n28
Lin Xiangru, 47, 213
Linda Walton, 205
Liu Bin (Liu Gongfu), 11, 227n16
Liu Chang, 80
Liu Gong (Liu Menggong), 193–95
Liu Huaisu, 233n51
Liu Huan, 200, 205, 208–9, 269n11
Liu Jingxuan, 233n51
Liu Kai, 11
Liu Liu, 84–85

Liu Lü, 122
Liu Shengmu, 45
Liu Shi, 46, 235n65
Liu Shu, 209, 270n11
Liu Xiang, 239n14, 245n87
Liu Xiaobiao, 230n17
Liu Xie, 252n66
Liu Xin, 229n2
Liu Yilong (Emperor Wen of Song), 81, 217–18
Liu Yimin, 54, 80, 88
Liu Yu (Emperor Wu of Song), 5, 81, 89–90, 158–60, 167, 170, 245n82
Liu Zai, 268n35
Liu Zhen (Liu Gonggan), 80, 243n59
Liu Zongyuan (Liu Zihou), 235n60
Liuyi shihua (Liuyi's Remarks on Poetry; Ouyang Xiu), 34
Lou Yue, 212
Lu, Mount (Mount Kuang), 79, 81–82, 88, 142–43, 197–217 passim, 258n36
Lu Ji, 100, 133–34, 247n14, 255n3, 259n40
Lu Qinli, 6, 184, 234n55, 245n80, 247n20, 263n89, 268n39
Lu Xiujing, 211–12, 215–16, 272n39
Lu Xun, 161–62
luben (copied version), 9–10
Luo You, 80, 126–28, 130, 255n90
Luoyang, 100, 265n113
Lushan houlu (The Second Account of Mount Lu; Zhou Bida), 210
Lushan ji (A Record of Mount Lu; Chen Shunyu), 200–201
Lushan jishi (A Record of Mount Lu; Sang Qiao), 204, 212
Lushan xiaozhi (A Short Account of Mount Lu; Cai Ying), 204, 211
Lushan xin daoyou (New Guide to Mount Lu), 210
Lushan zhi (The Record of Mount Lu; Mao Deqi), 204–5, 214, 270n15
Lushan zhi (The Record of Mount Lu; Wu Zongci), 204–5, 216

Ma Yongqing, 78, 231n26, 258n37
manuscript culture: compared with print culture, 4–9, 223–24; in late imperial China, 17, 221–22; and Tao Yuanming studies, 220–22; textual fluidity as central characteristic of, 7–9, 221, 224
Mao Deqi, 204–5, 214–15, 217, 270n15, 272n44
Mao Jin, 46, 48, 199
Mao Yi (filial son), 242n43
Mao Yi (Ming book collector), 45–49, 51, 291
Marcus, Leah S., 21, 224
McGann, Jerome J., 224
Mencius, 58, 95, 108, 127, 151, 206, 270n26
Meng Haoran, 271n27, 271n38
Meng Jia, 241n41, 242n49, 254n79
Meng Tao Zhai (Studio of Dreaming of Tao), 52
Mengxi xubitan (Continuation of the Notes of Dream Creek; Shen Gua), 32
Michael Puett, 251n50
Min Qihua, 231n27
"Ming xiang" (Clarification of the Image; Wang Bi), 26
Mo Youzhi ben (Mo Youzhi's edition), 293
Mu tianzi zhuan (The Biography of King Mu), 144, 148, 260n55

Nan shi (The Histories of the Southern Dynasties), 60, 68–94 passim, 201, 212, 214, 238n11, 272n44
Nankang, 196–215 passim, 270n11
Nenggaizhai manlu (Casual Records from Nenggaizhai Studio; Wu Zeng), 36
"Ni *Ye zhong ji*" (Imitations of *The Collection of Ye*; Xie Lingyun), 133
Nineteen Old Poems, 146; no. 13, 146; no. 15, 256n10, 259n41

Omar Khayyám, 174
Ouyang Jian, 230n11
Ouyang Xiu, 9, 34, 200, 205, 269n11
Ouyang Xuan, 272n42
Owen, Stephen, 228n28, 234n58, 237n3, 247nn18–19, 248n22, 251nn53–54, 253n73, 256n16

Pan Lei, 46
Pan Ni, 255n5
Pang Tongzhi, 80–82
Paradise Lost (Milton), 149
Pei Wei, 174
Peng Cheng, 32
The Peony Pavilion (Tang Xianzu), 252n64
philology, 222–23, 274n4; "new philology," 21
Pingzhou ketan (Zhu Yu), 234n59
Prince Qiao, 134–35, 139
printing, 4, 9, 16–17, 21, 221–24 passim, 227n26; before the age of print culture, 91, 97

Qian Jia xuepai (Qian-Jia school), 16
Qian Meixian, 48–49, 291
Qian Qianyi, 46–48, 235n66, 291
Qian Zeng (Qian Zunwang), 47–48, 51, 235n66, 236n68
Qian Zhongshu, 62
Qianlou, 61, 239n14; wife of, 61, 239n14
Qimin yaoshu (Essential Techniques for the Peasantry; Jia Sixie), 99, 250n37
qing tan (pure talk), 71
Qu Shaoji, 292
Qu Yong, 292
Qu Yuan, 104, 164
quan nong (encouraging the farmers), 119–20, 252n64
Quwei jiuwen (Old Stories Heard at Quwei; Zhu Bian), 10

Readers' reception, 8, 18
The Record of Rites, 127, 169, 195
Red Pine, 134, 139, 256n28
The Ring of the Dove (Ibn Hazm), 3
Ruan Hun, 254n77
Ruan Ji, 59, 78, 174, 243n50, 254n77
Ruan Xian, 254n77
Ruan Yu, 133
Ru'nan xianxian zhuan (Biographies of the Former Worthies of Ru'nan), 265n113

Said, Edward W., 223
Sang Qiao, 204, 212–14, 217
Seven Worthies of the Bamboo Grove, 126, 134, 174
shanben (fine edition), 9, 10, 17
Shang Mountain, 168–70, 264n103
Shang shan si hao (Four White-heads of Shang Mountain), 169–70, 191, 264n103
Shangjing, 109, 209–10, 216, 248n33, 273n58
Shanhai jing (The Classic of Mountains and Seas), 144, 148–49, 152–66 passim, 250n35, 259n50, 260n51
Shanjuan, 124
Shao Bowen, 231n26, 235n60
"Shao si ming" (Junior Master of Lifespans), 255n85
Shaoshi wenjian houlu (Shao Bowen), 231n26
Shaoxing ben (Shaoxing edition), 44–45, 291
Shen Gua, 32–33
Shen Yue, 60, 62–64, 66–67, 89–94, 134, 245n82, 253n74
Shi Chong, 142–44, 257n32, 257n34
Shi ji (Records of the Historian; Sima Qian), 229n6
Shi jing (The Classic of Poetry), 141, 165, 195, 229n3, 265n106, 267n16; "The Great Preface," 237n5; Zai shan, 121
Shi Ke, 272n39
Shi Zhecun, 161
"Shiba gaoxian zhuan" (Biographies of Eighteen High-minded Worthies), 243n60, 244n74
shifting cultivation, 246n10
Shilin shihua (Ye Mengde), 231n32
Shimen (Stone Gate), 29, 142–43, 145, 230n20
Shishuo xinyu (A New Account of Tales of the World), 27, 78, 80, 84, 126–27, 135, 239n24, 243n50, 254n77
Shu Guang and Shu Shou, 257n29
Shu Xi, 120, 252n66
Shun (emperor), 114, 116, 124, 264n96
Shuo yuan (The Garden of Tales), 26

Si Yue, 47, 91–92, 290
Si Yue ben (Si Yue's edition), 290
"Sihao lun" (On the Four White-heads; Huan Xuan), 170
Sima Guang, 46, 270n11
Sima Qian, 229n6, 248n25
Sima Xiangru, 136
Sima Xiuzhi, 159
Song ben (Song edition), 48, 290
Song Gaozong (Emperor Gaozong of Song), 293
Song Minqiu, 10–12, 21, 228n31
Song Qi, 226n10
Song shi jishi (An Account of Incidents around Song Poetry; Li E), 270n15
Song Shou, 21, 225
Song Xiang (Song Yuanxuan), 10, 47–48, 209, 271n33, 290
Song Xiang ben (Song Xiang's edition), 47–48, 227n12, 290
"Soushen houji" (A Sequel to *In Search of the Supernatural*), 249n35
Su Guo, 233n47, 258n37
Su Jun, 71
Su Shi (Su Dongpo, Su Wenzhong), 96, 128, 258n37; appraisal of *San xiao tu*, 272n39; copying out poems by previous poets, 235n60; discussion of *jian* and *wang*, 14, 31–36, 40, 231n27, 231n31; and Du Fu's poetry, 11; and Huang Tingjian, 213; and Huzhong Jiuhua, 38–39, 44, 234n59; as magistrate of Guangling, 232n33; sacrificial address for Chen Shunyu, 270n11; and Tao Yuanming, 4–6; and Tao Yuanming's collection, 232n32; on Tao Yuanming's zither, 87; variants in poetry of, 231n26; and Wang Jinqing, 39–40, 233n49
Su xie ben (Su Shi edition). *See* Su xie keben
Su xie keben (Su Shi edition), 16, 44–47, 113, 119, 291
Su Zhonghu, 231n26
Sui shu (The Sui History), 10, 68, 226n10
Sun Chu, 229n2
Sun Chuo, 258n38
Sun Kuang, 231n27
Sun Sheng, 126

Taiping huanyu ji (The Account of the Realm in the Taiping Era; Yue Shi), 199–200, 269n8
Taiping yulan (The Imperial Encyclopedia of the Taiping Era), 242n47
Tan Daoji, 73, 81, 83–84, 86, 89, 93
Tan Daoluan, 83
Tan Shao, 88–89
Tang Han (Tang Boji), 49–50, 184, 241n42, 293. See also *Tang Han ben*
Tang Han ben (Tang Han's edition), 14, 52, 184, 227n18, 236n69, 249n33, 259n42, 293–94
Tang Xianzu, 252n64
Tang Yijie, 168
Tang Yongtong, 26
Tao Dan, 28, 237n1
Tao Fan (Tao Hunu), 84
Tao Fuxiang (Ailu), 291
Tao Kan (Tao Shixing), 5, 57, 68–69, 79; background and character, 70–71; Eastern Jin aristocrats' attitude toward, 240n33; ethnicity of, 240n32; mother of, 48–49, 70; sons of, 84, 259n46
Tao Lu (Tao Cottage), 47, 51
Tao Mao, 69
Tao shi xi yi (An Analysis of the Meaning of Tao's Poetry; Huang Wenhuan), 295
Tao Shu, 148, 233n55, 241n42, 245n82, 296–97
Tao Shu ben (Tao Shu's edition), 296–97
Tao Tao Shi (Chamber of the Double Taos), 52
Tao Yuanming: and Buddhism, 20, 127, 247n16; biographies, 67–94; construction of Master Five Willows, 60–67; manuscript copies of works, 5, 10, 31, 226n10, 289–90; printed editions of works, 14, 16, 19, 44–45, 75, 78, 227n12, 290–97; and pursuit of immortality, 134–42

Tao Yuanming, works of: "Bingchen sui bayue zhong yu xiasun tian she huo" (Harvesting in the Farmstead at Xiasun in the Eighth Month in the *Bingchen* Year), 120; "Da Pang canjun" (In Reply to Aide Pang), 80; "Du Shanhai jing" (Reading *The Classic of Mountains and Seas*), 24, 149–67; "Gengxu sui jiuyue zhong yu xitian huo han dao" (Harvesting Dry Rice in the Western Fields in the Ninth Month of the Year *Gengxu*), 250n37; "Gui yuan tian ju" (Returning to Dwell in Gardens and Fields), 95–110, 125, 172; "Guimao sui shichun huai gu tian she" (Upon Thinking of the Ancient Farmers in Early Spring of the *Guimao* Year), 118, 246n8; "Guimao sui shieryue zhong zuo yu congdi Jingyuan" (Composed and Presented to My Cousin Jingyuan in the Twelfth Month of the *Guimao* Year), 125, 171–73; "Guiqulai ci" (Return), 38, 57, 76–79, 293; "He Guo zhubu" (Matching a Poem by Secretary Guo), 186–90; "He Hu xicao shi Gu Zeicao" (Matching the Poem of Clerk Hu, and to Be Shown to Sheriff Gu), 190–92; "He Liu Chaisang" (Answering a Poem by Liu Chaisang), 246n10; "Huan jiu ju" (Returning to My Former Residence), 109–10, 249nn33–35, 273n55; "Ji Chengshi mei wen" (elegy), 241n42; "Jin gu Zhengxi dajiangjun zhangshi Meng fujun zhuan" (The Biography of His Excellency Meng, the Former Chief of Staff to the Zhengxi General of the Jin), 241n41; "Jiuri xianju" (Living at Leisure on the Ninth Day), 86, 177–81, 195; "Lianyu duyin" (Drinking Alone during Incessant Rain), 70, 133–42, 249n35, 256n28; "Ming zi" (Charge to My Son), 57, 89–90, 241n40; "Nigu" (In Imitation of Ancient Poems), 25–26, 235n60; "Qi shi" (Begging for Food), 125, 127–31; "Quan nong" (Encouraging the Farmers), 120; "Rong mu" (The Blossoming Tree), 182–86; "Shan shang hua zan" (Appraisals of Fan Paintings), 251n49; *Shengxian qunfu lu* (A Record of Sages, Worthies, and Their Various Assistants), 289; "Shi yun" (Seasons Shift), 244n72; "Shi Zhou yuan Zu Xie" (To Be Shown to Secretary Zhou, and Zu and Xie), 89, 245n78; "Shi zuo Zhenjun canjun jing Qu'e" (Upon Passing through Qu'e When Beginning My Service as Aide to the General of Zhenjun), 57; "Shujiu" (An Account of Ale), 13, 292; *Si ba mu* (A Category of Fours and Eights), 289, 293; "Suimu he Zhang changshi" (At the End of the Year, Answering a Poem by Attendant Zhang), 80; "Taohuayuan ji" (The Record of Peach Blossom Spring), 262n78, 293; "Taohuayuan shi" (The Poem of Peach Blossom Spring), 292; "Ting yun" (Hanging Clouds), 134; "Wan ge shi" (Bearers' Songs), 162, 253n74; *Wu xiao zhuan* (The Biographies of Five Filial Pieties), 289, 293; "Wuliu xiansheng zhuan" (The Biography of Master Five Willows), 53, 58–62, 66–71, 80; "Wushen sui liuyue yu huo" (Encountering a Fire in the Sixth Month of the Year *Wushen*), 139; "Wuyue yi ri zuo he Dai zhubu" (Written on the First Day of the Fifth Month, Matching a Poem by Secretary Dai), 122; "Xianqing fu" (*Fu* on Stilling the Passions), 93; "Xing ying shen" (Body, Shadow, and Spirit), 225, 274n8; "Yi ju" (On Moving), 216; "Yinjiu" (On Drinking), 10, 23–24, 88, 97, 125, 134, 194–95, 202; "Yisi sui sanyue wei Jianwei canjun shidun jing Qianxi" (In the Third Month of the Year of *Yisi*, I Passed through

the Qian Creek on a Mission to the Capital When I Was Aide to the General of Jianwei), 41–44, 57; "Yong er Shu" (On the Two Shus), 257n29; "Yong pinshi" (On Impoverished Gentlemen), 150, 171–72, 192–94; "You hui er zuo" (Composed Upon Having an Encounter), 116; "You Xiechuan" (An Excursion to Xie Brook), 142–46, 257n32, 257n34, 273n57; "Yu zi Yan deng shu" (Letter to My Sons, Yan and Others), 50; "Yuan shi Chu diao shi Pang zhubu Deng zhizhong" (Resentful Poem in the Chu Mode, to Registrar Pang and Secretary Deng), 80; "Za shi" (Unclassified Poems), 23, 32, 43–44, 96–97, 159; "Zeng Changsha gong" (To the Duke of Changsha), 241n40; "Zeng Yang zhangshi" (To Chief of Staff Yang), 80, 167–71; "Zhuren gongyou Zhou jia mubai xia" (Partying under the Cypress Trees at the Zhou Family Graves), 146–48; "Ziji wen" (In Sacrifice for Myself), 91, 245n75
Tao Zhan, 259n46
textual variants: and editorial practice, 8–9, 11–12; in Tao Yuanming's works, 6–7, 10–19 passim, 220–21. *See also* Tao Yuanming, works of
Tian Guo, 242n43
"Tianwen" (Heavenly Questions), 258n39
tianyuan shi (farmstead poetry), 19
Tiaoxi yuyin conghua houji (Collected Comments of the Fisherman Recluse of Tiao Creek, Second Series; Hu Zi), 45
Tiaoxi yuyin conghua qianji (Collected Comments of the Fisherman Recluse of Tiao Creek, First Series; Hu Zi), 96
Tiger Stream, 211–12, 272n39
Tingzhai shihua (Zeng Jili), 290

Variants. *See* textual variants

Wang Anshi (Wang Jinggong), 11–12, 227n16
Wang Bi, 26, 98, 174
Wang Bo, 271n38
Wang Chong, 262n79
Wang Dao, 81
Wang Fuzhi, 117, 122, 147, 190
Wang Guoying, 59, 86, 246n87
Wang Hong, 79, 81–86, 93–94, 199
Wang Hongzhi, 243n50, 244n70
Wang Houzhi (Wang Zhongliang), 45
Wang Hui, 135
Wang Huzhi (Wang Xiuling), 84
Wang Ji, 6
Wang Jinqing (Wang Shen), 39–40, 233n49
Wang Kangju, 230n19
Wang Kui, 205
Wang Qishu, 200
Wang Shizhen, 236n66
Wang Shumin, 102, 135–36, 139, 246n2, 254n84, 259n49, 263n89
Wang Siren, 213–15
Wang Tanzhi, 97
Wang Wei (Nankang magistrate), 212
Wang Wei (Tang poet), 6, 253n73, 254n75, 271n38
Wang Xizhi, 142–45, 198, 257n32, 274n58
Wang Yao, 24, 229n3, 245n76
Wang Yi, 107
Wang Yun, 135
Wang Zhenbai, 202
Wang Zhu (Wang Yuanshu), 11–12
Wei Yingwu (Wei Suzhou), 6, 36–37
Wei's concubine, 8, 224
Weilei, 113–14
Wen Qiao, 70
Wen Runeng, 182
Wen Runeng ben (Wen Runeng's edition), 296
Wen xuan (An Anthology of Literature; Xiao Tong), 23, 32–33, 78, 97, 228n1, 232n43, 259n49; Li Shan's commentary on, 267n29
Wu Jun, 229n2
Wu Qi, 259n50
Wu Qian (Wu Kuili), 49–50, 236n70
Wu Renjie, 91, 238n12
Wu Song, 259n50, 264n91

Wu Xiu (Wu Zixiu), 51
Wu Zeng, 36–37
Wu Zhantai, 296
Wu Zhantai ben (Wu Zhantai's edition), 296
Wu Zhuo, 294
Wu Zixu, 254n76
Wu Zongci, 204–5, 215–16, 272n44, 273n54, 273n58, 274n60

Xi Kang, 65, 135–36, 174, 242n47
Xian, Mount, 53–55
Xiang Xiu, 174
Xiangyang, 54, 126, 255n90
Xiao Ben, 229n2
Xiao Daocheng, 250n45
Xiao Tong (Zhaoming Taizi or the Crown Prince Zhaoming), 6, 23; biography of Tao Yuanming, 60, 67–94 passim, 137, 245n78; preface to Tao Yuanming's collection, 226n11, 289
Xiao Tong ben (Xiao Tong's edition), 289
Xie An, 97
Xie Bingde, 245n82
Xie Brook, 142–44, 258nn36–37
Xie Fu, 247n16
Xie Jingyi, 89
Xie Lingyun (Xie Kangle), 35, 55, 85, 133, 167
Xie Shang (Xie Renzu), 84
Xijing zaji (A Miscellaneous Record of the Western Capital), 229n2, 267n14
"Ximen xing" (West Gate), 256n10
Xin Tang shu (The New Tang History), 226n10, 290
Xin Xiao, 229n2
Xingtian, 160–62
Xingzi County, 204, 214, 216, 273n52
xiuzhen ben (pocket-treasure edition), 292
Xiwangmu (Queen Mother of the West), 148, 151–57 passim, 162–64, 260nn51–53, 260nn55–56
Xu Jiaocen, 293
Xu Jin yangqiu (A Sequel to the Chronicle of Jin; Tan Daoluan), 83
Xu Xinjie, 205, 214–15
Xu Xun, 239n24
Xu Yinfang, 296
Xu You, 28, 230n16, 240n24
xuan yan (arcane discourse), 71
xuanxue (arcane learning), 26, 174, 266n1
xuanyan shiren (metaphysical poets), 252n55
xungu xue, 222
Xunyang, 6, 68–69, 84–85, 204, 259n46; "the three recluses of," 88
Xunyang ji (A Record of Xunyang), 200
Xunzi, 111, 116, 184–85

Yan Hui, 62, 137–38, 151, 172, 259n50
Yan Na (Yan Wenjing gong), 48
Yan Yanzhi, 6, 84–86, 244n70, 253n74; elegy for Tao Yuanming, 148, 227n11, 241n42, 242n43, 250n35, 289
Yan Zhan (Yan Dexin, Yue'an), 48
Yan Zhenqing, 207–8
Yan Zhitui, 70
Yang Hu, 54–55
Yang Jing, 116
Yang Shi, 35
Yang Shoujing, 200
Yang Songling, 79–80, 244n61
Yang Xiong, 266n7
Yang Xiuzhi (Yang Zilie, Vice Director Yang), 10, 209, 226n11, 289
Yang Yong, 234n55
Yang Yun, 248n25
Yanshi jiaxun (Yan Zhitui), 70
Yao (emperor), 114, 116, 188–89, 223
ye (vocation; achievements; amassed capital), 112, 184–88 passim, 192
Ye Mengde, 9, 33, 231n32
Yi jing (The Classic of Changes), 26, 175, 195, 233n52
"Yimin zhuan" (Biographies of Disengaged People; Fan Ye), 65
Yin Zhongkan, 170
Yin Zhongwen, 267n29
ying Song chao (facsimile of the Song edition), 49
"Yinyi zhuan" (Biographies of Recluses; Shen Yue), 62, 64, 89

Yiwen leiju (Classified Extracts from Literature), 23, 33, 87, 97, 259n49
yongshi shi (poems on history), 148, 257n29
You Mao, 206
"You Shimen shi bing xu" (Preface and Poem on a Journey to Stone Gate), 142
youxian shi (poems on roaming immortals), 133, 142, 146, 149, 151, 157
Yu Liang, 240n33
Yu Xin (Yu Yicheng), 35
Yuan An, 171–72, 265n113, 266n114
Yuan Can, 238n13
Yuan Ke, 159, 161
Yuan Shu, 64
Yuan Xingpei, 14–15, 258n37, 289–90
"Yuanming biezhuan" (An Official Biography of Yuanming), 272n39
"Yuanyou" (Far Roaming), 144
Yue Shi, 199
Yunxian sanlu (A Desultory Record of the Cloud Immortal), 271n39
Yunyu yangqiu (Ge Lifang), 92
Yutang ben (Jade Hall edition), 294

"Zai shan," 121
Zeng Guofan, 258n36
Zeng Hong, 160–61, 165
Zeng Ji, 208–10, 215
Zeng Ji ben (Zeng Ji's edition *or* the 1192 edition), 78, 97, 102, 239n14, 244n61, 249n33, 291–95
Zeng Jili, 290
Zhai, 89–90
Zhan, 48–49, 70
Zhang Gu, 202
Zhang Hua, 185, 262n73, 268n37
Zhang Jun, 149
Zhang Quan, 243n60
Zhang Rong, 242n50, 250n45
Zhang Xie, 133
Zhang Yanchang (Zhang Qitang), 49–50, 236n70
Zhang Ye, 79–80, 243n60
Zhang Zhan, 239n13
Zhang Zhongwei, 150, 193–95
Zhang Zilie, 295
Zhao Delin (also Zhao Lingzhi), 33, 232n32
Zhaoming Taizi. *See* Xiao Tong
Zhaoming Taizi ben (Crown Prince Zhaoming's edition), 289
Zhen yin zhuan (Biographies of Genuine Recluses; Yuan Shu), 64
zhenben (genuine copy), 10
Zhengde Nankang fuzhi (Zhengde Gazetteer of Nankang Prefecture), 202
zhi, 62, 105, 119, 184
Zhi Daolin, 28
Zhong Hui, 229n2
Zhong Rong, 133
Zhong Xing, 250n43
Zhong Youmin, 228n28, 273n52
Zhong Ziqi, 25–26
Zhou Bida (Yigong), 161–62, 210–11, 271n37
Zhou Chun, 49–52
Zhou Dunyi (Zhou Lianxi), 117
Zhou Fang (Chou Fang), 147, 259n46
Zhou Mi, 268n35
Zhou Wenkun, 296
Zhou Xuzhi, 88–89, 98–99
Zhu Bian, 10
Zhu Faji, 28, 230n17
Zhu Mu, 269n8
Zhu Xi (also Huiweng), 205–10, 212, 216, 270n11, 271n27
Zhu Yu, 234n59
Zhu Zhu, 269n8
Zhu Ziqing, 238n12, 255n2
Zhuangzi (also Zhuang Zhou), 24–26, 43, 66, 100, 113, 124, 136–42, 159, 166, 174–77, 181–82, 188–89
Zhuangzi, 181
Zigong, 118, 176
Zilu, 115, 239n20, 265n111
Zong Bing, 29–31
Zong Lin, 262n79, 267n14
Zu Qi, 89
zuben (base edition), 293
Zuo zhuan (Duke Yi), 56, 130

www.ingramcontent.com/pod-product-compliance
Lightning Source LLC
LaVergne TN
LVHW040200080826
844660LV00001B/48

* 9 7 8 0 2 9 5 9 8 5 5 3 4 *